Frommer's

W9-DGY-563

Chicago with Kids

2nd Edition

by Laura Tiebert

Here's what the critics say about Frommer's:

"Amazingly easy to use. Very portable, very complete."
—*Booklist*

"Detailed, accurate, and easy-to-read information for all price ranges."
—*Glamour Magazine*

"Hotel information is close to encyclopedic."
—*Des Moines Sunday Register*

"Frommer's Guides have a way of giving you a real feel for a place."
—*Knight Ridder Newspapers*

WILEY
Wiley Publishing, Inc.

About the Author

Laura Tiebert is a freelance writer whose travels have taken her from the frozen tundra of Dawson City in Yukon Territory to the wide beaches of Muscat, Oman. A native Midwesterner, she lived in New York City for years before returning to Chicago. Today, she stays a bit closer to home in Evanston, IL, where she lives with her husband Andrew and son Joel.

Published by:

Wiley Publishing, Inc.

111 River St.
Hoboken, NJ 07030-5774

ISBN 0-7645-7747-6

Editor: Christine Ryan
Production Editor: Blair J. Pottenger
Cartographer: Elizabeth Puhl
Photo Editor: Richard Fox
Production by Wiley Indianapolis Composition Services

For information on our other products and services or to obtain technical support, please contact our Customer Care Department within the U.S. at 800/762-2974, outside the U.S. at 317/572-3993 or fax 317/572-4002.

Wiley also publishes its books in a variety of electronic formats. Some content that appears in print may not be available in electronic formats.

Manufactured in the United States of America

5   4   3   2   1

Contents

List of Maps

An Invitation to the Reader

In researching this book, we discovered many wonderful places—hotels, restaurants, shops, and more. We're sure you'll find others. Please tell us about them, so we can share the information with your fellow travelers in upcoming editions. If you were disappointed with a recommendation, we'd love to know that, too. Please write to:

Frommer's Chicago with Kids, 2nd Edition
Wiley Publishing, Inc. • 111 River St. • Hoboken, NJ 07030-5774

An Additional Note

Please be advised that travel information is subject to change at any time—and this is especially true of prices. We therefore suggest that you write or call ahead for confirmation when making your travel plans. The authors, editors, and publisher cannot be held responsible for the experiences of readers while traveling. Your safety is important to us, however, so we encourage you to stay alert and be aware of your surroundings. Keep a close eye on cameras, purses, and wallets, all favorite targets of thieves and pickpockets.

Other Great Guides for Your Trip:

Frommer's Chicago
Frommer's Irreverent Guide to Chicago
Frommer's Portable Chicago
Chicago For Dummies

Frommer's Star Ratings, Icons & Abbreviations

Every hotel, restaurant, and attraction listing in this guide has been ranked for quality, value, service, amenities, and special features using a **star-rating system.** In country, state, and regional guides, we also rate towns and regions to help you narrow down your choices and budget your time accordingly. Hotels and restaurants are rated on a scale of zero (recommended) to three stars (exceptional). Attractions, shopping, nightlife, towns, and regions are rated according to the following scale: zero stars (recommended), one star (highly recommended), two stars (very highly recommended), and three stars (must-see).

In addition to the star-rating system, we also use **six feature icons** that point you to the great deals, in-the-know advice, and unique experiences that separate travelers from tourists. Throughout the book, look for:

Finds	Special finds—those places only insiders know about
Fun Fact	Fun facts—details that make travelers more informed and their trips more fun
Moments	Special moments—those experiences that memories are made of
Overrated	Places or experiences not worth your time or money
Tips	Insider tips—great ways to save time and money
Value	Great values—where to get the best deals

The following **abbreviations** are used for credit cards:

AE	American Express	DISC	Discover	V	Visa
DC	Diners Club	MC	MasterCard		

Frommers.com

Now that you have the guidebook to a great trip, visit our website at **www.frommers.com** for travel information on more than 3,000 destinations. With features updated regularly, we give you instant access to the most current trip-planning information available. At Frommers.com, you'll also find the best prices on airfares, accommodations, and car rentals—and you can even book travel online through our travel booking partners. At Frommers.com, you'll also find the following:

- Online updates to our most popular guidebooks
- Vacation sweepstakes and contest giveaways
- Newsletter highlighting the hottest travel trends
- Online travel message boards with featured travel discussions

How to Feel Like a
Chicago Family

What's the best part about visiting Chicago with your kids? On the positive side, Chicago is a big city. You'll find a rich diversity in cultures and languages and the opportunity to expose your kids to many different sights, sounds, and people. Free activities abound: Parks, a zoo, and the beach are a few of Chicago kids' favorite things—and they won't cost you a penny. Transportation is easy: Kids love the "El," carriage rides, trolley cars, and buses. And most activities are located around a compact city center—a brief bus or train ride from hotels on the Magnificent Mile or in River North or the Loop will get you to any of the downtown museums or the Lincoln Park Zoo. You'll always find a coffee shop just around the corner, great restaurants and shopping, and miles of walkable terrain for you and your kids.

The negatives? Again, Chicago is a big city. Streets, shops, and museums can get crowded in the summer. Panhandlers can be a problem in certain congested downtown areas. Traffic can be hazardous—you'll need to be extra-careful around busy intersections. (**Warning:** Cabs will not slow down for anyone— even families with kids). The "El" is not always stroller-friendly and getting through the station onto the train can be challenging. You may find yourself having to walk up flights of stairs carrying the diaper bag, stroller, and more.

Is it worth it? Millions of visitors who flock to our city every year can't be wrong.

As I wrote the first edition of this book, my husband and I were preparing to welcome our first child. As I write the second edition, we are seasoned parents of an energetic toddler, and we've road-tested many of this new edition's suggestions for experiencing Chicago with kids. And as we became part of the community of Chicago parents, many of them shared valuable, been-there, done-that advice. I have those Chicago parents to thank for the wide variety of activities and opinions you'll find in these pages.

In this book I am working on three assumptions: One is that when you travel with kids, there has to be something in it for them. You can't expect kids to enjoy a vacation filled with adult activities. (In fact, take a kid into a fancy department store or to a fine French restaurant and the parents are unlikely to enjoy it either!) But while we want to keep the kids happy, the goal of this book is to find activities that offer something for parents and kids alike.

The second assumption is a preference for the simple over the complex. Take your 3-year-old to the zoo and she may wind up spending more time watching squirrels chase each other across the lawn than the big cats emerging from their dens. And that's okay. Later on, she'll appreciate the larger animals! In this book I emphasize some off-the-beaten track, simple (and often inexpensive) ideas for entertaining your kids. Many of these ideas have been contributed by a cadre of Chicago parents.

The third is that you will seek out activities that are unique to Chicago. Now, some people are comfortable going to Hard Rock Cafe or Six Flags because they have them in their own city—and their kids like that sort of predictability. More power to you—and those places are certainly listed in this guidebook. My focus, however, is on transportation, museums, and food that say "Chicago."

Insiders in the travel business sometimes whisper that Chicago is to the United States as Frankfurt, Germany, is to Europe: a hub for conventions, a business destination, but otherwise often considered flyover or airport layover territory. In this book I intend to demonstrate to even the most sophisticated travelers that Chicago is a worthy destination. This city can be a magical place for families, filled with new discoveries and favorite places you'll want to visit again and again over the years. Many of my friends recall annual trips to Chicago with great fondness. Breakfast with Santa at the Walnut Room at Marshall Field's, Colleen Moore's Fairy Castle at the Museum of Science and Industry, Buckingham Fountain's invigorating spray on a windy day—and now, Millennium Park's bedazzling "bean" sculpture and its funhouse reflections will soon become part of your family lore, too.

1 Frommer's Favorite Chicago Family Experiences

Chicago has made vast strides in beautifying the city and developing visitor-friendly attractions. Millennium Park, a world-class destination on 25 acres near Michigan Avenue and the Art Institute, opened in 2004, and it is a knockout. The architectural highlight of the park is the Frank Gehry–designed Pritzker Music Pavilion, home of the free summer music concerts performed by the Grant Park Symphony Orchestra. Another popular attraction is the huge elliptical sculpture *Cloudgate* (immediately dubbed "the bean" by Chicagoans) by British artist Anish Kapoor—his first public work in the U.S. The dazzling $450 million park adds to the already excellent facilities for families, including Museum Campus, now (in my humble opinion) the number-one collection of museums located on one walkable campus in the country. Several years ago the city created the campus by linking three great Chicago institutions—the Field Museum of Natural History, John G. Shedd Aquarium, and Adler Planetarium & Astronomy Museum—by rerouting major streets to make the area more pedestrian-friendly.

Even as the city's donors feel the lightness of their empty pockets now that Millennium Park is complete, many of Chicago's cultural institutions are launching new fundraising drives that will continue to transform the landscape for visitors. Navy Pier was rehabilitated and opened in the mid-1990s, quickly becoming the city's number-one tourist destination. The North Loop theater district has risen from a decades-long slumber. And the retail expansion along the city's fabled Magnificent Mile has yet to slow down. Is it any wonder that natives of the city have the reputation of never wanting to live anywhere else?

From the simple pleasures of summer baseball to the complexities of the world of science, here are my favorite Chicago experiences for families:

- **Encountering Jurassic Wonders:** Sue, the largest T-rex skeleton ever uncovered, has made the Field Museum her home. (Don't be taken aback by her intimidating presence in the museum's grand entry hall.) But don't be surprised if your kids are just as much in awe of the Field's many classic kid charmers: a life-size Egyptian tomb, rooms of glittering gemstones, the royal Cameroon palace from Africa, and hundreds of stuffed animals (not of the teddy bear variety) in their habitat. Beware of the Field's mesmerizing qualities on adults and kids alike: A friend of mine began meditating in an Indian tepee, only to open his eyes and find the museum closed! See p. 151.

- **Exploring Underwater Life:** Most kids have a fascination for life under the sea, and an afternoon watching dolphins frolic and colorful tropical fish swim circles around a mammoth tank is sure to enthrall. John G. Shedd Aquarium, with its all-time favorite dolphin show and precious beluga whales, is a surefire winner with kids. See p. 154.

- **Marveling at the Innovations of Science and Industry:** You can't go wrong at the Museum of Science and Industry, Chicago's perennial kids' favorite. Watch chicks hatch in an incubator. Catch an IMAX movie at the Henry Crown space theater. Step aboard a retired 727 United Airlines jetliner. Travel deep into a replica of a Southern Illinois coal mine. And, as of spring 2005, the newly restored and always classic exhibit of a captured German U-boat goes back on display in a new, climate-controlled environment (years of sitting outside in the elements took their toll). With so much to do, you might want to divide and conquer by spending a couple of afternoons here. See p. 158.

- **Taking to the Water from Navy Pier:** Chicago's number-one tourist attraction is home to another kids' favorite—the Chicago Children's Museum. Navy Pier is also the jumping-off point for many of the boat tours of Lake Michigan, so find a vessel that's your speed, from powerboats to tall-masted schooners, and take to the water! See p. 159.

- **Talking to the Animals:** Located within Chicago's famous lakefront park, the Lincoln Park Zoo is convenient, compact, and charming. And what's not to love about a place that's open 365 days a year and never charges a cent for admission? This, the nation's oldest zoo, is famous for its major collection of gorillas, which live in the newly rebuilt Great Ape House, which gives its residents more outdoor living space (and the ability to control the temperature in their habitat, believe it or not). The adjoining Farm-in-the-Zoo allows urban kids to wander a working farm and meet cows, pigs, horses, chicks, and goats. And Pritzker Children's Zoo also recently received a makeover. See p. 185.

- **Riding the "El":** *L* is not just the 12th letter of the alphabet, but also the greatest, least expensive entertainment your kids will enjoy in Chicago (even though fares have jumped a quarter, to $1.75 per ride). Hop a southbound Brown Line elevated train toward the Loop, and watch the city unfold as the train crosses the Chicago River and screeches through downtown canyons. See "Kid-Friendly Tours," in chapter 6.

- **Cruising Chicago's Waterways:** A Chicago River cruise should be one of your first stops in our fair city. I didn't step aboard until I'd lived in the city for 2 years—and boy, did I miss out! Kids and adults alike will love the Chicago Architecture Foundation's river cruise. Or, head to Navy Pier and hop on one of the myriad vessels that stand ready to chauffer you around Lake Michigan. Whatever way you go, the best vantage point

Chicago & Vicinity

Chicago Dateline

1673 French explorers Marquette and Joliet discover portage at Chicago linking the Great Lakes region with the Mississippi River valley.

1779 Afro-French-Canadian trapper Jean Baptiste Point du Sable establishes a trading post on the north bank of the Chicago River. A settlement follows 2 years later.

1794 General "Mad" Anthony Wayne defeats the British in the Battle of Fallen Timbers; disputed Illinois Territory is finally ceded to the young American Republic by treaty a year later.

1803 Garrison of Fort Dearborn is established in Chicago, commanded by the grandfather of artist James McNeill Whistler.

1818 Illinois is admitted to the Union as the 21st state.

1833 Town of Chicago is officially incorporated, with little more than 300 residents.

1837 Chicago is incorporated as a city, with about 4,000 residents.

1847 The *Chicago Tribune* begins publishing.

1848 The 96-mile Illinois and Michigan Canal is opened, linking the Great Lakes with the Mississippi River.

1850 Chicago's population is roughly 30,000.

1856 Chicago is chief railroad center in the United States.

1870 Chicago's population numbers almost 300,000, making it perhaps the fastest-growing metropolis in history.

1871 The Great Chicago Fire burns large sections of the city; rebuilding begins while the ashes are still warm.

1882 The 10-story Montauk Building, the world's first skyscraper, is erected.

1892 The city's first elevated train goes into operation.

1893 Completely recovered from the Great Fire, Chicago hosts its first World's Fair, the World's Columbian Exposition. The world's first Ferris wheel is a big draw.

1905 Robert S. Abbott founds the *Chicago Defender,* which becomes the nation's premier African-American newspaper and later plays a major role in encouraging Southern blacks to move north during the "Great Migration" years.

for viewing Chicago's world-renowned architecture is from the water. See "Kid-Friendly Tours," in chapter 6.

- **Ogling Our Inland Ocean:** Chicago's magnificent lakefront is an emerald strand of parks and sand beaches, linked by running, walking, rollerblading, and biking trails. You'll appreciate the foresight of Chicago's forefathers even more when you compare our free and open public lakefront to that of other Great Lakes cities like Toronto, where much of the lakefront is used for industrial purposes or is privately owned. And at 22,300 square miles in size and reaching depths of 900 feet, our great lake will look more like the ocean to your kids. It's the only Great Lake that lies wholly in U.S. territory, and Chicago is blessed with 29 miles of lakefront for

1908 The Chicago Cubs win their second World Series. They haven't won one since.

1917 The Chicago White Sox win the World Series—and they also haven't won one since.

1920–33 During Prohibition, Chicago becomes a "wide-open town;" rival mobs battle violently throughout the city for control of distribution and sale of illegal alcohol.

1931 Notorious Chicago gangster Al Capone finally goes to jail—for tax evasion.

1942 Scientists, led by Enrico Fermi, create the world's first nuclear chain reactions under Stagg Field at the University of Chicago.

1955 Richard J. Daley begins his term as mayor; he is widely regarded as the "last of the big-city bosses."

1960 John F. Kennedy and Richard Nixon hold the first televised presidential debate in WBBM-TV's studios.

1966 Civil rights leader Martin Luther King, Jr., moves to Chicago to lead a fair-housing campaign.

1974 The 1,454-foot Sears Tower is completed, becoming the tallest building in the world.

1979 Jane Byrne becomes the first woman elected mayor of Chicago.

1983 Harold Washington becomes the first African-American mayor of Chicago.

1986 The Chicago Bears win their only Super Bowl.

1999 Michael Jordan, arguably the best basketball player ever, retires (for the second time) after leading the Chicago Bulls to six NBA championships in the previous 8 years.

2000 The Goodman Theatre opens its new $46 million theater complex in the Loop, completing the revitalization of the downtown theater district.

2004 Millennium Park, Chicago's largest public works project in decades, opens at the north end of Grant Park. The centerpiece—a steel-sheathed band shell—is designed by architect Frank Gehry.

biking, 'blading, or simply being. So get out there and enjoy the country's "third coast." See "Enjoying the 'Third Coast': Chicago's Beaches," in chapter 8.

- **Getting the Blues:** Even kids can get the blues, thanks to alcohol- and smoke-free nights at Blue Chicago (p. 255), one of the city's many fabled blues venues. The blues is the first original music of America and the basis for rock 'n' roll. It's an authentic piece of Chicago's heart and soul that you absolutely should not miss. If you want to learn more before your arrival in Chicago, read *Blues For Dummies,* written by the father-and-son team of Lonnie Brooks and Wayne Baker Brooks, two of Chicago's beloved blues musicians.

- **Rooting for the Home Team:** Win or lose (and sorry to say, historically speaking, it's usually lose—but as always, this may be our year!) an afternoon at Wrigley Field is a thrill for kids and adults alike. Even if the Cubbies aren't hitting them out of the park, hot dogs, peanuts in the shell, and a rousing rendition of "Take Me Out to the Ballgame" are sure to please. This most charming of major league ballparks is a slice of Americana that you should not miss. One afternoon spent in the embrace of the Friendly Confines will have you hooked on the sheer magic of Wrigley Field. See p. 263.

2 The Best Hotel Bets

Several years of expansion and new construction for Chicago hotels means the city offers a wide variety, from hip boutique hotels to huge facilities for convention-goers, and thankfully, a nice crop of family-friendly hotels. The downside: Room rates keep rising, making budget lodgings harder to find. One of the latest and greatest additions to the hotel scene includes the new **Hard Rock Hotel Chicago,** 230 N. Michigan Ave. (© **312/345-1000**), which might interest the teenagers in your crowd with its rock 'n' roll attitude (p. 73).

- **Most Family-Friendly:** With cribs, laundry service, free breakfast, and every room a suite, the **Embassy Suites Hotel Chicago— Downtown,** 600 N. State St. (© **800/362-2779**), is ideal for families looking for a little more space than the typical hotel room provides. The in-room Nintendo, indoor pool, and location near a couple popular kid-friendly venues—ESPN Zone and the Hard Rock Cafe—should keep Junior happy, too. See p. 94.

- **Newest Family-Friendly Hotel:** I always say that any hotel that's new is a good bet. New construction means fresh linens, fresh decor, updated heating and cooling systems—you get my drift. You'll get all this at the city's most recent family-friendly addition, **Courtyard by Marriott—Chicago Downtown/Magnificent Mile,** 165 E. Ontario St. (© **312/573-0800**), plus a great location just 1 block east of Michigan Avenue in the heart of the Magnificent Mile. There's also a brand-new pool, a rarity in downtown hotels, on the 10th floor. See p. 91.

- **Best Neighborhood Hotel:** Children 12 and under stay free at **Best Western Hawthorne Terrace Hotel,** 3434 N. Broadway (© **888/675-2378**). Rooms in this small hotel (just 59 rooms and junior suites) offer refrigerators, microwaves, and irons. Best of all, parking is a bargain at $16 a day—about half the going rate at Chicago's downtown hotels. p. 100.

- **Best Views:** This isn't an easy call. Peering over the elevated tracks, **Crowne Plaza Chicago—The Silversmith,** 10 S. Wabash Ave. (© **800/2CROWNE**), in the Loop, offers a distinctly urban vista (p. 73). But consider several other hotels for their mix of lake and city views: **Four Seasons Hotel Chicago** (p. 81), **The Drake** (p. 86), **The Ritz-Carlton Chicago** (p. 85), and **Park Hyatt Chicago** (p. 81).

- **When Hipness Is Important:** A hip hotel that's known for romance is using its small size— and sense of whimsy—to cater to kids. **Hotel Burnham,** 1 W. Washington, at State Street (© **877/294-9712**), keeps wee ones entertained with special offers for tea at American Girl Place Cafe and deals at the museums and theaters. During holidays, you'll find special

The Best Chicago Websites

The **World Wide Web** makes vacation planning simple. These Chicago-based sites provide up-to-date listings on everything from restaurants to walking tours.

- **www.877chicago.com** is your best bet for comprehensive tourism information on hotels, special promotions, and citywide events from the Chicago Convention and Tourism Bureau (and ℂ 877/CHICAGO also happens to be the phone number for the bureau's tourism information line).

- **www.metromix.com** is the *Chicago Tribune*'s entertainment-oriented site.

- **www.cityofchicago.org/Landmarks/index.html** is a city website that includes definitions of Chicago's architectural styles, tour information, and maps.

- **www.chicago.citysearch.com** offers reviews of restaurants, bars, shows, and shops.

- Two good general sites are **www.cityofchicago.com** (Chicago Office of Tourism) and **www.enjoyillinois.com** (Illinois Bureau of Tourism).

activities in the hotel lobby, including decorating gingerbread men at Christmas and hunting for eggs at Easter. Diaper bags, cribs, high chairs, changing tables, and more are available upon request. Rooms are clubby but glamorous, with plush beds, mahogany writing desks, and chaise lounges, and even the family pet is welcome. See p. 76.

- **When Price Is No Object:** The attention to detail, regal pampering, and well-connected concierges you will find at both the ultraluxe **Ritz-Carlton Chicago,** 160 E. Pearson St. (ℂ **800/621-6906;** p. 85), and **Four Seasons Hotel Chicago,** 120 E. Delaware Place (ℂ **800/332-3442;** p. 81), make them the hotels of choice for travelers who want to feel like royalty while in town. **The Peninsula Chicago,** 108 E. Superior St. (ℂ **866/288-8889;** p. 82), a newer entry onto the luxury scene in Chicago, also ascended into the ranks of the Ritz and Four Seasons

when it won *Travel & Leisure* magazine's 2004 award for top service in North America (and ranked in the top 10 in the world).

- **When Price Is Your Main Object: Red Roof Inn Chicago Downtown,** 162 E. Ontario St. (ℂ **800/733-7663;** p. 94), offers a fabulous location for a bargain price. But the **Hampton Inn & Suites Chicago—Downtown,** 33 W. Illinois St. (ℂ **800/HAMPTON;** p. 96), gets bonus points for being a bargain stay, plus having a pool.

- **Best Pool:** With its dazzling all-tile junior Olympic–size pool, constructed in 1929, the **Hotel InterContinental Chicago,** 505 N. Michigan Ave. (ℂ **800/327-0200**), takes this award easily. See p. 87.

- **Best Hotel Restaurant for Kids:** Go for **Atwood Cafe,** the stylish and funky restaurant fronting State Street at **Hotel Burnham,** 1 W. Washington (ℂ **877/294-9712**). Amazingly, this eclectic restaurant with a grown-up sophistication welcomes kids and features a special kids' menu. See p. 106.

- **Tops for Teens:** For a theatrical hotel experience, the **House of Blues Hotel,** 333 N. Dearborn St. (© **800/235-6397**), can't be beat, with its riotous mix of colors and playful attitude. See p. 95. Of course, this hotel is being given a run for its money by the brand-new **Hard Rock Hotel Chicago,** 230 N. Michigan Ave. (© **312/345-1000**), in the historic, distinctive, and freshly renovated Carbon Carbide skyscraper. See p. 73.

- **Tops for Toddlers: Homewood Suites,** 40 E. Grand Ave. (© **800/CALL-HOME**), offers cribs, high chairs, and babysitting services in a great location in River North—all great amenities for the toddling set. See p. 93.

3 The Best Dining Bets

With pizza and hot dogs among the city's signature dishes, Chicago is food heaven for kids. Before you run out and buy a case of antacids, however, take heart: Wonderful cuisine to please adults abounds, too. And I'm going to send you in that direction, right after I grab a garlic- and pepper-laden hot dog.

- **Best Views:** A location right on the Magnificent Mile means the **Hancock Observatory,** 875 N. Michigan Ave., offers an up-close-and-personal view of the city from its observation deck. For lunch, visit the observatory's **Signature Room at the 95th** (© **312/787-9596**), a sleek restaurant that offers a discounted lunch buffet for kids. On a clear day you can see 50 miles and part of three surrounding states—Michigan, Indiana, and Wisconsin. (Moms and daughters, make sure to visit the restroom—it's got the best views in the restaurant!) See p. 164.

- **Best Ice Cream:** Since the 1920s, **Margie's Candies,** 1960 N. Western Ave., at Armitage Avenue (© **773/384-1035**), has been serving up mammoth sundaes in conch shell–shaped dishes. Margie is gone now, but her husband Peter still mans the cash register. Don't miss the homemade hot fudge, real butterscotch, and caramel. The place hasn't changed much since 1940, and is stuffed with kitschy dolls, boxes of homemade candy, stuffed animals, and news clippings through the years. See p. 236.

- **Best Outdoor Eating:** Long tables and family-style dining reign in **Greektown,** making it a comfortable and fun destination for families and large groups; see "The Randolph Street Market District & Greektown," in chapter 5. At **Pegasus,** 130 S. Halsted St. (© **312/226-3377**), a rooftop garden allows diners a panoramic view of the Chicago skyline. The restaurant is so family- and large group–oriented, in fact, that when I called to make a reservation for a group of 10, the host replied, "Ten is not a big group!" See p. 116.

- **Most Kid-Friendly Service: Scoozi,** an Italian restaurant in River North at 410 W. Huron (© **312/943-5900**), is a family favorite for its Sunday afternoon pizza-making event that lets kids loose with tomato sauce and cheese to create their own pizzas (under the supervision of Scoozi chefs, who keep mess to a minimum and pop finished pizzas into the wood-burning oven). The evening is great for parents, too—they get a short break while their kids play chef to enjoy their meal and some grown-up conversation. Make a reservation, because your window of opportunity is small: The restaurant runs the program on Sunday only, from 5 to 6:30pm. See p. 126.

- **Best Kids' Menu:** How many times have you seen the big three on kids' menus? Burgers, chicken fingers, and buttered noodles are great, but when you want to expand your horizons (just a little), head for **Wishbone,** 1001 Washington St., at Morgan Street (© **312/850-2663**), or 3300 N. Lincoln Ave. (© **773/549-2663**). You'll find a little Southern flair to the kids' menu, with hoppin' John (black-eyed peas over rice), grilled ham, corn muffins, and home fries among the offerings. See p. 115.

- **Best Burgers:** The hamburger at **Mike Ditka's Restaurant,** 100 E. Chestnut St. (© **312/587-8989**), tastes more like chopped steak and can easily feed two. Sports fans will be entertained by football memorabilia and Bears fans can relive the glory days of former Coach Mike Ditka, who owns the place. Take your kids to the main dining room, though, because the bar vicinity tends to get a little foggy with cigar smoke. See p. 117.

- **Best Barbecue:** At longtime city favorite **Carson's,** 612 N. Wells St. (© **312/280-9200**), $20 gets you a full slab (nearly 2 pounds' worth) of incredible baby back ribs, accompanied by a bowl of Carson's almost-as-famous coleslaw and a choice of potatoes. See p. 125.

- **Best Breakfast:** Although the restaurant is located in the young professional haven of Lincoln Park, parents report that the managers and staff at **Toast,** 746 W.

Webster St., at Halsted Street (© **773/935-5600**), are baby- and kid-crazy. The pancakes and waffles are pretty crazy, too: Stacks arrive covered in fruit, yogurt, powdered sugar, and more. Go for brunch starting at 8am on weekends. See p. 137.

- **Best Family-Style Dining:** **Maggiano's,** 516 N. Clark St. (© **312/644-7700**), is a mecca for Italian family-style dining. Heaping plates of pasta meant to be shared make Maggiano's a good choice for a budget-conscious family. In fact, everything on the menu is supersize. Most steaks are more than a pound, and the full pasta dishes weigh in at over 25 ounces. (You can also get half-portions, which are still plentiful.) You're expected to share dishes, pass things around, and try a little bit of everything. See p. 126.

- **Best Asian Food:** If you eat at **Big Bowl,** 6 E. Cedar St., at Rush Street (© **312/640-8888**), at the beginning of your visit to Chicago, I guarantee you will make a repeat visit before you leave. The food here is addictive. From noodle soups to pad Thai (try the tofu and veggie version), your kids will find tons to love here. Each child gets a small bowl of white rice and crayons upon being seated. The restaurant bustles and kids will blend right in with the other activity. Make sure to grab a handful of individually wrapped fortune cookies on your way out! See p. 120.

- **Best Hot Dog: Gold Coast Dogs,** 159 N. Wabash Ave. (© **312/917-1677**). This River North fast-food stand serves up the authentic item, meaning a Vienna All-Beef Frank slathered with mustard, green relish, chopped onion, sliced tomato, hot peppers, and celery salt. Your kids might be brave enough to ask for and receive ketchup, but as an adult, I wouldn't risk the disapproving, raised-eyebrow look you'll get from the counter staff. You can round out the meal with cheese fries, made from Idaho potatoes and topped with a generous glob of Wisconsin cheddar. See p. 142.

- **Best Pizza:** In the town where deep-dish pies were born, Chicagoans take their out-of-town relatives to either **Gino's East,** 633 N. Wells St. (© **312/943-1124;** p. 128), or **Lou Malnati's Pizzeria,** 439 N. Wells St. (© **312/ 828-9800;** p. 140), to taste the real thing: mouthwatering slabs of pizza loaded with fresh ingredients atop delectably sweet crusts. Lou's fan base is so enamored that the restaurant has even instituted a popular overnight mail-order business to get expatriate Chicagoans with a deep-dish jones over the hump.

- **Best Fast Food:** Even though you're in the hometown of McDonald's, our vote goes to **foodlife** in Water Tower Place, 835 N. Michigan Ave. (© **312/ 335-3663**), a food court exemplar with everything from Asian noodles to pizza to smoothies. See p. 122.

- **Best Brunch:** Cajun and Southern cooking is in store for you at **Wishbone,** 1001 W. Washington Blvd. (© **312/850-2663**). Primitive art, bright colors, and a bustling crowd make this a great place for kids. A diverse crowd, from Harpo Studios employees (Oprah is headquartered right around the corner) to businesspeople in suits and ad agency types, frequent the place. For brunch, try the salmon cakes. See p. 115.

- **Best Girls' Day Out:** Can't help but notice those dark red bags that girls carry like badges of honor up and down Michigan Avenue? They come from **American Girl Place Cafe,** 111 E. Chicago Ave. (© **877/247-5223**), which also features a cafe and theater. Call well in advance for lunch reservations or to catch a performance of *The American Girls Revue* in the 150-seat theater. See p. 116.

- **Best Boys' Night Out:** What red-blooded American kid doesn't love baseball? **Harry Caray's,** 33 W. Kinzie St. (© **312/828-0966**), is one of Chicago's most flamboyant eateries, filled with uniforms, helmets, cards, and photographs. Be sure to check out the bar—it measures 60 feet, 6 inches, the exact distance from the plate on the pitcher's mound to home plate in a major-league park. See p. 124.

- **Best Neighborhood Hang-Out: Stanley's,** 1970 N. Lincoln Ave. (© **312/642-0007**), is a classic Lincoln Park restaurant with a family-friendly bent. There's a bar near the entrance, but the adjacent dining room, decorated with photos, quilts, bowling trophies, and children's drawings, feels like someone's family room. This popular family spot has a special kids' menu. On Saturday and Sunday from 11am to 4pm, there's an all-you-can-eat brunch buffet, featuring make-your-own omelets, build-your-own Belgian waffles, home-fried potatoes, fried chicken, and mashed potatoes. Daily specials are posted on the chalkboard out front. See p. 136.

- **Best Retro Diner:** Sure, it's a chain, but **Johnny Rocket's,** 901 N. Rush St. (© **312/337-3900**), does a wonderful job of replicating a 1950s diner. Burgers wrapped in paper, fries (which your friendly waitperson pours ketchup on for you), and flavored sodas from the fountain are sure to please kids. Kids' meals are available for $4.50, and kids can get menus to color. The location, just behind the 900 N. Michigan mall, makes the diner a perfect stop during a visit to the Magnificent Mile.

2

Planning a Family Trip to Chicago

Planning a trip is half the fun—and when kids are involved, planning is a chance to make them active participants in the upcoming family adventure. Ward off any potential kid meltdowns ("I didn't know we were going to do that!") by talking through the activities you all can enjoy. In this chapter we'll look at how to find up-to-date information on those activities, when to go, and how to get here.

1 Visitor Information

SOURCES OF INFORMATION

The best source of information is the Chicago Convention and Tourism Bureau, which operates an information line at © **877/CHICAGO** and a very helpful and up-to-date website at www.877chicago.com. **The Chicago Office of Tourism,** Chicago Cultural Center, 78 E. Washington St., Chicago, IL 60602 (© **312/744-2400** or TTY 312/744-2947; http://egov.cityofchicago.org), will mail you a packet of materials with information on upcoming events and attractions. The **Illinois Bureau of Tourism** (© **800/2CONNECT** or TTY 800/406-6418; www.enjoyillinois.com) will also send you a packet of information about Chicago and other Illinois destinations.

The number-one publication for families in the Chicago area is **Chicago Parent** (© **708/386-5555**), a monthly magazine that has won many awards as best regional parenting publication in the nation. Contact the magazine to request a copy of its June issue, which is the annual "Going Places" guide, a comprehensive listing of what to do with kids in the six-county metro area.

HELPFUL WEBSITES

Aside from official, government-run websites, some Chicago publications and other organizations have wonderful websites, some targeted to families. Check out *Chicago Parent* magazine's website, **www.chicagoparent.com**, prior to your visit, for a look at the calendar of events and excellent features on exploring Chicago with kids.

In addition, **www.gocitykids.com** provides a wealth of information, including current calendars of events for Chicago. You can search for activities, restaurants, and hotels, and see what's happening in specific neighborhoods. For information on baby gear, play spaces, and kid-friendly community events, check out **www.urbanbaby.com**.

Go to **www.digitalcity.com/chicago** for general information about Chicago provided by the *Chicago Tribune;* **www.metromix.com** is the *Tribune's* entertainment-oriented site. Also check out **www.chireader.com**, the site of the *Chicago Reader,* the city's alternative weekly paper.

Many of the city's performing-arts groups sell tickets online through **www.ticketweb.com**, so you can reserve seats before leaving home.

2 Money

ATMS

ATMs in Chicago are linked to a national network that most likely includes your bank at home. **Cirrus** (© **800/424-7787;** www.master card.com) and **PLUS** (© **800/843-7587;** www.visa.com) are the two most popular networks; check the back of your ATM card to see which networks your bank belongs to. Use the toll-free numbers to locate ATMs in Chicago. When you ask for directions to an ATM, Chicagoans may point you to the nearest "Cash Station," our local term (Cash Station is the biggest ATM network in the city); almost every machine labeled "Cash Station" is part of the Cirrus or PLUS network.

Be sure to check your daily withdrawal limit before you leave for your trip. And note that many banks have begun to impose a fee ranging from 50¢ to $3 every time you use an ATM in a different city. Your own bank may also charge you a fee for using ATMs from other banks. You can also withdraw cash advances from your credit cards at any bank (though you'll start paying hefty interest on the advance

Destination Chicago: Red Alert Checklist

- If you're driving, do you have all the directions you need and detailed road maps? If you're flying, are you carrying a current, government-issued ID, such as a driver's license or passport?
- Do any theater, restaurant, or travel reservations need to be booked in advance?
- Did you make sure your favorite attraction is open, or verify the dates of any special events you plan to attend? Call ahead for opening and closing times.
- If you purchased traveler's checks, have you recorded the check numbers and stored the documentation separately from the checks?
- Did you stop the newspaper and mail delivery, and leave a set of keys with someone reliable?
- Did you pack your camera and an extra set of camera batteries, and purchase enough film?
- Do you have a safe, accessible place to store money?
- Did you bring your ID cards that could entitle you to discounts, such as AAA and AARP cards, student IDs, and the like?
- Did you bring emergency drug prescriptions and extra glasses and/or contact lenses?
- Did you find out your daily ATM withdrawal limit?
- Do you have your credit card PINs? Is there a daily withdrawal limit on credit card cash advances?
- To check in at a kiosk with an e-ticket, do you have the credit card you bought your ticket with or a frequent-flier card?
- Did you leave a copy of your itinerary with someone at home?
- Do you have the measurements for those people you plan to buy clothes for on your trip?

> **Tips** **Small Change**
>
> Make sure you're carrying some small bills or loose change. Petty cash will come in handy for tipping and public transportation. Consider keeping the change separate from your larger bills, so that it's readily accessible and you'll be less of a target for theft.

the moment you receive the cash, and you won't receive frequent-flier miles for cash advances on an airline credit card).

CREDIT CARDS

Credit cards are invaluable when traveling. They are a safe way to carry money and provide a convenient record of all your expenses; you can withdraw cash advances from your credit cards at any bank (though you'll start paying hefty interest on the advance the moment you receive the cash), usually at the ATM if you know your personal identification number (PIN). If you've forgotten yours, call the number on the back of your credit card and ask the bank to send it to you, which usually takes 5 to 7 business days.

These days everyone pays with plastic, even for the smallest purchase. So go ahead and use your card for a cup of coffee and a bagel—few merchants will bat an eye. You can use just about any credit card here; one that might be more popular around Chicago than in other parts of the country is Discover, which is owned by Sears, the Chicago-based retailer.

TRAVELER'S CHECKS

These days, traveler's checks seem less necessary, but if you're withdrawing money every day, you might be better off with them—provided that you don't mind showing identification every time you want to cash a check. Most downtown restaurants, hotels, and shops in Chicago accept traveler's checks, and banks generally exchange them for cash (for a small fee). When you get away from downtown and the more affluent neighborhoods, however, smaller restaurants and shops may be reluctant to accept traveler's checks. American Express offices are open Monday through Saturday in Chicago. (See "Fast Facts: Chicago," in chapter 3 for office locations.) AAA members can obtain checks without a fee at most AAA offices.

WHAT TO DO IF YOUR WALLET IS LOST OR STOLEN

Almost every credit card company has an emergency toll-free number that you can call if your wallet or purse is lost or stolen. A representative may be able to wire you a cash advance off your credit card immediately and, in many places, can deliver an emergency credit card in a day or two. The **toll-free information directory** will provide the issuing bank's toll-free number if you dial ✆ 800/555-1212. **Citicorp Visa's** U.S. emergency number is ✆ 800/336-8472. **American Express** cardholders and traveler's check holders should call ✆ 800/221-7282 for all money emergencies. **MasterCard** holders should call ✆ 800/307-7309. If you opt to carry traveler's checks, be sure to keep a record of their serial numbers, separate from the checks, of course, so that you're guaranteed a refund in just such an emergency.

What Things Cost in Chicago	US$	UK£
Cab from O'Hare Airport to downtown hotel	30.00	16.80
Cab from Midway Airport to downtown hotel	24.00	13.45
Shuttle from O'Hare to downtown hotel	19.00	10.65
Shuttle from Midway to downtown hotel	14.00	7.85
Subway or bus ride	1.75	1.00
Transfer (good for two additional rides)	0.25	.15
Ticket to John Hancock Center Observatory	9.50 adults, 6.00 kids	5.30 adults, 3.35 kids
Ticket to Sears Tower Skydeck	9.95 adults, 6.95 kids	5.55 adults, 3.90 kids
Hot dog at Gold Coast Dogs	2.00	1.10
Movie ticket	8.75 adults, 5.50 kids	4.90 adults, 3.10 kids
20-ounce soft drink at drug or convenience store	1.29	.73
16-ounce apple juice	1.39	.78
Weekday *Chicago Tribune*	50¢	.28
Weekday *Chicago Sun-Times*	35¢	.20
Package of Pampers at drug store	12.99	7.25
1-quart can prepared Similac formula	4.99	2.80

3 When to Go

When should you go to Chicago? That depends on what kind of weather you like. Chicago has it all—heat and humidity, subzero temps, and wind, wind, wind. The city has a reputation for being really cold in the winter. In reality, it's about as cold as any other northern city. Maybe it's that wind that makes the cold seem more bitter. Still, most visitors prefer planning trips to Chicago in late spring through early fall. If you can't make it during prime time, err on the side of arriving later in fall rather than early in spring. Spring in Chicago can be notoriously late and fickle, but fall offers beautiful days that can extend to Thanksgiving.

Don't be afraid to try the off season: Museums are wide open, shops have sales (especially in Jan), and the streets aren't clogged with pedestrians. Chicago is definitely a four-season destination; its inhabitants are hardy enough to be out and about even in the depths of winter. As an added incentive to "off-season" travelers, hotel rates are rock bottom during the winter.

One thing is certain: Whenever you decide to go, you should be prepared for changeable weather. Chicagoans like to joke that if you don't like the weather here, just wait an hour. One beautiful summer afternoon, I left my apartment in jeans and a t-shirt, only to have to buy a sweatshirt downtown when the wind shifted and the temperature plummeted 15 degrees in 15 minutes. So even in July, make sure that you bring a light jacket or sweater. (And in the winter, however fashionable you are trying to be, don't think you can get by without a hat.)

For current conditions and **forecasts,** dial ✆ **312/976-1212** or check www.chicagotribune.com and click on "Weather."

Chicago's Average Temperatures & Precipitation

	Jan	Feb	Mar	Apr	May	June	July	Aug	Sept	Oct	Nov	Dec
High °F	20.2	33.9	44.3	58.8	70.0	79.4	85.3	82.1	75.5	64.1	48.2	35.0
°C	–6.5	1.0	6.8	14.9	21.1	26.3	29.6	27.8	24.4	17.8	8.99	1.67
Low °F	13.6	18.1	27.6	38.8	48.1	57.7	62.7	61.7	53.9	42.0	31.4	20.3
°C	–10.2	–7.7	–2.4	3.8	8.9	14.3	17	16.5	12.2	5.6	–0.3	–6.5
Rainfall (in.)	1.60	1.31	2.59	3.66	3.15	4.08	3.63	3.53	3.35	2.28	2.06	2.10

KIDS' FAVORITE CHICAGO EVENTS

Chicago is a festival city, with ethnic parades, food, music, art and flower fairs, and street celebrations packing the calendar. Particularly in the summer, it can be tough to choose among activities. In winter you'll have fewer choices, but some of the perennial favorites take place then.

To discover the latest and greatest special events in the city, ask the **Chicago Office of Tourism** (✆ 312/744-2400) or the **Illinois Bureau of Tourism** (✆ 800/2CONNECT) to mail you a copy of *Chicago Calendar of Events,* an excellent quarterly publication that surveys special events, including parades and street festivals, concerts and theatrical productions, and museum exhibitions. Also ask to be sent the latest materials produced by the **Mayor's Office of Special Events** (✆ 312/744-3315, or the Special Events Hot Line 312/744-3315, TTY 312/744-2964), which keeps current with citywide and neighborhood festivals. You'll find food, music and flower fairs, garden walks, and more.

Remember that new events might be added every year, and that occasionally special events are discontinued or rescheduled. So, to avoid disappointment, be sure to telephone in advance to the sponsoring organization, the Chicago Office of Tourism, or the Mayor's Office of Special Events to verify dates, times, and locations.

January

Chicago Cubs Convention. Even though April and Opening Day seem (and are) very far away in January, Cubs fans dream of next season at this convention, held at the Chicago Hilton and Towers. Players sign autographs and collectors buy, sell, and swap memorabilia. Call ✆ **773/404-CUBS** for more information. Mid-January.

Azalea and Camellia Flower Shows. Just when you and the kids are going to go stark-raving nuts from cabin fever, the **Lincoln Park Conservatory** (✆ 312/742-7737) and **Garfield Park Conservatory** (✆ 312/746-5100) come alive with spring-blooming flowers such as azaleas, tulips, and hyacinths. Late January or early February.

Chicago Boat, RV & Outdoor Show, McCormick Place, 23rd Street and Lake Shore Drive (✆ 312/946-6262). This extravaganza has been a Chicago tradition for nearly 70 years. All the latest boats and recreational vehicles are on display, plus there's trout fishing, a climbing wall, boating-safety seminars, and big-time entertainment. Late January.

February

Chinese New Year Parade, Wentworth and Cermak streets (✆ 312/326-5320). The twisting dragon is sure to please kids as it winds down the street at this annual celebration. Call to verify the date, which varies from year to year, depending on the lunar calendar (usually between Jan 21 and Feb 19).

Chicago Auto Show, McCormick Place, 23rd Street and Lake Shore

Drive (© **630/495-2282**). More than a thousand cars and trucks, domestic and foreign, are on display at this show, a tradition since 1901. Kids can get behind the wheel of the latest models at this event, which draws nearly a million car owners or wannabe owners a year. Mid-February.

International Cluster of Dog Shows, McCormick Place South, 23rd Street and South Lake Shore Drive (© **773/237-5100**). See canines great and small strut their stuff. They're all adorable, but only one can win Best in Show. More than 10,000 AKC (American Kennel Club) purebred dogs of all breeds heat up the competition. It's quite a scene, particularly in the poodle area, where you can see dogs getting their hair blow-dried until they look like canine rock stars. Third week in February.

March

Spring Flower Shows. Spring is sprung a little earlier in the conservatories than it is outside in the real world, and thank goodness. See the lilies, daffodils, tulips, pansies, and other flowering perennials at **Lincoln Park Conservatory** (© **312/742-7737**) and **Garfield Park Conservatory** (© **312/746-5100**). Throughout March and April.

St. Patrick's Day Parade. Even the Chicago River puts on the green for St. Patrick's Day—it's actually dyed Kelly green for the occasion. The parade runs along Dearborn Street from Wacker Drive to Van Buren; the best place to view it is around Wacker and Dearborn. Saturday closest to March 17.

April

Opening Day. Bundle up the kids and join the diehard fans at the ballpark (and diehard fans know to wear long underwear, so follow their lead). Optimism reigns supreme and fans hope again that this will be their season. And even if it's not, hot dogs and peanuts will take some of the edge off. For the Cubs, call © **773/404-CUBS;** for the White Sox, call © **312/674-1000.** Early April.

May

Buckingham Fountain Color Light Show, in Grant Park, at Congress Parkway and Lake Shore Drive. The water and the ever-changing colored lights put on their show in the landmark fountain nightly until 11pm. May 1 through October 1.

The Ferris Wheel and **Pier Walk,** at Navy Pier, 600 E. Grand Ave. (© **312/595-PIER**). Give your kids a bird's-eye view of Chicago from the Ferris wheel (those who are slightly less fond of heights can stay closer to earth on the carousel). Another seasonal event along the water is Pier Walk, a temporary installation of more than 150 large-scale sculptures displayed along the pier's South Dock. May through October.

Art Chicago, at Navy Pier's Festival Hall, 600 E. Grand Ave. This is one of the country's largest international contemporary-art fairs, and it's currently in flux. In the past more than 200 art galleries and 2,000 artists have participated in the 5-day event. With the show's decline in popularity among art cognoscenti, Art Chicago is changing up its offerings, and we'll see what the future brings. The event is usually preceded by a bus tour through the city's gallery districts in River North and Wicker Park. For information, call © **312/587-3300.** Mother's Day weekend.

Wright Plus Tour, at The Frank Lloyd Wright Home & Studio (© **708/848-1976**). Glimpse inside the brilliant mind of Frank Lloyd

Wright on this annual tour, which features 10 buildings in Oak Park, including Frank Lloyd Wright's home and studio, the Unity Temple, and several other notable Oak Park buildings in both Prairie and Victorian styles. Tickets go on sale March 1 and can sell out within 6 weeks. Third Saturday in May.

June

Ravinia Festival, Ravinia Park, in suburban Highland Park, north of Chicago (✆ 847/266-5100 for ticket reservations; www.ravinia. org). Summer wouldn't be summer without Ravinia, a Chicago tradition. Basically, it's an outdoor concert venue with a covered pavilion and plenty of lawn seating. Offerings range from classical to pop. Kids can enjoy a picnic on the lawn while parents revel in the music of the Chicago Symphony Orchestra. Pack a picnic, jump on the Metra commuter railroad, and join the crowds sitting under the stars on the lawn. *One warning:* Ravinia is so popular that many of the first-rate visiting orchestras, chamber ensembles, pop artists, and dance companies sell out in advance. June through September.

Chicago Blues Festival, Petrillo Music Shell, at Jackson Drive and Columbus Drive in Grant Park (✆ 312/744-3315). The lineup looks better every year at this festival. Admission is free, but get there in the afternoon to stake out a spot on the lawn for the evening shows. You'll discover young up-and-coming blues stars (including some who are the offspring of blues greats, such as Shamekia Copeland, daughter of Johnny Copeland). A shuttle bus will take you from the park to blues clubs. Call for information. First week in June.

57th Street Art Fair, at 57th and Kimbark streets in Hyde Park (✆ 773/493-3247; www.57th streetartfair.org). This is the oldest juried art fair in the Midwest—in 2004 it celebrated its 57th anniversary. Kids will especially enjoy the arts and crafts projects and the fun rides. First weekend in June.

Chicago Gospel Festival, Petrillo Music Shell, at Jackson Drive and Columbus Drive in Grant Park (✆ 312/744-3315). This is the largest outdoor, free-admission event of its kind. Blues may be the city's more famous musical export, but Chicago is also the birthplace of gospel music: Thomas Dorsey, the "father of gospel music," and the greatest gospel singer ever, Mahalia Jackson, were Southsiders. This 3-day festival offers music on three stages with more than 40 performances. Early June.

Printers Row Book Fair, on Dearborn Street from Congress to Polk (✆ 312/222-3986). One of the largest free outdoor book fairs in the country, this weekend-long event features readings by children's-book authors, book signings, and panel discussions on everything from writing your first novel to finding an agent. Also on offer are more than 150 booksellers displaying new, used, and antiquarian books for sale; a poetry tent; and special activities for children. Early June.

Old Town Art Fair, historic Old Town neighborhood, at Lincoln Park West and Wisconsin Street (✆ 312/337-1938; www.oldtown triangle.com). Children's art activities are on offer at this fair; adults will appreciate the more than 200 painters, sculptors, and jewelry designers from the Midwest and around the country. The fair also features an art auction, a garden walk, and food and drink. Second weekend in June.

Wells Street Art Festival, Wells Street from North Avenue to Division Street (℡ **312/951-6106**). Held on the same weekend as the Old Town Art Fair, this arts fest is still lots of fun, with 200 arts and crafts vendors, food, music, and carnival rides. Second weekend in June.

Andersonville Midsommarfest, along Clark Street from Foster to Balmoral avenues (℡ **773/728-2995**). You can relive the Scandinavian heritage of Andersonville, once Chicago's principal Swedish community. Parents rave about the Swedish American Museum's kids' exhibits, and don't miss the treats at the Swedish Bakery, located across the street from the museum. Second weekend in June.

Puerto Rican Fest, Humboldt Park, Division Street and Sacramento Boulevard (℡ **312/744-3315**). One of Chicago's animated Latino street celebrations, this festival includes 5 days of live music, theater, games, food, and beverages. It peaks with a parade that wends its way from Wacker Drive and Dearborn Street to the West Side Puerto Rican enclave of Humboldt Park. Mid-June.

Summer Solstice Celebration, Museum of Contemporary Art, 220 E. Chicago Ave. (℡ **312/280-2660**). Hip urbanites party for 24 hours straight on the longest day of the year, as the MCA transforms into a madcap festival of art, dance, music, and performance activities. General admission is $5; children 12 and under are admitted free. June 21 to 22.

Jammin' at the Zoo, Lincoln Park Zoo, 2200 N. Cannon Dr., at Fullerton Parkway (℡ **312/742-2000**). Family fun is the emphasis at this concert; however, depending on the featured musical act (which could be rock, zydeco, or reggae music), you might find that singles are more dominant at this perfect date venue. The lovely lawn south of the zoo's Park Place Café is certainly one of the more unusual outdoor venues in the city. The first of three summer concerts is held in late June.

Grant Park Music Festival, Pritzker Pavilion, in Millennium Park (℡ **312/742-4763**). The free outdoor musical concerts in the park begin the last week in June and continue through August. If your kids are old enough to stay up past 10, call to find out about the movies in the park, shown outdoors on a large screen.

Taste of Chicago, Grant Park (℡ **312/744-3315**). *Warning:* This food fest is hot, sweaty, and can get claustrophobic. If your kids are small or don't do well in crowds, avoid it. Going on a weekday morning will help you miss the heaviest crowds. Three-and-a-half million people eat their way through cheesecake, ribs, pizza, and more, all carted to food stands set up throughout the park by scores of Chicago restaurants. On the evening of July 3, things get pretty hairy when Chicago launches its Independence Day fireworks, and crowds are at their sweaty peak. Admission is free; you pay for the sampling, of course. Late June and the first week of July.

Chicago Country Music Festival, Petrillo Music Shell, at Jackson Drive and Columbus Drive in Grant Park (℡ **312/744-3315**), is less claustrophobic than Taste of Chicago and therefore more kid-friendly. And it's free! You'll see big-name entertainers of the country-and-western genre. Late June (during the first weekend of Taste of Chicago).

Gay & Lesbian Pride Parade, on Halsted Street, from Belmont Avenue to Broadway, south to Diversey Parkway, and east to Lincoln Park (© 312/744-3315). This parade is flamboyant and colorful, the culmination of a month of activities by Chicago's gay and lesbian community. The floats, marching units, and colorful characters will keep you entertained, so pick a spot on Broadway for the best view. Last Sunday in June.

Farmers markets open at two dozen sites all over the city at the end of the month and continue weekly through October. Downtown sites are Daley Plaza (every other Thurs) and Federal Plaza (every Tues). For other locations and times, call © 312/744-3315.

July

Independence Day Celebration (© 312/744-3315). Celebrated in Chicago on July 3, concerts and fireworks are the highlights of the festivities in Grant Park. The sight of fireworks exploding over and reflecting off of Lake Michigan is well worth braving the crowd. Take public transportation, or walk.

Irish-American Heritage Festival, Irish-American Heritage Center, 4626 N. Knox Ave., at Montrose Avenue (© 773/282-7035). If your kids are into Irish dancing, made famous by *Riverdance,* make sure to check out this festival, featuring Irish music, dance, food, readings, and children's entertainment. Second weekend in July.

Sheffield Garden Walk, starting at Sheffield and Webster avenues (© 773/929-WALK). One of Chicago's largest street parties, the Sheffield Garden Walk sounds a bit more refined than it actually is—but here's your chance to snoop into the lush backyards of Lincoln Park homeowners. There are also live bands, children's activities, and food and drink vendors on tap. Mid-July.

Chicago Yacht Club's Race to Mackinac Island (© 312/861-7777). Kids who love boats will get a kick out of watching the start of this 3-day competition. At Monroe Street Harbor, boats set sail on Saturday for the grandest of the inland water races. Mid-July.

Venetian Night, from Monroe Harbor to the Adler Planetarium (© 312/744-3315). Whimsical decorations on a carnival of illuminated boats make this a great kids' event. Fireworks and synchronized music by the Grant Park Symphony Orchestra complete the scene. Watch from the shoreline, or, if you can swing it, get onboard a friend's boat. End of July.

Newberry Library Book Fair and Bughouse Square Debates, 69 W. Walton St. and Washington Square Park (© 312/255-3501). For teens with an interest in history or a love of books, this fair will be a hit. Held over 4 days, Newberry Library sells tens of thousands of used books, most under $2. The highlight is soapbox orators re-creating the Bughouse Square Debates in Washington Square Park, just across the street. Pulitzer Prize–winning author Studs Terkel emcees the spirited chaos among left-wing agitators. Late July.

August

Chicago Air & Water Show, North Avenue Beach (© 312/744-3315). Kids love this hugely popular show, held on the lake at North Avenue Beach and overhead, where you'll see Stealth bombers, F-16s, and special appearances by the U.S. Air Force Thunderbirds and Navy Seals. Because the crowds are intense at North Avenue Beach, try grabbing a portable radio and hanging at Oak

Street Beach, along the Gold Coast. Admission is free. Mid-August.

Viva! Chicago Latin Music Festival, Petrillo Music Shell, at Jackson Drive and Columbus Drive in Grant Park (℡ 312/744-3370). Salsa, mambo, and the latest Latin rock groups hit the stage for this free festival. Last weekend in August.

Chicago Jazz Festival, Petrillo Music Shell, Jackson Drive and Columbus Drive in Grant Park (℡ 312/744-3315). This festival features Chicago-style jazz, with several national headliners always on hand. The event is free; kids are welcome. Late August to early September (Labor Day weekend).

September

Boulevard Lakefront Bike Tour. This 10-mile leisurely tour especially for families lets you explore the city, from neighborhoods and the lakefront to Chicago's historic link of parks and boulevards. It starts and ends at the University of Chicago in Hyde Park, which hosts the annual Bike Expo, with vendors and entertainment, the same day. Contact Chicagoland Bicycle Federation at ℡ 312/42-PEDAL. A Sunday in mid-September.

Mexican Independence Day Parade, along Dearborn Street between Wacker Drive and Van Buren Street (℡ 312/744-3315). Chicago is home to the nation's second-largest Mexican-American population, and that makes for a great parade. Another parade is held on the next day on 26th Street in the Little Village neighborhood (℡ 773/521-5387). Saturday in mid-September.

World Music Festival Chicago, various locations around the city (℡ 312/744-6630). This relatively new and enormously popular festival is a major undertaking by the city's Department of Cultural Affairs. Call ahead for tickets, because many events sell out. The festival is held at venues around town—notably, the Chicago Cultural Center, Museum of Contemporary Art, Old Town School of Folk Music, and Hot House. You'll see top performers from Zimbabwe to Hungary to Sri Lanka performing traditional, contemporary, and fusion music. Shows are a mix of free and ticketed ($10 or less) events. Call for information and to receive updates on scheduled performances. Late September.

Celtic Fest Chicago, Petrillo Music Shell, Jackson Drive and Columbus Drive in Grant Park (℡ 312/744-3315). The city's newest music festival celebrates the music and dance of Celtic traditions from around the world. Late September.

October

Chicago Marathon (℡ 888/243-3344 or 312/904-9800; www.chicagomarathon.com). Whether or not you or your kids are runners, cheering on the harriers is an uplifting experience. Sponsored by LaSalle Bank, Chicago's marathon is a major event on the international long-distance running circuit, with some of the world's top runners competing. It begins and ends in Grant Park, but can be viewed from any number of vantage points along the race route. Second Sunday in October.

Spooky Zoo Spectacular, Lincoln Park Zoo, 2200 N. Cannon Dr. at Fullerton Parkway (℡ 312/742-2000). Dress your tots in their Halloween finest for the free treats that are dispensed at various animal habitats. Bozo the Clown—himself a Chicago native—kicks things off with a parade through the zoo grounds. Late October.

November

The Big Top, United Center, 1901 W. Madison St. (© **312/455-4500**); and the Allstate Arena, 6920 N. Mannheim Rd., Rosemont (© **847/635-6601**). This is the month that Ringling Brothers, Barnum & Bailey comes to Chicago to set up its tent. Tickets are available from Ticketmaster (© **312/559-1212**). Throughout November.

State Street Thanksgiving Parade (© **312/781-5681**) is an annual event that takes place on Thanksgiving morning beginning at 8:30am. The parade marches up State Street, from Congress to Randolph.

Magnificent Mile Lights Festival (© **312/642-3570**). Beginning at dusk, a colorful parade of Disney characters makes its way south along Michigan Avenue, from Oak Street to the Chicago River, with holiday lights being illuminated block by block as the procession passes. Carolers, elves, and minstrels appear with Santa along the avenue throughout the day and into the evening, and many of the retailers offer hot chocolate and other treats. Saturday before Thanksgiving.

Christmas Tree Lighting, Daley Center Plaza, in the Loop (© **312/744-3315**). Combine the tree lighting with another Chicago Christmas tradition—the windows at Marshall Field's, at Randolph and State streets, just a few blocks east of Daley Center Plaza. The day after Thanksgiving, around dusk.

Zoo Lights Festival, Lincoln Park Zoo, 2200 N. Cannon Dr. (© **312/742-2000**). Colorful illuminated displays brighten long nights during the holidays. Another special tradition is the annual Caroling to the Animals, a daylong songfest on a Saturday early in the month. Late November through the first week in January.

December

A Christmas Carol, Goodman Theatre, 170 N. Dearborn St. (© **312/443-3800**). This is both a seasonal favorite and a Chicago institution; it's been performed for more than 2 decades. The show runs from around Thanksgiving to the end of December.

The Nutcracker, Joffrey Ballet of Chicago, Auditorium Theatre, 50 E. Congress Pkwy. The esteemed company performs its Victorian-American twist on this holiday classic. For tickets, call the Joffrey office at © **312/739-0120.** The production runs for 3 weeks from late November to mid-December.

4 What to Pack

As you have heard too many times already, Chicago's weather is changeable. So while I can give you general guidelines for packing for various seasons, always check out **www.weather.com** or **www.chicagotribune.com** for the long-range forecast. (Granted, in Chicago they seem to

---

Tips **Quick ID**

Tie a colorful ribbon or piece of yarn around your luggage handle, or slap a distinctive sticker on the side of your bag. This makes it less likely that someone will mistakenly appropriate it. And if your luggage gets lost, it will be easier to find.

Flying or Driving With Kids

FOR A PLANE TRIP

When traveling with kids, consider packing the following in your carry-on bag:

- The number of diapers your child wears in a day, plus an extra three
- A changing pad in case the tiny restroom in the airplane has no pull-out changing table
- A minimal number of toys—one coloring book and a stuffed animal will suffice
- Bottles for infants, sippy cups and snacks for toddlers
- A goodie bag with surprises, like a Discman with a CD of music or stories, books, or small plastic toys

For more comprehensive advice on flying with children, see "Getting There," later in this chapter, and pick up a copy of *Frommer's Fly Safe, Fly Smart* by Sascha Segan (Wiley, 2002).

FOR A CAR TRIP

If you will be renting a car in Chicago, inquire about reserving a child safety seat; most major rental-car agencies have these available for a small fee (Avis, for example, charges $5 per day or $25 per week).

Driving to Chicago? Long-distance car travel with kids presents a completely different packing challenge. Pack the following to help your car trip go more smoothly:

- A cooler with drinks, snacks, fruits, and veggies
- A flashlight to help locate items that have rolled under your seat for the 10th time in the last 5 minutes
- Window shades for the sun
- Audiotapes of stories or children's songs. Many parents put a TV/VCR in between the two front seats so kids can watch videos, which can be a great help for long stretches with nothing to do.

Other items to consider bringing include a first-aid kit, a box of wipes for clean-ups, blankets, plastic bags for motion sickness, and a change of clothes. Always have a cellphone in case of emergencies.

---

have it wrong at least half of the time, but it's better than a complete shot in the dark.) Ask yourself what you'd wear in your own city in this weather, and pack it. But leave some room in the suitcase, because you will undoubtedly buy items while traveling. In fact, one seasoned-traveler trick is to pack an empty nylon duffel bag in your suitcase. On the way home, you can stuff it with souvenirs and other Chicago loot.

Because you are apt to hit four seasons in just one Chicago day, here are some packing tips:

- **Pack a light sweater and jacket,** even for summer. The Windy City can get quite breezy, and that lake air has a chill at night. Theaters and restaurants can also overdo the air-conditioning, so a light sweater helps you ward off arctic chill.
- You are not too stylish to bring **practical headgear** to Chicago in

the winter. Believe me, you will appreciate this advice later. When it gets cold in Chicago, no one goes without head covering.

- Pack **shorts** for a late-spring or early-fall trip as well as for summer. You can always pair them with a sweatshirt if it gets chilly.
- **Bring layers.** You can always stuff that jacket into your backpack, but if you skip it altogether, you may end up regretting it. This way, you'll be able to stay out all day without running back to your hotel for frequent wardrobe adjustments.

As far as dress codes go, unless you and your kids are planning a big night out, like at the Pump Room at the Omni Ambassador East Hotel, for example, you will be just fine in "nice casual" attire. For men, that means a dress shirt, sports jacket, and tie for the fanciest places. For women, a long skirt with boots and a nice sweater goes just about anywhere in the winter. In the summer you'll be comfortable in cool slacks and cotton tops with sandals. If you are planning a very special night out, check to see if the restaurant enforces a dress code. Otherwise, you might end up borrowing a less-than-attractive tie and jacket from the maitre d'. You'll find that people dress more conservatively here than in New York or Los Angeles, and as a traveler you can blend in easily with a suitcase full of the basics: khakis, jeans, shorts, sandals, boots, and sweaters.

5 Insurance & Health

TRAVEL INSURANCE AT A GLANCE

Check your existing insurance policies before you buy travel insurance to cover trip cancellation, lost luggage, medical expenses, or car-rental insurance. You're likely to have partial or complete coverage. But if you need some, ask your travel agent about a comprehensive package. The cost of travel insurance varies widely, depending on the cost and length of your trip, your age and overall health, and the type of trip you're taking. Some insurers provide packages for specialty vacations, such as skiing or backpacking. More dangerous activities may be excluded from basic policies.

And keep in mind that in the aftermath of the September 11, 2001, terrorist attacks, a number of airlines, cruise lines, and tour operators are no longer covered by insurers. *The bottom line:* Always, always check the fine print before you sign on; more and more policies have built-in exclusions and restrictions that may leave you out in the cold if something does go awry.

For information, contact one of the following popular insurers:

- **Access America** (© 866/807-3982; www.accessamerica.com)
- **Travel Guard International** (© 800/826-4919; www.travelguard.com)
- **Travel Insured International** (© 800/243-3174; www.travelinsured.com)
- **Travelex Insurance Services** (© 888/457-4602; www.travelex-insurance.com)

STAYING HEALTHY

You won't need to take any unusual precautions when traveling to Chicago. The regular assortment of antacids, anti-diarrheals, and some acetaminophen or ibuprofen for headaches should suffice. Lake Michigan rarely gets rough enough to advise bringing motion sickness medication for boat tours; however, if you or your kids are particularly susceptible, or if you're planning a long fishing excursion, you may want to add some to your bag.

Avoiding "Economy Class Syndrome"

Deep vein thrombosis, or as it's know in the world of flying, "economy class syndrome," is a blood clot that develops in a deep vein. It's a potentially deadly condition that can be caused by sitting in cramped conditions—such as an airplane cabin—for too long. During a flight (especially a long-haul flight), get up, walk around, and stretch your legs every 60 to 90 minutes to keep your blood flowing. Other preventative measures include frequent flexing of the legs while sitting, drinking lots of water, and avoiding alcohol and sleeping pills. If you have a history of deep vein thrombosis, heart disease, or other condition that puts you at high risk, some experts recommend wearing compression stockings or taking anticoagulants when you fly; always ask your physician about the best course for you. Symptoms of deep vein thrombosis include leg pain or swelling, or even shortness of breath.

Pack prescription medications in your carry-on luggage, and keep them in their original containers. Also bring along copies of your prescriptions in case you lose your pills or run out. And don't forget sunglasses and an extra pair of contact lenses or prescription glasses.

WHERE TO GO IF YOU GET SICK AWAY FROM HOME

In downtown Chicago, the most centrally located hospital is **Northwestern Memorial Hospital,** 251 E. Huron St. (✆ **312/926-2000**), just east of Michigan Avenue. Their physician referral service is ✆ **312/926-8000.** The emergency department is at 250 E. Erie St., near Fairbanks Court (✆ **312/926-5188**).

MEDICAL INSURANCE

If you worry about getting sick away from home, consider purchasing **medical travel insurance** and remember to carry your ID card in your purse or wallet. Most health insurance policies cover you if you get sick away from home—but check, particularly if you're insured by an HMO. Members of **Blue Cross/Blue Shield** can now use their cards at select hospitals in most major cities worldwide (✆ **800/810-BLUE** or www.bluecares.com for a list of hospitals).

If you require additional insurance, try one of the following companies:

- **MEDEX International** (✆ **888/MEDEX-00** or 410/453-6300; www.medexassist.com)
- **Travel Assistance International** (✆ **800/821-2828;** www.travel assistance.com; for general information on services, call the company's **Worldwide Assistance Services, Inc.,** at ✆ 800/777-8710).

The cost of travel medical insurance varies widely. Check your existing policies before you buy additional coverage. Also, check to see if your medical insurance covers you for emergency medical evacuation: If you have to buy a one-way same-day ticket home and forfeit your nonrefundable round-trip ticket, you may be out big bucks.

If you suffer from a chronic illness, consult your doctor before your departure. For conditions like epilepsy, diabetes, or heart problems, wear a **MedicAlert Identification Tag** (✆ **800/825-3785;** www.medicalert. org), which will immediately alert doctors to your condition and give them access to your records through MedicAlert's 24-hour hot line.

6 Words of Wisdom on Traveling Safely with Kids in Chicago

The easiest way to stay safe in Chicago is to **hold hands with your kids.** It's safe and fun, without being overly protective. Keep your kids close and within eyeshot, and be extra careful around busy intersections. Cabs will not slow down for anyone—even families with kids. Do not cross anywhere but at traffic lights (it sounds obvious, but I've seen parents with strollers crossing in the middle of busy streets). Again, drivers won't stop for you in the city just because you have a stroller. Stay on major streets and avoid construction sites.

Visitors should steer clear of situations where kids could get lost in a crowd. At the ballpark, at the end of the game, wait until most of the crowd files out so kids can go at their own pace. Remember, Michigan Avenue and major attractions can get crowded in the summer. **Make contingency plans for reuniting,** even in the most ordinary situations. Start at the information desk at whatever attraction you're visiting, and make a plan to meet there in case you and your kids get split up.

Another tip is to **use public transportation.** If you are driving in to the city, park in a central location and walk or take the El or bus. Don't plan on taking a cab with small children unless you want to carry a car seat with you. Some parents find trains to be easier with children than the buses because you can roll strollers right onto trains, and you don't have to stand on a busy street corner like you would if waiting for the bus.

Finally, **travel light** and avoid being overburdened or distracted by too much gear. Carry water, juice, and snacks (downtown, you will pay a ton to buy these items). Also, be prepared for a lack of chain fast-food outlets. When visiting major attractions, you may be able to avoid taking a stroller because most places rent them. If you do feel the need to bring a stroller, make sure it's light and narrow—some of the sturdy but wide strollers are hard to maneuver through city crowds and narrow store aisles.

Several books on the market offer additional tips to help you travel with kids. *How to Take Great Trips with Your Kids* (The Harvard Common Press; $9.95), is full of good general advice that can apply to travel anywhere. *Family Travel Times* (© 888/822-4FTT; www.familytraveltimes.com) is an excellent online newsletter updated twice monthly. Subscriptions are $39 a year, $49 for 2 years. Sample articles are available on the newsletter's website. Other recommended family travel Internet sites include **Family Travel Forum** (www.familytravelforum.com), a comprehensive site that offers customized trip planning; **Family Travel Network** (www.familytravelnetwork.com), an award-winning site that offers travel features, deals, and tips; and **Family Travel Files** (www.thefamilytravelfiles.com), which offers an online magazine and a directory of off-the-beaten-path tours and tour operators for families.

7 Planning Your Trip Online

SURFING FOR AIRFARES

The "big three" online travel agencies, **Expedia.com, Travelocity.com,** and **Orbitz.com** sell most of the air tickets bought on the Internet. (Canadian travelers should try expedia.ca and travelocity.ca; U.K. residents can go for expedia.co.uk and opodo.co.uk.). Each has different business deals with the airlines and may offer different fares on the same flights, so it's wise to shop around. Expedia and Travelocity will also send you **e-mail notification** when a cheap fare becomes available to your favorite destination. Of the smaller travel agency websites, **Side-Step** (www.sidestep.com) has garnered the best reviews from Frommer's authors. It's a browser add-on that purports to "search 140 sites at once," but in reality only beats competitors' fares as often as other sites do.

Also remember to check **airline websites,** especially those for low-fare carriers such as Southwest, JetBlue, AirTran, WestJet, or Ryanair, whose fares are often misreported or simply missing from travel agency websites. Even with major airlines, you can often shave a few bucks from a fare by booking directly through the airline and avoiding a travel agency's transaction fee. But you'll get these discounts only by **booking online:** Most airlines now offer online-only fares that even their phone agents know nothing about. For the websites of airlines that fly to and from your destination, go to "Getting There," later in this chapter.

Great **last-minute deals** are available through free weekly e-mail services provided directly by the airlines. Most of these are announced on Tuesday or Wednesday and must be purchased online. Most are only valid for travel that weekend, but some (such as Southwest's) can be booked weeks or months in advance. Sign up for weekly e-mail alerts at airline websites or check megasites that compile comprehensive lists of last-minute specials, such as **Smarter Living** (smarter living.com). For last-minute trips, **site59.com** and **lastminutetravel. com** in the U.S. and **lastminute.com** in Europe often have better air-and-hotel package deals than the major-label sites. A website listing numerous bargain sites and airlines around the world is **www.itravelnet.com**.

If you're willing to give up some control over your flight details, use what is called an **"opaque" fare**

service like **Priceline** (www.priceline. com; www.priceline.co.uk for Europeans) or its smaller competitor **Hotwire** (www.hotwire.com). Both offer rock-bottom prices in exchange for travel on a "mystery airline" at a mysterious time of day, often with a mysterious change of planes en route. The mystery airlines are all major, well-known carriers—and the possibility of being sent from Philadelphia to Chicago via Tampa is remote; the airlines' routing computers have gotten a lot better than they used to be. But your chances of getting a 6am or 11pm flight are pretty high. Hotwire tells you flight prices before you buy; Priceline usually has better deals than Hotwire, but you have to play their "name our price" game. If you're new at this, the helpful folks at **BiddingForTravel** (www.biddingfortravel.com) do a good job of demystifying Priceline's prices and strategies. Priceline and Hotwire are great for flights within North America and between the U.S. and Europe. But for flights to other parts of the world, consolidators will almost always beat their fares. *Note:* In 2004 Priceline added nonopaque service to its roster. You now have the option to pick exact flights, times, and airlines from a list of offers—or opt to bid on opaque fares as before.

For much more about airfares and savvy air-travel tips and advice, pick up a copy of *Frommer's Fly Safe, Fly Smart* (Wiley Publishing, Inc.).

SURFING FOR HOTELS

Shopping online for hotels is generally done one of two ways: by booking through the hotel's own website or through an independent booking agency (or a fare-service agency like Priceline; see below). These Internet hotel agencies have multiplied in mind-boggling numbers of late, competing for the business of millions of consumers surfing for accommodations around the world. This competitiveness can be a boon to consumers

Frommers.com: The Complete Travel Resource

For an excellent travel-planning resource, we highly recommend **Frommers.com** (www.frommers.com), voted Best Travel Site by *PC Magazine*. We're a little biased, of course, but we guarantee that you'll find the travel tips, reviews, monthly vacation giveaways, bookstore, and online-booking capabilities thoroughly indispensable. Among the special features are our popular **Destinations** section, where you'll get expert travel tips, hotel and dining recommendations, and advice on the sights to see for more than 3,500 destinations around the globe; the **Frommers.com Newsletter,** with the latest deals, travel trends, and money-saving secrets; our **Community** area featuring **Message Boards,** where Frommer's readers post queries and share advice (sometimes even our authors show up to answer questions); and our **Photo Center,** where you can post queries and share money-saving tips. When your research is done, the **Online Reservations System** (www.frommers.com/book_a_trip) takes you to Frommer's preferred online partners for booking your vacation at affordable prices.

who have the patience and time to shop and compare the online sites for good deals—but shop they must, for prices can vary considerably from site to site. And keep in mind that hotels at the top of a site's listing may be there for no other reason than that they paid money to get the placement.

Of the "big three" sites, **Expedia** offers a long list of special deals and "virtual tours" or photos of available rooms so you can see what you're paying for (a feature that helps counter the claims that the best rooms are often held back from bargain booking websites). **Travelocity** posts unvarnished customer reviews and ranks its properties according to the AAA rating system. Also reliable are **Hotels.com** and **Quikbook.com.** An excellent free program, **Travelaxe** (www.travelaxe.net), can help you search multiple hotel sites at once, even ones you may never have heard of—and conveniently lists the total price of the room, including the taxes and service charges. Another booking site, **Travelweb** (www.travelweb.com), is partly owned by the hotels it represents (including the Hilton, Hyatt, and Starwood chains) and is therefore plugged directly into the hotels' reservations systems—unlike independent online agencies, which have to fax or e-mail reservation requests to the hotel, a good portion of which get misplaced in the shuffle. More than once, travelers have arrived at the hotel only to be told that they have no reservation. To be fair, many of the major sites are undergoing improvements in service and ease of use, and Expedia will soon be able to plug directly into the reservations systems of many hotel chains—none of which can be bad news for consumers. In the meantime it's a good idea to **get a confirmation number** and **make a printout** of any online booking transaction.

In the opaque website category, **Priceline** and **Hotwire** are even better for hotels than for airfares; with both, you're allowed to pick the neighborhood and quality level of your hotel before offering up your money. Priceline's hotel product even covers Europe and Asia, though it's much better at getting five-star lodgings for three-star prices than at finding anything at the bottom of the scale. On the downside, many hotels stick Priceline guests in their least desirable rooms. Be sure to go to the BiddingForTravel website (see above) before bidding on a hotel room on Priceline; it features a fairly up-to-date list of hotels that Priceline uses in major cities. For both Priceline and Hotwire, you pay upfront, and the fee is nonrefundable. *Note:* Some hotels do not provide loyalty program credits or points or other frequent-stay amenities when you book a room through opaque online services.

SURFING FOR RENTAL CARS

For booking rental cars online, the best deals are usually found at rental-car company websites, although all the major online travel agencies also offer rental-car reservations services. Priceline and Hotwire work well for rental cars too; the only "mystery" is which major rental company you get, and for most travelers the difference between Hertz, Avis, and Budget is negligible.

8 The 21st-Century Traveler

INTERNET ACCESS AWAY FROM HOME

Travelers have any number of ways to check their e-mail and access the Internet on the road. Of course, using your own laptop—or even a PDA (personal digital assistant) or electronic organizer with a modem—gives you the most flexibility. But even if you don't have a computer, you can still access your e-mail and even your office computer from cybercafes.

WITHOUT YOUR OWN COMPUTER

It's hard nowadays to find a city that *doesn't* have a few cybercafes. Although there's no definitive directory for cybercafes—these are independent businesses, after all—two places to start looking are at **www.cybercaptive.com** and **www.cybercafe.com**. You'll do best looking in neighborhoods that house students, such as Lincoln Park, which is home to DePaul University.

Aside from formal cybercafes, most **youth hostels** nowadays have at least one computer you can get to the Internet on. And most **public libraries** across the world offer Internet access free or for a small charge. Avoid **hotel business centers** unless you're willing to pay exorbitant rates.

Most major airports now have **Internet kiosks** scattered throughout their gates. These kiosks, which you'll also see in shopping malls, hotel lobbies, and tourist information offices around the world, give you basic Web access for a per-minute fee that's usually higher than cybercafe prices. The kiosks' clunkiness and high price mean they should be avoided whenever possible.

To retrieve your e-mail, ask your **Internet Service Provider (ISP)** if it has a Web-based interface tied to your existing e-mail account. If your ISP doesn't have such an interface, you can use the free **mail2web** service (www.mail2web.com) to view and reply to your home e-mail. For more flexibility, you may want to open a free, Web-based e-mail account with **Yahoo! Mail** (http://mail.yahoo.com). (Microsoft's Hotmail is another popular option, but Hotmail has severe spam problems.) Your home ISP may be able to forward your e-mail to the Web-based account automatically.

If you need to access files on your office computer, look into a service called **GoToMyPC** (www.gotomypc.com). The service provides a Web-based interface for you to access and manipulate a distant PC from anywhere—even a cybercafe—provided your "target" PC is on and has an always-on connection to the Internet (such as with Road Runner cable).

The service offers top-quality security, but if you're worried about hackers, use your own laptop rather than a cybercafe computer to access the GoToMyPC system.

WITH YOUR OWN COMPUTER

Wi-fi (wireless fidelity) is the buzz-word in computer access, and more and more hotels, cafes, and retailers are signing on as wireless "hotspots" from where you can get high-speed connection without cable wires, net-working hardware, or a phone line (see below). You can get wi-fi connection one of several ways. Many laptops sold in the last year have built-in wi-fi capability (an 802.11b wireless Ether-net connection). Mac owners have their own networking technology, Apple AirPort. For those with older computers, an 802.11b/**wi-fi card** (around $50) can be plugged into your laptop. You sign up for wireless access service much as you do cell-phone service, through a plan offered by one of several commercial compa-nies that have made wireless service available in airports, hotel lobbies, and coffee shops, primarily in the U.S.

(followed by the U.K. and Japan). **T-Mobile Hotspot** (www.t-mobile. com/hotspot) serves up wireless con-nections at more than 1,000 Starbucks coffee shops nationwide. **Boingo** (www.boingo.com) and **Wayport** (www.wayport.com) have set up net-works in airports and high-class hotel lobbies. IPass providers (see below) also give you access to a few hundred wireless hotel lobby setups. Best of all, you don't need to be staying at the Four Seasons to use the hotel's net-work; just set yourself up on a nice couch in the lobby. The companies' pricing policies can be Byzantine, with a variety of monthly, per-connection, and per-minute plans, but in general you pay around $30 a month for lim-ited access—and as more and more companies jump on the wireless band-wagon, prices are likely to get even more competitive.

There are also places that provide **free wireless networks** in cities around the world. To locate these free hotspots, go to **www.personaltelco.net/index. cgi/WirelessCommunities**.

Most business-class hotels through-out the world offer dataports for lap-

---

Digital Photography on the Road

Many travelers are going digital these days when it comes to taking vaca-tion photographs. Not only are digital cameras left relatively unscathed by airport X-rays, but with digital equipment, you don't need to lug arm-loads of film with you as you travel. In fact, nowadays you don't even need to carry your laptop to download the day's images to make room for more. With a **media storage card,** sold by all major camera dealers, you can store hundreds of images in your camera. These "memory" cards come in different configurations—from memory sticks to flash cards to secure digital cards—and different storage capacities (the more megabytes of memory, the more images a card can hold) and range in price from $30 to over $200. (**Note:** Each camera model works with a spe-cific type of card, so you'll need to determine which storage card is com-patible with your camera.) When you get home, you can print the images out on your own color printer or take the storage card to a camera store, drugstore, or chain retailer. Or have the images developed online with a service like **Snapfish** (www.snapfish.com) for something like 25¢ a shot. See "Flying with Film & Video," on p. 47.

Online Traveler's Toolbox

Veteran travelers usually carry some essential items to make their trips easier. Following is a selection of handy online tools to bookmark and use.

- **Airplane Seating and Food.** Find out which seats to reserve and which to avoid (and more) on all major domestic airlines at www.seatguru.com. And check out the type of meal (with photos) you'll likely be served on airlines around the world at www.airlinemeals.com.
- **Intellicast** (www.intellicast.com) and **Weather.com** (www.weather.com). Gives weather forecasts for all 50 states and for cities around the world.
- **Mapquest** (www.mapquest.com). This best of the mapping sites lets you choose a specific address or destination, and in seconds it will return a map and detailed directions.
- **Subway Navigator** (www.subwaynavigator.com). Download subway maps and get savvy advice on using subway systems in dozens of major cities around the world.
- **Time and Date** (www.timeanddate.com). See what time (and day) it is anywhere in the world.
- **Visa ATM Locator** (www.visa.com) for locations of PLUS ATMs worldwide, or **MasterCard ATM Locator** (www.mastercard.com) for locations of Cirrus ATMs worldwide.

top modems, and a few thousand hotels in the U.S. and Europe now offer free high-speed Internet access using an Ethernet network cable. You can bring your own cables, but most hotels rent them for around $10. **Call your hotel in advance** to see what your options are.

In addition, major Internet Service Providers (ISPs) have **local access numbers** around the world, allowing you to go online by simply placing a local call. Check your ISP's website or call its toll-free number and ask how you can use your current account away from home, and how much it will cost.

If you're traveling outside the reach of your ISP, the **iPass** network has dial-up numbers in most countries around the world. You'll have to sign up with an iPass provider, who will then tell you how to set up your computer for

your destination(s). For a list of iPass providers, go to www.ipass.com and click on "Individuals Buy Now." One solid provider is **i2roam** (www.i2roam.com; © **866/811-6209** or 920/235-0475).

Wherever you go, bring a **connection kit** of the right power and phone adapters, a spare phone cord, and a spare Ethernet network cable—or find out whether your hotel supplies them to guests.

USING A CELLPHONE

Just because your cellphone works at home doesn't mean it'll work elsewhere in the U.S. (thanks to our nation's fragmented cellphone system). It's a good bet that your phone will work in major cities—although some services work better in Chicago than others. U.S. Cellular is based here, so if that's your service, you're in luck. But whatever your wireless company, take a look at the coverage map on its website before heading out—T-Mobile, Sprint, and Nextel are particularly weak in rural areas. If you need to stay in touch at a destination where you know your phone won't work, **rent** a phone that does from **InTouch USA** (© **800/872-7626;** www.intouchglobal.com) or a rental car location, but beware that you'll pay $1 a minute or more for airtime.

If you're not from the U.S., you'll be appalled at the poor reach of our **GSM (Global System for Mobiles) wireless network,** which is used by much of the rest of the world (see below). Your phone will probably work in most major U.S. cities; it definitely won't work in many rural areas. (To see where GSM phones work in the U.S., check out www.t-mobile.com/coverage/national_popup.asp.) And you may or may not be able to send SMS (text messaging) home—something Americans tend not to anyway, for various cultural and technological reasons. (International budget travelers like to send text messages home because it's much cheaper than making international calls.) Assume nothing—call your wireless provider and get the full scoop. In a worst-case scenario, you can always rent a phone; InTouch USA delivers to hotels.

9 Getting There

BY PLANE
THE MAJOR AIRLINES
Domestic carriers that fly regularly to O'Hare include **American** (© 800/433-7300; www.aa.com), **Continental** (© 800/525-0280; www.continental.com), **Delta** (© 800/221-1212; www.delta.com), **Northwest** (© 800/225-2525; www.nwa.com), **United** (© 800/864-8331; www.united.com), and **US Airways** (© 800/428-4322; www.usairways.com). Commuter service is also provided by several regional airlines. Airlines that fly to Chicago's Midway Airport are **America West** (© 800/235-9292; www.americawest.com), **AirTran Airways** (© 800/247-8726; www.airtran.com), **ATA** (© 800/435-9282; www.ata.com), **Continental** (© 800/525-0280; www.continental.com), **Frontier** (© 800/432-1359; www.frontierairlines.com), **Northwest** (© 800/225-2525; www.nwa.com), and **Southwest** (© 800/435-9792; www.iflyswa.com). The toll-free numbers listed are for use in the United States and Canada.

FLYING FOR LESS: TIPS FOR GETTING THE BEST AIRFARES
Airfares are a great example of capitalism at work: Passengers within the

---

Tips Kids with Colds

It's more difficult for kids to make their ears pop during takeoff and landing than it is for adults. The eustachian tube is especially narrow in children; the passage is even tighter when mucous membranes are swollen. This can make ascent and descent especially painful—even dangerous—for a child with congested sinuses. If your little one is suffering from a cold or the flu, it's best to keep him grounded until he recuperates, if that's an option. If you must travel with your child as scheduled, give them an oral child's decongestant an hour before ascent and descent or administer a spray decongestant before and during takeoff and landing.

Tips Don't Stow It—Ship It

If ease of travel is your main concern and money is no object, you can ship your luggage and sports equipment with one of the growing number of luggage-service companies that pick up, track, and deliver your luggage (often through couriers such as Federal Express) with minimum hassle for you. Traveling luggage-free may be ultraconvenient, but it's not cheap: One-way overnight shipping can cost from $100 to $200, depending on what you're sending. Still, for some people, especially the elderly or the infirm, it's a sensible solution to lugging heavy baggage. Specialists in door-to-door luggage delivery are **Virtual Bellhop** (www.virtualbellhop. com), **SkyCap International** (www.skycapinternational.com), **Luggage Express** (www.usxpluggageexpress.com), and **Sports Express** (www.sports express.com).

---

same airplane cabin rarely pay the same fare for their seats. Rather, each pays what the market will bear. Business travelers who need to purchase tickets at the last minute, change their itinerary at a moment's notice, or get home before the weekend pay the premium rate, known as the full fare. Passengers who can book their ticket long in advance, who don't mind staying over Saturday night, or who are willing to travel on a Tuesday, Wednesday, or Thursday after 7pm will pay a fraction of the full fare. On most flights, even the shortest hops, the full fare is close to $1,000, but a 7-day or 14-day advance purchase ticket is closer to $200 to $300. Here are a few other easy ways to save:

- Periodically, airlines lower prices on their most popular routes. Check your newspaper for advertised discounts, or call the airlines directly and ask if any **promotional rates** or special fares are available. You'll almost never see a sale during the peak summer vacation months of July and August, or during the Thanksgiving or Christmas seasons; in periods of low-volume travel, however, you should pay no more than $400 for a cross-country flight. If your schedule is flexible, ask if you can secure a cheaper fare by staying an

extra day or by flying midweek. (Many airlines won't volunteer this information.) If you already hold a ticket when a sale breaks, it may even pay to exchange your ticket, but keep in mind you'll usually incur a change fee of as much as $100 to do so.

Note: The lowest-priced fares often are nonrefundable, require advance purchase of 1 to 3 weeks and a certain length of stay, and carry penalties for changing dates of travel.

- **Consolidators,** also known as bucket shops, are a good place to find low fares. Consolidators buy seats in bulk from the airlines and then sell them back to the public at prices below even the airlines' discounted rates. Their small ads usually run in the Sunday travel section of your newspaper at the bottom of the page. Before you pay, however, ask for a confirmation number from the consolidator, and then call the airline itself to confirm your seat. Be prepared to book your ticket with a different consolidator if the airline can't confirm your reservation. Also be aware that bucket-shop tickets are usually nonrefundable or rigged with stiff cancellation penalties,

Air Travel Security Measures

In the wake of the terrorist attacks of September 11, 2001, the airline industry implemented sweeping security measures in airports. Although regulations vary from airline to airline, you can expedite the check-in process and alleviate airport stress by taking the following steps:

- **Arrive early.** Times vary from airport to airport, depending on their size. Figure on arriving for check-in anywhere from a minimum of an hour in advance to at least 2 hours before your scheduled flight.
- **Don't count on curbside check-in.** Some airlines and airports have stopped curbside check-in altogether, whereas others offer it on a limited basis. For up-to-date information, check with the individual airline.
- **Be sure to carry plenty of documentation.** An up-to-date, government-issued photo ID (federal, state, or local) is now required. You may need to show this at various checkpoints. With an e-ticket, you may be required to have with you printed confirmation of purchase, and perhaps even the credit card with which you bought your ticket. This varies from airline to airline, so call ahead to make sure you have the proper documentation.
- **Know what you can carry on—and what you can't.** Travelers in the United States are now limited to one carry-on bag, plus one personal bag (such as a purse or a briefcase). The **Transportation Security Administration (TSA)** has also issued a list of banned carry-on items; for more information, check the TSA website at www.tsa.gov. Your airline may have additional restrictions on carry-on items, so call ahead to avoid problems.
- **Prepare to be searched.** Expect spot-checks. Electronic items (such as a laptop or cellphone) should be readied for additional screening. Be prepared to place your jewelry, loose change, and any other metallic items on your person in bins before you go through security.
- **It's no joke.** If anyone asks you security-related questions, don't be flip. The agents will not hesitate to call security.

often as high as 50% to 75% of the ticket price.

STA Travel (© **800/777-0112;** www.statravel.com) caters especially to young travelers, but their bargain-basement prices are available to people of all ages. **1800airfare** (© **800/AIR-FARE;** www. 1800airfare.com) was formerly owned by TWA but now offers the deepest discounts on many other airlines, with a 4-day advance purchase. Other reliable consolidators include **1-800-FLY-CHEAP** (www.1800flycheap. com); **TFI Tours International** (© **800/745-8000** or 212/736-1140), which serves as a clearinghouse for unused seats; or "rebators" such as **Travel Avenue** (© **800/333-3335**), which rebates part of its commissions to you.

- Search **the Internet** for cheap fares. Great last-minute deals are available through free weekly e-mail services provided directly by the airlines. Websites such as **Frommers.com** (www.frommers.com), **Travelocity** (www.travelocity.com), **Expedia** (www.expedia.com), **Qixo** (www.qixo.com), and **Orbitz** (www.orbitz.com) allow consumers to comparison-shop for airfares, access special bargains, book flights, and reserve hotel rooms and rental cars. See the section "Planning Your Trip Online," earlier in this chapter.

- Join a travel club such as **Moment's Notice** (© 718/234-6295; www.moments-notice.com) or **Travelers Advantage** (© 877/259-2691; www.travelersadvantage.com), which supply unsold tickets at discounted prices. You pay an annual membership fee to get the club's hot line number. Of course, you're limited to what's available, so you have to be flexible.

- Join **frequent-flier clubs.** It's best to accrue miles on one program, so you can rack up free flights and achieve elite status faster. But it makes sense to open as many accounts as possible, no matter how seldom you fly a particular airline. It's free, and you'll get the best choice of seats, faster response to phone inquiries, and prompter service if your luggage is stolen, your flight is canceled or delayed, or if you want to change your seat.

CHICAGO'S AIRPORTS

The one experience most Chicago visitors share is **O'Hare International Airport** (© 773/686-2200). O'Hare has long battled with Atlanta's Hartsfield for the title of the world's busiest airport. The airport reigns as a major hub for making connections worldwide. O'Hare boasts its own police force, zip code, medical center, cemetery, and chapel.

O'Hare is located northwest of the city proper, about a 25- to 30-minute drive from downtown, depending, of course, on the traffic. A cab ride into the city will cost you about $30 to $35. You can also ask the taxi-stand attendant to arrange a shared ride for you, which will cost about $15 per person.

For $1.75, you can take the El (vernacular for the elevated train), which will efficiently get you downtown in about 40 minutes, regardless of traffic. Trains leave every 6 to 10 minutes during the day, and every half-hour in the evening and overnight. O'Hare also has outposts for every major car-rental company (see "Getting Around" in chapter 3 for details).

O'Hare has information booths in all five terminals, most located on the baggage level. The multilingual personnel, who are outfitted in red jackets, can assist travelers with everything from arranging ground transportation to getting information about local hotels. The booths also offer a plethora of useful tourism brochures. The booths, labeled "Airport Information," are open daily from 9am to 8pm.

On the opposite end of the city, the southwest side, is Chicago's other major airport, **Midway** (© 773/838-0600). A new terminal has eased considerable crowding problems and expanded the selection of restaurants

---

Fun Fact O'Hare, Oh My

Chicago's O'Hare International Airport handles more passengers and aircraft operations than any other airport in the world. Approximately 200,000 travelers pass through O'Hare each day, generating about 500,000 jobs for the region. O'Hare is completely self-supporting, requiring no local taxpayer dollars to keep it going.

Travel in the Age of Bankruptcy

Airlines can go bankrupt, so protect yourself by **buying your tickets with a credit card,** as the Fair Credit Billing Act guarantees that you can get your money back from the credit card company if a travel supplier goes under (and if you request the refund within 60 days of the bankruptcy). **Travel insurance** can also help, but make sure it covers against "carrier default" for your specific travel provider. And be aware that if a U.S. airline goes bust midtrip, a 2001 federal law requires other carriers to take you to your destination (albeit on a space-available basis) for a fee of no more than $25, provided you rebook within 60 days of the cancellation.

and shops. Although it's smaller than O'Hare and fewer airlines have routes here, Midway is closer to the Loop and you may be able to get a cheaper fare flying into this airport. (Always check fares flying into both airports if you want to find the best deal.) The El Orange Line extends to Midway, so you can make it downtown in about half an hour for $1.75. Please note that the Orange Line stops operating each night at about 11:30pm and resumes service by 5am. Trains leave the station every 6 to 15 minutes. Most major car-rental companies have counters at Midway as well.

You can find the latest information on both airports at the city's Department of Aviation website: **www. ohare.com.**

Continental Airport Express (© 800/654-7871 or 312/454-7800; www.airportexpress.com) serves most first-class hotels in Chicago with its blue-and-white Airport Express vans; ticket counters are located at both airports near the baggage claim (outside Customs at the international terminal at O'Hare). For transportation to the airport, reserve a spot from one of the hotels (check with the bell captain). The cost is $21 one-way ($39 roundtrip) to or from O'Hare and $16 one-way ($30 round-trip) to or from Midway. The shuttles operate from 6am to 11:30pm. For limo service from either O'Hare or Midway, call **Carey Limousine of Chicago** (© 773/631-7200), or **Chicago Limousine**

Services (© 312/726-1035). Depending on the number of passengers and whether you opt for a sedan or stretch limo, the service will cost about $80 to $130, including gratuity and tax.

With 1 week's notice, **CTA paratransit** offers door-to-door lift services to and from O'Hare for travelers with disabilities. Visitors must be registered with a similar program in their home city. For information, call © 312/432-7025 or TTY 312/917-1338.

SAFE SEATS FOR KIDS

The practice of allowing children younger than 2 to ride for free on a parent's lap may be prohibited by the time you read this. At press time the FAA was writing a rule that would require all children under 40 pounds to have their own tickets and be secured in a child seat.

All the major American airlines except Delta now offer discounted infant tickets for children 2 years of age or younger, to make it more affordable for you to reserve a separate adjacent seat for your baby and a restraining device.

(Most airlines require that an infant be 2 weeks old to travel—bring a birth certificate. American and Continental only require that the child be 7 days old. Alaska lets babies fly as soon as they're born.)

For now, if a seat adjacent to yours is available, your lap child can sit there free of charge. When you check in, ask if the flight is crowded. If it isn't, explain your situation to the agent and ask if you can reserve two seats—or simply move to two empty adjacent seats once the plane is boarded. You might want to shop around before you buy your ticket and deliberately book a flight that's not very busy. Ask the reservationist which flights tend to be most full and avoid those. Only one extra child is allowed in each row, however, due to the limited number of oxygen masks.

On international journeys children already can't ride free on parents' laps. On flights overseas a lap fare usually costs 10 percent of the parent's ticket price. Children who meet the airline's age limit (which ranges from 11–15 years old) can purchase international fares at 50% to 75% of the lowest coach fare in certain markets. Some of the foreign carriers make even greater allowances for children.

Children riding for free will usually not be granted any baggage allowance.

All airlines offer child meals if requested in advance. Ticketed babies can get "infant meals" on America West, Delta, and US Airways, and all major airlines except Alaska and Southwest will warm bottles on request.

CHILD SEATS: THEY'RE A MUST

According to *Consumer Reports Travel Letter*, the National Transportation Safety Board says that, since 1991, the deaths of five children and injuries to four could have been prevented had the children been sitting in restraint systems during their flights. Even in the event of moderate turbulence, children sitting on a parent's lap can be thrust forward and injured. When you consider that a commercial aircraft hits a significant amount of turbulence at least once a day on average, you'd do well to think about investing a few hundred dollars for a safety seat.

The FAA recommends that children under 20 pounds ride in a rear-facing child-restraint system, and says children that weigh 20 to 40 pounds should sit in a forward-facing child-restraint system. Children over 40 pounds should sit in a regular seat and wear a seat belt.

All child seats manufactured after 1985 are certified for airline use, but make sure your chair will fit in an airline seat—it must be less than 16 inches wide. You may not use booster seats or seatless vests or harness systems. Safety seats must be placed in window seats—except in exit rows, where they are prohibited, so as not to block the passage of other travelers in the case of an emergency.

The airlines themselves should carry child safety seats onboard. Unfortunately, most don't. To make matters worse, overzealous flight attendants have been known to try to keep safety seats off planes. One traveler recounts in the November 2001 issue of *Consumer Reports Travel Letter*

The Custody Trap

Because of concern about parental abductions, special requirements exist for children flying to many foreign countries, including Mexico. If they're with one parent, they must bring a notarized consent document from the other parent—even if the missing parent is the one waving goodbye at the airport! A decree of sole custody or parental death certificate will also do. Minors traveling alone to these countries must bring either two consent forms, a decree of sole custody and one consent form, or applicable death certificates. Ask your airline what's required when you book the ticket.

how a Southwest attendant attempted to block use of a seat because the red label certifying it as safe for airline use had flaked off. That traveler won her case by bringing the owner's manual and appealing to the pilot—you should do the same.

Getting safety seats on an international flight may be even more difficult. Ask to make sure you can use your safety seat when you book a flight on a foreign airline.

Until the new FAA rule comes into effect, if you can't afford the expense of a separate ticket, book a ticket toward the back of the plane at a time when air travel is likely to be slowest—and the seat next to you is most likely to be empty. The reservationist should also be able to recommend the best (meaning the least busy) time for you to fly.

CHILDREN TRAVELING SOLO

Although individual airline policies differ (check with the specific airline for details), for the most part children ages 5 to 11 pay the regular adult fare and can travel alone as unaccompanied minors on domestic flights only with an escort from the airlines—a flight attendant who seats the child, usually near the galley, where the flight crew is stationed; watches over the child during the flight; and escorts the child to the appropriate connecting gate or to the adult who will be picking up the child. Unaccompanied minors typically board first and disembark last.

On domestic flights, the service costs between $30 and $75, depending on the airline and whether the child will have to change planes. On all the major airlines, several children traveling together from the same family will only have to pay one fee.

Unaccompanied children are never left alone; escorts stay with them until turning them over to an escort on the connecting flight or to a designated guardian. Airlines require attending adults to furnish a name, address, and government-issued photo ID. The adult who drops the child off at the airport must then designate the name and address of the adult who is authorized to pick the child up. At the destination city, the airline will not release the child to anyone but the authorized adult, after receiving a signature and seeing a photo ID.

Children ages 5 to 7 generally may travel unaccompanied on direct and nonstop flights only; in other words, they're not allowed to change planes for connecting flights at that age. (Northwest and Delta allow all children to travel on connecting flights.) Children ages 8 to 11 may make connecting flights with an escort, with the exception of Southwest and America West, which do not allow any unaccompanied child under the age of 12 to take a connecting flight. America West's policy is relatively new, started in 2001 after two embarrassing incidents where the airline sent one child to the wrong destination and neglected to tell a parent about another child's flight delay.

Children over the age of 12 are considered adults and may travel without an escort on every major carrier but Northwest, which requires escorts until age 14. They still qualify for assistance from the airline for the extra fee. Southwest is the only airline that does not allow children to use the escort service once they are able to fly without one, at age 12.

Because airlines want to avoid the responsibility of having to shepherd children overnight, minors are usually not allowed to take the last connecting flight of the day, when the risk of missed connections is greatest. Minors are usually not allowed to travel on standby, and they must have confirmed reservations.

On connecting flights, ask when you book if the child will be flying on more than one airline. (With the new airline alliances, your child may end up on a Northwest aircraft, even though you booked the flight through Continental.) If so, make sure you know each airline's policy for unaccompanied minors. Once you receive the ticket, review it yourself to make sure the city of origin and the destination are accurate. Review the ticket carefully with your child and explain simply how it works.

If you're booking a flight for your child, the airlines will request your name, telephone number, and address—along with the name, number, and address of the guardian who will meet your child at the destination city. An adult guardian must accompany the child to the gate or plane, furnish reasonable proof that another adult will meet the child at the final destination, and remain at the airport until the plane is in the air. The accompanying adult at the destination will have to sign a release form and furnish government-issued photo identification, such as a license or passport. If a child is unusually big or small, it's wise to bring a birth certificate to the airport as proof of age.

Solo Minors on International Flights

Major carriers' policies for minors traveling alone are basically the same for both domestic and international travel, although fees are higher on international flights. Children may be prohibited from boarding an international flight under poor weather conditions that could require that the plane be rerouted.

Parents should seriously consider using European airlines for international trips because of the extra services they provide for kids. British Airways has a toy chest on its planes, and Virgin Atlantic treats kids like royalty, with special entertainment channels, toys, and treats.

If you're booking a ticket for a minor on an international flight, you should call the consulate of the destination country to find out about visas and other special entry requirements.

Minor Orientation

With stricter security measures at airports, parents must now get a pass from the ticket agent for permission to escort their children to the departure gate. (Adults picking up unaccompanied minors at arrival gates also need this permission slip.) If your child has never flown before, it makes sense to show up at the airport a little early to wander around, watch other planes take off and land, and prepare your child in advance for how flight is going to feel. Be sure to discuss the danger of talking to strangers—even if you have had the same discussion before. You will be allowed to escort your child to the gate, but not onto the plane.

Some airlines allow unaccompanied minors to board first, so the flight crew has more time to meet the child, orient the child to the location of bathrooms and emergency exits, store carry-ons, review safety procedures, and—kids love this part—introduce the child to the cockpit crew. Make sure minors understand that they should contact an attendant in case of any type of problem—from sickness to a malfunctioning headset to a bothersome neighbor. If you can't make it all the way on to the plane, be sure to introduce your child to the gate attendant and ensure the child will receive help boarding if necessary.

Some airlines offer special meals for children, such as hamburgers, hot dogs, or peanut butter sandwiches, which must be ordered in advance, when you make the reservation. It's still wise to send your child off with a bagged lunch, snack, and drinks. Also pack books and other entertainment in a carry-on and make sure your child knows how to get at them onboard the plane.

Make sure your child has cash and knows how to make a collect phone call. In one place, record your child's name, your own name, address, and phone number, along with the names and phone number of your child's hosts at the final destination. Review the information with your child and place it in a safe purse, pocket, or neck pouch. Be sure, however, that your child knows not to share this information with strangers—not even a friendly neighbor in the cabin.

If your child is taking medication, it may be wise to postpone the trip unless you are certain your child is responsible for self-administering dosages properly. Flight attendants are not allowed to administer drugs to minors.

EASING TRAVEL WITH THE TOTS IN TOW

Several books on the market offer tips to help you travel with kids. Most concentrate on the U.S., but two, *Family Travel & Resorts: The Complete Guide* (Lanier Publishing International; $19.95) and *How to Take Great Trips with Your Kids* (The Harvard Common Press; $9.95), are full of good general advice that can apply to travel anywhere. Another reliable tome, with a worldwide focus, is *Adventuring with Children* (Foghorn Press; $14.95).

Family Travel Times (© 888/822-4FTT; www.familytraveltimes.com) is an excellent online newsletter updated twice monthly. Subscriptions are $39 a year, $49 for 2 years. Sample articles are available on the newsletter's website.

If you plan carefully, you can actually make it fun to travel with kids:

- If you're traveling with children, you'll save yourself a good bit of aggravation by **reserving a seat in the bulkhead** row. You'll have more legroom, and your children will be able to spread out and play on the floor underfoot. You're also more likely to find sympathetic

company in the bulkhead area, as families with children tend to be seated there.

- Be sure to **pack items for your children in your carry-on luggage.** In case you're forced to check one of your carry-ons, consolidate the children's things in one bag or in your purse. If you're forced to check a carry-on, be sure to choose the one that holds the kid's things. When you're deciding what to bring, ready yourself for the worst: long, unexpected delays without food, bathrooms without changing tables, airline meals that feature your children's least favorite dishes.

- Have **a long talk with your children** before you depart for your trip. If they've never flown before, explain to them what to expect. If they're old enough, you may even want to describe how flight works and how air travel is even safer than riding in a car. Explain to your kids the importance of good behavior in the air—how their own safety can depend upon their being quiet and staying in their seats during the trip.

- **Pay extra careful attention to the safety instructions** before takeoff. Consult the safety chart behind the seat in front of you and show it to your children. Be sure you know how to operate the oxygen masks, as you will be expected to secure yours first and then help your children with theirs. Be especially mindful of the location of emergency exits. Before takeoff, plot out an evacuation strategy for you and your children in your mind's eye.

- Ask the flight attendant **if the plane has any special safety equipment for children.** Make a member of the crew aware of any medical problems your children have that could manifest during flight.

- **Be sure you've slept sufficiently** for your trip. If you fall asleep in the air and your child manages to break away, there are all sorts of sharp objects that could cause injury. Especially during meal-times, it's dangerous for a child to be crawling or walking around the cabin unaccompanied by an adult.
- **Be sure your child's seatbelt remains fastened properly,** and try to reserve the seat closest to the aisle for yourself. This will make it harder for your children to wander off—in case, for instance, you're taking the redeye or a long flight overseas and you do happen to nod off. You will also protect your child from jostling passersby and falling objects—in the rare but entirely possible instance that an overhead bin pops open.

  In the event of an accident, unrestrained children often don't make it—even when the parent does. Experience has shown that it's impossible for a parent to hold onto a child in the event of a crash, and children often die of impact injuries.

  For the same reason, sudden turbulence is also a danger to a child who is not buckled into his own seat belt or seat restraint. According to *Consumer Reports Travel Letter,* the most common flying injuries result when unanticipated turbulence strikes and hurtles passengers from their seats. (See "Child Seats: They're a Must," above, for suggestions regarding FAA-promoted child-restraint systems.)
- **Try to sit near the lavatory,** though not so close that your children are jostled by the crowds that tend to gather there. Consolidate trips there as much as possible.
- Try to **accompany children to the lavatory.** They can be easily bumped and possibly injured as they make their way down tight aisles. It's especially dangerous for children to wander while flight attendants are blocking passage with their service carts. On crowded flights, the flight crew may need as much as an hour to serve dinner. It's wise to encourage your kids to use the restroom as you see the attendants preparing to serve.
- Be sure to **bring clean, self-containing compact toys.** Leave electronic games at home. They can interfere with the aircraft navigational system, and their noisiness, however lulling to children's ears, will surely not win the favor of your adult neighbors. Magnetic checker sets, on the other hand, are a perfect distraction, and small coloring books and crayons also work well, as do card games like Go Fish.

  Visit the library before you leave home and check out children's books about flying or airplane travel. Geography-related books and coloring books that include their departure point and destination will also help engage them during air travel.

  A Walkman with a few favorite recordings will also come in handy—especially if you throw in some sleepy-time tunes. By all means, don't leave home without a favorite blanket or stuffed animal—especially if it's your kid's best friend at bedtime.
- Some airlines **serve children's meals first.** When you board, ask a flight attendant if this is possible, especially if your children are very young or seated toward the back of the plane. After all, if your kids have a happy flight experience, everyone else in the cabin is more likely to as well.
- You'll certainly be grateful to yourself for **packing tidy snacks**

In-Flight Fun For Kids

With one of these children's game books onboard, even the longest plane ride will go faster.

Great Games for Kids on the Go: Over 240 Travel Games to Play on Trains, Planes, and Automobiles
by Penny Warner
Retail price: $12.95
Ages 4 to 8
This book is full of entertaining educational games to help your kids while away the miles. Each game is highly engaging and entertaining and requires few materials and very little space.

Brain Quest for the Car: 1,100 Questions and Answers
All About America
by Sharon Gold
Retail price: $10.95
Ages 7 to 12
This book features cards with questions about American geography, culture, and customs.

Vacation Fun Mad Libs: World's Greatest Party Game
by Roger Price
Retail price: $3.99
Ages 8 and up
As suggested by the title, this book is chock-full of Mad Libs. Your kids will want to keep playing even after you've touched down.

like rolled dried fruit, which are much less sticky and wet and more compact and packable than actual fruit. Blueberry or raisin bagels also make for a neat, healthy sweet and yield fewer crumbs than cookies or cakes. Ginger snaps, crisp and not as crumbly as softer cookies, will also help curb mild cases of motion sickness. And don't forget to stash a few resealable plastic bags in your purse. They'll prove invaluable for storing everything from half-eaten crackers and fruit to checker pieces and matchbox cars.

- **Juice or cookies** will not only keep them distracted during ascent and descent—often the scariest parts of flight for a child—they will also help their little ears pop as cabin air pressure shifts rapidly. Juice (paper cartons travel best) will also keep them swallowing and help them to stay properly hydrated. Avoid giving young children gum or hard candies, since sudden turbulence may cause them to choke.

- If your children are very young, **bring pacifiers.** The act of sucking will keep their ears clear. By the same logic, takeoff and landing are the perfect times for feedings. Your kids will be distracted from the deafening cabin noise, and their ears will pop more easily. If your schedule won't allow this, try placing drops of water on an infant's tongue, to facilitate swallowing. Don't forget to pack bottles and extra milk or formula as well, as these are unavailable on most aircraft. Many airlines prohibit flight attendants from preparing formula, so it's best to pack your baby's food premixed.

TASTELESS: DEALING WITH AIRLINE FOOD

Most airlines have cut back on food service recently—and even if you do get a "meal" on a domestic flight, it's likely to be a limp turkey sandwich. Your best bet is to brown-bag homemade sandwiches. Unlike fruit, for example, they have no leftover parts to throw away, and you won't have to tussle with airport security over silverware. But if you insist on eating economy-class cuisine, some tips:

- **Order a special meal.** Most airlines allow coach-class passengers to order from a range of special meals, including low-fat, low-cholesterol, vegetarian, and children's meals (usually a hamburger or hot dog). These meals aren't necessarily fresher than the standard ones, but at least you'll know what's in them. Call your airline 2 days before your flight to secure your meal. Then double-check when you check in.
- **Become a vegetarian.** Dieticians and frequent fliers say vegetarian and vegan meals are often better than standard airline fare. Vegan meals skip cheese and sweets, leading to a healthier but more spartan platter.
- **Fly a tasty airline.** The Zagat organization rates airline food annually. For 2001, Midwest Express had the best economy-class meals (including fresh chocolate-chip cookies and real plates), while America West rated the worst of the airlines that actually serve meals (think that aforementioned turkey sandwich.)

In general, coach-class passengers now only get meals on flights crossing two-thirds of the country or more; everyone else gets peanuts or other minibags of snacks. (Continental and Alaska are welcome exceptions, but "meals" on Continental flights under 3½ hours are of the dreaded turkey sandwich variety.)

Most low-fare airlines generally only serve snacks (except for Midwest Express), even on cross-country flights. But some offer better snacks than others. Southwest offers a nonyummy bag of salted peanuts. But JetBlue serves up classy blue potato chips, and Frontier goes even further with chicken wraps and specialty bagels.

Zagat's Top-Rated Airline Meals

Economy Class
1. Midwest Express
2. Alaska Airlines
3. National Airlines, United Airlines (tie)*
5. Hawaiian Airlines

Premium Class
1. Hawaiian Airlines
2. Alaska Airlines, Continental Airlines (tie)
4. United Airlines, American Airlines (tie)

*National Airlines is no longer in business.

Source: 2001 Zagat Airline Survey, found at www.zagat.com

The Economy-Class Meal Policies of Major Airlines

- **Alaska:** Food served on flights of 2 hours or more. Meal times: breakfast 6 to 8:30am; lunch 10:30am to 1:30pm; dinner 4 to 7pm.
- **America West:** Food served only on flights between the East Coast and Phoenix. Breakfast 6 to 9am; lunch 11am to 1pm; dinner 5 to 7pm.
- **American:** Food served only on nonstop, transcontinental flights. Breakfast 5 to 8:30am; lunch noon to 1pm; dinner 5:30 to 7pm.
- **Continental:** Food served on flights of 2 hours or more. Breakfast 7 to 9am; lunch 11am to 1pm; dinner 5 to 7pm.
- **Delta:** Food served only on flights of more than 1,750 miles. Breakfast 5 to 8:30am; lunch noon to 1pm; dinner 6:30 to 7:30pm.
- **Northwest:** Food served only on flights between Detroit/Minneapolis/Memphis and the West Coast. Breakfast 6 to 9:45am; lunch 11am to 1:15pm; dinner 4:30 to 7:15pm.
- **United:** Food served only on flights of more than 1,635 miles. Breakfast 5 to 9:59am; lunch 11am to 1:29pm; dinner 4:50 to 7:29pm.
- **US Airways:** Food served only on nonstop, transcontinental flights. Breakfast 6 to 10am; lunch 11am to 1pm; dinner 4 to 7pm.

BY CAR

Chicago is served by interstate highways from all major points on the compass. I-80 and I-90 approach from the east, crossing the northern sector of Illinois, with I-90 splitting off and emptying into Chicago via the Skyway and the Dan Ryan Expressway. From here, I-90 runs through Wisconsin, following a northern route to Seattle. I-55 snakes up the Mississippi Valley from the vicinity of New Orleans and enters Chicago from the west along

the Stevenson Expressway, and in the opposite direction it provides an outlet to the Southwest. I-57 originates in southern Illinois and forms part of the interstate linkage to Florida and the South, connecting within Chicago on the west leg of the Dan Ryan. I-94 links Detroit with Chicago, arriving on the Calumet Expressway and leaving the city via the Kennedy Expressway en route to the Northwest.

Here are a few approximate driving distances in miles to Chicago: from **Milwaukee,** 92; from **St. Louis,** 297; from **Detroit,** 286; from **Denver,** 1,011; from **Atlanta,** 716; from **Washington, D.C.,** 715; from **New York City,** 821; and from **Los Angeles,** 2,034.

BY TRAIN

Rail passenger service, although it may never approach the grandeur of its heyday, has made enormous advances in service, comfort, and efficiency since the creation of Amtrak in 1971. As in the past, but on a reduced scale, Chicago remains the hub of the national passenger rail system. Traveling great distances by train is certainly not the quickest way to go, nor always the most convenient. But many travelers still prefer it to flying or driving.

For tickets, consult your travel agent or call **Amtrak** (② **800/USA-RAIL;** www.amtrak.com). Ask the reservations agent to send you Amtrak's useful travel planner, with information on train accommodations and package tours.

When you arrive in Chicago, the train will pull into **Union Station** at 210 S. Canal, between Adams and Jackson streets (② **312/655-2385**). Bus nos. 1, 60, 125, 151, and 156 all stop at the station, which is just west across the river from the Loop. The nearest El stop is at Clinton Street and Congress Parkway (on the Blue Line), which is a fair walk away, especially when you're carrying luggage.

Flying with Film & Video

Never pack film—developed or undeveloped—in checked bags, as the new, more powerful scanners in U.S. airports can fog film. The film you carry with you can be damaged by scanners as well. X-ray damage is cumulative; the faster the film and the more times you put it through a scanner, the more likely the damage. Film under 800 ASA is usually safe for up to five scans. If you're taking your film through additional scans, U.S. regulations permit you to demand hand inspections. In international airports, you're at the mercy of airport officials. On international flights, store your film in transparent baggies, so you can remove it easily before you go through scanners. Keep in mind that airports are not the only places where your camera may be scanned: Highly trafficked attractions are X-raying visitors' bags with increasing frequency.

Most photo supply stores sell protective pouches designed to block damaging X-rays. The pouches fit both film and loaded cameras. They should protect your film in checked baggage, but they also may raise alarms and result in a hand inspection.

You'll have little to worry about if you are traveling with **digital cameras.** Unlike film, which is sensitive to light, the digital camera and storage cards are not affected by airport X-rays, according to Nikon. Still, if you plan to travel extensively, you may want to play it safe and hand-carry your digital equipment or ask that it be inspected by hand. See "Digital Photography on the Road," on p. 32.

Carry-on scanners will not damage **videotape** in video cameras, but the magnetic fields emitted by the walk-through security gateways and handheld inspection wands will. Always place your loaded camcorder on the screening conveyor belt or have it hand-inspected. Be sure your batteries are charged, as you may be required to turn the device on to ensure that it's what it appears to be.

BY BUS

The **Greyhound Bus Station** in Chicago is at 630 W. Harrison (© **800/231-2222** travel information; www.greyhound.com), not far from Union Station. Several city buses (nos. 60, 125, 156, and 157) pass in front of the terminal building, and the nearest El stop is at Clinton Street and Congress Parkway on the Blue Line.

10 Show & Tell: Getting Kids Interested in Chicago

Kids will be most interested in your upcoming adventure when they have input into the activities you plan. Use this book to tell your kids about the great adventures awaiting them in Chicago—riding the El, climbing into a captured World War II U-boat at the Museum of Science and Industry, riding a high-speed elevator to see the sights from the John Hancock Center,

or going to a McDonald's that's also a rock 'n' roll museum.

Movie-wise, you can rent *Blues Brothers* (1979) and show Jake and Elmo jumping the bridge across the river and careening down the street under the El tracks. The movie features a classic multicar pileup in the center of downtown Daley Plaza. *Ferris Bueller's Day Off* (1985) is the ultimate teenage wish-fulfillment movie, set in Chicago and the suburbs. In fact, most of the John Hughes movies (*Pretty in Pink, Sixteen Candles,* and *The Breakfast Club*) are set in the Chicago area.

Children's books set in Chicago that will be readily available at your local library or bookstore include *Fair Weather* by Richard Peck, in which a 19th-century farming family is turned upside down by a visit to Chicago for the 1893 World's Columbian Exposition; *Playoff Dreams* by Fred Bowen, in which a boy attends a ball game with his uncle at Wrigley Field and learns the story of the legendary Cubs player and Hall of Fame member Ernie Banks; and *The Dragon of Navy Pier* by Kate Noble, in which Charlie, a young dragon on a carousel, comes alive one night and sets out to explore Navy Pier.

Show your kids photos of landmarks—Wrigley Field is a familiar sight to most of us. You might also find photos of Soldier Field, United Center (with its statue to Michael Jordan), the soaring John Hancock Center (with its girded black X's crisscrossing all the way up the building), the Chicago Water Tower (the only building to survive the fire of 1871, allegedly started by Mrs. O'Leary's cow), Sears Tower, and the lakefront. Discuss the El trains and show kids photos of the elevated tracks. Show them the Chicago bridges that raise and lower, stopping traffic so boats can make their way to the lake. Tell them that the Chicago River that these bridges span runs from the lake (rather than into it, as most rivers do)—and about the engineering marvel that reversed its flow.

Getting to Know Chicago

The best advice on orienting yourself on Chicago's streets? Look for our inland ocean. Whenever you spot Lake Michigan dead ahead, you are facing east. Another directional no-brainer? If you are on the Magnificent Mile, or in the Loop, look up. The tallest building around is that black glass behemoth, the Sears Tower, and it's to the south.

The orderly configuration of Chicago's streets and the excellent public transportation system make this city more accessible than most of the world's other large cities. This chapter provides an overview of the city's design, as well as some suggestions for how to maneuver within it. The chapter also lists some resources that traveling families frequently need, from babysitters to 24-hour pharmacies.

1 Orientation

VISITOR INFORMATION

The **Chicago Convention and Tourism Bureau** runs a toll-free visitor hot line (© **877/CHICAGO;** www.877chicago.com). The **Chicago Office of Tourism** offers information at 312/744-2400, TTY 312/744-2947, and http://city ofchicago.org/exploringchicago and operates three visitor information centers staffed with people who can answer questions and stocked with plenty of brochures on area attractions, including materials on everything from museums and city landmarks to lakefront biking maps and even fishing spots. The main visitor center, located in the Loop and convenient to many places that you'll likely be visiting, is on the first floor of the **Chicago Cultural Center,** 78 E. Washington St. (at Michigan Ave.). The center has a phone that you can use to make hotel reservations and several couches and a cafe where you can study maps and plan your itinerary. The center is open Monday through Friday from 10am to 6pm, Saturday from 10am to 5pm, and Sunday from 11am to 5pm; it's closed on holidays.

A second, smaller center is located in the heart of the city's shopping district, in the old pumping station at Michigan and Chicago avenues. Recently renamed the **Chicago Water Works Visitor Center,** its entrance is on the Pearson Street side of the building, across from the Water Tower Place mall. It's open daily 7:30am to 7pm. This location has the added draw of housing a location of Hot Tix, which offers both half-price day-of-performance and full-price tickets to many theater productions around the city, as well as a gift shop. Part of the building has been converted into a theater, including a small cabaret space for tourist-oriented shows and a larger playhouse for the acclaimed Lookingglass Theatre.

The **Illinois Bureau of Tourism** (© **800/2CONNECT** or TTY 800/406-6418; www.enjoyillinois.com) can provide general and specific information 24 hours a day. The agency also has staff at the information desk in the lobby of the **James R. Thompson Center,** 100 W. Randolph St. (© **312/814-9600**), in the

Helmut Jahn–designed building at LaSalle and Randolph streets in the Loop. The desk is open Monday through Friday from 8:30am to 4:30pm.

INFORMATION BY TELEPHONE The **Mayor's Office of Special Events** operates a recorded hot line (℃ **312/744-3370;** www.cityofchicago.org) listing current special events, festivals, and parades occurring throughout the city. The city of Chicago also maintains a 24-hour information line for those with hearing impairments; call ℃ **312/744-2964.**

PUBLICATIONS Pick up a free copy of *Chicago Parent* magazine at any bookstore, public library, park district building, or children's specialty shop. You will also find copies in newspaper vending boxes on Michigan Avenue. Each issue includes a daily calendar of events and a museum page that keeps readers abreast of new openings of interest to kids. Each June, the magazine publishes its annual *Going Places* guide. Call the magazine's offices in Oak Park at ℃ **708/386-5555** to order one.

Chicago's major daily newspapers are the *Tribune* and the *Sun-Times.* Both have cultural listings, including movies, theaters, and live music, not to mention reviews of the very latest restaurants that are sure to have appeared in the city since this guidebook went to press. The Friday editions of both papers contain special pullout sections with more detailed, up-to-date information on special events happening over the weekend. Both papers have also launched weekday tabloids aimed at younger readers: The *Tribune* publishes *Red Eye*, while the *Sun-Times* puts out *Red Streak*. Both carry a similar mix of "lite" news items, entertainment news, and quirky features, making them pretty much interchangeable.

Chicago magazine is an upscale monthly with good restaurant listings. For a look at the city's beautiful people, pick up *CS* (formerly *Chicago Social*), a glossy monthly magazine filled with photos from charity galas and ads for high-priced local boutiques.

In a class by itself is the *Chicago Reader*, a free weekly that is an invaluable source of entertainment listings, classifieds, and well-written articles on contemporary issues of interest in Chicago. Published every Thursday (except the last

---

Value Insider Tours—for Free!

Want your kids to see the city from a native's point of view? A new program, **Chicago Greeter**, run by the Chicago Office of Tourism, matches tourists with local Chicagoans who serve as volunteer guides. Visitors can request a specific neighborhood or theme (everything from Polish heritage sites to Chicago movie locations), and a greeter gives a free 2- to 4-hour tour. (Greeters won't escort groups of more than six people). Kids of all ages are welcome (bringing newborns on the tours, however, is discouraged). When you call, please specify that you will be using a stroller so that your guide can plan accordingly for accessing public transportation. Chicago Greeter offers a special "Kids Activities" tour that includes Navy Pier. Other popular family tours include Lincoln Park Zoo and the Shedd Aquarium (see the website or call for details). Specific requests for these kid-friendly tours should be made at least a week in advance, but "InstaGreeters" are also available on a first-come, first-served basis at the Chicago Cultural Center, 77 E. Randolph St., Friday through Sunday. For details, call ℃ **312/744-8000** or visit www.chicagogreeter.com.

week of Dec), the weekly has a wide distribution downtown and on the North Side; it is available in many retail stores, in building lobbies, and at the paper's offices, 11 E. Illinois St. (© 312/828-0350), by about noon on Thursday.

Another free weekly, *New City* (© 312/243-8786), also publishes excellent comprehensive listings of entertainment options. Appealing to a slightly younger audience than the *Reader,* its editorial tone tends toward the edgy and irreverent. Published every Wednesday, it's available in the same neighborhoods and locations as the *Reader.*

Most Chicago hotels stock their rooms or lobbies with at least one informational magazine, such as *Where Chicago,* that lists the city's entertainment, shopping, and dining locales.

CITY LAYOUT

The **Chicago River** forms a Y that divides the city into its three geographic zones: North Side, South Side, and West Side (Lake Michigan is where the East Side would be). The downtown financial district is called **the Loop.** The city's key shopping street is **North Michigan Avenue,** also known as the **Magnificent Mile.** In addition to department stores and vertical malls, this stretch of property north of the river houses many of the city's most elegant hotels. North and south of this downtown zone, Chicago stretches along 29 miles of Lake Michigan shoreline that is, by and large, free of commercial development, reserved for public use as green space and parkland from one end of town to the other.

Chicago proper today has about three million inhabitants living in an area about two-thirds the size of New York City; another five million make the suburbs their home. The villages north of Chicago now stretch in an unbroken mass nearly to the Wisconsin border; the city's western suburbs extend 30 miles to Naperville, one of the fastest-growing towns in the nation over the past 2 decades. The real signature of Chicago, however, is found between the suburbs and the Loop, where a colorful patchwork quilt of residential neighborhoods gives the city a character all its own.

FINDING AN ADDRESS   Having been a part of the Northwest Territory, Chicago is laid out in a **grid system,** with the streets neatly lined up as if on a giant piece of graph paper. Because the city itself isn't rectangular (it's rather elongated), the shape is a bit irregular, but the perpendicular pattern remains. Easing movement through the city are a half-dozen or so major diagonal thoroughfares.

Point zero is located at the downtown intersection of State and Madison streets. **State Street** divides east and west addresses, and **Madison Street** divides north and south addresses. From here, Chicago's highly predictable addressing system begins. Making use of this grid, it is relatively easy to plot the distance in miles between any two points in the city.

Virtually all of Chicago's principal north-south and east-west arteries are spaced by increments of 400 in the addressing system—regardless of the number of smaller streets nestled between them. And each addition or subtraction of 400 numbers to an address is equivalent to a half mile. Thus, starting at point zero on Madison Street and traveling north along State Street for 1 mile, you will come to 800 N. State St., which intersects Chicago Avenue. Continue uptown for another half mile and you arrive at the 1200 block of North State Street at Division Street. And so it goes, right to the city line, with suburban Evanston located at the 7600 block north, 9½ miles from point zero.

The same rule applies when you're traveling south, or east to west. Thus, heading west from State Street along Madison Street, Halsted Street—at 800 W.

Fun Fact   A River Runs Through It

The Chicago River remains one of the most visible of the city's major physical features. It's spanned by more movable bridges (52 at last count) than any city in the world. An almost-mystical moment occurs downtown when all the bridges spanning the main and south branches—connecting the Loop to both the near–West Side and the near–North Side—are raised, allowing for the passage of some ship or barge or contingent of high-masted sailboats. The Chicago River has long outlived the critical commercial function that it once performed. Most of the remaining millworks that still occupy its banks no longer depend on the river alone for the transport of their materials, raw and finished. The river's main function today is to serve as a fluvial conduit for sewage, which, owing to an engineering feat that reversed its flow inland in 1900, no longer pollutes the waters of Lake Michigan. Recently, Chicagoans have begun to discover another role for the river, that of leisure resource, providing short cruises on its water, park areas, cafes, and public art installations on its banks, and the beginnings of a riverside bike path that connects to the lakefront route near Wacker Drive. Actually, today's developers aren't the first to wonder why the river couldn't be Chicago's Seine. A look at the early-20th-century Beaux Arts balustrades lining the river along Wacker Drive, complete with comfortably spaced benches—as well as Parisian-style bridge houses—shows that Chicago-based architect Daniel Burnham knew full well what a treasure the city had.

Madison St.—is a mile's distance, while Racine Avenue, at the 1200 block of West Madison Street, is 1½ miles from the center. Madison Street then continues westward to Chicago's boundary with the near suburb of Oak Park along Austin Avenue, which, at 6000 W. Madison, is approximately 7½ miles from point zero.

The key to understanding the grid is that the side of any square formed by the principal avenues (noted in dark or red ink on most maps) represents a distance of half a mile in any direction. Understanding how Chicago's grid system works is of particular importance to those visitors who want to do a lot of walking in the city's many neighborhoods and who want to plot in advance the distances involved in trekking from one locale to another.

The other ingeniously convenient aspect of the grid is that every major road uses the same numerical system. In other words, the cross street (Division St.) at 1200 N. Lake Shore Dr. is the same as at 1200 N. Clark St., which is the same as at 1200 N. LaSalle St., and so on.

STREET MAPS   A suitably detailed map of Chicago is published by **Rand McNally,** available at many newsstands and bookstores for less than $5 (the smaller, more manageable laminated versions cost $6.95). Rand McNally operates a thoroughly stocked retail store at 444 N. Michigan Ave. (© **312/321-1751**), just north of the Wrigley Building. Maps are also available at the city's visitor information centers at the **Chicago Cultural Center** and the **Chicago Water Works Visitor Center** (see "Visitor Information," near the beginning of this chapter).

NEIGHBORHOODS IN BRIEF

The Loop & Vicinity

Downtown In the case of Chicago, downtown means the Loop. The Loop refers literally to a core of primarily commercial, governmental, and cultural buildings contained within a corral of elevated train tracks, but greater downtown Chicago overflows these confines and is bounded by the Chicago River to the north and west, by Michigan Avenue to the east, and by Roosevelt Avenue to the south. The main attractions for families in the Loop are Millennium Park, the Art Institute, the Cultural Center, and the Harold Washington Library. If you are catching a show, you'll find the revitalized theater district in the North Loop. Marshall Field's on State Street, famous for its window decorations during the holidays, anchors a strip of retail shopping.

The North Side

Near North/Magnificent Mile North Michigan Avenue is known as the Magnificent Mile, from the bridge spanning the Chicago River to its northern tip at Oak Street. Many of the city's best hotels, shops, and restaurants are to be found on and around elegant North Michigan Avenue. Here you'll find the Terra Museum of American Art and the Museum of Contemporary Art—but the focus is shopping, not museums. The area stretching east of Michigan Avenue to the lake is also sometimes referred to as "Streeterville"—the legacy of George Wellington "Cap" Streeter, an eccentric, bankrupt showman who staked out 200 acres of self-created landfill here about a century ago after his steamship had run aground on the shore, and then declared himself "governor" of the "District of Lake Michigan." True story.

River North Just to the west of the Mag Mile's zone of high life and sophistication is an old warehouse district called River North. It's also the site of most chain restaurants that cater to the kid set. Over the past 15 to 20 years, the area has experienced a rebirth as one of the city's most vital commercial districts, and today it is filled with many of the city's hottest restaurants, nightspots, art galleries, and loft dwellings. Several large-scale residential loft-conversion developments have lately been sprouting on its western and southwestern fringes.

The Gold Coast Some of Chicago's most desirable real estate and historic architecture are found along Lake Shore Drive, between Oak Street and North Avenue and along the adjacent side streets. Despite trendy little pockets of real estate popping up elsewhere, the moneyed class still prefers to live by the lake. This residential area doesn't offer much for kids, but it does have beautiful scenic streets for walking. On the neighborhood's western edge, the northern stretch of State Street just south of Division Street has, in recent years, developed into a thriving zone of restaurants, bars, and nightclubs.

Old Town West of LaSalle Street, principally on North Wells Street between Division Street and North Avenue, is the nightlife district of Old Town. On Wells Street, a few blocks east and a few blocks west of North Avenue, you'll find plenty of families and strollers during the day. This area was a hippie haven in the 1960s and '70s, but in recent years its residential areas have been rapidly gentrified as Cabrini Green, America's most notorious housing project, has finally fallen to the wrecking ball. Old Town's biggest claim to fame, the legendary Second City comedy club, has served up the lighter side of life to Chicagoans for more than 30 years.

Lincoln Park Chicago's most popular residential neighborhood is fashionable Lincoln Park. The neighborhood is notable for visiting families because it is bordered on the east by the huge park of the same name, which is home to two major museums and one of the nation's oldest zoos (established in 1868). The trapezoid formed by Clark Street, Armitage Avenue, Halsted Street, and Diversey Parkway also contains many of Chicago's most happening bars, restaurants, retail stores, music clubs, and off-Loop theaters—including the nationally acclaimed Steppenwolf Theatre Company.

Lakeview & Wrigleyville Wrigleyville is the name given to the neighborhood in the vicinity of Wrigley Field—home of the Chicago Cubs—at Sheffield Avenue and Addison Street. Many homesteaders have moved into these areas in recent years, and a slew of nightclubs and restaurants have followed in their wake. Midway up the city's North Side is a one-time blue-collar, now mainstream middle-class and bohemian quarter called Lakeview. It has become the neighborhood of choice for many gays and lesbians, recent college graduates, and a growing number of residents priced out of Lincoln Park. The main thoroughfare is Belmont Avenue, between Broadway and Sheffield Avenue.

Uptown & Andersonville Uptown, along the lake and about as far north as Foster Avenue, is where the latest wave of immigrants—including internal migrants from Appalachia and the Native American

reservations—has settled. Vietnamese and Chinese immigrants have transformed Argyle Street between Broadway and Sheridan Road into a teeming market for fresh meat, fish, and all kinds of exotic vegetables. Slightly to the north and west is the old Scandinavian neighborhood of Andersonville, whose main drag is Clark Street, between Foster and Bryn Mawr avenues. This neighborhood is friendly to families, with the feel of a small Midwestern village, albeit one with an eclectic mix of Middle Eastern restaurants, a distinct cluster of women-owned businesses, and a burgeoning gay and lesbian community. You'll find Ann Sather restaurant, the Swedish-American Museum, the Swedish Bakery, and Women and Children First, a great bookstore.

Lincoln Square Families flock to Old Town School of Folk Music's theater and education center, a beautiful restoration of a former library building, in this neighborhood located west of Andersonville and slightly to the south, where Lincoln, Western, and Lawrence avenues intersect. Lincoln Square was the home to Chicago's once-vast German-American community. Lincoln Square now also has a distinctly Greek flavor, with several restaurants of that nationality, to boot. The surrounding leafy residential streets are now experiencing an influx of white middle-class families.

Rogers Park Rogers Park, which begins at Devon Avenue, is located on the northern fringes of the city bordering suburban Evanston. Its western half has been a Jewish neighborhood for decades. The eastern half, dominated by Loyola University's lakefront campus, has become the most cosmopolitan enclave in the entire city: Asians, East Indians, Russian Jews, and German Americans live side by side

Chicago Neighborhoods

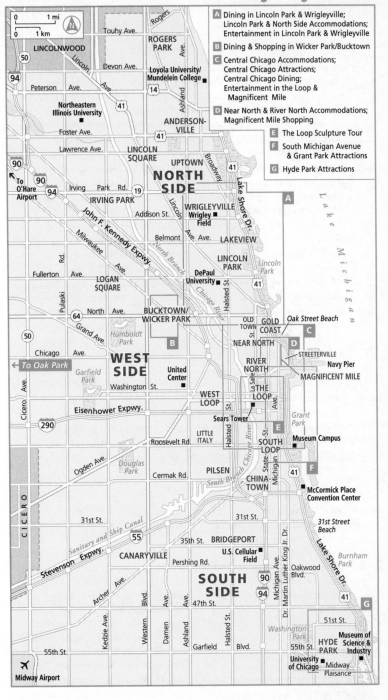

A	Dining in Lincoln Park & Wrigleyville; Lincoln Park & North Side Accommodations; Entertainment in Lincoln Park & Wrigleyville
B	Dining & Shopping in Wicker Park/Bucktown
C	Central Chicago Accommodations; Central Chicago Attractions; Central Chicago Dining; Entertainment in the Loop & Magnificent Mile
D	Near North & River North Accommodations; Magnificent Mile Shopping
E	The Loop Sculpture Tour
F	South Michigan Avenue & Grant Park Attractions
G	Hyde Park Attractions

Moments **Frommer's Favorite Oh-So-Chicago Experiences**

- **Strolling the Lakefront.** Chicagoans use the lakefront in every possible way: for walking, rollerblading, biking, running, swimming, picnicking, and playing volleyball. Summers on the lakefront can get a little crowded, but that's part of the fun. Even in winter, you can see hardy souls out for a run while waves crash onto the shoreline. Most activity takes place around Oak Street Beach and North Avenue Beach.

- **Sightseeing on the Chicago River and Lake Michigan.** By far the best way to scope out the city is by taking a boat tour. Getting onto the water gives you a fresh perspective on a city that grew up around a lake and a river. Options include dinner cruises, the "ducks" (amphibian land/water transports), speedboats, and tall ships. See "Kid-Friendly Tours," in chapter 6, for suggestions.

- **Visiting Marshall Field's around the Holidays.** Marshall Field's State Street store puts on a real show during the holidays. The unveiling of the windows is a much-anticipated event, and having breakfast or lunch around the gigantic Christmas tree in the stately Walnot Room is a time-honored tradition for generations of Chicagoans.

- **Cheering the Cubbies.** Wrigley Field is not to be missed. In fact, Chicagoans regularly play hooky to hang out in the bleachers on a perfect summer afternoon. Eat a hot dog. Exercise your lungs during the singing of "Take Me Out to the Ballgame." I'm sure you'll leave agreeing with me that Wrigley Field is the most charming ballpark in America.

- **Riding the El.** The noisy, dirty El (Chicagos' elevated train), which blocks sunlight from the streets beneath its tracks, is a quintessential part of Chicago. Even if you have nowhere in particular to go, hop on the El and ride around the Loop. The brown line heading

with African Americans and the ethnically mixed student population drawn to the Catholic university. Much of Rogers Park has a neo-hippie ambience, but the western stretch of Devon Avenue is a Midwestern slice of Calcutta, settled by Indians who've transformed the street into a veritable restaurant row of tandoori chicken and curry-flavored dishes.

The West Side

West Loop Also known as the Near West Side, the neighborhood just across the Chicago River from

the Loop is the city's newest gentrification target, as old warehouses and once-vacant lots are transformed into trendy condos. The stretch of Randolph Street just west of Highway 90/94 and the surrounding blocks are known as "Restaurant Row" for the many dining spots that cluster there. Nearby, on Halsted Street between Adams and Monroe streets, is Chicago's old "Greek Town," still the Greek culinary center of the city. Much of the old Italian neighborhood in this vicinity was the south takes you on an up-clos-and-personal view of Chicago's financial center. See "Getting Around," later in this chapter, for more in riding the El. Also see the box "Sky Train: Chicago's El" for more on the history of the trains.

- **Getting the Blues.** This most American of music forms is venerated by Chicagoans, who keep the blues alive nightly in the city's clubs. Chicago-style blues is what most people think of when you mention live blues played in a nightclub setting. Catching a blues act is a great way for grown-ups to spend a night out on the town (see the box "If You Have a Sitter: The Music Scene" in chapter 10).

- **Discovering Wonders at Chicago's Museums.** Generations of Chicagoans recall permanent exhibits at Chicago museums with nostalgia. I remember Colleen Morre's Fairy Castle at the Museum of Science and Industry—the most fantastic dollhouse you'll ever see. My brother will never forget the Santa Fe Model Railway at the same museum. Whatever you family's fancy, you can find an exhibit about it somewhere among the Adler Planetarium & Astronomy Museum, Field Museum of Natural History, Art Institute of Chicago, Museum of Science and Industry, John G. Shedd Aquarium, or Museum of Contemporary Art.

  And don't miss out on Chicago's Museum Campus—a landscaped 57-acre area with terraced gardens and broad walkways that's home to the Field Museum of Natural History, John G. Shedd Aquarium, and the Adler Planetarium & Astronomy Museum. In my humble opinion, the Museum Campus is the most impressive collection of museums in the most beautiful setting anywhere in the country.

  For more on Chicago's museums, see chapter 6.

victim of urban renewal, but remnants still survive on Taylor Street; the same is true for a few old delis and shops on Maxwell Street, dating from the turn of the 20th century when a large Jewish community lived in the area.

Bucktown/Wicker Park Centered near the confluence of North, Damen, and Milwaukee avenues, where the Art Deco Northwest Tower is the tallest thing for miles, this resurgent area is said to be home to the third-largest concentration of artists in the country.

Over the past century, the area has hosted waves of German, Polish, and, most recently, Spanish-speaking immigrants (not to mention writer Nelson Algren). In recent years, it has morphed into a bastion of hot new restaurants, alternative culture, and loft-dwelling yuppies surfing the gentrification wave that's washing over this still-somewhat-gritty neighborhood.

The South Side

South Loop The generically rechristened South Loop area was Chicago's original "Gold Coast" in the late 19th century, with Prairie Avenue (now a historic district) as its most exclusive address. But in the wake of the 1893 World's Columbian Exposition in Hyde Park, and continuing through the Prohibition era of the 1920s, the area was infamous for its Levee vice district, home to gambling and prostitution, some of the most corrupt politicians in Chicago history, and Al Capone's headquarters at the old Lexington Hotel. However, in recent years, its prospects have turned around. The South Loop—stretching from Harrison Street's historic Printers Row south to Cermak Road (where Chinatown begins), and from Lake Shore Drive west to the south branch of the Chicago River—is one of the fast-growing residential neighborhoods in the city.

Pilsen Originally home to the nation's largest settlement of Bohemian-Americans, Pilsen (which derives its name from a city in Bohemia) was for decades the principal entry point in Chicago for immigrants of every ethnic stripe. Centered at Halsted and 18th streets just southwest of the Loop, it is now the second-largest Mexican-American community in the United States. One of the city's most vibrant and colorful neighborhoods, Pilsen has been happily invaded by the outdoor mural movement launched years earlier in Mexico, and it boasts a profusion of authentic taquerias and bakeries. The neighborhood's annual Day of the Dead celebration, which begins in September, is an elaborate festival that runs for 8 weeks. The artistic spirit that permeates the community isn't confined to Latin American art. In recent years artists of every stripe, drawn partly by the availability of loft space in Pilsen, have nurtured a small but thriving artists' colony.

Bridgeport & Canaryville Bridgeport, whose main intersection is 35th and Halsted streets, has been the neighborhood of two Mayor Daleys, father and son (the son moved not too long ago to the new Central Station development in the South Loop area). After the old Comiskey Park was torn down, the Chicago White Sox stayed in Bridgeport, inaugurating their new stadium there. Nearby Canaryville, just south and west, is typical of the "back of the yard," blue-collar neighborhoods that once surrounded the Chicago Stockyards. Neither area offers much to the typical visitor; in fact, "outsiders" aren't all that welcome.

Hyde Park Hyde Park's main attraction for families is the world-famous Museum of Science and Industry. Hyde Park is like an independent village within the confines of Chicago, right off Lake Michigan and roughly a 30-minute train ride from the Loop. The main drag is 57th Street, and the University of Chicago—with all its attendant shops and restaurants—is the neighborhood's principal tenant. The most successful racially integrated community in the city, Hyde Park is an oasis of furious intellectual activity and liberalism that, ironically, is hemmed in on all sides by neighborhoods suffering some of the highest crime rates in Chicago.

2 Getting Around

The best way to tour Chicago is by walking its streets. Fortunately, it's also one of the easiest ways to get around with kids. But when walking is not practical—such as when moving between distant neighborhoods or getting around on cold winter days—Chicago's public train and bus systems are efficient modes of transportation. In fact, they may be the least expensive way of entertaining your child while visiting the city.

BY PUBLIC TRANSPORTATION

The **Chicago Transit Authority (CTA)** operates an extensive system of trains and buses throughout the city of Chicago. The sturdy system carries about 1.5 million passengers a day. Subways and elevated trains (known as the El) are generally safe and reliable, although it's advisable to avoid long rides through unfamiliar neighborhoods late at night.

The bus and the El each has its pros and cons when traveling with kids. Parents with infants might prefer the El, since carrying a baby and a stroller up the bus steps (then paying the fare and finding a seat as the bus lurches into traffic) requires strength, coordination, and nerves of steel. Until your child can climb up steps, the easy-on, easy-off advantage of the El makes it the better choice (in spite of the fact that you might have to carry your stroller up and down stairs to reach the train platform).

Fares for the bus, subway, and El are $1.75, with an additional 25¢ for a transfer that allows CTA riders to make two transfers on the bus or El within 2 hours of receipt. Children under 7 ride free, and those between the ages of 7 and 11 pay 85¢ (15¢ for transfers). Seniors can also receive the reduced fare if they have the appropriate reduced-fare permit (call ℂ **312/836-7000** for details on how to obtain one, although this is probably not a realistic option for a short-term visitor).

Adopting a system used by other urban transit agencies, the CTA uses credit card–size fare cards that automatically deduct the exact fare each time you take a ride. The reusable cards can be purchased with a preset value already stored ($17.50 for 10 rides), or riders can obtain cards at vending machines located at all CTA train stations and charge them with whatever amount they choose (a minimum of $1.75 and up to $100). If within 2 hours of your first ride you transfer to a bus or the El, the turnstiles at the El stations and the fare boxes on buses will automatically deduct from your card just the cost of a transfer (25¢). If you make a second transfer within 2 hours, it's free. The same card can be recharged continuously.

Fare cards can be used on buses, but you can't buy a card on the bus. If you get on the bus without a fare card, you'll have to pay $1.75 cash (either in coins or in dollar bills); the bus drivers cannot make change, so make sure that you've got the right amount before hopping onboard.

⸜Tips⸝ Free Ride

During the summer, the city of Chicago operates kid-pleasing free trolleys daily between Michigan Avenue and the Museum Campus (site of the Adler Planetarium, the Field Museum of Natural History, and the Shedd Aquarium); the trolleys run only on weekends in the fall and spring. Free trolleys also run year-round between Navy Pier and the Grand/State Street El station on the Red Line. Check out the routes and get details on schedules at www.metrarail.com. The trolleys are supposed to make stops every 30 minutes, but waits can be far longer during peak tourist season—and the trolleys aren't air-conditioned. If you get tired of waiting, remember that CTA public buses travel the same routes for only $1.75 per person.

CTA INFORMATION The CTA operates a useful telephone information service ((C) **836-7000** or TTY 836-4949 from any area code in the city and suburbs) that functions daily from 5am to 1am. When you want to know how to get from where you are to where you want to go, call the CTA. Make sure that you specify any conditions you might require—the fastest route, for example, or the simplest (the route with the fewest transfers or the least amount of walking), and so forth. You can also check out the CTA's website at **www.transitchicago. com**. Excellent comprehensive CTA maps, which include both El and bus routes, are usually available at subway or El stations, or by calling the CTA. The CTA also has added a toll-free customer service hot line ((C) **888/YOUR-CTA** or TTY 888/CTA-TTY1 Mon–Fri 7am–8pm, with voice mail operating after hours) to field questions and feedback. Although the new fare-box system has eliminated the need for ticket agents, agents are still available at some El stations to offer customer assistance.

BY THE EL & THE SUBWAY The rapid transit system operates five major lines, which the CTA recently began identifying by color (although Chicagoans often still refer to them by their points of origin): the **Red Line** (also known as the Howard/Dan Ryan Line) runs north-south; the **Green Line** (also known as the Lake St. Line) runs west-south; the **Blue Line** (also known as the O'Hare Line) runs west-northwest to O'Hare Airport; the **Brown Line** (also known as the Ravenswood Line) runs in a northern zigzag route; and the **Orange Line** runs southwest, serving Midway airport. The **Purple Line,** which runs on the same Loop elevated tracks as the Orange and Green lines, serves north suburban Evanston only during rush hour.

Study your CTA map carefully (there's one printed on the inside back cover of this guide) before boarding any train. Most trains run every 5 to 20 minutes, decreasing in frequency in the off-peak and overnight hours, but some stations close after work hours (as early as 8:30pm) and remain closed on Saturday, Sunday, and holidays. The Orange Line train does not operate from about 11:30pm to 5am, the Brown Line operates only north of Belmont after about 9:30pm, the Blue Line's Cermak branch has ceased operating overnight and on weekends, and the Purple Line does not run overnight.

The CTA has posted timetables on the El platforms so that you can determine when the next train should arrive.

BY BUS Chicago's comprehensive system of public buses means virtually every place in the city is within close walking distance of a bus stop. Other than on foot

---

Tips **Ticket to Ride**

Consider buying a **Visitor Pass,** which works like a fare card and allows individual users unlimited rides on the El and CTA buses over a 24-hour period. The cards cost $5 and are sold at airports, hotels, museums, Hot Tix outlets, transportation hubs, and Chicago Office of Tourism visitor information centers. You can also buy them in advance online at www.transit chicago.com or by calling (C) **888/YOUR-CTA**. Also available now are 2-, 3-, and 5-day passes. Although the passes save you the trouble of feeding the fare machines yourself, remember that they're economical only if you plan to make at least three distinct trips at least 2 or more hours apart. (You get two additional transfers for an additional 25¢ on a regular fare.)

Purple Line (Evanston Express)
Red Line
Blue Line (O'Hare Airport)
Brown Line
Orange Line (Midway Airport)
Green Line

Clark/Lake State/Lake

Lake Transfer

Washington/ Wells

Washington/ Dearborn

Randolph/ Wabash

Washington/ State

Madison/ Wabash

Monroe/ Dearborn

Monroe/State

Adams/Wabash

Quincy/Wells

Jackson/ Dearborn

Jackson/State

LaSalle/Van Buren

Library (State/Van Buren)

Free Train Connections

LaSalle/Congress

or bicycle, the best way to get around Chicago's warren of neighborhoods—the best way to actually see what's around you—is by riding a public bus. (The view from the elevated trains can be pretty dramatic too; the difference is that on the trains you get the backyards, while on the bus you see the buildings' facades and the street life.) Look for the **blue-and-white signs** to locate bus stops, which are spaced about 2 blocks apart.

A few buses that are particularly handy for many visitors are the **no. 146 Marine/Michigan,** an express bus from Belmont Avenue on the North Side that cruises down North Lake Shore Drive (and through Lincoln Park during non-peak times) to North Michigan Avenue, State Street, and the Grant Park museum campus; the **no. 151 Sheridan,** which passes through Lincoln Park en route to inner Lake Shore Drive and then travels along Michigan Avenue as far south as Adams Street, where it turns west into the Loop (and stops at Union Station); and the **no. 156 LaSalle,** which goes through Lincoln Park and then into the Loop's financial district on LaSalle Street.

Pace buses (© **836-7000** from any Chicago area code, or 847/364-7223, Mon–Fri 8am–5pm; www.pacebus.com) cover the suburban zones that surround Chicago. They run every 20 to 30 minutes during rush hour, operating until midevening Monday through Friday and early evening on weekends. Suburban bus routes are marked no. 208 and above, and vehicles may be flagged down at intersections because few of the lines have bus stops that are marked.

Fun Fact Sky Train: Chicago's El

It's a rare Hollywood film or TV series set in the Windy City that doesn't frame its stars against that most archetypal of Chicago images: the city's elevated train system, more commonly known as the **"El."** But the origin of the El has nothing to do with its celebrated gritty, rumbling, rail-screeching urban aesthetic.

Chicago made a miraculous recovery after the Great Fire of 1871—within 20 years, a sea of neighborhoods appeared on former prairies and swamps, and the downtown district overflowed with people, streetcars, wagons, horses, and horse droppings. The boom created two problems: It was hard to get downtown quickly in the pre-automobile era, and once you got downtown, it was impossible to actually move around.

So Chicago took to the sky, building a system of elevated trains 15 feet above all the madness. The South Side line (part of today's Green Line) was the first, opening in 1892 and running to 39th Street, about 5 miles south from downtown; the following year, the line was extended to Jackson Park, bringing commuters to the World's Fair. In 1893, the Lake Street line (also part of today's Green Line) began running to the West Side, and the Metropolitan West Side Elevated (part of today's Blue Line, serving the Northwest and West sides) opened in 1895.

The first El trains on the South Side and Lake Street lines were steam-powered, but the Metropolitan West Side Line debuted with a new-fangled electric style of train. The cleaner, quieter trains were a hit, and the other El lines followed the West Side's lead. In 1896, the Lake Street Line started using electricity, and the South Side Line got wired in 1898. These lines were run by competing companies, and each line had its own terminal on the outskirts of downtown, so commuters still had to negotiate the traffic and the filth of downtown streets once they got off the train.

In 1895, the three El companies collaborated to build a set of tracks into and around the central business district that all the lines would then share. By 1897, the "Loop" was up and running, but it would take almost 100 years before the "El" would connect the whole city.

Chicago's El wasn't the nation's first. That honor belongs to New York City, which started running its elevated trains in 1867, 25 years before Chicago. But the New York El has almost disappeared, moving underground and turning into a subway early last century. With 289 miles of track, Chicago has the biggest El in the country, and the second-largest public transportation system.

BY COMMUTER TRAIN

If you plan to visit suburban destinations, your best public transportation bet is the **Metra** commuter railroad (© **312/322-6777** or TTY 312/322-6774 Mon–Fri 8am–5pm; at other times, call Regional Transportation Authority [RTA] at © 312/836-7000 or TTY 312/836-4949; www.metrarail.com). The Metra serves the six-county suburban area around Chicago with 12 train lines.

Several terminals are located downtown, including **Union Station** at Adams and Canal streets, **LaSalle Street Station** at LaSalle and Van Buren streets, **North Western Station** at Madison and Canal streets, and **Randolph Street Station** at Randolph Street and Michigan Avenue.

To visit some of the most affluent suburbs in the country, take the **Union Pacific North Line** (previously known as the North Western train), which departs at the North Western Station, and select from among the following destinations: Kenilworth, Winnetka, Glencoe, Highland Park, and Lake Forest.

The **Metra Electric** (once known as the Illinois Central–Gulf Railroad, or the IC) runs close to Lake Michigan on a track that occupies some of the most valuable real estate in Chicago. It will take you to Hyde Park. You can catch the Metra Electric in the Loop at the Randolph Street Station and at the Van Buren Street Station at Van Buren Street and Michigan Avenue (both these stations are underground).

Commuter trains have graduated fare schedules based on the distance you ride. On weekends and holidays and during the summer, Metra offers a family discount that allows up to three children under age 12 to ride free when accompanying a paid adult. The commuter railroad also offers a $5 weekend pass for unlimited rides on Saturday and Sunday.

BY TAXI

I don't recommend taking taxis with infants and very young children because unless the taxi is a new model, you may not be able to latch your car seat in the back. With older children, however, taxis are a pretty affordable way to get around the Loop and to get to the dining, shopping, and entertainment options found beyond downtown, such as on the near–North Side, in Old Town and Lincoln Park, and on the near–West Side. But for longer distances, the fares will add up.

Taxis are easy to hail in the Loop, on the Magnificent Mile and the Gold Coast, in River North, and in Lincoln Park, but if you go much beyond these key areas, you might need to call. Cab companies include **Flash Cab** (*©* 773/ **561-1444**), **Yellow Cab** (*©* 312/TAXI-CAB or 312/829-4222), and **Checker Cab** (*©* 312/CHECKER or 312/243-2537).

The meter in Chicago cabs currently starts at $1.90 and increases $1.60 for each mile, with a 50¢ surcharge for each additional rider age 12 to 65.

BY CAR

Chicago is laid out so logically that it's relatively easy for visitors to get around the city by car. Although rush-hour traffic jams are just as frustrating as they are in other large U.S. cities, traffic runs fairly smoothly at most times of the day. The combination of wide streets and strategically spaced expressways makes for generally easy riding. But Chicagoans have learned to be prepared for unexpected delays; it seems that at least one major highway and several downtown streets are under repair throughout the spring and summer months. (Some say we have two seasons here: winter and construction.)

Diagonal corridors—such as Lincoln Avenue, Clark Street, and Milwaukee Avenue—slice through the grid pattern at key points in the city and shorten many a trip that would otherwise be tedious on the checkerboard surface of the Chicago streets. **Lake Shore Drive** (also known as the Outer Dr.) has to be one of the most scenic and useful urban thoroughfares anywhere. You can travel the length of the city (and beyond), never far from the Great Lake that is Chicago's most awesome natural feature.

DRIVING RULES   One bizarre anomaly in the organization of Chicago's traffic is the occasional absence of signal lights off the principal avenues, notably in the River North and Streeterville neighborhoods. A block east or west of the Magnificent Mile (North Michigan Ave.)—one of the most traveled streets in the city—you will in some cases encounter only stop signs to control the flow of traffic. Once you've become accustomed to the system, it works very smoothly, with everyone—pedestrians and motorists alike—advancing in their proper turn.

Unless otherwise posted, a right turn on red is allowed after stopping and signaling.

PARKING   Parking regulations are vigorously enforced throughout the city. Read signs carefully: The streets around Michigan Avenue have no-parking restrictions during rush hour—and believe me, your car will be towed immediately. Many neighborhoods have adopted resident-only parking that prohibits others from parking on their streets, usually after 6pm each day (even all day in a few areas, such as Old Town). The neighborhood around Wrigley Field is off-limits during Cubs night games, so look for yellow sidewalk signs alerting drivers during the dozen-and-a-half or so times the Cubs play under lights. You can park in resident-only permit zones if you're visiting a friend, who can provide you with a pass to stick on your windshield. Beware of tow zones, and, if visiting in winter, make note of curbside warnings regarding snow plowing.

A safe bet is valet parking, which most restaurants provide for $6 to $9. Downtown you can also opt to park in a public garage, but you might have to pay the premium prices common in any metropolitan area. (Several garages connected with malls or other major attractions offer discounted parking with a validated ticket.)

The very best parking deal in the Loop is the city-run **Millennium Park garage** (© 312/742-7644), which charges $12 for 12 hours or less (enter on Columbus Dr., 1 block east of Michigan Ave., between Monroe and Randolph sts.). Also relatively affordable and superconvenient is the public parking underneath **Grant Park,** with entrances at Michigan Avenue at Van Buren Street (© 312/745-2862) and Michigan Avenue and Madison Street (© 312/742-7530). Parking costs $9 for the first hour, $12 for 1 to 2 hours, $15 for 2 to 10 hours, and $18 for 24 hours. You'll find higher prices at most other downtown lots, including **McCormick Place Parking,** 2301 S. Lake Shore Dr. (© 312/791-7000); **Midcontinental Plaza Garage,** 55 E. Monroe St. (© 312/986-6821); and **Navy Pier Parking,** 600 E. Grand Ave. (© 312/595-7437).

CAR RENTAL   Hertz (© 800/654-3131), **Avis** (© 800/831-2847), **National** (© 800/227-7368), and **Budget** (© 800/527-0700) all have offices at O'Hare Airport and at Midway Airport. Each company also has at least one office downtown: Hertz at 401 N. State St., Avis at 214 N. Clark St., National at 203 N. LaSalle St., and Budget at 65 E. Lake St.

BY BOAT

Boat transport is a great way to get around with kids. And boat traffic in Chicago has been stirring up a bigger wake recently. **Shoreline Sightseeing** (© **312/222-9328**) has started ferrying passengers on the lake between Navy Pier and the Shedd Aquarium, and on the Chicago River between Navy Pier and the Sears Tower (Adams St. and the river). The **water taxis** operate daily Memorial Day to Labor Day every half-hour and cost $6 for adults, $5 for seniors, and $3 for children.

If you are staying in the suburbs and traveling to the Magnificent Mile, kids will love a ride on the Metra commuter train followed by a ride on a shuttle boat operated by **Wendella Commuter Boats** (© 312/337-1446), which float daily April through October between a dock below North Western Station, the commuter train station across the river from the Loop, and the Wrigley Building (the boats dock on the northwest side of the Michigan Ave. bridge). The ride, which costs $1.50 each way (or 10 rides for $11) and takes about 8 minutes, is popular with both visitors and commuters. The service operates every 10 minutes from 7am to 7pm.

Wendella recently added a water taxi of its own, a 38-foot, 74-passenger river bus operating daily between the North Western and Union Station train stations and the River East pier (just east of the Michigan Ave. bridge) beginning at 9am. A one-way fare costs $2.

BY BICYCLE

I wouldn't recommend trying to ride bicycles on the city streets with kids. Although the city of Chicago has earned kudos for its efforts to improve conditions for bicycling (designated bike lanes have been installed on stretches of Wells St., Roosevelt Rd., Elston Ave., and Halsted St.), it can still be rough trying to compete with cars and their drivers, who aren't always so willing to share the road. If you are determined to bike with your kids, though, you might want to take to the lakefront path or area parks. Make sure you wear a helmet at all times!

Bike Chicago (© 800/915-BIKE; bikechicago.com), with five locations including Navy Pier, rents all sorts of bikes, including tandems and four-seater "quadcycles," baby seats, and in-line skates. Bikes rent for $8.75 an hour or $25 a day. Bike Chicago leads free bike tours of Lincoln and Grant parks from Navy Pier at 10:30am and 1:30pm daily, and from North Avenue Beach at 11am and 2pm. Helmets, pads, and locks are free. The shop is open daily from 8am to 10pm in June, July, and August, weather permitting. From September through May the shop is open daily from 9am to 7pm.

The **Chicagoland Bicycle Federation** (© 312/42-PEDAL; www.chibikefed. org), a nonprofit advocacy group, is a good resource for bicyclists. The group publishes several bicycling maps with tips on recommended on-street routes and parkland routes, and a guide to safe cycling in the city.

Bike and Roll also rents all types of bikes and in-line skates from two locations: Navy Pier (© 312/595-9600) and North Avenue Beach (© 773/327-2706). Bikes rent for $9.75 per hour or $34 per day. The shops are open daily from 9am to 7pm, weather permitting.

3 Planning Your Outings

Planning a day of touring a city with kids is a little like mapping out a military campaign: You should have a list of sights to hit, and a precise idea of how you will get from one activity to the next, leaving time in between for potty breaks and snack stops. If you plan carefully and center all your days' activities in close proximity, you can save yourself a lot of wasted transit time.

Prime areas for families include the **Magnificent Mile,** with the John Hancock Center, American Girl Place, FAO Schwarz, Niketown, and other shopping destinations; **Streeterville,** home of Navy Pier and the Museum of Contemporary Art; **River North,** with lots of chain establishments, including ESPN Zone, Hard Rock Cafe, Rock 'n' Roll McDonald's, and Ed Debevic's; **Lincoln Park,** with the park, zoo, and botanical gardens; **Museum Campus,** with four museums within walking distance of each other; and **Hyde Park,** home to the Museum of Science and Industry.

FINDING A RESTROOM

The number-one tip for visitors from Chicago parents: Know where the nearest restroom is at all times! First order of business: Always use the bathroom at your hotel before you leave, and stop in the restroom before you leave any museum or restaurant. Failing that, key restrooms in prime locations include: **900 N. Michigan Avenue mall,** on the second and fifth floors; **John Hancock Center,** in the lower level; **Water Tower Place;** and **Nordstrom's,** located in the Westfield North Bridge mall on Michigan Avenue, just south of the Chicago River. Most **Starbucks Coffee** shops have restrooms—just ask the barista for the key. **Barnes & Noble** and **Borders** bookstores typically have bathrooms near the children's section. Major hotel lobbies are also good bets. Most restaurants will take pity on a distressed child, so just ask; some store owners may do the same. If you are really concerned about mapping out nearby bathrooms, there's even a website dedicated to the topic. The Bathroom Diaries (www.thebathroomdiaries. com) lists 10,000 bathrooms around the world, everywhere from Cambodia to Antarctica, with a focus on the U.S. Readers rank bathrooms according to cleanliness, safety, and aesthetic beauty (believe it or not!).

NURSING MOMS & INFANTS

Chicago is slightly more conservative than other big cities: While most people will see a nursing mom and look the other way, some might stare rudely. If you need to breast-feed an infant, you'll probably feel most comfortable in women's lounges in major department stores (**Nordstrom** is best).

FAST FACTS: Chicago

American Express Travel-service offices are located in the Loop at 55 W. Monroe St. (℃ **312/541-5440**) and across from the Virgin Megastore, at 605 N. Michigan Ave. (℃ **312/943-7840**).

Area Codes The **312** area code applies to the Loop and the neighborhoods closest to it, including River North, North Michigan Avenue, and the Gold Coast. The rest of the city is under the **773** area code. Suburban area codes are **847** (north), **708** (west and southwest), and **630** (far west). You must dial "1" plus the area code for all telephone numbers, even if you are making a call within the same area code.

Babysitters Check with the concierge or desk staff at your hotel, who are likely to maintain a list of reliable sitters with whom they have worked in the past. Many of the hotels work with the **American ChildCare Service** (℃ **312/644-7300**), a state-licensed babysitting service that can match you with a sitter. The sitters are required to pass background checks, provide multiple child-care references, and be trained in infant and child CPR. It's best to make a reservation 24 hours in advance; the office is open from 9am to 5pm. Rates are about $17 per hour, with a 4-hour minimum and a $10 fee for transportation.

Business Hours Shops generally keep normal business hours, Monday through Saturday from 10am to 6pm. Most stores generally stay open late at least 1 evening a week. And certain businesses, such as bookstores, are almost always open during the evening hours all week. Most shops (other than those in the Loop) are now open on Sunday as well, usually from noon to 5pm. Malls are generally open until 7pm and on Sunday as well. Banking hours in Chicago are normally from 9am (8am, in some cases) to 5pm Monday through Friday, with select banks remaining open later on specified afternoons and evenings.

Car Rentals See "Getting Around," earlier in this chapter.

Dentists The 24-hour referral service of the **Chicago Dental Society** (*Ⓒ* **630/978-5745**) can refer you to an area dentist. You also might try your hotel concierge or desk staff, who often keep a list of dentists.

Doctors In the event of a medical emergency, your best bet—unless you have friends who can recommend a doctor—is to rely on your hotel physician or go to the nearest hospital emergency room. The **Chicago Medical Society** (*Ⓒ* **312/670-2550**; www.cmsdocs.org) makes free referrals on weekdays from 8:30am to 4:30pm. **Northwestern Memorial Hospital** also has a **Physician Referral Service** (*Ⓒ* **877/926-4664**). See also "Hospitals," below.

Driving Rules See "Getting Around," earlier in this chapter.

Drugstores **Walgreens,** 757 N. Michigan Ave., at E. Chicago Street (*Ⓒ* **312/664-4000**), is open 24 hours. Two other 24-hour locations are 641 N. Clark St., at W. Ontario Street (*Ⓒ* **312/587-0904**), and 1200 N. Dearborn, at W. Division Street (*Ⓒ* **312/943-0971**). **Osco Drugs** has a toll-free number (*Ⓒ* **800/654-6726**) that you can call to locate the 24-hour pharmacy nearest you.

Embassies & Consulates See appendix A, "For International Visitors."

Emergencies For fire or police emergencies, call *Ⓒ* **911.** The nonemergency phone number for the Chicago Police Department is *Ⓒ* **311.** The city of Chicago proclaims the following policy: "In emergency, dial 911 and a city ambulance will respond free of charge to the patient. The ambulance will take the patient to the nearest emergency room according to geographic location." If you desire a specific, nonpublic ambulance, call **Chicago Ambulance** (*Ⓒ* **773/521-7777**).

Hospitals The best hospital emergency room in Chicago is, by consensus, at **Northwestern Memorial Hospital,** 251 E. Huron St. (*Ⓒ* **312/926-2000**; www.nmh.org), a state-of-the-art medical center right off North Michigan Avenue. The emergency department (*Ⓒ* **312/926-5188** or 312/944-2358 for TDD access) is located at 251 E. Erie St., near Fairbanks Court. For an ambulance, dial *Ⓒ* **911.**

Internet Access Many Chicago hotels have business centers with computers available for guests' use. Computers with Internet access are also available to the public at the **Harold Washington Library Center,** 400 S. State St. (*Ⓒ* **312/747-4300**) and at the Internet cafe inside the **Apple** computer store, 679 N. Michigan Ave. (*Ⓒ* **312/981-4104**).

Liquor Laws Most bars and taverns have a 2am license, allowing them to stay open until 3am Sunday (Sat night); some have a 4am license and may remain open until 5am on Sunday.

Maps See "City Layout," in section 1, "Orientation," earlier in this chapter.

Newspapers & Magazines The *Chicago Tribune* (① 312/222-3232; www.chicagotribune.com) and the *Chicago Sun-Times* (① 312/321-3000; www.suntimes.com) are the two major dailies. The *Chicago Reader* (① 312/828-0350; www.chireader.com) is a free weekly that appears each Thursday, with all the current entertainment and cultural listings. *Chicago* magazine (www.chicagomag.com) is a monthly that is widely read for its restaurant reviews. *CS* is a free lifestyle monthly that covers nightlife, dining, fashion, shopping, and other cultural pursuits. The *Chicago Defender* covers local and national news of interest to the African-American community. The Spanish-language *La Raza* (www.laraza.com) reports on stories from a Latino point of view. The *Chicago Free Press* (www.chicago freepress.com) and *Windy City Times* (www.outlineschicago.com) both publish both news and feature articles about gay and lesbian issues.

Police For emergencies, call ① **911**. This is a free call (no coins required). For nonemergencies, call ① **311**.

Post Office The main post office is at 433 W. Harrison St. (① **312/983-8182**); free parking is available. You can also find convenient branches in the Sears Tower, the Federal Center Plaza at 211 S. Clark St. (designed by Mies van der Rohe, no less), the James R. Thompson Center at 100 W. Randolph St., and a couple of blocks off the Magnificent Mile at 227 E. Ontario St.

Radio **WBEZ** (91.5 FM) is the local National Public Radio station, which plays jazz in the evenings. **WFMT** (98.7 FM) specializes in fine arts and classical music. **WXRT** (93.1 FM), a progressive rock station whose DJs don't stick to corporate-sanctioned play lists but mix things up with shots of blues, jazz, and local music. If it's Top 40 you want to hear, tune in to 101.9 FM. On the AM side of the dial, you'll find talk radio on **WGN** (720) and **WLS** (890)—two longtime stations that got their names from their immodest owners (respectively, that would be the *Chicago Tribune,* the "World's Greatest Newspaper," and Sears, the "World's Largest Store"). News junkies should tune to **WBBM** (780) for nonstop news, traffic, and weather reports, and sports fans will find company on the talk station **WSCR** (1160).

Safety Chicago has all the crime problems of any urban center, so use your common sense and stay cautious and alert. At night you might want to stick to well-lighted streets along the Magnificent Mile, River North, Gold Coast, and Lincoln Park (stay out of the park proper after dark, though), which are all high-traffic areas late into the night. Don't walk alone at night, and avoid wandering down dark residential streets, even those that seem perfectly safe. Muggings can—and do—happen anywhere.

After dark, you might want to avoid neighborhoods such as Hyde Park, Wicker Park (beyond the busy intersection of Milwaukee, Damen, and North aves.), and Pilsen, which border areas with more troublesome reputations. You can also ask the concierge at your hotel or an agent at the tourist visitor center for recommendations about visiting a particular area of the city.

The El is generally quite safe, even at night, although some of the downtown stations can feel eerily deserted late in the evening. When you're traveling with kids, I always recommend that when in doubt, spring for a taxi. Buses are a safe option too, especially nos. 146 and 151, which pick up along North Michigan Avenue and State Street and connect to the North Side via Lincoln Park.

Blue-and-white police cars are a common sight, and officers also patrol by bicycle downtown and along the lakefront and by horseback at special events and parades. There are police stations in busy nightlife areas, such as the 18th District station at Chicago Avenue and LaSalle Street in the hopping restaurant-and-entertainment mecca of River North, and the 24th District station (known as Town Hall) at Addison and Halsted streets, located near the busy strip of sports bars and nightclubs in Wrigleyville.

Taxes The local sales tax is 8.75%. Restaurants in the central part of the city, roughly the 312 area code, are taxed an additional 1%, for a total of 9.75%. The hotel room tax is a steep 14.9%.

Time Zone All of Illinois, including Chicago, is located in the Central time zone, so clocks are set 1 hour earlier than those on the East Coast and 2 hours later than those on the West Coast. Chicago switches to daylight saving time on the first Sunday in April, and back to Standard Time on the last Sunday in October.

Transit Info The **CTA** has a useful number to find out which bus or El train will get you to your destination: ℂ **836-7000** (from any area code in the city or suburbs) or TTY 836-4949.

Weather For the **National Weather Service**'s current conditions and fore-cast, dial ℂ **312/976-1212** (for a fee), or check the weather on the Web at www.weather.com.

4

Family-Friendly Accommodations

Downtown Chicago is packed with hotels, and the good news for families is that although most of the hotels are oriented to the city's convention trade, plenty cater to families. In the last few years, a building boom in the high-end market has brought international players such as the Peninsula and Sofitel into the Midwestern market—wonderful hotels, but not the kind that most families can afford. But even though budget lodgings are becoming harder to find anywhere near downtown, you won't have a problem finding midrange, family-friendly hotels in the most convenient neighborhoods, such as River North. Chicago is not a city where luxury hotels have dibs on all the prime real estate.

Because Chicago's hospitality industry caters first and foremost to the business traveler, the hotels tend to empty out by Friday. (Keep in mind, though, that rooms are sometimes available at rock-bottom rates during conventions if a hotel is unable to book to capacity.) Hotels are sometimes willing to reduce prices on the weekends to push up their occupancy rates. And many hotels known as "business hotels" have made efforts to add family-friendly amenities to entice families to stay the weekend. Still, the hotel industry has been so strong in Chicago in recent years that you won't find reservation agents as willing or able to wheel and deal as they once were.

Warning: You never know when a huge convention will gobble up all the desirable rooms in the city, even on a weekend. You'd be wise to book a room well in advance whenever you plan to visit. To find out if an upcoming convention coincides with the dates you plan to visit Chicago, contact the **Chicago Convention & Visitors Bureau** (© 312/567-8500; www.choosechicago.com—click on "Meeting Professionals," then "Convention Calendar").

If the city has a slow season, it's the depth of winter, when outsiders tend to shy away from the cold and the threat of being snowed in at O'Hare. Serious bargain hunters might choose to visit then. The Convention & Visitors Bureau usually offers a special promotion, "Winter Delights," from January to March. Call © 877/244-2246 for a brochure, or check out www.877chicago.com. The brochure includes discounts on many of Chicago's leading hotels and restaurants.

Tip: If you'd like to watch your pennies but the idea of traveling in the dead of winter—and bundling the kids up 20 times a day as you pop in and out of attractions, restaurants, and your hotel—doesn't appeal to you, another option is to stay in a less expensive hotel during the week and move into swell digs for the weekend finale.

ACCESSIBILITY Most hotels are prepared to accommodate travelers with physical disabilities (and for families traveling with children and the accompanying strollers and other equipment), but you should always inquire when you make reservations to make sure that the hotel can meet your particular needs.

RESERVE IN ADVANCE Whatever hotel or hotels you choose, regardless of season, making reservations well in advance will help ensure that you get the best rate available. I've provided toll-free phone numbers for all the hotels reviewed in this chapter, but you might find better rates by calling the hotel's reservations office directly. Most hotels have check-in times somewhere between 3 and 6pm; if you are going to be delayed, call ahead and reconfirm your reservation to prevent cancellation.

RESERVATION SERVICES For discounted rooms at more than 30 downtown hotels, try **Hot Rooms** (℃ **800/468-3500** or 773/468-7666; www.hotrooms.com). I've used this service and was very pleased to get a night in a top-rated downtown hotel for about half the regular price—and that was during the height of the busy summer season. The service is free, but if you cancel a reservation (and you must adhere to each individual hotel's cancellation policy), you're assessed a $25 fee. Another source of information on reservations is the annual *Illinois Hotel-Motel Directory,* which also provides information about weekend packages. Call the **Illinois Bureau of Tourism** at ℃ **800/ 2CONNECT** for a copy.

BED & BREAKFAST RESERVATIONS A centralized reservations service called **Bed & Breakfast/ Chicago Inc.,** P.O. Box 14088, Chicago, IL 60614 (℃ **800/375-7084** or 773/394-2000; fax 773/394-2002; www.chicago-bed-breakfast. com), lists more than 70 accommodations in Chicago. If you're of an adventurous bent, you'll find options ranging from high-rise and loft apartments to guest rooms carved from a former private club on the 40th floor of a Loop office building. Most lie within 3 miles of downtown (many are located in the Gold Coast, Old Town, and Lincoln Park) and will run you $135 to $300 for apartments, and as low as $85 for guest rooms in private homes. *Note:* Most B&Bs require a minimum stay of 2 or 3 nights; also, many have restrictions on children. Some accept only children over age 10, for example, and others will not accept kids of any age. It's always wise to ask if children are welcome when making reservations.

LANDING THE BEST ROOM Somebody has to get the best room in the house: It might as well be you. You can start by joining the hotel's frequent-guest program, which may make you eligible for upgrades. A hotel-branded credit card usually gives it owner "silver" or "gold" status in frequent-guest programs for free. Always ask about a corner room. They're often larger and quieter, with more windows and light, and they often cost the same as standard rooms. When you make your reservation, ask if the hotel is renovating; if it is, request a room away from the construction. Ask about nonsmoking rooms, rooms with views, rooms with twin, queen-, or king-size beds. If you're a light sleeper, request a quiet room away from vending machines, elevators, restaurants, bars, and discos. Ask for a room that has been most recently renovated or redecorated.

If you aren't happy with your room when you arrive, ask for another one. Most lodgings will be willing to accommodate you.

A NOTE ABOUT PRICES In this chapter I've divided hotels into four price categories: **Very Expensive** means double-occupancy rooms typically cost upwards of $350 per night; **Expensive** rooms cost around $250 to $350; **Moderate,** about $150 to $250; and **Inexpensive,** $85 to $150.

The rates given in this chapter are per night and do not include taxes, which are quite steep at 14.9%, nor do they take into account any discounts. Prices are always subject to availability and vary according to day of the week and seasonally. (The lower rates tend to be offered Jan–Mar and on nonholiday weekends.)

1 The Loop

Strictly speaking, "downtown" in Chicago means the Loop—the central business district, a 6-by-8-block rectangle enveloped by elevated tracks on all four sides. An outer circle beyond this literal loop of tracks is bounded on the north and west by the Chicago River and its south branch, forming an elbow on two sides; on the east by Michigan Avenue running along the edge of Millennium Park and Grant Park; and on the south by the Congress Expressway. Within these confines are the city's financial institutions, trading markets, and municipal government buildings, making for, as you might expect, quite a lot of hustle and bustle Monday through Friday. Come Saturday and Sunday, however, the Loop is pretty dead, despite the fact that it is also home to major music and theater venues and is near the Art Institute. On a nice day, it's easy to walk south from the Loop to the Museum Campus, home to the Field Museum of Natural History and John G. Shedd Aquarium.

For visitors who want a real "city" experience, the Loop offers dramatic urban vistas or skyscrapers and a feeling that you're in the center of weekday action. The Loop has an interesting mix of grand old hotels, such as the Palmer House, and brash new upstarts, most notably the hip triad run by the West Coast–based Kimpton Group: the Hotel Burnham, Hotel Monaco, and Hotel Allegro. Despite their differences, all offer undeniable convenience for families who prefer to be at the center of the city.

VERY EXPENSIVE

Fairmont Hotel ★★ The Fairmont is easily one of the city's most luxurious hotels, offering an array of deluxe amenities and services. This is the kind of place that regularly hosts high-level politicians and CEOs (but not rock stars). The overall effect is chic but a bit impersonal. The entrance looks out on anonymous office towers, and you're likely to wander the circular lobby a bit before finding the check-in desk. Still, families rave about the huge rooms and bend-over-backwards service; although families aren't the hotel's primary market, you will be made to feel more than welcome.

The large rooms are decorated in a comfortable, upscale style. (Ask for one with a lake view, although even the city-view rooms offer some distance from neighboring offices.) The posh bathrooms feature extra-large tubs, separate vanity areas, and swivel TVs. The windows even open (a rarity in high-rise hotels), so you can enjoy the breeze drifting off Lake Michigan. Suites have one or two bedrooms, a living room, a dining area, and a built-in bar—and all come with lake views. You can access Lakeshore Athletic Club without walking outside. The club has a pool, but unfortunately the club is open to children only after 2pm on Saturday and all day on Sunday. The hotel is connected to the city's underground pedway system (one of my favorite activities to do with kids), through which you can walk all the way to Marshall Field's on State Street on inclement days without stepping outside.

200 N. Columbus Dr. (at Lake St.), Chicago, IL 60601. © **800/526-2008** or 312/565-8000. Fax 312/856-1032. www.fairmont.com. 692 units. $129–$389 double; $229–$539 suite. Kids under 18 stay free in parent's room.

Rollaways $25/night; cribs free. AE, DC, DISC, MC, V. Valet parking $30 with in/out privileges. Subway/El: Red, Green, Orange, Brown, or Blue Line to State/Lake. Small pets accepted. **Amenities:** Restaurant; lounge; access to Lakeshore Athletic Club, one of the top health clubs in the city (w/full-court basketball, climbing wall, pool, and spa); concierge; business center; salon; 24-hr. room service; babysitting; laundry service; 24-hr. dry cleaning. *In room:* A/C, TV w/pay movies, fax, minibar, hair dryer, iron, CD player, high-speed Internet access.

EXPENSIVE

Crowne Plaza Chicago—The Silversmith ★ *Finds*   You might call the Silversmith a hidden gem. The landmark building, designed by the celebrated firm of D. H. Burnham and Company, was built in 1897 to serve the jewelry and silver trade on Wabash Avenue, still known as Jeweler's Row. While the hotel isn't a traditional "family" hotel, it does provide cribs, babysitting service, and toys and games. Word about The Silversmith has been slow getting out (even many Loop office workers who pass by it every day don't know it's there), so it doesn't book up as quickly as other hotter spots. That's good news for families on vacation because it means that the hotel is more willing to make a deal on room rates. (The suites—perfect for families—often get discounted, I hear.) There is also more likely to be room at this inn during the busy convention season.

Rooms come in varying configurations, with 12-foot-high ceilings, 10-foot picture windows, handsome Frank Lloyd Wright–inspired wrought-iron fixtures, armoires, and homey bedding; bathrooms are generously sized. Because buildings surround this very urban hotel, most rooms along the hotel's main corridor tend to be dark (with windows looking into neighboring office buildings). For a better—and quintessentially Chicago—view, get a room at the front on the fifth floor or higher, overlooking Wabash Avenue and the El tracks. In the evening stop by the lobby for a wine-and-cheese reception and complimentary desserts (including Eli's cheesecake, one of the city's signature sweet treats).

10 S. Wabash Ave. (at Madison St.), Chicago, IL 60603. ℭ **800/2CROWNE** or 312/372-7696. Fax 312/372-7320. www.silversmith.crowneplaza.com. 143 units. $149–$279 double; from $289 suite; weekend rates available. Rollaways $20/night; cribs free. AE, DC, DISC, MC, V. Valet parking $28 with in/out privileges. Subway/El: Brown, Green, or Orange Line to Madison/Wabash, or Red Line to Washington/State. **Amenities:** Restaurant; lounge; tiny fitness room (w/access to nearby health club for a fee); concierge; business center and secretarial services; limited room service; babysitting; laundry service; dry cleaning; club-level rooms. *In room:* A/C, TV w/pay movies, dataport, minibar, coffeemaker, hair dryer, iron, safe.

Hard Rock Hotel Chicago ★   The good news: This hotel is not located on top of the supertouristy Hard Rock Cafe, which is located about a mile away in River North. In fact, the hotel is a relatively restrained rehab of one of the city's historic skyscrapers, the 40-story Carbide and Carbon Building. As you might expect, the theme here is music: Pop tunes echo through the lobby, TV monitors show videos, and glass cases display pop-star memorabilia. If your kids are in the age range that considers wearing a Hard Rock T-shirt from exotic locales a badge of honor, they may well get a kick from a stay here. But for the grown-ups in your crowd, the mix of old and new can be somewhat jarring. The black-and-gray lobby feels like a nightclub, but the marble-and-gold-trimmed elevator bank still says "high-rise office building." Don't expect too much rock-star attitude; to date, the Hard Rock appears to be populated by youngish business travelers and families. The guest rooms are neutral in decor with modern furnishings. The building's larger-than-average windows let in plenty of natural light. The Hard Rock Rooms on the corners of each floor are larger than the standard double rooms and feature chaise longues for stretching out. Families should inquire about the suites, located in the tower at the top of the building, which come in various one- and two-bedroom configurations.

Central Chicago Accommodations

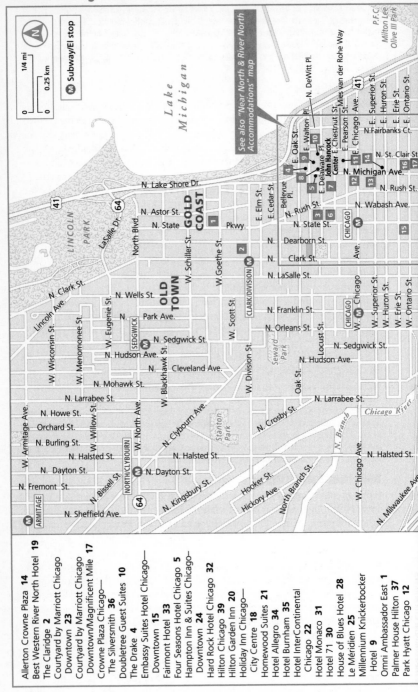

See also "Near North & River North Accommodations" map

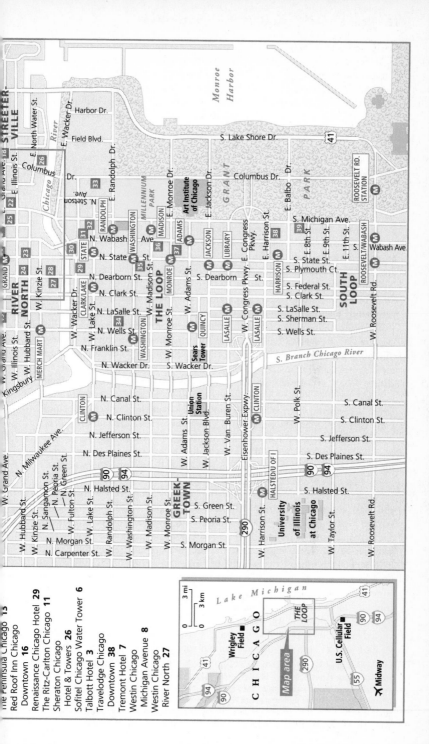

The Peninsula Chicago 13
Red Roof Inn Chicago
  Downtown 16
Renaissance Chicago Hotel 29
The Ritz-Carlton Chicago 11
Sheraton Chicago
  Hotel & Towers 26
Sofitel Chicago Water Tower 6
Talbott Hotel 3
Travelodge Chicago
  Downtown 38
Tremont Hotel 7
Westin Chicago
  Michigan Avenue 8
Westin Chicago
  River North 27

The hotel's restaurant, China Bar & Grill, serves up Asian fusion cuisine in a high-energy setting, and the street-level bar, open until 4am, features live music and DJs most nights. Despite its efforts to become a Chicago hipster hangout, the place still has the feel of a hotel bar. The hotel is actively courting rock bands who come through town on tour, but my guess is that the hotel will be hard-pressed to convince the likes of U2 to exchange their ultraluxury digs at the Park Hyatt for the Hard Rock.

230 N. Michigan Ave. (at Lake St.), Chicago, IL 60601. ✆ **877/ROCK-HOTEL** or 312/345-1000. Fax 312/345-1012. www.hardrockhotelchicago.com. 381 units. $169–$239 double; from $1,500 suite. Kids under 12 stay free in parent's room. No rollaways; cribs free. Weekend rates available. AE, DC, DISC, MC, V. Valet parking $35 with in/out privileges. Subway/El: Red Line or Blue Line to Lake. **Amenities:** Restaurant; bar; exercise room; concierge; business services; 24-hr. room service; same-day laundry service; dry cleaning. *In room:* A/C, TV w/DVD player and video games, minibar, coffeemaker, hair dryer, iron, safe, CD player, high-speed Internet access.

Hotel Burnham ★★★   Here's my pick for Chicago's most distinctive hotel, one that took a historic location and jazzed it up with a dash of colorful modern style. This hip hotel uses its sense of whimsy to embrace, not exclude, families. Don't come to the Burnham if you're looking for extensive amenities—the lobby is tiny, as is the exercise room, and there's no pool. But it's my top choice for families in this price category, provided you book a suite, which will offer your family plenty of space.

The result of a brilliant restoration of the historic Reliance Building—one of the first skyscrapers ever built and a highly significant architectural treasure—this intimate boutique hotel (named for Daniel Burnham, whose firm designed the Reliance Building in 1895) is the work of the Kimpton Group, the trend-setting West Coast–based chain behind the Allegro and Monaco hotels (both reviewed later in this section). It occupies a prime spot in the heart of State Street, across from Marshall Field's and 1 block south of the hopping North Loop theater district. The Burnham is a must for architecture buffs: Wherever possible, the restoration retains period elements—most obviously in the hallways, which recall the original office corridors with terrazzo tile floors, white marble wainscoting, mahogany door and window frames, and room numbers painted on the translucent glass doors.

Rooms are clubby but glamorous, with plush beds, mahogany writing desks, and chaise longues. The hotel's 19 suites feature a separate living-room area and CD stereo systems. To keep wee ones entertained, the hotel offers coloring books and crayons, games, and Super Nintendo. During holidays you'll find special activities in the hotel lobby, including decorating gingerbread men around Christmas and hunting for eggs at Easter. Diaper bags, cribs, high chairs, changing tables, and more are available upon request. And there's a turndown service with cookies and milk. The hotel's restaurant offers a children's menu. Ask the concierge for special offers for tea at American Girl Place Cafe and deals at the museums and theaters. And don't leave Fido at home: Pets are positively welcomed here. The hotel provides pet beds, treats, food and water bowls, and dog-walking services (and they'll even clean out your in-room kitty litter box!).

1 W. Washington (at State St.), Chicago, IL 60602. ✆ **866/690-1986** or 312/782-1111. Fax 312/782-0899. www.burnhamhotel.com. 122 units. $149–$299 double; $199–$349 suite. Kids 17 and under stay free in parent's room. No rollaways available; cribs free. AE, DC, DISC, MC, V. Valet parking $29 with in/out privileges. Subway: Red or Blue Line to Washington/State. Pets allowed. **Amenities:** Restaurant; small fitness room (and access to nearby health club); concierge; business services; 24-hr. room service; laundry service; dry cleaning. *In room:* A/C, TV, fax, dataport, minibar, hair dryer, iron.

Hotel Monaco ⭐⭐ More California-chic than French Riviera–suave, this playful 14-story boutique hotel greets guests with derby-hatted doormen, funky house music, and a goldfish for your room that comes with its own name. (Naturally, the ability to acquire a personal goldfish tends to be kids' favorite aspect of this hotel.) Given the hotel's playful spirit, it attracts a younger clientele, with an overall vibe that is laid-back and friendly rather than so-hip-it-hurts. (This is Chicago, after all, not New York.)

The plush, jewel-toned 1930s French Deco decor at the Kimpton Group's most upscale Chicago property infuses sizable rooms resembling theatrical set pieces—eclectic furnishings include Deco armoires, mahogany writing desks, and marshmallow-soft beds. The lack of a pool is somewhat compensated for by the luxurious Jacuzzi bathtubs. Families enjoy the suites, some of which adjoin rooms with two double beds. (For your wannabe Mick Jagger, there's a "Party Like a Rock Star" suite with a Sony 52-disc CD player, rock costume replicas, an electric guitar and amplifier, concert photographs of rock icons, and a 19-in. TV set that appears to have been thrown through the window.) Rooms on the top three floors give you a vista of the Chicago River and surrounding skyscrapers. The cozy lobby is the spot for free morning coffee and an evening wine reception. You'll find the concierge happy to help with a list of kid-friendly attractions. And feel free to bring the family pet along—the hotel has welcomed every creature from parrots to poodles. Make sure to tell them about your pet when you make a reservation, as pet food and dog walking services are available, too.

225 N. Wabash Ave. (at Wacker Dr.), Chicago, IL 60601. ℂ **800/397-7661** or 312/960-8500. Fax 312/960-1883. www.monaco-chicago.com. 192 units. $139–$299 double; $279–$429 suite. Kids 17 and under stay free in parent's room. Rollaways and cribs free. AE, DC, DISC, MC, V. Valet parking $28 with in/out privileges. Subway/El: Brown, Green, or Orange Line to Randolph/Washington or Red Line to State/Lake. Pets allowed. **Amenities:** Restaurant (South Water Kitchen, p. 111); fitness room (and access to nearby health club); concierge; business center; 24-hr. room service; in-room massage; babysitting; laundry service; dry cleaning. *In room:* A/C, TV w/pay movies, fax, dataport, minibar, coffeemaker, hair dryer, iron.

Hotel 71 ⭐⭐ The city's newest hotel is actually a complete renovation of a rather drab 1950-era high-rise. The spacious rooms are the draw for families here—they're among the largest in the city, and a bargain at the price. Don't let the boring exterior fool you. With over 400 rooms and 30-plus stories, Hotel 71 is too big to be considered a "boutique" hotel, but it is filled with unique touches that reflect the boutique sensibility. The rather cramped lobby has a nightclub look, with black curtains covering the walls and atmospheric trance music wafting from the stereo system. By contrast, the rooms are bright and cheery, and the decor is brand-new, with yellow-checked linens and curtains and spotless white bathrooms. Rooms have well-lit work desks and minibars stocked with gourmet treats from Dean & DeLuca (keep it locked to prevent the kids from charging up a storm!). Rooms on the north side of the hotel overlook the Chicago River and have the best views. Request a room on the west end of the building for a gorgeous northwest view down the river and across to the Magnificent Mile. Suites come with either a living room or meeting room and a bedroom down the hall (One negative: The bathrooms are actually smaller than those in the regular rooms), but a family of three or four could fit into a standard room with two queen beds.

71 E. Wacker Dr. (at Wabash Ave.), Chicago, IL 60601. ℂ **800/621-4005** or 312/346-7100. Fax 312/346-1721. www.hotel71.com. 454 units. $149–$249 double. Kids under 18 stay free in parent's room. Rollaways $30/night; cribs free. Weekend rates available. AE, DC, DISC, MC, V. Valet parking $32 with in/out privileges. Subway/El: Brown, Green, or Orange Line to Randolph/Wabash, or Red Line to Washington/State. **Amenities:** Restaurant; fitness room; concierge; business services; 24-hr. room service; laundry service; dry cleaning. *In room:* A/C, TV, minibar, hair dryer, iron, CD player, high-speed Internet access.

Fun Fact **Did You Know?**

Merriel Abbott, the dance choreographer who booked all the acts at the Palmer House's famed Empire Room—one of the nation's leading supper clubs from the 1930s to the 1950s—gave Liberace and Bob Fosse their first breaks. Liberace, a cocktail pianist at the club, was "discovered" in Milwaukee by Abbott, who is credited with dressing up the flamboyant entertainer's piano with a candelabra to lend his act some pizzazz. Fosse, a native Chicagoan, made his debut at age 18 as part of a dance team. He and his partner made $500 a month in 1947; Liberace was paid a miserly $1,100 for 5 weeks in 1946.

Palmer House Hilton *Overrated*   Chicago's oldest hotel, the namesake of legendary State Street merchant prince Potter Palmer, is decidedly from another era (although this building is actually the third Palmer House). The massive complex feels somewhat lost in time, as the elegance of the lobby isn't translated into the rooms, which are decorated in an anonymous midlevel hotel style. Clientele tends heavily toward conventioneers. Some rooms are more recently upgraded and redecorated than others, so be sure to ask for a refurbished room when making reservations. Bathrooms are on the smallish size, though some rooms come with two bathrooms, a plus for families. Kids might appreciate the sheer palatial size of the place, with plenty of room to wander, and the location is good for access to the Museum Campus. Ask about Vacation Station, a kids' welcome packet that includes information on kids' activities around the city, plus games and snacks. Despite the hotel's excellent location, you shouldn't expect grand views of surrounding skyscrapers (most rooms look out into offices across the street). The Palmer House's days as one of Chicago's top hotels are definitely past.

17 E. Monroe St. (at State St.), Chicago, IL 60603. (C) **800/HILTONS** or 312/726-7500. Fax 312/917-1797. www.hilton.com. 1,640 units. $129–$350 double; $450–$1,500 suite. Kids 18 and under stay free in parent's room. Rollaways $25/stay; cribs free. AE, DC, DISC, MC, V. Valet parking $31 with in/out privileges; self-parking across the street $21. Subway/El: Red Line to Monroe/State. **Amenities:** 4 restaurants (including the legendary but dated Trader Vic's, a Polynesian restaurant); 2 lounges; indoor pool; health club; Jacuzzi; sauna; children's programs; concierge; business center; shopping arcade; room service until 2am; babysitting referrals; laundry service; overnight dry cleaning; executive rooms. *In room:* A/C, TV w/video games, minibar, coffeemaker, hair dryer, iron.

Renaissance Chicago Hotel *★★*   The Renaissance is the most understated upscale hotel in the city, located at the top of State Street, just across the bridge from the Magnificent Mile and steps from the Loop's attractions. Although business travelers are the Renaissance's bread and butter, I was happy to discover that the hotel has bent over backwards to accommodate families traveling with children. One huge plus: A pool on the fourth floor is open from 6:30am to 10pm, with no restrictions on children's use. The hotel's restaurants offer kids' menus for breakfast, lunch, and dinner, offering everything from French toast to ravioli. Kids will appreciate the PlayStation games on the television.

The hotel embraces its location with bay windows offering stunning views of the river and the towers of North Michigan Avenue. The rooms are tasteful and rather understated. Standard double rooms include a small sitting area with a couch and smallish bathrooms; deluxe doubles have much bigger bathrooms (some with separate showers and bathtubs) and two couches. Club-level rooms, located on the top four floors, are half a room larger and have their own concierge in a private lounge, where complimentary continental breakfast and evening hors d'oeuvres and pastries are served. Families often request connecting rooms, one of which has a king bed and the other, two queen-size beds. I'd also recommend requesting a room on the 20th floor or higher on the east side for views of both the Chicago River and Lake Michigan. Other good bets are rooms on the hotel's north side, all of which have river views.

1 W. Wacker Dr. (at State St.), Chicago, IL 60601. (C) 800/468-3571 or 312/372-7200. Fax 312/372-0093. www.renaissancehotels.com. 553 units. $159–$259 double; $189–$289 Club Level double; $500–$2,500 suite. Kids under 12 stay free in parent's room. Rollaways at no charge in Club Lounge rooms only; cribs free. Weekend rates available. AE, DC, DISC, MC, V. Valet parking $34 with in/out privileges. Subway/El: Brown Line to State/Lake, or Red Line to Washington/State. Small pets accepted. **Amenities:** Restaurant; lounge; indoor pool w/skylights; health club w/sauna and whirlpool; concierge; 24-hr. Kinko's business center; salon; 24-hr. room service; babysitting; laundry service; club-level rooms. In room: A/C, TV w/pay movies and PlayStation, minibar, coffeemaker, hair dryer, iron, high-speed Internet access, wet bar in some rooms.

MODERATE

Hotel Allegro ⭐ (Value)   For families in search of a fun, light-hearted vibe, the Kimpton Group's splashy Allegro is a good value. Although its published rates are similar to those of its sister properties, the Hotel Monaco and Hotel Burnham, the Allegro is far larger and therefore more likely to offer special rates to fill space, especially on weekends and in the winter. Guests enter a whimsical lobby that feels like a cartoon with its plush, eclectic, and boldly colorful furnishings, but the overarching theme here is musical entertainment. Adjoining the hotel is the historic Palace Theatre, a former vaudeville house reopened in 1999 as a venue for first-run Broadway shows. Suites have robes, VCRs, and two-person Jacuzzi tubs. For a family of three or more, the hotel recommends a king suite with a two-person Jacuzzi tub; the room includes a living room and separate bedroom with a king bed.

As befits a place where the concierge wears a stylish leather jacket and the doorman hums along to the tunes playing on speakers out front, the Allegro appeals to younger travelers. The hotel's restaurant, 312 Chicago, attracts nonguests in search of excellent Italian-American cuisine. There's no kids' menu, but the restaurant is accommodating to families. Like the other Kimpton Group hotels in Chicago, Hotel Allegro welcomes pets.

171 W. Randolph St. (at LaSalle St.), Chicago, IL 60601. (C) 800/643-1500 or 312/236-0123. Fax 312/236-0917. www.allegrochicago.com. 483 units. $149–$299 double; $225–$399 suite. Kids 17 and under stay free in parent's room. Rollaways are free available depending on room; cribs free. AE, DC, DISC, MC, V. Valet parking $30 with in/out privileges. Subway/El: All lines to Washington. Pets allowed. **Amenities:** Restaurant; lounge; exercise room (and access to nearby health club w/indoor pool); concierge; business services; salon; limited room service; same-day laundry service; dry cleaning. In room: A/C, TV w/pay movies, fax, minibar, hair dryer, iron, high-speed Internet access (upon request).

2 South Loop

Unlike the area surrounding North Michigan Avenue—the "Mag Mile"—the South Loop is less about glamour and more about old Chicago. Running the length of Grant Park, South Michigan Avenue is ideal for a long city stroll, passing grand museums, imposing architecture, and the park's greenery and statuary. But although this stretch was once Chicago's most regal hotel row, it's certainly the worse for wear today. Over the last decade, however, the surrounding neighborhood has been revitalized, with the conversion of industrial buildings into loft apartments. Old-timers might complain about gentrification, but it's good news for visitors, who now find more restaurant options and livelier street life. For families, the proximity to Millennium Park, Grant Park, and State Street shopping makes the area attractive, particularly when summer music festivals or holiday shopping is on the agenda.

VERY EXPENSIVE

Hilton Chicago ★★   When it erupted onto Michigan Avenue in 1927, this massive brick-and-stone edifice billed itself as the largest hotel in the world. It certainly owns one of the most colorful histories of any Chicago hotel. Guests have included Queen Elizabeth, Emperor Hirohito, and every president since FDR. The classical-rococo public spaces—including the Versailles-inspired Grand Ballroom and Grand Stair Lobby—are magnificent, but the rest of the hotel is firmly entrenched in the present. The hotel is a solid choice for families: There's plenty of space to wander, and it's close to all of the major museums and Grant Park (great for when the kids need to burn off some energy). Even better, there's a heated swimming pool and a fitness center with a whirlpool and sauna, all open to kids.

Some rooms are on the small side, but all are comfortable and warm, and many of the standard rooms have two bathrooms—great for families. Adjoining rooms are available; ask when you call for reservations. The views from those higher up facing Michigan Avenue offer a sweeping view of Grant Park and the lake. The hotel's Tower section offers a separate registration area, upgraded amenities (including robes, fax machines, and VCRs), and a lounge open from 6am to 11pm, serving complimentary continental breakfast and evening hors d'oeuvres and cocktails (you'll pay about $50 above the standard rate for these rooms).

720 S. Michigan Ave. (at Balbo Dr.), Chicago, IL 60605. © **800/HILTONS** or 312/922-4400. Fax 312/922-5240. www.chicagohilton.com. 1,544 units. $124–$324 double; from $139–$339 junior suite. Kids 18 and under stay free in parent's room. Rollaways $25/stay; cribs $25/stay. AE, DC, DISC, MC, V. Valet parking $32; self-parking $29. Subway/El: Red Line to Harrison/State. **Amenities:** 4 restaurants; 2 lounges; indoor pool; health club w/indoor track, hot tubs, sauna, and steam room; concierge; business center; 24-hr. room service; massage; babysitting; laundry service; 24-hr. dry cleaning. *In room:* A/C, TV w/pay movies, dataport, minibar, coffeemaker, hair dryer, iron.

INEXPENSIVE

Travelodge Chicago Downtown *Value*   You won't be reveling in luxury, but Travelodge promises and delivers neat, clean rooms at reasonable prices. The hotel's location near the Loop and Museum Campus is excellent: You are half a block from Grant Park and all the summer festivals, and only 4 blocks from the Field Museum. This 12-story hotel is one of few budget lodgings you'll find in the heart of the Loop. The hotel was built in 1925 as the Harrison Hotel, and for many years was one of the premier hotels in the city. Ever since Travelodge acquired the property, they've been promoting it as "a touch of old Chicago" and working to restore the property. To date, all guest rooms and the lobby have been renovated.

Families should request one of the "Sleepy Bear Den" rooms, which offer privacy for parents and for kids—but not too much privacy. The room is separated into two areas with an archway: On one side is a king bed for the parents, and on the other side is a double bed for the kids, specially decorated with whimsical curtains and bedding. Each side has its own television and VCR; the kids' side is stocked with children's movies. Also included are a microwave and refrigerator. Other rooms suitable for families offer two beds and two bathrooms. There's no pool, but two restaurants cater to families: Chicago Carry-Out offers full breakfasts and sandwiches, and Charming Wok offers inexpensive Chinese fare from 11am to 11pm.

65 E. Harrison St. (at S. Wabash Ave.), Chicago, IL 60605. ℂ **888/515-6375** or 312/427-8000. Fax 312/427-8261. www.travelodge.com. 250 units. $105–$165 double. Kids 17 and under stay free in parent's room. Rollaways $10/night; cribs free. AE, DC, DISC, MC, V. Indoor garage parking $15 car or small van, includes 1 in/out per day at no charge. Subway/El: Red Line to State/Harrison. **Amenities:** 2 restaurants. *In room:* A/C, TV w/pay movies, fax, dataport, minibar, coffeemaker, hair dryer, iron.

3 Near North & the Magnificent Mile

Along the Magnificent Mile—a stretch of Michigan Avenue running north of the Chicago River to Oak Street—you'll find most of the city's premium hotels. The location can't be beat.

VERY EXPENSIVE

Four Seasons Hotel Chicago ⭐⭐⭐   A fabulous pool and indulgences for kids make this hotel a thumbs-up for families in search of luxury. Consistently voted one of the top hotels in the world by frequent travelers, the Four Seasons occupies a rarefied aerie between the 30th and 46th floors above the Mag Mile's most upscale vertical mall. The overall look is that of an English country manor rather than a glitzy getaway, but the real attraction here is the service, not the decor. Rooms have English furnishings, custom-woven carpets and tapestries, and dark wood armoires. Each has windows that open to let in the fresh air. Bathrooms boast such indulgences as a lighted makeup mirror, oversize towels and robes, scales, and Bulgari toiletries.

Kid-friendly services include little robes, balloon animals, video games, a special room-service menu, and milk and cookies. Ask about the "Kids for All Seasons" weekend package, which includes small gifts and discounts from kids' retailers. With the package, children under 12 eat free from the kids' room-service menu—and receive a complimentary gift from the ice cream man. Yes, it's true—as a special treat for wee ones, the hotel has an ice cream man who will visit your room and let kids choose an ice cream and toppings, including Oreo pieces, gummy bears, M&Ms, sprinkles, freshly whipped cream, and chocolate sauce and caramel sauce. Most indulgent of all, however, are the twin beds—so soft that the hotel's gift shop sells about a hundred of them each year for $1,200 a piece.

An 18-foot-high white marble fountain marks the entrance to the opulent Seasons Restaurant (the hotel's other restaurant, The Café, offers kids' menus). I'd recommend that families make reservations for the Sunday brunch at Seasons, which takes place from 10:30am to 1:30pm. Children are welcome to join the fun in their own section of the restaurant, where a Harry Potter castle houses arts and crafts. The activities are supervised by a babysitter, and you can enjoy the best brunch in Chicago while your kids are within view. Kids can join you to eat, then run off to enjoy their own experience in the castle. Bon appétit!

120 E. Delaware Place (at Michigan Ave.), Chicago, IL 60611. ℂ **800/332-3442** or 312/280-8800. Fax 312/280-1748. www.fourseasons.com. 343 units. $435–$535 double; $585–$3,500 suite. Weekend rates from $305. Kids under 18 stay free in parent's room. Rollaways and cribs free. AE, DC, DISC, MC, V. Valet parking $36 with in/out privileges; self-parking $26. Subway/El: Red Line to Chicago/State. Pets accepted. **Amenities:** 2 restaurants; lounge; indoor pool (unrestricted access for kids); fitness center; concierge; business center; 24-hr. room service; babysitting; laundry service; 24-hr. dry cleaning. *In room:* A/C, TV/VCR w/pay movies and Nintendo, minibar, coffeemaker, hair dryer, iron, high-speed Internet access.

Park Hyatt Chicago ⭐⭐⭐   For those in search of chic modern luxury, the Park Hyatt is the coolest hotel in town. The hotel occupies one of the most desirable spots on North Michigan Avenue, overlooking Water Tower Square, and the best rooms are those that face east, overlooking the bustle of Michigan Avenue and the lake in the distance.

Luxury might be the watchword here, but the look is anything but stuffy: The lobby feels like a sleek modern art gallery. German painter Gerhard Richter's *Piazza del Duomo Milan* masterpiece is the visual centerpiece of the space, providing ample evidence of what visual treats lie in store for guests. Rooms feature Eames and Mies van der Rohe reproduction furniture, and window banquettes with stunning city views (the windows actually open). The bathrooms are especially wonderful: You can pull back a sliding cherrywood wall and enjoy a view of the city while you soak in the oversize tub.

Families often book connecting rooms, one with a king bed and one with two double beds. Every room has CD and DVD players with a flat-screen TVs, and the concierge will loan from the hotel's library of DVDs (including kids' movies) at no cost. The health club is only open to those over 16, but the pool welcomes kids—and it's a stunner, with city views looking south and bronze-colored tiles. If you plan to spend significant time at American Girl Place, ask about the hotel's special package, which includes breakfast for two at the hotel, outfits for the doll, and a special turndown service—for your child's doll, too, of course. The "Kids-cierge" program for children up to age 14 includes a backpack with a camera, maps, and coupons to redeem at the hotel, including a coupon for a tour of the behind-the-scenes workings of the hotel, which includes the kitchen (kids get a cookie and chef's hat), housekeeping, and more.

The crown jewel of the Park Hyatt is NoMI, a restaurant nestled on the seventh floor. Serving French-inspired cuisine and featuring an *Architectural Digest*–worthy interior, with an adjoining outdoor terrace, NoMI (an acronym for North Michigan) continues to receive stellar reviews. Parents will want to book a sitter for an evening out here—it's far too chic to be kid-friendly.

800 N. Michigan Ave., Chicago, IL 60611. **©** **800/233-1234** or 312/335-1234. Fax 312/239-4000. www. hyatt.com. 203 units. $375–$425 double; $695–$3,000 suite. Kids 18 and under stay free in parent's room. No rollaways; cribs free. AE, DC, DISC, MC, V. Valet parking $36 with in/out privileges. Subway/El: Red Line to Chicago/State. **Amenities:** Restaurant (French/American); lounge; indoor pool; health club w/Jacuzzi and spa; concierge; business center w/computer technical support; 24-hr. room service; massage; babysitting; laundry service; 24-hr. dry cleaning. *In room:* A/C, TV w/DVD player and pay movies, dataport, minibar, coffeemaker, hair dryer, iron, CD player.

The Peninsula Chicago ★★★   Do believe the hype. The first Midwest location from the luxury Peninsula hotel group promised to wow us, and it does not disappoint. Taking design cues from the chain's flagship Hong Kong hotel, the Peninsula Chicago mixes an Art Deco sensibility with modern, top-of-the-line amenities. Service is practically a religion here: In fact, in 2004 frequent travelers ranked this hotel number-one in North America for service (and among the top 10 worldwide).

Rooms are average in size (except for the rather small "junior suites," which have living rooms that can comfortably seat only about four people). Rooms that are popular with families include suites with two double beds, or adjoining rooms that offer one room with a king bed and one with two double beds. The hotel's in-room technology is cutting-edge: A small silver "command station" by every bed allows guests to control all the lights, curtains, and room temperature without getting out from under the covers. The marble-filled bathrooms have separate shower stalls and tubs, spacious vanities, and another "command station" by the bathtub. Add in the flat-screen TVs and DVD players, and you've got a classic hotel that's very much attuned to the present.

Kids' amenities include a treat upon arrival: milk and cookies (or popcorn and soda if they prefer). Rooms can be equipped with video games, DVDs, and a

Near North & River North Accommodations

Allerton Crowne Plaza **12**
Best Western River North Hotel **17**
Courtyard by Marriott Chicago Downtown **24**
Courtyard by Marriott Chicago Downtown/Magnificent Mile **5**
Doubletree Guest Suites **5**
The Drake **1**
Embassy Suites Hotel Chicago—Downtown **16**

Four Seasons Hotel Chicago **4**
Hampton Inn & Suites Chicago–Downtown **23**
Hilton Garden Inn **18**
Holiday Inn Chicago—City Centre **15**
Homewood Suites **19**
Hotel InterContinental Chicago **20**
House of Blues Hotel **26**
Le Méridien **22**

Millennium Knickerbocker Hotel **2**
Park Hyatt Chicago **10**
The Peninsula Chicago **11**
Red Roof Inn Chicago Downtown **14**
The Ritz-Carlton Chicago **9**
Sheraton Chicago Hotel & Towers **21**
Sofitel Chicago Water Tower **8**
Talbott Hotel **3**
Tremont Hotel **6**
Westin Chicago Michigan Avenue **7**
Westin Chicago River North **25**

Making the Most of the Concierge

Nearly all upscale hotels have concierges, and many smaller inns offer concierge services from the front desk. Too often, these people go underutilized by guests who don't know the full range of services concierges can provide. Beyond merely giving directions to Navy Pier, concierges are there to act as guests' problem solvers. The best ones take real pleasure in helping, and the more challenging the request, the better. When you're on vacation, why not truly relax, and let the concierge be your personal assistant during your stay?

House Cars: Upper-end hotels often have house cars available to drop off guests in the Loop or elsewhere within 5 miles of the hotel. Businesspeople use the service most, but any guest can enjoy this perk. If you want to take the kids to watch the White Sox play at U.S. Cellular Field, or you need a ride to a restaurant, request a house car through the concierge desk. There's usually no charge, but you may tip the driver at your discretion.

Restaurants: Every concierge will make dinner reservations for guests, and I recommend having the concierge phone ahead no matter where you are dining. If a restaurant is booked, the concierge may have more pull squeezing you in than you would on your own. But don't ask the concierge for any old restaurant recommendation. (I've been to some unremarkable, touristy places that way.) It's more effective to name two or three options and have the concierge tell you more about each one.

Other Services: You needn't limit requests to restaurant reservations. Concierges can also book cruises on Lake Michigan, car rentals, or even spa treatments—whatever requires a phone call. They can buy tickets to a sporting or entertainment venue or amend airline reservations.

Solutions: Did a child get sick? Head right to the concierge, who will make it a personal mission to ensure your kid is seen by a doctor as soon as possible. Concierges will also oblige less urgent requests, like reserving doggy day care or finding a last minute gift. You don't even have to be checked into the hotel. You can fax and e-mail the concierge with your arrival date and particular request. If he or she does go beyond the call of duty, gratuities are always appreciated—although never expected.

library of kids' movies—make sure to request them when you make your reservation. The bright, airy spa and fitness center fill the top two floors—check out the view from the outdoor deck. The spa has an Olympic-size pool, and one lane is always reserved for family swim. The 20th-floor health club is also open to children, with no restrictions. You can obtain child-care services through the concierge.

The sultry hotel bar—hidden from the lobby behind curved, leather-covered walls—is a top spot for a romantic evening with your mate. The Lobby is the best in-hotel restaurant bet for families, with a kids' menu. Don't miss breakfast at Pierre Gourmet, located just outside the hotel at the corner of Superior and Rush streets, for some of the best baked goods on the Magnificent Mile. The hotel's other restaurants, including The Avenue and Shanghai Terrace, do offer children's menus, but I'd recommend that the meal be an adults-only affair.

108 E. Superior St. (at Michigan Ave.), Chicago, IL 60611. ℂ 866/288-8889 or 312/337-2888. Fax 312/751-2888. www.chicago.peninsula.com. 339 units. $445–$455 double; $500–$4,500 suite. Kids 17 and under stay free in parent's room. Rollaways and cribs free. AE, DC, DISC, MC, V. Valet parking $36 with in/out privileges. Subway/El: Red Line to Chicago/State. Pets accepted. **Amenities:** 4 restaurants (seafood, Asian, Continental, and European bakery); bar; indoor pool with outdoor deck; fitness center; spa; hot tub; sauna; concierge; business center; 24-hr. room service; in-room massage; babysitting; laundry service; same-day dry cleaning. *In room:* A/C, TV w/pay movies (VCRs and DVD players upon request), fax, dataport, minibar, fridge (upon request), hair dryer, safe.

The Ritz-Carlton Chicago ★★★   Perched high atop Water Tower Place, the Ritz-Carlton casts a soothing presence on guests as they're deposited into the airy 12th-floor lobby. Not surprisingly, the quality of the accommodations is of the highest caliber. The standard rooms have traditional furnishings; suites are especially suited to families, with an additional living area furnished with a sofa and chair, a writing desk, a second TV and VCR, and a stereo. Lake views cost more but are spectacular (although in all the rooms, you're up high enough that you're not staring into surrounding condominium buildings). Families will find this luxury crash pad quite welcoming: Every child receives a gift and can borrow toys and games from a stash kept by the concierge. Video games are available, and kids' food can be delivered by room service 24 hours a day. Teenagers receive a special gift pack upon arrival.

Guests staying in Premier Suites are treated to a gratis wardrobe pressing upon arrival, personalized stationery, Bulgari toiletries, and fresh flowers. Service is the Ritz-Carlton's selling point, whether it's the "compcierge" who helps guests with computer problems or the "allergy-sensitive" rooms that are cleaned with special nonirritating products and come stocked with nonfeather duvets and pillows, plus hypoallergenic bath products on request.

Whether or not you stay here, the Ritz-Carlton is an elegant place for afternoon tea, served at 2:30 and 4:30pm in the lobby. At one end of the lobby is the Greenhouse restaurant, designed with a glass roof and wall that seems to jut out over the city. The hotel's gastronomic claim to fame is The Dining Room, one of Chicago's finest, serving French cuisine under the direction of acclaimed chef Sarah Stegner. The hotel's excellent Sunday brunch includes a special buffet for children replete with M&Ms, macaroni and cheese, chicken nuggets, and peanut-butter-and-jelly sandwiches.

160 E. Pearson St., Chicago, IL 60611. ℂ 800/621-6906 or 312/266-1000. Fax 312/266-1194. www.four seasons.com/chicagorc. 435 units. $395–$535 double; $545–$4,000 suite. Weekend rates from $310. Kids under 18 stay free in parent's room. Rollaways and cribs free. AE, DC, DISC, MC, V. Valet parking $36 with in/out privileges; self-parking $26 with no in/out privileges. Subway/El: Red Line to Chicago/State. Pets accepted. **Amenities:** 4 restaurants; 2 lounges; indoor pool; health club w/spa, hot tub, and sauna; concierge; business center; 24-hr. room service; in-room massage; babysitting; laundry service; same-day dry cleaning; premier suites. *In room:* A/C, TV w/VCR and pay movies, fax, dataport, minibar, hair dryer.

Sofitel Chicago Water Tower ★★★   Whether or not you stay here, you'll quickly spot the Sofitel, thanks to its striking white stone-and-glass facade and geometric shape: A narrow prism tower rising from a square base. Located 1 block west of the Magnificent Mile, the Sofitel doesn't cater specifically to families, but service is so accommodating that you and your kids will be made to feel right at home. The interior is stylish, with a funky, modern flair and color combos that stray far from the traditional, with deep purples and reds combining with black and white graphics. The place has a whimsical air that will appeal to kids: Luminescent floor tiles in the lobby change color in a never-ending light show. Most employees seem to hail from exotic French-speaking locales such as Morocco, giving the hotel an international flair that you won't find in most of Chicago's hotels. Foreign-language magazines are scattered on tables throughout the lobby.

Of the 415 rooms, 55 are suites that offer pullout sofas and striking views of the lake and city. (To comfortably fit a crib in the room, you'll want a suite.) Up to two children can stay in a room for no extra charge—try a suite or a standard room with two double beds. And speaking of beds, they're outfitted with fabulously fluffy and inviting duvets. Closets are spacious, and the bathtub is stocked with candles and fresh flowers. Babysitting services are available upon request, and little guests receive their own Sofitel teddy bear.

20 E. Chestnut St. (at Wabash St.), Chicago, IL 60611. ℂ **800/SOFITEL** or 312/324-4000. Fax 312/324-4026. www.sofitel.com. 415 units. $199–$459 double; $459–$599 suite. Kids under 18 stay free in parent's room. No rollaways; cribs free. AE, DC, DISC, MC, V. Valet parking $35. Subway/El: Red Line to Chicago/State. Small pets accepted. **Amenities:** Restaurant (French cafe); bar; fitness center; concierge; business center; 24-hr. room service; babysitting; laundry service; same-day dry cleaning. *In room:* A/C, TV w/pay movies, fax, mini-bar, coffeemaker, hair dryer, iron, high-speed Internet access.

EXPENSIVE

Doubletree Guest Suites ⭐   This full-service all-suite hotel is a very good choice for families seeking something with a little less starch. Best of all is its location: just off the Mag Mile and next door to the Hancock Building and Water Tower Place.

Suites might not be huge, but they're warm, inviting, and immaculate to boot. All feature a separate living room (with pullout sofa) and bedroom. The price depends on bed size, floor (some have spectacular lake views), and furnishings. The hotel doesn't feel that different from other Doubletree properties, but that consistency might be just what some people are looking for.

The homespun service and little touches are what count here: fresh flowers in the lobby and freshly baked chocolate-chip cookies presented to guests on check-in. The hotel's high spot—literally—is the fitness center on the 30th floor, with a pool that's surrounded by stunning views of Navy Pier and the Magnificent Mile; kids are welcome at both. (Stop by on a summer Wed or Sat evening for a great view of the fireworks at Navy Pier). The hotel also is home to Mrs. Park's Tavern, a family-friendly place featuring creative American fare. The restaurant has a kids' menu and sidewalk seating that offers prime people-watching in the shadow of the John Hancock building.

198 E. Delaware Place, Chicago, IL 60611. ℂ **800/222-TREE** or 312/664-1100. Fax 312/664-8627. www.doubletreehotels.com. 345 units. Kids under 18 stay free in parent's room. No rollaways (sofa beds in every suite); cribs free. AE, DC, DISC, MC, V. Valet parking $34 with in/out privileges. Subway/El: Red Line to Chicago/State. **Amenities:** Restaurant; lounge; indoor pool; fitness room; hot tub; sauna; concierge; business center; 24-hr. room service; babysitting; laundry room; dry cleaning. *In room:* A/C, TV w/pay movies, dataport, minibar, fridge, coffeemaker, hair dryer, iron.

The Drake ⭐⭐⭐   If ever the term "grande dame" fit a hotel, it fits The Drake. Fronting East Lake Shore Drive with a prominent rooftop marquee that has a signature on the city's skyline, the landmark building opened in 1920 and soon became one of the city's finest hotels. Although it's owned by Hilton, longtime Chicagoans still think of The Drake with possessive pride; it's our version of New York's Plaza or Paris's Ritz.

For all its old-time glamour, the hotel seems a bit of a dowager when compared to gleaming newer upscale hotels such as the Park Hyatt or Peninsula (both reviewed earlier in this chapter), but this, of course, is part of The Drake's charm. The Drake welcomes families, but the lack of a pool, game room, or other kid-friendly amenities (many of which its competitors offer) may be a negative. Still, plenty of families have made it a tradition to stay here.

Parents will be happy to know that the typical room is generous in size and furnished comfortably with a separate sitting area; some have two bathrooms. Rooms and suites on the slightly more expensive "executive floors" provide such additional amenities as personalized stationery, disposable cameras, a generous continental breakfast in a private lounge, and free cocktails and hors d'oeuvres, plus a daily newspaper, and valet assistance for polishing shoes, packing and unpacking, and securing theater tickets. The fourth and fifth floors have a lounge open to all guests, where soft drinks and fresh-brewed coffee and tea are available without charge. The lake-view rooms are lovely, and—no surprise—you'll pay more for them. Be forewarned that city-view rooms on the lower floors look out onto a facing building on Walton Place, so you'll probably be keeping your drapes shut.

Even if you don't stay at the hotel, take your kids to the lavishly decorated Palm Court for afternoon tea, which is accompanied by a harpist. The hotel's restaurants include the Oak Terrace, a large dining room serving up American fare and some great views of the lake and Michigan Avenue; the Cape Cod Room, a local favorite for seafood; and Coq d'Or, one of Chicago's most atmospheric piano bars. All of the restaurants have kids' menus, but I'd recommend dining at Oak Terrace, the most casual of the three.

140 E. Walton Place (at Michigan Ave.), Chicago, IL 60611. © **800/55-DRAKE** or 312/787-2200. Fax 312/787-1431. www.thedrakehotel.com. 537 units. $255–$295 double; $335–$430 executive floor; from $600 suite. Weekend rates start at $289 with continental breakfast. Kids 18 and under stay free in parent's room. Rollaways and cribs free. AE, DC, DISC, MC, V. Valet parking $32 with in/out privileges. Subway/El: Red Line to Chicago/State. **Amenities:** 3 restaurants; 2 lounges; fitness center; concierge; business center; shopping arcade (including a Chanel boutique); barbershop; 24-hr. room service; babysitting; in-room massage; laundry service; 24-hr. dry cleaning; executive-level rooms. *In room:* A/C, TV w/pay movies, dataport, minibar, coffeemaker, hair dryer, iron.

Hotel InterContinental Chicago ★★   The newer hotels might be getting all the attention, but the Hotel InterContinental remains a sentimental favorite for many Chicagoans, ranking right up there with The Drake in our affections. Built as an athletic club in 1929, the building's original lobby features truly grand details: marble columns, hand-stenciled ceilings, and historic tapestries. The addition of a drab, impersonal modern tower in the 1960s added more rooms but gave the InterContinental a somewhat schizophrenic quality. A recent renovation integrated the two sides into a cohesive whole, and brought the guest rooms up several notches in quality.

A soaring, four-story rotunda, topped by a 50-foot-wide dome, serves as the new entry point to the hotel, offering a suitably dramatic welcome. All rooms have been completely renovated to make them consistent throughout the property. You'll find classic mahogany furnishings, subdued but elegant decor, and smallish bathrooms (this is an older property, after all). Families might want to request an executive suite in the North Tower, which provides a room with a king bed that connects by French doors to a second room with a sofa bed. Rooms in the South Tower have a more distinctive feel, but be prepared for smaller bathrooms. Rooms in that tower also vary widely in size.

While you're here, take your kids to the best pool in the city: The InterContinental's main claim to fame is the junior Olympic-size pool on the top floor. One of the first aboveground swimming pools ever built, it's decorated in a lavish

"Venetian" style, with mosaics, marble columns, and painted tiles. Also be sure to ask about the "Kids in Tow" family package when making your reservation. Upon check-in, kids are presented with a backpack containing a T-shirt and other goodies, a coupon for a free in-room movie, and a 50% discount on all kids' meals in the hotel. Complimentary parking is part of the package, as are the milk and cookies that will be delivered to your room at turndown time.

The hotel's restaurant, Zest, is the only street-level restaurant on Michigan Avenue, and it offers a kids' menu. (Try to grab a table by the front windows to enjoy the never-ending street scene.)

505 N. Michigan Ave. (at Grand Ave.), Chicago, IL 60611. © **800/327-0200** or 312/944-4100. Fax 312/944-1320. www.chicago.intercontinental.com. 807 units. $249–$350 double; $500–$3,000 suite; weekend and promotional rates from $145. Kids under 18 stay free in parent's room. Rollaways available in historic South tower only for $25/night; cribs free. AE, DC, DISC, MC, V. Valet parking $27–$34 with in/out privileges. Subway/El: Red Line to Grand/State. **Amenities:** Restaurant; 2 lounges; indoor pool; fitness center w/sauna; concierge; business center; 24-hr. room service; massage; babysitting; laundry service; same-day dry cleaning; executive rooms. *In room:* A/C, TV w/pay movies, dataport, minibar, coffeemaker, hair dryer, iron.

Le Méridien ★★ Tucked into the back of Westfield North Bridge mall, Le Méridien is a fairly recent addition to the competitive high-end Chicago hotel market, and it seems the general public has yet to discover it. I'd recommend it for families seeking a luxurious option in the wintertime, thanks to the convenience of having a whole mall just a few steps away. You can get out without even bundling the kids up—an attractive proposition when it's icy outside. A quick elevator ride connects you with stores such as Nordstrom and Kenneth Cole or Chicago's Magnificent Meal food court, where you can grab anything from a Fluky's hot dog to Italian fare at Tuscany Cafe.

Le Méridien touts its design philosophy as "European with a French accent," which, in this case, means marble floors, vaguely 18th-century-inspired furniture, and some whimsical artwork (a large painting of a Napoleonic figure with the head of a dog hangs in the lobby). A terrace offers outdoor seating, and a casual bistro is hidden away in the back of the lobby (depending on your perspective, it's either pleasantly secluded or isolated). Rooms are on the small side (especially the least expensive ones on the north side of the hotel). Amenities are top-of-the-line: Every room offers a cordless phone, high-speed Internet access, and an in-room safe that allows you to plug in and charge your laptop or cellphone while it's locked away.

High rollers will want to book one of the suites overlooking Michigan Avenue; a few even come with private terraces, something few hotels in this city can offer. Some say the Grand Terrace Suite is the best hotel room in the city. The private terrace is twice the size of the room itself and, situated above Michigan Avenue, it offers a jaw-dropping, unobscured, picture-postcard view of the Magnificent Mile all the way to Oak Street Beach. And even though you are outdoors and right in the hustle and bustle of a major city, on a busy weekday you can hardly hear the people and traffic below.

Le Méridien can't quite compete with the Park Hyatt or the Peninsula (reviewed earlier in this chapter) in the glamour department, but its cozy style should appeal to travelers looking for something a little more personal.

521 N. Rush St. (at Grand St.), Chicago, IL 60611. © **800/543-4300** or 312/645-1500. Fax 312/645-1550. www.chicago.lemeridien.com. 311 units. $129 double; $375–$3,500 suite. Kids under 12 stay free in parent's room. Free rollaways and cribs. AE, DC, DISC, MC, V. Valet parking $33 with in/out privileges. Subway/El: Red Line to Chicago/State. Pets accepted. **Amenities:** Restaurant; bar; health club w/spa, Jacuzzi, and steam room; concierge; business center; 24-hr. room service; in-room massage; babysitting; laundry service; same-day dry

cleaning. *In room:* A/C, TV w/pay movies and video games, dataport, minibar, fridge, coffeemaker, hair dryer, iron, safe, CD player, high-speed Internet access.

Millennium Knickerbocker Hotel ⭐   Another historic hotel that's undergone a face-lift, the Knickerbocker looks spiffy from the lobby but retains a shabby-chic feel on the guest floors. The epitome of Jazz Age indulgence when built in 1927 as the Davis, the Knickerbocker has since undergone more transformations than Madonna. During the Capone era it was rumored to have shady underworld connections. In the 1970s Hugh Hefner turned it into the gaudy Playboy Towers and invited the leisure-suit set to a perpetual disco inferno on the hotel's famed illuminated ballroom floor. By the time the 1980s rolled around, the Knickerbocker had been through the ringer.

But thanks to a $20 million renovation, the Knickerbocker once more exudes vintage charm. Weekends are popular with families, thanks to the hotel's superb location a block from Oak Street Beach and across the street from The Drake. You'll be in the heart of Magnificent Mile shopping, and walking distance from the American Girl Place.

The rooms aren't especially spacious, but they are warm and comfortable. Bathrooms are small but nicely done. *One caveat:* Views are often rather dismal, but you can catch a glimpse of the lake in all rooms ending in 18, and corner rooms (ending in 17, 28, or 35) look onto Michigan Avenue. Families might consider staying on the Club level, which features upgraded rooms and a private lounge with complimentary breakfast, coffee, munchies, and board games. If you tell the staff that you'll be traveling with kids, they will provide some family-friendly amenities such as milk and cookies at turndown, and the pay-per-view movies always feature a children's program.

163 E. Walton Place (½ block east of Michigan Ave.), Chicago, IL 60611. ☎ **800/621-8140** or 312/751-8100. Fax 312/751-9663. www.milleniumhotels.com. 305 units. $129–$299 double; $285–$1,000 suite. Kids under 17 stay free in parent's room. Rollaways $20/night; cribs free. AE, DC, DISC, MC, V. Valet parking $35 with in/out privileges; self-parking $24 with in/out privileges. Subway/El: Red Line to Chicago/State. **Amenities:** Restaurant; bar; exercise room; concierge; business center; 24-hr. room service; babysitting; laundry service; dry cleaning; club-level rooms. *In room:* A/C, TV w/pay movies, fax, dataport, minibar, coffeemaker, hair dryer, iron.

Sheraton Chicago Hotel & Towers ⭐   Here's a beautifully situated hotel, perched on the riverfront with a view of the lake. Families will appreciate being only a short walk away from Navy Pier and steps from Michigan Avenue, with all its shopping and entertainment, and buses to whisk you to the Museum Campus. You'll also be close to walking paths along the river and lakefront, and near the Michigan Avenue Bridge leading to Millennium Park.

You can request a room with views of the Chicago River, Lake Michigan, or the city skyline, and suites are available. The indoor pool and sun deck on the seventh floor has wraparound views; the pool has recently been renovated. There's a charge for using the fully equipped health club, with treadmills, lifecycles, elliptical cross trainers, life steps, and weight training, plus a sauna and massage therapy. If parents want to spend time on their own, babysitting services are available through the concierge.

The hotel boasts five restaurants and lounges, including Shula's Steakhouse. For families wanting a quick bite, there's also a snack bar and cafe.

301 E. North Water St., Chicago, IL 60611. ☎ **877/242-2558** or 312/464-1000. Fax 312/464-9140. www.sheratonchicago.com. 1,209 units. $299 double; from $450 suite. Kids under 18 stay free in parent's room. Rollaways $25/night; cribs free. AE, DC, DISC, MC, V. Valet parking $34 with in/out privileges. Bus: 151 to Michigan Ave. Bridge; walk east. **Amenities:** 3 restaurants and lounges; indoor pool; health club; sauna; business center; 24-hr. room service; massage. *In room:* A/C, TV w/ video games, dataport, minibar, coffeemaker, hair dryer, iron, safe.

Talbott Hotel ★★ *Finds*   The family-owned Talbott is a small, European-style gem that's a fine choice for families. Constructed in the 1920s as an apartment building, the Talbott was converted to a hotel in 1989. That's great news for families, because the hotel has many suites with two bedrooms and two bathrooms, plus kitchen facilities. The location just off the Magnificent Mile is superb and close to family-friendly restaurants such as Johnny Rocket's. The wood-paneled lobby, decorated with leather sofas and velvety armchairs, two working fireplaces, tapestries, and numerous French horns used for fox hunts, is intimate and inviting—all the better in which to enjoy your complimentary continental breakfast. Kids' amenities are sparser here than at some larger hotels, but the homey, nonchain hotel atmosphere, large suites, availability of kitchens, and prime location make this one of my favorites for families.

Rooms aren't quite as distinctive, although they are decorated in a perfectly comfortable midrange hotel style; they vary in size, so ask when making reservations. Suites and the hotel's "executive king" rooms entice with Jacuzzi tubs; suites have separate sitting areas with sofa beds and dining tables. The Talbott is not for families in need of extensive hotel facilities, but the cozy atmosphere and personal level of service appeals to visitors looking for the feeling of a small inn rather than a sprawling, corporate hotel.

20 E. Delaware Place (between Rush and State sts.), Chicago, IL 60611. © 800/TALBOTT or 312/944-4970. Fax 312/944-7241. www.talbotthotel.com. 149 units. $149–$289 double; $319–$449 suite. Kids under 18 stay free in parent's room. Rollaways $20/night; cribs free. AE, DC, DISC, MC, V. Self-parking $21. Subway/El: Red Line to Chicago/State. **Amenities:** Lounge; access to nearby health club; concierge; business services; 24-hr. room service; laundry service; dry cleaning; executive rooms. *In room:* A/C; TV, minibar, hair dryer, iron, safe.

Tremont Hotel   Slightly more upscale than the Talbott but with the same small, European-style feel, the Tremont caters mainly to adults. Suites are the only realistic family option, as most guest rooms tend to be on the small (or shall we say, "intimate") side. In fact, all rooms except the suites have only one bed and accommodate two people. Rooms in the Tremont House—a separate building next door—have kitchenettes. Suites are designed so one room includes a king bed with its own television, minibar, and bathroom. The adjoining living room offers a sofa bed, a television, minibar, and bathroom. The cozy lobby with a fireplace sets the mood from the start. The furnishings are tasteful without being somber, and rooms are cheery, with yellow walls and large windows.

The steak-and-chops restaurant off the lobby, the memorabilia-filled **Mike Ditka's Restaurant** (p. 117), is co-owned by the legendary former Chicago Bears football coach.

100 E. Chestnut St. (1 block west of Michigan Ave.), Chicago, IL 60611. © 800/621-8133 or 312/751-1900. Fax 312/751-8650. www.tremontchicago.com. 130 units. $119–$279 double; $199–$299 suite. Kids under 18 stay free in parent's room. Cribs free; no rollaways (most rooms are too small). AE, DC, DISC, MC, V. Valet parking $34. Subway/El: Red Line to Chicago/State. **Amenities:** Restaurant; small exercise room (and access to nearby health club); concierge; business services; massage; babysitting; laundry service; dry cleaning. *In room:* A/C, TV/VCR, minibar, coffeemaker, hair dryer, iron, safe, CD player.

MODERATE

Allerton Crowne Plaza ★   A historic hotel that received a fairly bland makeover a few years ago, the Allerton was built in 1924 as a "club hotel" providing permanent residences for single men and women. It's now been converted into the flagship hotel of the upscale Crowne Plaza chain. The Italian Renaissance–inspired exterior has been painstakingly restored to its original dark-red brickwork and stone carvings and limestone base. Too bad the distinctive exterior style wasn't replicated inside. However, visitors who want to stay in a place that feels new—without being too trendy—should be satisfied with the reinvented Allerton. Because it was built for single men and women, even the suites aren't that big; families should also ask about adjoining rooms. The Allerton is an old-time Chicago hotel, so don't expect to find loads of family-friendly amenities such as a pool or game room. There's a fitness center, but kids aren't allowed. Rooms, however, might make up for the lack of amenities with their warm and homey feel. Snag one overlooking Michigan Avenue to get the best views (or at least stop by the hotel's Renaissance Ballroom for a peek at the Mag Mile).

701 N. Michigan Ave. (at Huron St.), Chicago, IL 60611. ℭ 800/227-6963 outside Illinois or 312/440-1500. Fax 312/440-1819. www.allertonchi.crowneplaza.com. 443 units. $109–$229 double; $159–$399 suite. Kids 19 and under stay free in parent's room. Rollaways $25/night; cribs free. AE, DC, DISC, MC, V. Valet parking $34 with in/out privileges. Subway/El: Red Line to Chicago/State. **Amenities:** Restaurant; lounge; fitness center (w/excellent city views); sauna; concierge; business center; 24-hr. room service; laundry service; same-day dry cleaning. *In room:* A/C, TV w/pay movies, dataport, minibar, coffeemaker, hair dryer, iron.

Courtyard by Marriott Chicago Downtown   Marriott's lower-budget chain offers families good value in the heart of River North. You're a short walk from Michigan Avenue, the Loop, and the many theme restaurants of River North, including the ESPN Zone. The trolley to Navy Pier stops a block from the hotel (on State St.). Plus, you'll get access to an indoor pool, fitness center (kids 12 and under must be supervised by an adult), whirlpool, sauna, and sun deck. Guest rooms are newly renovated and feature granite vanities, high-speed Internet access, and sofas, some with pull-out beds. Rooms especially good for families include connecting rooms (both double-bedded and king), and suites that offer a bedroom plus a sitting room with a sofa bed. The 30 East Café and Lounge offers breakfast buffet (with a special price of $7 for kids), lunch, dinner, and room service. There's no kids' menu, but most kids will be able to find something they like among the kid-friendly, sandwich-and-soup options on the regular menu.

30 E. Hubbard St. (at State St.), Chicago, IL 60611. ℭ 800/321-2211 or 312/329-2500. Fax 312/329-0293. www.marriott.com. 337 units. $119–$209 double; $159–$400 suite. Kids 18 and under stay free in parent's room. Rollaway beds and cribs free. AE, DC, DISC, MC, V. Valet parking $33 with in/out privileges; self-parking $21. Subway/El: Red Line to Grand/State. **Amenities:** Restaurant; lounge; exercise room; indoor pool; concierge; room service; laundry service and self-service laundry. *In room:* A/C, TV w/pay movies, dataport, coffeemaker, hair dryer, iron, high-speed Internet access.

Courtyard by Marriott Chicago Downtown/Magnificent Mile   This brand-new hotel is located in the heart of the Magnificent Mile, just a half-block east of Michigan Avenue. Sure, it's not the place to indulge in luxuries, but it's a great choice for families, with a killer location plus that rarest of rarities in downtown hotels: a brand-new pool, on the 10th floor. There's even a large fitness room with great views. Rooms here are generally larger than at the Courtyard's sister hotel in River North. Double rooms with two beds feature two queen beds (not two double beds, which is standard in the industry)—a nice option for families of four. King suites have a kitchen with a refrigerator and microwave, plus a pull-out couch in the living area. Rooms offer city views, some of Michigan Avenue. Another family-friendly feature in the room design is the shower and bathtub area, which is separate from the vanity and dressing area, a plus when multiple people are trying to get ready in the morning. The lobby decor is Art Deco, and the room decor is pretty standard, but everything is clean and new. An American cafe, Viand Bar & Kitchen, is kid-friendly and also provides room service. And when mom and dad need a pick-me-up, they can get a cup of coffee from the Starbucks in the lobby.

165 E. Ontario St. (just east of Michigan Ave.), Chicago, IL 60611. ✆ **312/573-0800**. Fax 312/573-0573. www.marriott.com. 306 units. $249 double; $309 king suite. Kids 18 and under stay free in parent's room. Rollaway beds and cribs free. AE, DC, DISC, MC, V. Valet parking $35 with in/out privileges; self-parking $25, no in/out privileges. Subway/El: Red Line to Grand/State. **Amenities:** Restaurant; lounge; exercise room; indoor pool; concierge; room service; laundry service and self-service laundry. *In room:* A/C, TV w/pay movies, dataport, coffeemaker, hair dryer, iron.

Hilton Garden Inn 😊   Although it might seem out of place in these urban climes, this Hilton Garden Inn, located on prime real estate between North Michigan Avenue and the River North neighborhood, is every inch a big-city player. The hotel caters to business types, but families certainly won't feel out of place here: The building is adjacent to ESPN Zone, a Virgin Megastore, and the new Shops at North Bridge mall. The hotel features weekend packages for families, so ask for current deals when you call. The hotel doesn't have much personality—the lobby is strictly business and feels cold. What the place does have going for it—besides location—is a high-rise sensibility that should appeal to families looking for an urban experience. The ample rooms are located between the 13th and the 23rd floors. Views higher up, especially on the east side and from corner suites facing north and south, afford dramatic vistas of the cityscape and skyline. The hotel's six suites include a parlor area, wet bar, and dining table, with possible connections to adjacent rooms.

10 E. Grand Ave. (at State St.), Chicago, IL 60611. ✆ **800/HILTONS** or 312/595-0000. Fax 312/595-0955. www.hilton.com. 357 units. $169–$309 double; $400–$700 suite. Kids 18 and under stay free in parent's room. Rollaways $20/night; cribs free. AE, DC, DISC, MC, V. Valet parking $34 with in/out privileges; self-parking $20 with no in/out privileges. Subway/El: Red Line to Grand/State. **Amenities:** Restaurant; lounge; indoor pool; fitness center w/Jacuzzi and sauna; concierge; business center; limited room service; babysitting; laundry service; same-day dry cleaning. *In room:* A/C, TV w/pay movies, dataport, fridge, coffeemaker, hair dryer, iron.

Holiday Inn Chicago—City Centre ⭐⭐ *Value*   Enter the soaring modern atrium, with its vases of blooming fresh flowers, and you won't believe that this place is kin to Holiday Inn's assembly-line roadside staples. Its location is a nice surprise as well: east of the Magnificent Mile and close to the Ohio Street Beach and Navy Pier. Although the rooms are pretty basic, the amenities make this one of the best values in the city.

The Holiday Inn is a good bet for the budget-conscious family: Not only do kids under 18 stay free in their parent's room, but those 12 and under also eat free in the hotel's restaurants when accompanied by a parent. There's a large outdoor pool, and you're located very near to Ohio Street and Oak Street beaches. Leave the pay-per-view movies one night and head to the new AMC theaters nearby, where all 21 screens offer stadium seating.

Fitness devotees will rejoice because the Holiday Inn is located next door to the Lake Shore Athletic Club, where guests may enjoy the extensive facilities free of charge. Have the concierge check on family hours at the pool, which are generally a couple hours in the morning, a few hours in the afternoon, and all day on Sunday. The gym is only available to adults over 18. The hotel also has its own spacious outdoor pool and sun deck. The views are excellent, especially looking north toward the Hancock Building and Monroe Harbor. Even the standard room should fit a family of three or four comfortably. You might want to splurge on one of the "master suites," which boast large living-room areas with wet bars, along with a Jacuzzi-style tub and sauna in the bathroom.

300 E. Ohio St. (at Fairbanks Court), Chicago, IL 60611. ✆ **800/HOLIDAY** or 312/787-6100. Fax 312/787-6259. www.chicc.com. 500 units. Weekend and promotional rates $99–$119. Kids under 18 stay free in parent's room. Rollaways $25/night; cribs free. AE, DC, DISC, MC, V. Self parking $22. Subway/El: Red Line to Grand/State. **Amenities:** 2 restaurants; bar; outdoor and indoor pools; access to nearby

health club; hot tub; sauna; children's programs; concierge; business services; limited room service; babysitting; laundry room; dry cleaning. *In room:* A/C, TV w/pay movies, coffeemaker, hair dryer, iron, high-speed Internet access.

Homewood Suites ⭐

An excellent choice for families, this hotel offers a handy location and fresh, clean rooms with some nice extras. Because all of the rooms are suites with full kitchens, you can prepare your own meals, and there's plenty of room for everyone to spread out. Housed just off the Mag Mile in a sleek tower above retail shops, offices, and a health club—and adjacent to ESPN Zone—the hotel's design aesthetic is best described as "Italian Renaissance meets Crate & Barrel." Distressed-leather sofas, Mediterranean stone tile, wrought-iron chandeliers, and beaded lampshades adorn its sixth-floor lobby.

Rooms—one- and two-bedroom suites and a handful of double-double suites, which can connect to king suites—feature velvet sofas that are all sleepers, and the beds have big, thick mattresses. Each comes with a full kitchen, a dining-room table that doubles as a workspace, and decent-size bathrooms. The hotel provides a complimentary buffet breakfast and beverages and hors d'oeuvres every evening; there is also a free grocery-shopping service and free access to an excellent health club next door.

40 E. Grand Ave. (at Wabash St.), Chicago, IL 60611. ② **800/CALL-HOME** or 312/644-2222. Fax 312/644-7777. www.homewoodsuiteschicago.com. $99–$249 for a 2-room suite. Kids under 18 stay free in parent's room. Rollaways and cribs free. AE, DC, DISC, MC, V. Valet parking $32 with in/out privileges. Subway/El: Red Line to Grand/State. **Amenities:** Fitness room w/small pool and nice views of the city; concierge; business services; babysitting; laundry machines on all floors; dry cleaning. *In room:* A/C, TV w/pay movies, fully equipped kitchen, coffeemaker, hair dryer, iron.

Westin Chicago Michigan Avenue ⭐⭐

Located across the street from the John Hancock Center, this hotel is right on the Magnificent Mile, steps from Bloomingdale's and Water Tower Place. In past years the Westin looked a bit shabby, but renovations have spruced up the lobby, fitness center, and guest rooms. Newly renovated rooms feature a marble foyer, expanded bathroom, and new furnishings and carpeting.

This hotel offers the Westin Kids Club for kids 12 and under. Other notable family amenities are the many baby and toddler accessories available to guests, from bottle warmers and cribs to night lights and electrical outlet covers. Kids are greeted with Westin Kids Club sports bottles or sippy cups, which are filled with complimentary beverages at meals. Also available are coloring books, bathtub toys, and a story line on the hotel phone that plays age-appropriate bedtime stories when you dial a four-digit number. The hotel restaurant will make sure kids' meals are ready when you arrive if you call in advance and special menus are available through room service, too. Older kids can while away the hours with in-room PlayStations.

The Grill on the Alley has been winning great reviews and offers American cuisine in a contemporary atmosphere. You'll be comfortable bringing the kids here, and the kids' menu features pastas and burgers. A lobby cafe is a good stop for breakfast. The small fitness center is open to kids and includes free weights, treadmills, lifecycles, and Stairmasters, and men's and women's locker rooms feature saunas.

909 N. Michigan Ave., Chicago, IL 60611. ② **800/228-3000** or 312/943-7200. Fax 312/397-5580. www.westinmichiganave.com. 751 units. $179–$250 double; $600–$800 suite. Kids 18 and under stay free in parent's room. Rollaways $25/night and cribs free. AE, DC, DISC, MC, V. Valet parking with in/out privileges $33. Bus: No. 151 to Delaware St. Pets accepted with $25 fee. **Amenities:** Restaurant (American); cafe; health club; sauna; children's programs; 24-hr. room service. *In room:* A/C, TV w/video games, minibar, coffeemaker, hair dryer, iron, high-speed Internet access.

INEXPENSIVE

Red Roof Inn Chicago Downtown ★ Value This hotel is your best bet for the lowest-priced lodgings in downtown Chicago. The location is its main selling point: right off the Magnificent Mile (and within blocks of the Ritz-Carlton and Peninsula, where rooms will cost you at least three times as much). The guest rooms are stark and small (much like the off-the-highway Red Roof Inns), but all have new linens and carpeting. Ask for a room facing Ontario Street, where you'll get western exposure and some natural light (rooms in other parts of the hotel look right into neighboring office buildings). For a family of three or four, go for the king suite, which has a sofa bed, microwave, and refrigerator. Room service is available through Coco Pazzo Café (p. 119), an excellent northern Italian restaurant around the corner from the hotel's front door.

162 E. Ontario St. (½ block east of Michigan Ave.), Chicago, IL 60611. © 800/733-7663 or 312/787-3580. Fax 312/787-1299. www.redroof.com. 195 units. $86–$102 double; $110–$159 king suite. Kids 17 and under stay free in parent's room. No rollaways; cribs free. AE, DC, DISC, MC, V. Valet parking $18 with no in/out privileges. Subway/El: Red Line to Grand/State. **Amenities:** Business services; free morning coffee in lobby. *In room:* A/C, TV w/pay movies, dataport, hair dryer, iron.

4 River North

The name "River North" designates a vast area parallel to the Magnificent Mile. The zone is bounded by the river to the west and south, and roughly by Clark Street to the east and by Chicago Avenue to the north. The earthy redbrick buildings that characterize the area were once warehouses of various kinds and today form the core of Chicago's art-gallery district. The neighborhood also has spawned many of the city's trendiest restaurants. You'll find many of the city's family-friendly hotels here. That, coupled with the proximity of tourist draws such as the Hard Rock Cafe, Rainforest Café, and ESPN Zone, means River North is an area families should consider when booking a hotel.

EXPENSIVE

Embassy Suites Hotel Chicago—Downtown ★★ You might fancy yourself in Florida when you first set foot in this hotel, where a gushing waterfall and palm- and fern-lined landscaped ponds lie at the bottom of the huge central atrium. But you're not in the tropics: You're in one of Chicago's most family-friendly hotels, even though it bills itself as a business hotel and does a healthy convention business. Accommodations are spacious enough for parents and kids: All suites have two rooms, consisting of a living room with a sleeper sofa, a round table, and four chairs; and a bedroom with either a king-size bed or two double beds. Guests staying on the VIP floor get nightly turndown service and in-room fax machines and robes. At one end of the atrium, the hotel serves a complimentary cooked-to-order breakfast and, at the other end, supplies complimentary cocktails and snacks in the evening. And yes, there's a pool. On the weekends, step into the elevator and you'll find plenty of Chicago-area families with kids wrapped in towels making good use of the hotel as a weekend getaway.

Off the lobby is an excellent restaurant, Papagus Greek Taverna, and next door is a Starbucks with outdoor seating.

Embassy Suites has opened another location at 511 N. Columbus Dr. (© 312/836-5900), just a few blocks from Navy Pier. Highly recommended!

600 N. State St. (at W. Ohio St.), Chicago, IL 60610. © 800/EMBASSY or 312/943-3800. Fax 312/943-7629. www.embassysuites.com. 358 units. $199–$259 king suite; $269–$299 double suite. Kids 17 and under stay free in parent's room. Few rollaways available, ask upon check-in (sofa beds in every suite); cribs free. AE, DC, DISC, MC, V. Valet parking $34 with in/out privileges. Subway/El: Red Line to Grand/State. **Amenities:** Restaurant; coffee bar; indoor pool; exercise room w/whirlpool and sauna; concierge; business center; limited room

service; babysitting; laundry machines; dry cleaning; VIP rooms. *In room:* A/C, TV w/pay movies and video games, dataport, kitchenette, coffeemaker, hair dryer, iron.

House of Blues Hotel ★★★   The funky vibe makes this a great hotel for teenagers and anyone who wants a hotel to be an experience—not just a place to sleep. Blending Gothic, Moroccan, East Indian, and New Orleans influences, the House of Blues lobby is a riot of crimsons and deep blues. In fact, if you're in the Marina Towers vicinity, stop by to check it out, even if you're not staying here.

You can catch your breath in the lighter, whimsical rooms, which feature some of the most exciting Southern folk art you'll ever come across. The casually dressed, friendly staff invents creative nightly turndowns for guests—such as fragrant mood crystals or a written thought for the day left on your pillow. One of the hotel's biggest selling points is its location in the entertainment-packed Marina Towers complex. Within steps of the hotel, you've got a bowling alley, a marina with boat rentals, the riverside Smith & Wollensky steakhouse (an outpost of the New York restaurant), the innovative Bin 36 wine bar and restaurant, and, of course, the House of Blues Music Hall and Restaurant. (Don't miss the Sun brunch at which gospel choirs perform—kids can order off the menu at a reduced rate.)

333 N. Dearborn St. (at the river), Chicago, IL 60610. © **800/235-6397** or 312/245-0333. Fax 312/923-2444. www.loewshotels.com. 365 units. $139–$349 double; $500–$1,250 suite. Weekend and promotional rates available. Kids 18 and under stay free in parent's room. Rollaways and cribs free. AE, DC, DISC, MC, V. Valet parking $28 with in/out privileges. Subway/El: Brown Line to Clark/Lake, or Red Line to Grand/State. Pets accepted. **Amenities:** Lounge; access to Crunch Health & Fitness Club; concierge; business center; 24-hr. room service; babysitting; laundry service; same-day dry cleaning. *In room:* A/C, TV/VCR w/pay movies and video games, fax, dataport, minibar, coffeemaker (upon request), hair dryer, iron, CD player.

Westin Chicago River North ★★★   Located on the northern bank of the Chicago River, the Westin River North has the personality of a business hotel but has made an effort to be family-friendly. Especially notable are the many baby and toddler accessories available to guests, from bottle warmers and cribs to night lights, jogging strollers, and electrical-outlet covers. Like the Westin Michigan Avenue (reviewed in the previous section), this hotel offers the Westin Kids Club for kids 12 and under. Kids are greeted with Westin Kids Club sports bottles or sippy cups, which are filled with complimentary beverages at meals. Other perks include coloring books, bathtub toys, and a story line on the hotel phone that plays age-appropriate bedtime stories when you dial a four-digit number. Kids' meals are available at the hotel restaurant with advance notice, and special menus are available through room service.

Rooms are handsome, with furniture and artwork that give them a residential feel. For the best view, request a room facing south, overlooking the Chicago River. For those who feel like splurging, a suite on the 19th floor more than satisfies, with three enormous rooms, including a huge bathroom and a large window offering a side view of the river.

320 N. Dearborn St. (on the river), Chicago, IL 60610. © **800/WESTIN1** or 312/744-1900. Fax 312/527-9650. www.westinchicago.com. 424 units. $199–$498 double; $419–$2,800 suite; weekend rates $199–$249. Kids 18 and under stay free in parent's room. Rollaways $25/night; cribs free. AE, DC, DISC, MC, V. Valet parking $34 with in/out privileges; self-parking $16. Subway/El: Brown, Orange, or Green Line to State/Lake. **Amenities:** Restaurant; lounge; fitness center; concierge; business center; 24-hr. room service; babysitting; laundry service, same-day dry cleaning. *In room:* A/C, TV w/pay movies and video games, fax, dataport, minibar, coffeemaker, hair dryer, iron.

MODERATE

Best Western River North Hotel *Value*   This former motor lodge and cold-storage structure conceals a very attractive, sharply designed interior that

scarcely resembles any Best Western in which you're likely to have spent the night. One of the few hotels located right in the midst of one of the busiest nightlife and restaurant zones in the city, it lies within easy walking distance of interesting boutiques and Chicago's art-gallery district. Rooms are spacious, and the bathrooms are spotless (though no-frills). One-room suites have a sitting area, while other suites have a separate bedroom; all suites come with a sleeper sofa. The Best Western's reasonable rates and rooftop pool (with sweeping views) will appeal to families on a budget—and the almost-unheard-of free parking can add up to significant savings for anyone planning to stay a week or more.

125 W. Ohio St. (at LaSalle St.), Chicago, IL 60610. (©) **800/528-1234** or 312/467-0800. Fax 312/467-1665. www.rivernorthhotel.com. 150 units. $105–$149 double; $250 suite. Kids under 18 stay free in parent's room. Rollaways $10/night; cribs free. AE, DC, DISC, MC, V. Free parking for guests (1 car per room). Subway/El: Red Line to Grand/State. **Amenities:** Restaurant (American); lounge; indoor pool with sun deck; exercise room; business services; limited room service; laundry service; VIP rooms. *In room:* A/C, TV w/pay movies and video games, dataport, minibar, coffeemaker, hair dryer, iron, safe.

Hampton Inn & Suites Chicago—Downtown ✦ *Value*   The Hampton, with its combination of rooms, two-room suites, and studios, is a smart choice for families. Kids will appreciate the indoor pool and in-room video games and VCRs after a busy day of sightseeing. You won't have far to go to find dinner: The Hard Rock Cafe and Rainforest Café are both a few blocks' walk away.

Rooms are residential and warm, with framed collages of vintage Chicago postcards on the walls. Request a room overlooking Illinois Street if you crave natural light; most rooms don't offer much of a view. The apartment-style suites feature galley kitchens with fridges, microwaves, dishwashers, and cooking utensils. You won't have to cook breakfast though, since the hotel offers a complimentary breakfast buffet. Off the lobby is an American diner, and a second-floor skywalk connects to Ruth's Chris Steakhouse next door.

33 W. Illinois St. (at Dearborn St.), Chicago, IL 60610. (©) **800/HAMPTON** or 312/832-0330. Fax 312/832-0333. www.hamptoninn.com. 230 units. $129–$179 double; $189–$229 suite. Kids under 18 stay free in parent's room. Rollaways $10/night and cribs free. AE, DC, DISC, MC, V. Valet parking $32 with in/out privileges; self-parking $14 with no in/out privileges. Subway/El: Red Line to Grand/State. **Amenities:** Restaurant (American diner); indoor pool with sun deck; exercise room w/sauna; business services; room service; laundry machines. *In room:* A/C, TV, coffeemaker, hair dryer, iron, safe, high-speed Internet access.

5 The Gold Coast

The Gold Coast begins approximately at Division Street and extends north to North Avenue, bounded on the west by Clark Street and on the east by the lake. The area encompasses a short strip of some of the city's priciest real estate along Lake Shore Drive. From the standpoint of social status, the streets clustered here are among the finest addresses in Chicago. It's a lovely neighborhood for a stroll among the graceful town houses and the several lavish mansions that remain, relics from a glitzier past. The hotels here tend to be upscale without hitting the peak that some of the nearby Michigan Avenue hotels reach.

To locate these hotels, see the "Central Chicago Accommodations" map on p. 74.

EXPENSIVE

Omni Ambassador East ✦   The ring-a-ding glory days of the Ambassador East, when stars including Frank Sinatra, Humphrey Bogart, and Liza Minnelli shacked up here during layovers or touring stops in Chicago, are ancient history. But even though big-name celebs tend to ensconce themselves at the Peninsula or Park Hyatt these days, the Ambassador name still evokes images of high glamour in these parts. For the past 50 years, celebrities who have come to town to mingle with Chicago's Gold Coast society have done so most publicly from the revered Booth One in the ritzy Pump Room restaurant. Less pricey than the Peninsula or Park Hyatt, and located on a beautiful tree-lined street in the Gold Coast, the Omni East is a good choice for families looking for accommodations near, but not on, the Magnificent Mile.

The Ambassador suffered a slow decline in the 1960s and 1970s, which didn't turn around until 1986, when Omni bought and renovated the property. Today, after a recent second face-lift, the Ambassador East has reclaimed its strut and splendor. Rooms have been spruced up; bathrooms feature the usual higher-end amenities. Executive suites have separate sitting areas, but most extravagant is the Presidential Suite, which boasts a canopied terrace and marble fireplace. If money's no object, families will want to go for celebrity suites (named for the stars who've crashed in them), each with a separate bedroom, two bathrooms, a small kitchen, and dining room. The Ambassador East offers a Kids' Program and makes an extra effort for guests with disabilities, offering equipment such as TDD telephones and strobe fire alarms for hearing-impaired guests.

1301 N. State Pkwy. (1 block north of Division St.), Chicago, IL 60610. (C) **800/843-6664** or 312/787-7200. Fax 312/787-4760. www.omnihotels.com. 285 units. $160–$200 double; $259–$799 suite. Kids 18 and under stay free in parent's room. Rollaways and cribs free. AE, DC, DISC, MC, V. Valet parking $34 with in/out privileges. Subway/El: Red Line to Clark/Division. **Amenities:** Restaurant; small fitness room (and access to nearby health club); concierge; business services; 24-hr. room service; babysitting; 24-hr. laundry service; dry cleaning. *In room:* A/C, TV w/pay movies, dataport, minibar, coffeemaker, hair dryer, iron.

MODERATE

The Claridge ⭐ *Finds*   If a modest, cost-effective option in a lovely setting within walking distance of both Michigan Avenue and Lincoln Park's many attractions sounds pretty good to you, look into the Claridge. Ask for a room above the eighth floor that overlooks the tree-lined street (kings and double-doubles are spacious and sunny); avoid at all cost the dark "king superior" rooms, which look onto the fire escape. Some deluxe accommodations have sitting areas, and three executive suites on the 14th floor have working fireplaces.

The Claridge won't overwhelm you with facilities; the hotel's restaurant and bar are both quite small. Where this small hotel really wins its Brownie points is for the very pleasant staff and nice touches. Kids will love the freshly baked cookies at turndown. In the lobby there's a small sitting area where your family can enjoy a complimentary hot breakfast buffet. The surrounding neighborhood of elegant town houses makes a great place for a stroll—without the traffic and noise of other downtown neighborhoods.

1244 N. Dearborn Pkwy. (1 block north of Division St.), Chicago, IL 60610. (C) **800/245-1258** or 312/787-4980. Fax 312/266-0978. www.claridgehotel.com. 163 units. $175–$250 double; $475–$750 suite. Kids under 18 stay free in parent's room. Rollaways and cribs free. AE, DC, DISC, MC, V. Valet parking $34 with in/out privileges. Subway/El: Red Line to Clark/Division. Pets accepted. **Amenities:** Restaurant; lounge; exercise room; concierge; business services; limited room service; laundry service; same-day dry cleaning. *In room:* A/C, TV w/pay movies, dataport, minibar, coffeemaker, hair dryer, iron.

6 Lincoln Park & the North Side

If you prefer the feel of living amid real Chicagoans in a residential neighborhood, several options await you in Lincoln Park and farther north. Not only do these hotels tend to be more affordable than those closer to downtown, but they also provide a different vantage point from which to view Chicago. If you stay at the Majestic Hotel or the City Suites Hotel, for example, you can join the

Lincoln Park & North Side Accommodations

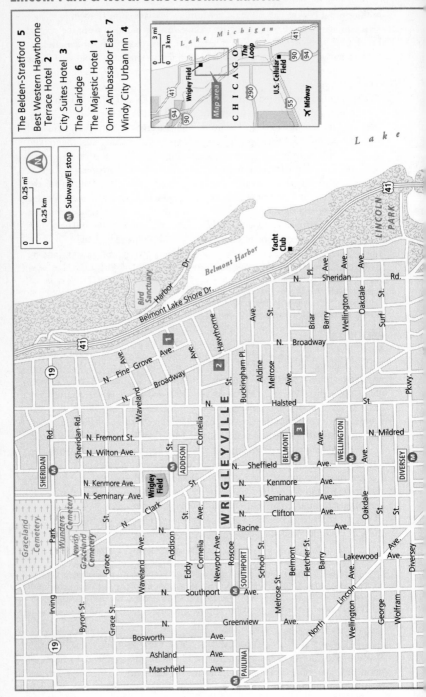

The Belden-Stratford **5**
Best Western Hawthorne Terrace Hotel **2**
City Suites Hotel **3**
The Claridge **6**
The Majestic Hotel **1**
Omni Ambassador East **7**
Windy City Urban Inn **4**

0.25 mi
0.25 km

Ⓜ Subway/El stop

3 mi
3 km
Lake Michigan
Wrigley Field
The Loop
U.S. Cellular Field
CHICAGO
Map area
✈ Midway

Lake   Shore   Dr.

Diversey Harbor

Michigan

North Pond

N. Lakeview Ave.

Wrightwood

Deming
Pl.
Arlington Pl.

N. Orchard   St.

N. Burling St.

N.   Halsted   St.

Ave.

LINCOLN
PARK

Wrightwood

Ave.

St.

Montana

N. Racine

Ave.

Schubert Ave.

Wayne

N.   Southport

N. Greenview

N.   Ashland

Ave.

John Cannon Dr.

Stockton
N. Lincoln Park West

Clark

N. Cleveland Ave.

Lincoln

Ave.

North

Ave.

OZ PARK

No. 276
Park

Ave.

FULLERTON Ⓜ

DePaul University

Belden

Webster

Montana

Ave.

Trebes
Park

Fullerton

Lakewood Ave.

Ave.

North

North

Ave.

LINCOLN
PARK
ZOO

Dr.

*South
Pond*

5

St.

Armitage

N.   Dayton   St.

N.   Fremont   St.

N.   Ave. Bissell   St.

N. Sheffield   Ave.

Dickens

Clifton   St.

ARMITAGE Ⓜ

Clybourn

North

Cortland

N.

North Branch

Chicago River

LINCOLN   PARK

*Chicago
Historical
Society*

N.   Wells   St.

N. Park

Eugenie   Ave.

N.   Sedgwick

Wisconsin St.

Menomonee

Armitage   Ave.

Lincoln

N.   Orchard   St.

N.   Burling   St.

N.   Halsted

Wisconsin St.

Willow

Ave.

64

Schiller

SEDGWICK Ⓜ

N.   Cleveland Ave.

N. Mohawk   St.

N. Larrabee   St.

OLD TOWN

Avenue

NORTH/CLYBOURN Ⓜ

Ave.

North

W.

Kingsbury

Chicago River

*Turning
Basin*

64

Elston

Kennedy

Expwy.

90 94

N.   Wood   St.

North Avenue
Beach

41

Burton Pl.

N. Burton Pl.   St.

N. State St.   7 →

N. Dearborn St.

N. Clark St.   6 →

N. La Salle St.

Weed St.

Ave.

Noble

N. Greenview

N. Bosworth

N.   Ashland

Altgeld

99

locals on a pedestrian pilgrimage to Wrigley Field for a Cubs game. The area is flush with restaurants, and public transportation via the El or buses is a snap.

EXPENSIVE

The Belden-Stratford ⭐ *Finds*   This north-side hotel is a great option for families who want to do as the natives do in a neighborhood atmosphere. Actually a condominium building that offers 25 hotel rooms, the two-story lobby feels grandly European, and paneled entry doors lead the way to airy rooms with 9-foot-high ceilings, crown molding, and plush carpeting. Rooms are large, the doorman greets you as if you were a resident, and Lincoln Park, where kids can run free, is across the street. You are right across from the Lincoln Park Zoo and the Conservatory, and steps from the lake and buses that will take you downtown in a matter of minutes.

Be sure to ask for a room with a park view, so you can watch runners pass and couples stroll. (Some rooms feature wraparound views with south, west, and east exposures.) Even though it's a condominium building, there's maid and valet service and a rooftop sun deck. One downside: Because the Belden-Stratford is not a full-service hotel, there's no room service or concierge.

2300 N. Lincoln Park W., Chicago, IL 60614. (🎧 **800/800-6261** or 773/281-2900. Fax 773/880-2039. www. beldenstratford.com. 25 units. $209–$299 double. Kids under 18 stay free in parent's room. Rollaways $20/night; cribs free. AE, DC, DISC, MC, V. Valet parking $25 with in/out privileges. Subway/El: Red Line to Fullerton. **Amenities:** Fitness center; spa; salon; coin-op laundry. *In room:* A/C, TV; hair dryer and iron upon request.

MODERATE

Best Western Hawthorne Terrace Hotel ⭐ *Value*   A fantastic bargain for families who don't mind staying a bit north of the beaten track, this hotel offers plenty of space for a great price. The Hawthorne Terrace, located near Wrigley Field on the Near North side, was remodeled 5 years ago. The junior suites provide a room with two double beds, and an adjoining living room with a pullout couch; families of four will fit comfortably in one of these suites, which can also accommodate a crib. Amazingly, for the price, you also have access to a fitness center with a sauna and Jacuzzi. (Young children should be supervised by an adult.) A continental breakfast is offered in the lobby every morning. Best of all? Parking is a bargain at $16 a day—about half the going rate of most downtown hotels.

3434 N. Broadway, Chicago, IL 60657. (🎧 **888/675-2378** or 773/244-3434. Fax 773/244-3435. www.best western.com. 59 units. $175 double; $185 suite. Kids 12 and under stay free in parent's room. Rollaways free (sofa beds provided in junior suites); cribs free. AE, DC, DISC, MC, V. Parking $16 in nearby lot with in/out privileges. Subway/El: Red Line to Belmont. **Amenities:** Exercise room; laundry service and laundry room. *In room:* A/C, TV, fridge, coffeemaker, hair dryer, iron.

Windy City Urban Inn ⭐⭐ *Finds*   Children over the age of 10 are welcome at this grand 1886 home, located on a tranquil side street just blocks away from busy Clark Street and Lincoln Avenue—both chock-full of shops, restaurants, and bars. The inn is charming enough, but the true selling point of the Windy City Inn is hosts Andy and Mary Shaw. He's a well-known political reporter, and she has 20 years of experience in the Chicago bed-and-breakfast business. Together, they are excellent resources for anyone who wants to get beyond the usual tourist sites. Subtle Chicago touches give guests a distinctive experience: Blues and jazz play during the buffet breakfast, and local food favorites offered to guests include the famous cinnamon buns from Ann Sather's restaurant and beer from Goose Island Brewery.

The remodeled building has a more open feel than the typical Victorian home. The five rooms in the main house and three apartments in a coach house are each named after Chicago writers. Families should choose one of the two coach-house apartments that can sleep four: two in an upstairs bedroom and two on a bed that folds up against the wall. (Custom-made for the Shaws, these feature top-quality mattresses, making them much more comfortable than the Murphy beds of old.) These apartments have kitchens and are wonderfully cozy with their fireplaces and Jacuzzi tubs.

In good weather, guests are invited to eat breakfast on the back porch or in the garden between the main house and the coach house. There, you can sit back and imagine that you're living in your very own Chicago mansion—the type of home that many Chicagoans wish they could live in themselves.

607 W. Deming Place, Chicago, IL 60614. ℂ 877/897-7091 or 773/248-7091. Fax 773/248-7090. www. chicago-inn.com. 8 units. $115–$185 double. Kids age 10 to 18 stay free in parent's room (coach-house apts only). No rollaways or cribs. Rates include buffet breakfast. AE, DC, DISC, MC, V. Parking $6 in nearby lot with in/out privileges. Subway/El: Red Line to Fullerton. **Amenities:** Laundry machines. In room: A/C, TV, kitchenette; coffeemaker, hair dryer, and iron available upon request.

INEXPENSIVE

City Suites Hotel (Value   A few doors down from the elevated train stop on Belmont Avenue, this charming small hotel has a 1930s Art Deco aesthetic, and feels more along the lines of an urban bed-and-breakfast than a big hotel. Most rooms are suites, with separate sitting rooms and bedrooms, all furnished with first-rate pieces and decorated in a homey and comfortable style. Families should ask about the king suite, with a king bed and sitting area with sofa bed; they can also accommodate a crib. The amenities are excellent for a hotel in this price range, including local limousine service, plush robes, and complimentary continental breakfast. Families will be happy to know that fridges and microwaves are available upon request in suites.

A bonus—or drawback, depending on your point of view—is the hotel's neighborhood setting. Most rooms can be fairly noisy; those facing north overlook Belmont Avenue, where nightlife continues into the early-morning hours, and those facing west look right out over rumbling El tracks. On your way in and out of the hotel, you'll mingle with plenty of locals, from young professional families to gay couples to punks in full regalia. Blues bars, nightclubs, and restaurants abound hereabouts, making the City Suites a find for the bargain-minded and adventuresome. Room service is available from **Ann Sather,** a Swedish diner and neighborhood institution (p. 138).

933 W. Belmont Ave. (at Sheffield Ave.), Chicago, IL 60657. ℂ 800/248-9108 or 773/404-3400. Fax 773/ 404-3405. www.cityinns.com. 45 units. $99–$169 double. Rates include continental breakfast. Kids 12 and under stay free in parent's room. No rollaways (sofa beds in suites); cribs free. AE, DC, DISC, MC, V. Parking $18 in nearby lot with in/out privileges. Subway/El: Red Line to Belmont. **Amenities:** Exercise room; business services; concierge; limited room service; laundry service; same-day dry cleaning. In room: A/C, TV w/pay movies, dataport, minibar, coffeemaker, hair dryer, iron.

The Majestic Hotel (★★ (Finds   Owned by the same group as the City Suites Hotel, the Majestic blends seamlessly into its residential neighborhood. Located on a charming tree-lined street (but convenient to the many restaurants and shops of Lincoln Park), the hotel welcomes kids with open arms. Guests receive a complimentary continental breakfast and afternoon tea in the lobby. Some of the larger suites—the most appealing are those with sun porches—offer butler's pantries with a fridge, microwave, and wet bar. Families should ask about the two-room king suite, which features a bedroom with king bed, a living room with a sofa bed, and a kitchenette with refrigerator and microwave. Other than the larger suites, many of the rooms are fairly dark because you're surrounded by apartment buildings on almost all sides. Avoid the claustrophobic single rooms with alley views. The hotel is ideally suited for enjoying the North Side and is only a short walk from both Wrigley Field and the lake.

528 W. Brompton St. (at Lake Shore Dr.), Chicago, IL 60657. © 800/727-5108 or 773/404-3499. Fax 773/404-3495. www.cityinns.com. 52 units. $99–$179 double. Rates include continental breakfast. Kids under 12 stay free in parent's room; age 12 and over, $10 per person. No rollaways (sofa beds in suites); cribs free. AE, DC, DISC, MC, V. Self-parking $19 in nearby garage with no in/out privileges. Subway/El: Red Line to Addison; walk several blocks east to Lake Shore Dr. and then 1 block south. **Amenities:** Exercise room; business services; limited room service; laundry service; same-day dry cleaning. *In room:* A/C, TV w/pay movies, dataport, minibar, coffeemaker, hair dryer, iron.

Family-Friendly Dining

Chicago has come into its own as a major dining destination, and that's not limited to the chic, see-and-be-seen spots. Plenty of options await families, too. In addition to those stylish restaurants, you'll find an amazing array of steakhouses, family-style Italian restaurants, and just about every kind of ethnic cuisine you could possibly crave. You'll be surprised at the number and range of restaurants that welcome kids in Chicago. Even restaurants that don't offer a specialized kids' menu often will provide half-size portions for children. Whether you're looking for a restaurant for your family's big night out or simply a no-frills spot to dig in, in this chapter you'll find places the locals go to when they want to eat well.

Chicagoans have a passion for two foods your kids are probably passionate about, too: hot dogs and pizza. Don't run out to buy a case of antacids just yet—options for adult stomachs also exist. And although I've covered the obvious family-friendly choices

like Rainforest Cafe and Ed Debevic's, in this chapter I've tried to focus more on unique dining ideas that are Chicago's own.

A NOTE ON PRICES Unfortunately, Chicago is no longer the budget-dining destination it once was. (Hipness doesn't come cheap.) I've divided restaurants into three price categories: "Expensive" means that dinner for a family of four will cost $75 and up; "Moderate," $40 to $75; and, at an "Inexpensive" place, you'll pay about $40 or less. But just because the prices have risen doesn't mean that the attitude has. Restaurants in Chicago might have gotten trendy, but we're still friendly.

To find out more about restaurants that opened since this book went to press, check out the *Chicago Tribune*'s entertainment website (**www.metromix.com**), the website for *Chicago* magazine (**www.chicagomag.com**), and the entertainment/nightlife website **www.chicago.citysearch.com**.

1 Restaurants by Cuisine

ALSATIAN
Brasserie Jo ✦ (River North, $$$, p. 124)

AMERICAN
American Girl Place Cafe ✦✦✦ (Magnificent Mile & the Gold Coast, $$$, p. 116)
Ann Sather ✦✦ (Wrigleyville & the North Side, $, p. 138)
Café Brauer ✦ (Lincoln Park, $, p. 135)

Carson's ✦ (River North, $$, p. 125)
Charlie's Ale House on Navy Pier ✦ (Magnificent Mile & the Gold Coast, Lincoln Park, $, p. 121)
Cheesecake Factory (Magnificent Mile & the Gold Coast, $$, p. 119)
Dave & Buster's (River North, $, p. 127)

Key to Abbreviations: $$$ = Expensive $$ = Moderate $ = Inexpensive

ESPN Zone (Magnificent Mile & the Gold Coast, $$, p. 120)

Goose Island Brewing Company (Lincoln Park, $$, p. 131)

Hard Rock Cafe (River North, $, p. 128)

Harry Caray's ★★ (River North, $$$, p. 124)

Houston's (River North, $$, p. 125)

Jack Melnick's Corner Tap (Magnificent Mile & the Gold Coast, $$, p. 120)

John Barleycorn (Lincoln Park, $, p. 136)

John's Place ★★★ (Lincoln Park, $, p. 136)

Mr. Beef ★ (River North, $, p. 129)

Northside Café ★ (Wicker Park/Bucktown, $, p. 140)

Oak Street Beachstro ★ (Magnificent Mile & the Gold Coast, $$$, p. 117)

Oak Tree ★ (Magnificent Mile & the Gold Coast, $, p. 123)

O'Brien's Restaurant (Lincoln Park, $$$, p. 131)

O'Donovan's (Wrigleyville & the North Side, $, p. 139)

Rainforest Cafe (River North, $, p. 130)

South Water Kitchen ★ (the Loop, $$, p. 111)

Stanley's ★★ (Lincoln Park, $, p. 137)

Toast ★ (Lincoln Park, $, p. 137)

ASIAN

Big Bowl ★ (Magnificent Mile & the Gold Coast, $, p. 120)

Flat Top Grill (Lincoln Park, Wrigleyville & the North Side, Randolph Street Market District, $, p. 135)

Penny's Noodle Shop ★ (Wrigleyville & the North Side, $, p. 139)

BARBECUE

Carson's ★ (River North, $$, p. 125)

Twin Anchors ★ (Lincoln Park, $, p. 137)

BISTRO

Bistro 110 ★★ (Magnificent Mile & the Gold Coast, $$, p. 119)

BREAKFAST

Ann Sather ★★ (Wrigleyville & the North Side, $, p. 138)

Billy Goat Tavern ★ (Magnificent Mile & the Gold Coast, $, p. 121)

Bourgeois Pig ★ (Lincoln Park, $, p. 134)

Corner Bakery (Magnificent Mile & the Gold Coast and citywide, $, p. 122)

House of Blues (River North, $$, p. 129)

Lou Mitchell's ★★ (the Loop, $, p. 112)

Oak Tree ★ (Magnificent Mile & the Gold Coast, $, p. 123)

Toast ★ (Lincoln Park, $, p. 137)

Uncommon Ground ★ (Wrigleyville & the North Side, $, p. 139)

Wishbone ★★★ (Randolph Street Market District, $, p. 115)

BURGERS

Billy Goat Tavern ★ (Magnificent Mile & the Gold Coast, $, p. 121)

Ed Debevic's ★ (River North, $, p. 127)

Flapjaw Café (Magnificent Mile & the Gold Coast, $, p. 122)

Green Door Tavern (River North, $, p. 128)

John Barleycorn (Lincoln Park, $, p. 136)

Northside Café ★ (Wicker Park/Bucktown, $, p. 140)

CAJUN/CREOLE

Heaven on Seven ★★ (the Loop, $, p. 112)

House of Blues (River North, $$, p. 129)

Wishbone ★★★ (Randolph Street Market District, $, p. 115)

CONTINENTAL

Bistro 110 ✯✯ (Magnificent Mile & the Gold Coast, $$, p. 119)

DINER

Ed Debevic's ✯ (River North, $, p. 127)

Heaven on Seven ✯✯ (the Loop, $, p. 112)

Lou Mitchell's ✯✯ (the Loop, $, p. 112)

Manny's Coffee Shop & Deli ✯ (near the Loop, $, p. 112)

Nookies (Lincoln Park, $, p. 137)

Silver Cloud Bar & Grill ✯ (Wicker Park/ Bucktown, $, p. 140)

Twisted Spoke ✯ (River North, $, p. 130)

ECLECTIC

Atwood Cafe (The Loop, $$$, p. 106)

foodlife ✯✯ (Magnificent Mile & the Gold Coast, $, p. 122)

Oak Street Beachstro ✯ (Magnificent Mile & the Gold Coast, $$$, p. 117)

FONDUE

Geja's Café ✯ (Lincoln Park, $$$, p. 131)

FRENCH

Brasserie Jo ✯ (River North, $$$, p. 124)

La Creperie ✯✯ (Lincoln Park, $, p. 136)

GERMAN

The Berghoff ✯ (the Loop, $$, p. 107)

GREEK

Artopolis (Greektown, $, p. 116)

Athena (Greektown, $$, p. 116)

Costas (Greektown, $$, p. 116)

Greek Islands (Greektown, $$, p. 116)

Parthenon (Greektown, $$, p. 116)

Pegasus (Greektown, $$, p. 116)

Santorini (Greektown, $$, p. 116)

HOT DOGS

Fluky's (Magnificent Mile & the Gold Coast, $, p. 142)

Gold Coast Dogs (Magnificent Mile & the Gold Coast, $, p. 142)

Murphy's Red Hots (Wrigleyville, $, p. 142)

Portillo's (River North, $, p. 142)

Superdawg Drive-In (Far North Side, $, p. 142)

The Wieners Circle (Lincoln Park, $, p. 142)

ITALIAN

Buca di Beppo (Wrigleyville & the North Side, $$, p. 138)

Coco Pazzo Café ✯ (Magnificent Mile & the Gold Coast, $$, p. 119)

Harry Caray's ✯✯ (River North, $$$, p. 124)

La Cantina Enoteca (the Loop, $$, p. 110)

Leona's (River North, $$, p. 125)

Maggiano's ✯ (River North, $$, p. 126)

Ranalli's Pizzeria, Libations & Collectibles (Lincoln Park, $, p. 142)

Rosebud on Taylor ✯✯ (near the Loop, $$, p. 110)

Scoozi ✯ (River North, $$, p. 126)

Tufano's Vernon Park Tap (near the Loop, $, p. 113)

Tuscany ✯ (near the Loop, $$$, p. 107)

The Village ✯ (the Loop, $$, p. 111)

Vivere ✯ (the Loop, $$, p. 111)

JAPANESE

Kabuki (Lincoln Park, $$, p. 134)

Ron of Japan (Magnificent Mile & the Gold Coast, $$$, p. 117)

Sai Café ✯ (Lincoln Park, $$, p. 134)

MEXICAN

El Jardin (Lincoln Park, $, p. 135)

MIDDLE EASTERN

Reza's ✿✿ (River North, $$,
p. 126)

NOODLES

Penny's Noodle Shop ✿
(Wrigleyville & the North Side,
$, p. 139)

PIZZA

California Pizza Kitchen (Magnifi-
cent Mile & the Gold Coast,
$, p. 121)

Chicago Pizza & Oven Grinder
(Lincoln Park, $, p. 142)

Edwardo's (Magnificent Mile &
the Gold Coast, South Loop,
and Lincoln Park; $; p. 141)

Gino's East ✿✿ (River North,
$, p. 128)

Leona's (River North, $$, p. 125)

Leona's Pizzeria (Wrigleyville,
$, p. 142)

Lou Malnati's Pizzeria ✿ (River
North, $, p. 141)

Pat's Pizzeria (Wrigleyville,
$, p. 142)

Pizzeria Due (River North,
$, p. 129)

Pizzeria Uno ✿ (River North,
$, p. 129)

Ranalli's Pizzeria, Libations &
Collectibles (Lincoln Park,
$, p. 142)

SANDWICHES

Bourgeois Pig ✿ (Lincoln Park,
$, p. 134)

Corner Bakery (Magnificent Mile
& the Gold Coast and citywide;
$, p. 122)

Mrs. Levy's Delicatessen (Loop,
$, p. 113)

Potbelly Sandwich Works (the
Loop, $, p. 113)

Uncommon Ground ✿
(Wrigleyville & the North Side,
$, p. 139)

SEAFOOD

La Cantina Enoteca (the Loop, $$,
p. 110)

SOUTHERN

House of Blues (River North, $$,
p. 129)

Wishbone ✿✿✿ (Randolph Street
Market District, $, p. 115)

SOUTHWESTERN

Bandera (Magnificent Mile & the
Gold Coast, $$$, p. 116)

SPANISH/TAPAS

Cafe Iberico ✿✿ (River North, $,
p. 127)

STEAKHOUSE

Houston's (River North, $$,
p. 125)

Mike Ditka's Restaurant ✿✿
(Magnificent Mile & the Gold
Coast, $$$, p. 117)

SWEDISH

Ann Sather ✿✿ (Wrigleyville &
the North Side, $, p. 138)

2 The Loop

Chicago's business power center isn't exactly attuned to family dining—what
you'll find here are corporate types on expense accounts. (Because of the area's
business orientation, keep in mind that some of the downtown eateries are
closed on Sun.) But in case you're spending the day touring the Loop's many
attractions, we've pegged some great sandwich stops and reasonable dining
options. The good news: Just west of the Loop, Little Italy offers inexpensive
ethnic dining.

EXPENSIVE

Atwood Cafe ECLECTIC   Colorful and offbeat, this stylish eatery in the
Hotel Burnham provides enough fun for kids, and enough sophistication for
adults, all while serving up a fresh take on American comfort food. Tuck your

---

Tips **Chilling Out with an Italian Ice**

When in Little Italy, do as the Italians do: Cool off with an Italian ice. In a heat wave, **Mario's Italian Lemonade,** at 1068 W. Taylor St., has been the place to chill for 35 years. They're open from 11am to midnight from May to mid-September. Lemon is the most popular flavor, but piña colada, fruit cocktail, or chocolate might appeal to more adventurous kids.

---

family into a cozy banquette in one of the room's nooks and crannies, and take in the bustle of State Street from the comfort of your own table. Adults won't want to miss the mussels in a garlicky tomato sauce with crusty, grilled home-made bread. Kids will love the banana and white chocolate bread pudding—if they manage to save room for dessert.

1 W. Washington St. (at State St.). © 312/368-1900. High chairs, boosters. Reservations recommended. Kids' menu available, $10. Main courses $18–$26. AE, DC, DISC, MC, V. Mon–Fri 7am–10am, 11:30am–3:45pm, and 5–10pm; Sat 8–10am, 11:30am–3:45pm, and 5–10pm; Sun 8am–3pm and 5–10pm. Subway/El: Red Line to Washington/State.

Tuscany ✦ NORTHERN ITALIAN Tuscany is one of the most reliable restaurants on Taylor Street, which is Chicago's version of Little Italy, home to a host of time-honored, traditional, hearty Italian restaurants. In contrast to the city's more fashionable Italian spots, family-owned Tuscany has the comfortable feel of a neighborhood gathering place. Although the food is of high enough quality to draw a fine-dining crowd, the unpretentious atmosphere means you'll find big tables of families, so don't worry about disturbing the peace. As you might expect, the extensive menu features the culinary fare of the Tuscany region, including pastas, pizzas, veal, chicken, and a risotto of the day, and the portions are large. Specials include anything cooked on the wood-burning grill and Tuscan sausage dishes. There's no kids' menu, but half-orders are available. You'll find a second location in Wrigleyville, across from Wrigley Field at 3700 N. Clark St. (© 773/404-7700).

1014 W. Taylor St. (between Racine Ave. and Halsted St.). © 312/829-1990. www.stefanirestaurants.com. High chairs, boosters. Reservations recommended. Main courses $9.25–$27. AE, DC, DISC, MC, V. Mon–Fri 11am–3:30pm; Mon–Thurs 5–11pm; Fri–Sat 5pm–midnight; Sun 2–9:30pm. Subway/El: Blue Line to Polk.

MODERATE

The Berghoff ✦ GERMAN Spaetzle and sauerbraten are hot sellers at this longtime German landmark in Chicago's Loop. Having celebrated its centennial in 1998, the immense, 700-seat restaurant is housed in one of the first buildings constructed in the Loop after the Chicago Fire, and one of only two remaining buildings in the city with a cast-iron facade. The Berghoff holds Chicago liquor license no. 1, issued at the close of Prohibition, and it still serves its own brand of beer. (*Good news for kids:* The Berghoff also serves its own root beer.) If you decide to belly up at the stand-up bar, you might notice that the bar clientele is still overwhelmingly male; the stand-up bar at The Berghoff didn't admit women until 1969.

The menu rotates seasonally, but the German standard-bearers are always available. The Berghoff serves hundreds of orders of Wiener schnitzel every day, plus bratwurst, sauerbraten, corned beef, and the like. Sides of choice include spaetzle, creamed spinach, and red cabbage. Because some of us have arteries to worry about, the third and fourth generations of family management have

Central Chicago Dining

American Girl Place
Cafe **14**
Artopolis **50**
Athena **49**
Bandera **36**
The Berghoff **57**
Big Bowl **4**
Billy Goat Tavern **39**
Bistro 110 **9**
Brasserie Jo **41**
Cafe Iberico **26**
California Pizza
Kitchen **13**
Carson's **18**
Charlie's Ale House
on Navy Pier **30**
Cheesecake Factory **11**
Coco Pazzo Café **32**
Corner Bakery **3**
Costas **51**
Dave & Buster's **2**
Ed Debevic's **23**
Edwardo's **1**
ESPN Zone **35**
Flapjaw Café **8**
Fluky's **38**
foodlife **12**
Gino's East **22**
Gold Coast Dogs **40**
Greek Islands **48**
Green Door Tavern **21**
Hard Rock Cafe **27**
Harry Caray's **43**
Heaven on Seven **45**
House of Blues **42**
Houston's **37**
Jack Melnick's
Corner Tap **29**
Johnny Rocket's **6**

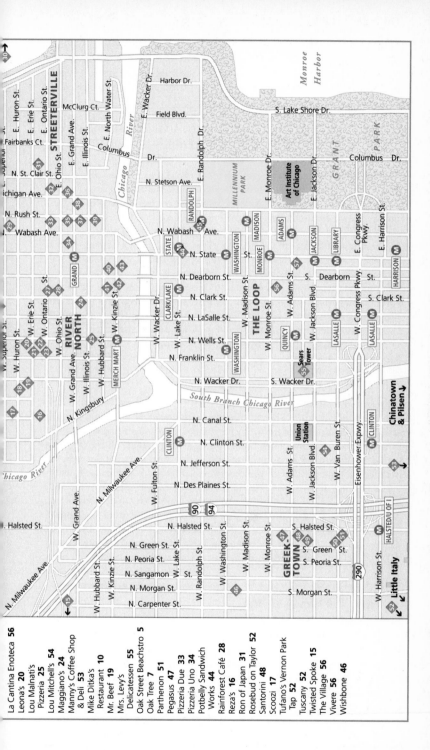

La Cantina Enoteca **56**
Leona's **20**
Lou Malnati's
Pizzeria **25**
Lou Mitchell's **54**
Maggiano's **24**
Manny's Coffee Shop
& Deli **53**
Mike Ditka's
Restaurant **10**
Mr. Beef **19**
Mrs. Levy's
Delicatessen **55**
Oak Street Beachstro **5**
Oak Tree **7**
Parthenon **51**
Pegasus **47**
Pizzeria Due **33**
Pizzeria Uno **34**
Potbelly Sandwich
Works **44**
Rainforest Café **28**
Reza's **16**
Ron of Japan **31**
Rosebud on Taylor **52**
Santorini **48**
Scoozi **17**
Tufano's Vernon Park
Tap **52**
Tuscany **52**
Twisted Spoke **15**
The Village **56**
Vivere **56**
Wishbone **46**

added some lighter fare in the form of salads, broiled fish, and vegetarian dishes. There's a children's menu with smaller portions of the dishes on the regular menu. The Berghoff also holds a popular Oktoberfest celebration each year in mid-September, serving brats, chicken, and pretzels, and hosting live music in the street.

17 W. Adams St. (between State and Dearborn sts.). © 312/427-3170. www.berghoff.com. Kids' menu, high chairs, boosters. Reservations recommended. Main courses $7.95–$12 lunch, $11–$17 dinner; kids' menu items around $5. AE, MC, V. Mon–Thurs 11am–9pm; Fri 11am–9:30pm; Sat 11am–10pm. Subway/El: Red or Blue Line to Jackson or Monroe.

La Cantina Enoteca *Value* ITALIAN/SEAFOOD   La Cantina is the most casual and moderately priced of the three restaurants in the Italian Village. It makes the most of its basement location by creating the feel of a wine cellar. During the day the restaurant attracts a daily regular clientele of lawyers, judges, and the like, many of whom eat at the bar. During pretheater dining hours, you'll find plenty of other families eating here. Specializing in seafood, La Cantina offers at least five fresh varieties every day, plus a fish soup appetizer, macaroni with scallops and shrimp in a garlic pesto sauce, and seafood-filled ravioli. Nonseafood items include your basic pasta favorites (there are no surprises where the pasta is concerned—all the reliable standards are here) and some beef and veal dishes. The dinner menu offers a big-time bargain: A la carte dishes (most under $20) include a salad, and for $2 more you also get soup, dessert, and coffee.

71 W. Monroe St. (between Clark and Dearborn sts.). © 312/332-7005. www.italianvillage-chicago.com. Sassy seats. Reservations recommended. Main courses $11–$23 lunch, $12–$27 dinner. AE, DC, DISC, MC, V. Mon–Fri 11:30am–2:30pm; Mon–Thurs 5–11pm; Fri–Sat 5pm–midnight; Sun 4:30–8pm (seasonally). Subway/El: Red or Blue Line to Monroe.

Rosebud on Taylor ★★ *Value* ITALIAN   If you want a real Chicago dining experience, this is it: At Rosebud you'll be surrounded by locals, not tourists. The old-style, dark rooms are filled with families celebrating birthdays and older couples who have been coming here for years. If your kids are on the verge of a hunger meltdown, ask for some breadsticks to tide them over: You can expect to wait well beyond the time of your reservation. Rosebud is known for its enormous helpings of pasta, served up in massive white bowls. Expect to walk out with a doggy bag, or—even better—have your whole table share a few dishes. But the portions aren't just large, they're delicious. Most pastas lean toward heavy Italian-American favorites: deep-dish lasagna and fettuccine Alfredo that defines the word rich. But the menu has been hipped up with more modern takes on Italian cooking. Any of the pastas with vodka sauce are out of this

---

Finds **The Italian Village**

The building at 71 W. Monroe St. houses three separate Italian restaurants, collectively known as the Italian Village, a downtown dining landmark. Each restaurant has a unique take on Italian ambience and cooking; they also share an exemplary wine cellar and fresh produce grown in a family garden. Each of the three restaurants in the Italian Village is detailed in this section. Families with young children will be most comfortable at moderately priced La Cantina Enoteca; if you have older kids, they might enjoy the atmospheric Village, designed to re-create a dining experience in the Italian countryside. Vivere is the most upscale of the three restaurants.

---

world. Rosebud also offers pasta lovers five different *cavatelli* dishes, a house specialty, and a tempting selection of *secondi*—meat, fish, and poultry dishes.

If you don't feel like trekking to the original, Rosebud offers another, trendier version just off the Mag Mile at 720 N. Rush St., at Superior Street (© **312/ 266-6444**).

1500 W. Taylor St. (1 block east of Ashland Ave.). © **312/942-1117.** High chairs, boosters. Reservations recommended, especially on weekends. Main courses $5.95–$13 lunch, $11–$30 dinner. AE, DC, DISC, MC, V. Mon–Thurs 11am–10pm; Fri 11am–11pm; Sat 5–11pm; Sun 4–10pm. Subway/El: Blue Line to Polk.

South Water Kitchen ⭐ AMERICAN   Although South Water Kitchen isn't breaking any new culinary ground, it deserves a mention as one of the few places in the Loop that welcomes kids while featuring food sophisticated enough for discerning moms and dads. The dining room evokes the spirit of an old-fashioned city saloon, and the menu goes the retro route as well. Entrees include modern twists on familiar favorites, including a pork chop with sage bread pudding; free-range chicken fricassee with herb dumplings; and a different "blueplate special" every night (at $14, it's an excellent deal for the neighborhood). The restaurant provides not only kids' menus but also games to keep the little ones occupied. Best of all, half the proceeds of all children's meals go to the Chicago Coalition for the Homeless.

In the Hotel Monaco, 225. N. Wabash Ave. (at Wacker Dr.). © **888/306-3507.** www.swk.citysearch.com. Kids' menu, high chairs, boosters. Reservations accepted. Main courses $8–$17 lunch, $14–$22 dinner; kids' menu items around $5. AE, DC, MC, V. Mon–Fri 11:30am–2:30pm; daily 5–9pm. Subway/El: Red Line to State/Lake.

The Village ⭐ SOUTHERN ITALIAN   Upstairs in the Italian Village is The Village, with its charming interpretation of alfresco dining in a small Italian town, complete with a midnight-blue ceiling, twinkling "stars," and banquettes tucked into private, cavelike little rooms. It's the kind of Pan-Chicago place where you might see one man in a tux and another in shorts. The massive 200-item menu includes some time-warp appetizers (oysters Rockefeller, shrimp *de jonghe*) and the old-time, hearty southern Italian standards. This is old-school Italian: eggplant *parmigiana*, a heavy spaghetti *alla carbonara*, veal scaloppini, calves' liver, and yes, even pizza. The food is good rather than great, but what sets The Village apart as a place for families is the bordering-on-corny faux-Italian atmosphere that will delight your kids, and an old-time waitstaff that somehow keeps up with the nonstop flow of patrons.

71 W. Monroe St. (between Clark and Dearborn sts.). © **312/332-7005.** www.italianvillage-chicago.com. Sassy seats. Reservations recommended (accepted for parties of 3 or more). Main courses (including salad) $8–$20 lunch, $10–$30 dinner. AE, DISC, MC, V. Mon–Thurs 11am–midnight; Fri–Sat 11am–1am; Sun noon–midnight. Subway/El: Red or Blue Line to Monroe.

Vivere ⭐ REGIONAL ITALIAN   On the main floor of the Italian Village is Vivere, the Italian Village's take on gourmet cooking. Teenagers might enjoy this upscale—but not snobbish—take on Italian fare. The bold interior, with rich burgundies, textured walls, spiraling bronze sculptures, and fragmented mosaic floors, makes dining a theatrical experience. No spaghetti and meatballs here: The pasta dishes feature upscale ingredients, from the *pappardelle* with braised duck to the *agnolottini* filled with pheasant. Fresh fish is always on the menu (a recent entree selection was salmon with spiced carrot broth), along with a good selection of meats and game. Grilled venison medallions are served with foie gras ravioli, while roasted duck is accompanied by a potato terrine and sautéed spinach.

71 W. Monroe St. (between Clark and Dearborn sts.). ✆ **312/332-4040.** www.italianvillage-chicago.com. Sassy seats. Reservations recommended. Main courses $11–$22 lunch, $12–$33 dinner. AE, DC, DISC, MC, V. Mon–Fri 11:30am–2:30pm; Mon–Thurs 5–10pm; Fri–Sat 5–11pm. Subway/El: Red or Blue Line to Monroe.

INEXPENSIVE

Heaven on Seven ★★ *Finds* CAJUN/DINER   Kids will love the "every day is Mardi Gras" feel of this highly popular spot, a favorite of local office workers. Just check out the lunchtime crowd that packs the restaurant, located on the seventh floor of the Garland Building, across from Marshall Field's. Chef/owner Jimmy Bannos's Cajun and Creole specialties come with a cup of soup, and include such Louisiana staples as red beans and rice, a catfish po' boy sandwich, and jambalaya. If your kids don't have a taste for Tabasco, the enormous coffee-shop-style menu covers all the traditional essentials: grilled-cheese sandwiches, omelets, tuna, the works. Indulge in chocolate pecan pie or chicory coffee crème brûlée for dessert. Usually open only for breakfast and lunch, on the third Friday of the month, Heaven on Seven serves dinner from 5:30 to 9pm. Although the Loop original has the most character, in the past couple of years, more Mardi Gras–infused locations have opened along the Mag Mile at 600 N. Michigan Ave. (✆ **312/280-7774**), adjacent to a cineplex, and in Wrigleyville at 3478 N. Clark St. (✆ **773/477-7818**); unlike the original location, both accept reservations and credit cards. Of the newer locations, I'd recommend the Mag Mile restaurant for kids, where you'll be in the company of many families; the Wrigleyville location attracts big groups and singles.

111 N. Wabash Ave. (at Washington St.), 7th floor. ✆ **312/263-6443.** Kids' menu, high chairs, boosters. Reservations not accepted. Menu items $3.95–$13; kids' menu around $5 (includes soda and an ice cream sandwich). No credit cards. Mon–Fri 8:30am–5pm; Sat 10am–3pm; 3rd Fri of each month 5:30–9pm. Subway/El: Red Line to Washington/State.

Lou Mitchell's ★★ *Finds* BREAKFAST/DINER   Lou Mitchell's is the genuine article and a Loop dining institution, located across the south branch of the Chicago River from the Loop, a block farther west than Union Station. A French food critic passing through Chicago rated Lou Mitchell's the number-one breakfast spot in America, home of the "five-star breakfast." Quirky touches bound to amuse kids are everywhere: If the waiter discovers you're from out of town, don't be surprised if a table flag of your home state or country is plopped down on your table.

Don't worry about the line to get in; female patrons get boxes of Milk Duds, and everyone gets free donut holes while they wait. Turnover is continuous and service efficiently attentive. If your kids are old enough, you might shorten the wait for a table by grabbing a counter seat. One specialty here is the airy omelets served in sizzling skillets; you'll double your pleasure (and cholesterol) with Mitchell's use of double-yolk eggs. Orders arrive with thick slabs of toasted Greek bread and homemade marmalade. You might also have the best bowl of oatmeal you've ever eaten—deliciously creamy. Orange juice and grapefruit juice are freshly squeezed. At the end of your meal, a small paper cup of vanilla soft-serve ice cream will be offered up, gratis. If you eat breakfast here, you'll likely be full enough to make it practically to dinner without even noticing that you missed a meal.

565 W. Jackson Blvd. (at Jefferson St.). ✆ **312/939-3111.** High chairs, boosters. Reservations accepted for groups of 8 or more. Breakfast items $1.95–$6.95. No credit cards. Mon–Sat 5:30am–3pm; Sun 7am–3pm. Subway/El: Blue Line to Clinton.

Manny's Coffee Shop & Deli ★ *Value* DINER   If your itinerary includes a trip back in time, make sure you visit Manny's, a South Side institution since

---

Moments **Watching the World Float by from Chicago's Riverwalk**

The outdoor cafes along the banks of the Chicago River's main branch, between Wabash Avenue and Wells Street, are run by restaurants that change from year to year, so we can't recommend specific restaurants or dishes. But food is almost an afterthought: Kids will thrill to the parade of schooners and speedboats cruising along the Chicago River on their way to Lake Michigan. Open seasonally.

1942. Kid highlights include spaghetti, beef stew, rice pudding, German chocolate cake, and the occasional special, from franks and beans to chop suey. Adults can grab a tray and navigate the fast-moving line. Even if they go for more standard fare, kids will be awed by the carving station known for its enormous corned-beef sandwiches (about half a lb.), Reubens, world-class hot pastrami, and steamship rounds the size of VW Beetles. Gruff yet friendly staff in paper hats take their métier seriously, and the effect—and the food—is absolutely reassuring. Seat yourself and snarf down knishes, borscht, liver and onions, meatloaf, tongue, and stewed prunes. Introduce your kids to the old-fashioned joys of cream soda and Green River.

1141 S. Jefferson St. (☎) **312/939-2855.** www.mannysdeli.com. High chairs, boosters. Reservations not accepted. Main courses $4.95–$8.95. No credit cards. Mon–Sat 5am–4pm. Subway/El: Red Line to Roosevelt.

Mrs. Levy's Delicatessen SANDWICHES   Should you be planning a trip up the Sears Tower, here's the perfect place to stop and fortify your family first. This retro deli displays signed photos of famous patrons and offers up deli staples such as knishes, blintzes, and homemade soups. Sandwiches are piled high and include corned beef, beef brisket, and pastrami; soup of the day might include sweet-and-sour cabbage, chicken matzo ball, or mushroom barley.

233 S. Wacker Dr. (Sears Tower), 2nd floor. (☎) **312/993-0530.** High chairs. Reservations not accepted. All main courses under $8. AE, DC, DISC, MC, V. Mon–Sat 11am–5pm. Subway/El: Brown Line to Wells/Franklin.

Potbelly Sandwich Works *Value* SANDWICHES   Ask a Chicagoan where to go for a great sandwich, and he'll invariably point the way to Potbelly. Yes, there's a potbelly stove inside, as well as a player piano and other Old West saloon-type memorabilia, but go here for the mouthwatering made-to-order sandwiches. (That's all they serve.) Prepared on homemade sub rolls stuffed with turkey, Italian meats, veggies, pizza ingredients, and more, and layered with lettuce, tomato, onion, pickles, and Italian seasonings, they're warmed in a countertop toaster oven. Even with all the fixin's, each is around $5. Tempting milkshakes keep the blender mighty busy. Potbelly has nearly 20 other locations throughout the city, including one in The Shops at North Bridge, 520 N. Michigan Ave. ((☎) **312/527-5550**), that is convenient for Loop and Magnificent Mile sightseers and shoppers.

190 N. State St. (at Lake St.). (☎) **312/683-1234.** High chairs, boosters. Reservations not accepted. Main courses $3.50–$5.50. No credit cards. Mon–Fri 10am–9pm; Sat 10am–7pm; Sun 11am–6pm. Subway/El: Red Line to State.

Tufano's Vernon Park Tap ITALIAN   Taking the family to the United Center to suffer along with the Chicago Bulls? Here's a great spot to fortify your family for the long evening ahead. Located on the eastern edge of Little Italy,

Tufano's is a popular place that's been family-owned for 60 years—and it's attracted neighborhood regulars as well as celebrities and politicians. (Check out the wall of photos that includes everyone from Tommy LaSorda to Dolly Parton.)

Tips   **Suburban Safaris**

If you have access to a car, you'll want to explore suburban Chicago's highways and byways. These restaurants alone are worth a special trip:

- **Phil Smidt's,** 1205 N. Calumet Ave., Hammond, Indiana (© 800/376-4534; www.froglegs.com). Northwest Indiana is just a hop, skip and jump across the Chicago Skyway (and close to the Indiana gambling boats). The fried perch dinners (all-you-can-eat, a boon for families with growing kids) will make your kids reconsider their preference for frozen fish sticks. For dessert, try the tart gooseberry pie. Closed on Monday.

- **White Fence Farm,** 11700 Joliet Rd., Lemont, Illinois (© 630/739-1720; www.whitefencefarm.com). For the best fried chicken north of the Mason-Dixon line, Chicagoans in the know head to White Fence Farm. And what better kid-pleaser than a fried chicken dinner with all the fixings?

- **Robinson's No. 1 Ribs,** 940 Madison St., Oak Park, Illinois (© 708/383-8452; http://rib1.com). Backyard Chef Charlie Robinson parlayed a win in the late Chicago journalist Mike Royko's first annual rib cook-off into this large and extremely popular venue. After a day touring the Oak Park's architectural gems, go low-brow and dive right in to a plate of smoky ribs slathered in a secret sauce made with 17 herbs and spices.

- **Hecky's Barbecue,** 1902 Green Bay Rd., Evanston, Illinois. (© 847/492-1182; www.heckys.com). When in Evanston, do as the locals do and indulge at this rib joint. Since the place isn't big on atmosphere (there is a dining room, two doors down the street, so you must pick up your food and go), the best plan is to get dinner to go, head back to your hotel and dive in (don't skimp on the napkins). Other specialties include hot pork links, chicken and turkey drumsticks. If your travel plans don't include a visit to Evanston, head to Hecky's new Chicago branch, at 1234 N. Halsted St. (© 312/377-7427).

- **Homer's Ice Cream,** 1237 Green Bay Rd., Wilmette, Illinois. (© 847/251-0477; www.homersicecream.com). Homer's is the kind of place where you feel good about feeding your kids burgers and ice cream. And in fact, Homer's is all about the ice cream, which is the best I've had. (Adults should try the cappuccino chip; kids go for peppermint stick.) Seasonal flavors might include pumpkin in the fall, and prairie berry and peach in the summer. The burgers, hot dogs and chicken sandwiches are fresh and grilled to order. The red-and-white signage outside and matching decor inside evokes good old ice cream parlor fun. Homer's is a convenient stop after a tour of the North Shore and a welcome relief from the usual fast food.

The bar is a Chicago classic, and the cuisine is Italian. The traditional pasta dishes and Tufano's lemon chicken with potatoes are always good bets. On the weekends, go for the homemade ravioli and cavatelli. On Friday, regulars choose the seafood salad.

1073 W. Vernon Park Place. © 312/733-3393. High chairs, boosters. Reservations not accepted. Menu items $7–$13. Cash only. Tues–Thurs 11am–10pm; Fri 11am–11pm; Sat 4–11pm; Sun 3–9pm. Subway/El: Blue Line to UIC/Halsted.

3 The Randolph Street Market District & Greektown

Much of the Market District is about the "scene"—and when traveling with kids, making the scene ranks pretty low. But you might want to make a trip to the district just to dine at **Wishbone**, or to experience adjacent **Greektown**, filled with cheap eats and noisy, boisterous restaurants where kids blend right in. Greektown sits on the district's eastern border. There's nothing much to do here besides eat—but if you have a few days in Chicago, try to make it here for at least one meal.

Transportation to Greektown and the Market District is easy, by the way—it's about a $7 cab ride from Michigan Avenue or a slightly longer trek by bus (no. 8 or 9) or El, with stops at Halsted and Lake, a block from the restaurants. The walk from the Loop is very pleasant and totally secure in the daytime, but at night, save your stroll for Michigan Avenue.

MARKET DISTRICT

Wishbone ★★★ SOUTHERN/CAJUN/BREAKFAST This Southern-style restaurant has much to recommend it for families. First, it's a homegrown restaurant, not a chain, with a casual ambience. Second, children can be kept busy looking at the large and surrealistic farm-life paintings on the walls or reading a picture book, *Floop the Fly*, loaned to diners (written and illustrated by the parents of the owners). The food is diverse enough that both adults and kids can find something to their liking, but there's also a menu geared just to children. The sprawling, loft-style space is quirky enough to be fun (plenty of folk art), but still relaxed and attitude-free.

Known for Southern food and big-appetite breakfasts, Wishbone's extensive, reasonably priced menu blends hearty, home-style choices with healthful and vegetarian items. Brunch is the 'Bone's claim to fame, when an eclectic crowd of bedheads packs in for the plump and tasty salmon cakes, omelets, and red eggs (a lovely mess of tortillas, black beans, cheese, scallions, ancho chile sauce, salsa, and sour cream). Brunch can be a mob scene, though, so to avoid a long wait, try lunch or dinner; offerings run from "yardbird" (charbroiled chicken with sweet red-pepper sauce) and blackened catfish to hoppin' John or Jack (vegetarian variations on the black-eyed-pea classic). Variety is Wishbone's strong point: Every entree comes with a choice of sides, so diners can mix and match to their hearts' content. The restaurant provides outdoor seating in nice weather.

There's a newer location at 3300 N. Lincoln Ave. (© 773/549-2663), but the original location has more character.

1001 Washington St. (at Morgan St.). © 312/850-2663. www.wishbone.epagecity.com. Kids' menu, high chairs, boosters. Reservations accepted, except for weekend brunch. Main courses $5.25–$9.50 breakfast and lunch, $6.95–$14 dinner; kids' menu around $6. AE, DC, DISC, MC, V. Mon–Fri 7am–3pm; Sat–Sun 8am–3pm; Tues–Fri 5–9pm; Sat 5–10pm.

GREEKTOWN

A short cab ride from the Loop across the south branch of the Chicago River will take you to the city's Greektown, a row of moderately priced and inexpensive

Greek restaurants clustered on Halsted Street between Van Buren and Washington streets. Many restaurants have wonderful outdoor seating and spectacular views of the city—plus, long tables of families and shouts of "Opa!" make quite a ruckus that will keep your kids entertained. **Greek Islands,** 200 S. Halsted St. (© **312/782-9855**); **Santorini,** 800 W. Adams St., at Halsted Street (© **312/829-8820**); **Parthenon,** 314 S. Halsted St. (© **312/726-2407**); and **Costas,** 340 S. Halsted St. (© **312/263-0767**), are all good bets for gyros, Greek salads, shish kabobs, and the classic moussaka. My top pick for families is **Athena,** 212 S. Halsted St. (© **312/655-0000**), which has a stunning three-level outdoor seating area, a fantastic choice for a warm summer evening. It's paved with brick and landscaped with 30-foot trees, flower gardens, and even a waterfall. Best of all: an incredible view of the downtown skyline with the Sears Tower right in the middle. **Pegasus,** 130 S. Halsted St. (© **312/226-3377**), has a rooftop patio serving drinks, appetizers, and desserts. **Artopolis,** 306 S. Halsted St. (© **312/559-9000**), is another casual option offering up tasty Greek and Mediterranean specialties, wood-oven pizzas, and wonderful breads and French pastries.

4 The Magnificent Mile & the Gold Coast

Yes, the Mag Mile is all about designer shopping—and designer eating—and you'll be pleasantly surprised to discover that plenty of those eateries welcome kids. In fact, a great many families who visit Chicago never stray far from the Magnificent Mile and the adjoining Gold Coast area. From the array of restaurants, shops, and pretty streets in the area, it's not hard to see why.

EXPENSIVE

American Girl Place Cafe 😸😸😸 AMERICAN   Dining with dolly has never been done in a more appealing manner than at the cafe located inside the American Girl Place store. Not to be sexist, but most boys will be less than thrilled about spending time here surrounded by girls, dolls, and dresses: It's really best for a girls' day out. With an eye-popping black, white, and red polka-dot-and-stripe decor, the cafe has loads of kid appeal. The view of the water tower and surrounding street life from the third-floor cafe is wonderful. Parents and daughters can bond over lunch, dinner, or tea, and dolly (only of the American Girl species, of course) can join in, settled on a special booster seat. Treats on the menu include fresh cinnamon buns, frittata quiche, chicken fingers, macaroni and cheese, and tic-tac-toe pizza. Top your meal off with a sugar cookie, carrot cake, or chocolate pudding flowerpot, and wash everything down with a pink lemonade or hot chocolate. American Girl Place is a destination for many families visiting Chicago, so plan well in advance to avoid disappointing the American girl in your life. The cafe recommends booking 8 to 12 weeks in advance.

111 E. Chicago Ave. © **877/247-5223.** High chairs, boosters. Reservations required. Prix-fixe menu (includes gratuity) lunch $17, tea $16, dinner $18. AE, DC, DISC, MC, V. Lunch seatings 11am and 12:30pm daily; tea seatings 2:30 and 4pm daily; dinner 5:30 Mon–Thurs, 7:30 Fri–Sat. Subway/El: Red Line to Chicago/State.

Bandera SOUTHWESTERN   The open-range ambience here is created by the chicken roasting over a hickory-burning fire. Some complain that the room even gets a bit too smoky from that open fire, but in the wintertime it gives Bandera a cozy rustic Western feel. If your kids will eat cornbread and roasted chicken with mashed potatoes, they'll do fine here. Menu offerings include roasted prime rib, pork tenderloin with barbecue sauce, Western beef back ribs, and wood-roasted salmon. This is a national chain, so the restaurant might look awfully familiar, but a location on Michigan Avenue that affords views of the street life below makes this branch particularly well situated.

535 N. Michigan Ave. ⓒ 312/644-3524. Kids' menu, high chairs, boosters. Main courses $15–$25; kids' menu $5–$10. AE, DC, MC, V. Mon–Thurs 11:30am–10pm; Fri–Sat 11:30am–11pm, Sun noon–10pm. Subway/El: Red Line to Grand. Bus: 151 and 157.

Mike Ditka's Restaurant ⭐⭐ STEAKHOUSE   For many Chicago football diehards, the glory days of former coach "Iron" Mike Ditka, who led the Bears to victory in Super Bowl XX in 1985, are still alive and well. Football memorabilia lines the walls of this restaurant, filled with amber light and dark wood. Kids who are at all into the game might inadvertently get a little history lesson— even the Bears' 1985 victory, seemingly still fresh in the minds of Bears' fans who love to relive the glory days, probably qualifies as ancient history to your kids. Televisions in the posh bar allow patrons to simultaneously sip Scotch and pray for "da Coach" to return. Upstairs, there's a cigar lounge that gets pretty pungent: Families would be best off in the downstairs dining room. The hamburger here (really, a chopped steak burger) is one of the best in the city and easily feeds two. Appetizers here are called "Kickoffs" and include a "Duck Cigar," a hand-rolled pastry with a hearty duck-and-mushroom filling, and a "Souper Bowl" of corn chowder. There are lots of salads, pastas, and seafood dishes to choose from, but why be a wimp? Go for the "Fullback Size" filet mignon, with spinach and homemade onion rings, or "Da Pork Chop," surrounded by warm cinnamon apples and a green peppercorn sauce.

100 E. Chestnut St. (in the Tremont Hotel, between Michigan Ave. and Rush St.). ⓒ 312/587-8989. www.mikeditkaschicago.com. Kids' menu, high chairs, boosters. Main courses $9–$13 lunch; $15–$30 dinner.; kids' menu around $8. AE, DC, DISC, MC, V. Mon–Thurs 11am–10pm; Fri 11am–11pm; Sat 10am–11pm; Sun 10am–10pm. Subway/El: Red Line to Chicago Ave.

Oak Street Beachstro ⭐ AMERICAN/ECLECTIC   Could a location be more prime? Settled on the curve of Oak Street Beach, this bistro offers tables on the sand. (The cafe is open in warm weather only and opens in early May.) Take a dip in the lake with your family, then head up the beach for specialties such as the grilled salmon sandwich, Cobb salad, and salmon filet. Less exotic offerings such as salads, sandwiches, and pasta should please kids. For the grown-ups, beer and wine is available, and frozen drinks can be made sans alcohol for the kids. Outdoor seating provides some of the best people-watching around. Saturday and Sunday you'll find a breakfast buffet from 8 to 11:30am. Come at twilight and you'll be treated to a beautiful violet sky.

1001 N. Lake Shore Dr. (at Oak Street Beach). ⓒ 312/915-4100. High chairs, boosters. Reservations accepted for parties of 6 or more only. Main courses $15–$25. AE, DC, DISC, MC, V. May–Oct (weather permitting) Mon–Fri 11am–9:30pm; Sat–Sun 8am–9:30pm. Subway/El: Red Line to Chicago. Bus: 145, 146, 147, or 151.

Ron of Japan JAPANESE   The heyday of teppanyaki dining (you know, Japanese chefs chopping and grilling at your table, with the accompanying flashing knives and flying shrimp tails) passed decades ago, but the show is still a kid-pleaser. Specialties include shrimp with egg yolk sauce, filet mignon, prime rib served on a samurai sword, and Shogun dinner (lobster and steak). Grilled on an iron plate set into each table, the food is cut, seasoned, and served by chefs who dish up amazing flair as well as flavor. The restaurant has 14 such tables— larger ones accommodate up to 10 diners, the smaller ones, six or so. As knives and pepper shakers fly through the air, meats sizzle on the hot iron plate. Above each grill/table is a retractable hood that keeps smoke out of everyone's eyes.

Tips Dining Out in Peace

- **Set the ground rules.** Before entering a restaurant, remind kids that you are going to a special place and that a few key rules apply, such as inside voices and good manners.

- **Bring entertainment.** Crayons, markers, paper, stickers, etc. will give your children something to do while awaiting their food. If the kids are old enough, bring postcards for them to write.

- **Try word games.** "I Spy" is a good one. Another word game involves one person naming something in a category, such as food. The next person names a word in the same category that starts with the last letter of the previous word. (For example: orange, eggplant, tomato, onion...)

- **Remember the value of conversation.** Talk with your kids about what you did during the day or what you have planned for the next one. That will help pass the time and encourage restaurant-appropriate behavior.

- **Decide who's "on duty."** Decide ahead of time which adult will have to interrupt his or her meal, should a child act up. Take turns at each meal.

- **Use time-outs.** If your normally polite child acts up, immediately and quietly take him or her outside. This will avoid embarrassment, and will be a lesson to the child. You shouldn't have to do this more than a few times before your child gets the message.

- **Make exceptions.** Your child may normally drink milk with dinner. Permit him or her to have a Shirley Temple (7Up and grenadine with a cherry). This will make dinner out seem special.

- **Use rewards and bribery.** Tell kids that if they behave well and eat their dinner, they'll get a bowl of vanilla ice cream for dessert.

- **Be flexible.** If the kids are tired, skip the appetizers or order food that is quick to prepare. If they've reached their limit, have one parent take them outside to stretch their legs or hunt down a dessert spot while the other parent pays the bill.

- **Slow down.** Before dinner, take them back to the hotel for a nap to rest up or to a playground to let loose some pent-up energy.

- **Eat early.** If you plan to eat at a more elegant restaurant or if it's the weekend, arrive early, before the restaurant gets full. (Plan a post-dinner walk or activity, such as strolling Navy Pier in summer or the John Hancock Center's Christmas tree in winter.)

- **Do lunch.** Some of the city's finer restaurants are open for lunch. Why not make lunch your special meal of the day? The ambience may be more kid friendly, the prices lower, and your children better behaved. Then you can all have pizza for dinner, and you won't feel you've missed out.

- **Relax.** Chicagoans are very friendly, and most restaurants are delighted to have children dining with them.

230 E. Ontario St. ℂ 312/644-6500. Kids' menu, high chairs, boosters. Reservations accepted for parties of 8 or more only. Main courses $15–$25; kids' menu $13–$15. AE, DC, DISC, MC, V. Mon–Thurs 5–9:30pm; Fri 5–10:30pm; Sat 5–10pm; Sun 4:30–9pm. Subway/El: Red Line to Chicago/State. Bus: 151 or 157.

MODERATE

Bistro 110 ★★ BISTRO/CONTINENTAL   Bistro 110 enjoys a prime location just half a block west of North Michigan Avenue. A neighborhood crowd gathers here for the bistro's changing weekly specials, posted on a chalkboard, where you can also check out the weather forecast and other local news. This popular spot opened in 1987, putting it on the cutting edge of the bistro-style dining trend. The restaurant is much larger than an authentic bistro would be, with plenty of hustle and bustle that helps families fit right in.

The menu covers a broad price range and several bistro classics, such as escargots in puff pastry, mussels in white-wine sauce, French onion soup, cassoulet, and steak au poivre. More ambitious items include a spice-rubbed lamb (roasted and braised for 18 hr.), and wood-roasted Maine sea scallops over spinach and basmati rice. Chicago holds Bistro 110 dear for the roasted heads of garlic served with crusty bread and its wood-roasted meats and vegetables. (The wood-roasted items, including a delicious, savory half chicken and a bountiful roast vegetable plate, are among your best bets here—some of the other items can be inconsistent.) The kids' menu ranges from beef tenderloin to grilled cheese. Sunday brunch, complete with a jazz trio from New Orleans, is a good time to bring your kids. (Yes, the trio will visit your table and "serenade" you—rather loudly.) Brunch is extremely popular, so get there early to avoid a long wait.

110 E. Pearson St. (just west of Michigan Ave.). ℂ 312/266-3110. www.levyrestaurants.com. Kids' menu, high chairs, boosters. Main courses $13–$28; kids' menu $6–$14. AE, DC, DISC, MC, V. Mon–Wed 11:30am–10pm; Thurs–Sat 11:30am–11pm; Sun 10am–10pm. Subway/El: Red Line to Chicago/State.

Cheesecake Factory AMERICAN   It really must take a factory to produce the 34 flavors of cheesecake offered here. While this restaurant is one of the usual "kid-friendly" suspects, a handy location on Michigan Avenue and the prospect of outdoor dining on the John Hancock Center Plaza makes this better than your average chain dining experience. The restaurant is big and noisy, and be prepared for your name to be added to a long list when you arrive. (You'll be given a pager for the wait.) The odd decor, with copper-colored metal sculpted into aerodynamic shapes that overhang the entryways, gives kids plenty to gawk at while you wait.

Even picky eaters will find something to order on the enormous menu. There's no kids' menu, but the regular menu features chicken strips and minicheeseburgers, among other tot treats. Baja chicken tacos, barbecued ranch chicken salad, and avocado egg rolls are a few of the items on the wide-ranging menu. And the cheesecake! Save room for white chocolate raspberry truffle, chocolate peanut butter cookie dough, or seasonally, pumpkin cheesecake. Why they also serve fudge cake, carrot cake, and ice cream sundaes, I'll never know—apparently some misguided diners don't opt for cheesecake!

875 N. Michigan Ave. (in the plaza of the John Hancock Center). ℂ 312/337-1101. High chairs, boosters. Main courses $8.95–$16. AE, DC, DISC, MC, V. Mon–Thurs 11:30am–11pm; Fri–Sat 11:30am–12:30am; Sun 10am–11:30pm. Subway/El: Red Line to Chicago/State.

Coco Pazzo Café ★ NORTHERN ITALIAN   Here's the perfect combination for families: food sophisticated enough for grown-ups, simple enough for kids. An added plus is a scenic sidewalk cafe for that rare perfect-weather day in

Chicago. The cafe is the more casual version of Coco Pazzo restaurant. The decor is colorful, with ceramic tile, wall murals, and a copper-topped bar. Cuisine is rustic Tuscan and northern Italian. The menu includes focaccia, thin-crust pizza, seafood, veal, chicken dishes, and pasta. For adults, specialties include fish *cartoccio* (fresh fish in parchment paper), gnocchi with tomato and basil, and tagliolini with wild mushrooms. Sunday brunch features a fixed-price menu that varies every week.

636 N. St. Clair St. (C) 312/664-2777. High chairs, boosters. Reservations recommended. Main courses $8–$15. AE, DISC, V. Mon–Thurs 11:30am–10:30pm; Fri–Sat 11:30am–11pm; Sun 11:30am–10pm. Subway/El: Red Line to Chicago. Bus: 3, 157, 151, 145, 146 or 147.

ESPN Zone AMERICAN   Kids will love it, but grown-ups prone to indigestion might want to tread carefully. (Maybe you'll want to skip dining here and just hit the arcade?) The frenetic activity inside this temple of televised athletics will likely please your kids (and please you, too, if you have trouble keeping them entertained) but can be a bit overwhelming. Every wall is covered with television screens or sports art, with a full-on visual and audio assault on your senses. This massive 35,000-square-foot sports-themed dining-and-entertainment complex features three components: the Studio Grill, designed with replicas of studio sets from the cable networks' shows (including *SportsCenter*); the Screening Room, a sports pub featuring a 16-foot screen and an armada of TV monitors and radio sets carrying live broadcasts of games; and the Sports Arena, a gaming area with interactive and competitive attractions. Good news for adults: The food here is better-than-average tavern fare, including quite a few salads and upscale items such as a salmon filet baked on cedar and served with steamed rice and grilled vegetables.

43 E. Ohio St. (at Wabash Ave.). (C) 312/644-3776. Kids' menu, high chairs, boosters. Main courses $7.25–$20; kids' menu $5–$8. AE, DISC, MC, V. Sun–Thurs 11am–midnight; Fri–Sat 11am–1am. Subway/El: Red Line to Grand.

Jack Melnick's Corner Tap AMERICAN   This casual neighborhood pub provides a comfortable, welcoming, and fun environment—a local hangout where folks can "come as they are." Specialties include burgers done seven ways, chopped salads, and home-style specials such as barbecued ribs and chicken. A 50-foot old-fashioned bar is the epicenter of Jack's, featuring an extensive bottle and tap beer selection from around the world "from Old Style to Newcastle." Patrons can catch just about any sporting event from baseball to hockey on the 16 screens featuring DirecTV, or play a game of darts. The dining room has always been one of my favorite spots on the Magnificent Mile, with a screened-in porch area that lets in the lake breeze in the summer, and a stone fireplace and deep booths that make for cozy dining in the wintertime. Desserts include apple pie, banana cream pie, and a chocolate-chip-cookie skillet sundae. On Sunday catch brunch from 11am to 3pm.

41 E. Superior St. (at Wabash Ave.). (C) 312/266-0400. Kids' menu, high chairs, boosters. Reservations only accepted for parties of 10 or more. Main courses $8–$15; kids' menu $4. AE, DC, DISC, MC, V. Mon–Wed 11:30am–midnight; Thurs–Sat 11:30am–2pm; Sun 11am–11pm. Subway/El: Red Line to Chicago/State.

INEXPENSIVE

Big Bowl ★ *(Value* ASIAN   You know you're in a kid-friendly Asian restaurant when you sit down and crayons and a bowl of white rice are brought to the table. Big Bowl also has a great kids' menu—no cheeseburgers, just smaller portions of the same Asian food the adults eat. Okay, so the restaurant is yet another creation of Rich Melman's Lettuce Entertain You empire. But it's friendly, affordable, and the kind of place that's got dishes so addictive, I dare you to only go once during your visit. Start with a glass of the signature fresh ginger ale or a fresh-brewed fruit-flavored iced tea; either will wake up your taste buds. The menu covers a range of Asian specialties, including Chinese pot stickers, Thai curries, and Vietnamese spring rolls. The indecisive can go with one of several combinations, each offering a mix of soup, salad, appetizers, or noodles. The straightforward crunchy sesame chicken is a reliable standby, mixing crispy chicken pieces with fresh Asian vegetables in a light soy sauce. Other good bets are the teriyaki beef and spicy flat noodles with tofu and veggies. You can also put together your own mix of flavors at the large stir-fry bar. If you're looking for delivery, Big Bowl will rush pot stickers to your hotel, no problem. Big Bowl has another Chicago location, which re-creates the same upscale diner decor, at 60 E. Ohio St., just off the Magnificent Mile and near kid-frequented spots such as ESPN Zone (© 312/951-1888).

6 E. Cedar St. (at Rush St.). © 312/640-8888. www.bigbowl.com. Kids' menu, high chairs, boosters. Reservations not accepted. Main courses $8–$15; kids' menu $5–$8. AE, DC, DISC, MC, V. Sun–Thurs 11:30am–10pm; Fri–Sat 11:30am–11pm. Subway/El: Red Line to Clark/Division.

Billy Goat Tavern ★ *Value* BURGERS/BREAKFAST   "Cheezeborger, Cheeze-borger—No Coke . . . Pepsi." Viewers of the original *Saturday Night Live* will certainly remember the classic John Belushi routine, a moment in the life of a crabby Greek short-order cook. The comic got his material from the Billy Goat Tavern, located under North Michigan Avenue near the bridge that crosses to the Loop (you'll find it by walking down the steps across the street from the Chicago Tribune building). Just BUTT IN ANYTIME says the sign on the red door with the picture of the billy goat on it. The tavern has traditionally been a hangout for the newspaper workers and writers who occupy the nearby Tribune Tower and Sun-Times Building, but its *Saturday Night Live* fame attracts droves of tourists, a la the *Cheers* bar in Boston. The tavern offers beer and greasy food (including, of course, "cheezeborgers"). Families will feel most at home during lunchtime, when tourists and office workers pop in for a quick burger.

430 N. Michigan Ave. © 312/222-1525. Kids' menu. Reservations not accepted. Menu items $4–$8; kids' menu $2–$4. No credit cards. Mon–Fri 7am–2am; Sat 10am–2am; Sun 11am–2am. Subway/El: Red Line to Chicago/State.

California Pizza Kitchen PIZZA   Way, way back in the early 1990s, "CPK" was plying its new concept of exotic toppings made on individual-size pies. The concept is a bit stale, but kids still get a kick out of creating and swapping pieces of their individual pizzas. Names like tandoori chicken, Hawaiian, BLT, Peking duck, and grilled burrito might cause an "Ewwwww!" reaction from your kids, but you'll likely be safe with tamer options such as barbecued chicken. Traditional meat-and-cheese pizzas are also available, as are soups, salads, pasta dishes, and desserts. If all else fails, there's a children's menu with pepperoni pizza; Caesar salad topped with cheddar goldfish crackers; buttered noodles; and brownies. There are three additional Chicago locations, at 52 E. Ohio St. (© 312/787-6075), in the Shops at North Bridge, 520 N. Michigan Ave. (© 312/327-2300), and 939 W. North Ave. (© 312/337-1281).

835 N. Michigan Ave. (Water Tower Place, 7th floor). © 312/787-7300. Kids' menu, high chairs, boosters. Reservations not accepted. Menu items $7–$10; kids' menu items $5. AE, DC, DISC, MC, V. Mon–Sat 11am–10pm; Sun noon–9pm. Subway/El: Red Line to Chicago/State.

Charlie's Ale House on Navy Pier ★ AMERICAN   One of several outdoor dining options along Navy Pier, this outpost of the Lincoln Park restaurant wins for lip-smacking pub fare and a great location on the southern promenade overlooking the lakefront and Loop skyline. It's a great vantage point for Wednesday- and Friday-night fireworks, too. The Navy Pier location is handy for sightseers; kids will like the burgers, meatloaf, and, maybe, the chicken potpie. The original location in Lincoln Park triumphs with a wonderful beer garden, which is welcoming to families. (The restaurant says everyone is welcome—except dogs!) It's spacious, surrounded by tall ivy-covered brick walls, and buzzing with activity and good vibes. The Lincoln Park restaurant is at 1224 W. Webster Ave. (© **773/871-1440**); take the Red Line to Sheffield.

700 E. Grand Ave. © **312/595-1440**. Kids' menu, high chairs, boosters. Reservations accepted only for parties of 15 or more. Main courses $11–$17; kids' menu $5. AE, DC, DISC, MC, V. Mon–Fri 11am–midnight; Sat–Sun 11am–1am. Subway/El: Red Line to Grand/State; transfer to Navy Pier's free trolley.

Corner Bakery BREAKFAST/SANDWICHES   In case of emergency hunger meltdown, it's a good idea to locate the nearest Corner Bakery ahead of time. A very popular destination (and justifiably so), there are about 40 outlets in Chicago and its suburbs. It's easy to get addicted to the coffee and sweets here: In fact, when my former office mates and I counted up our visits each week, we decided to dub our local branch "Corner Bankruptcy." Sandwiches, salads, fruit, and amazing baked-good desserts are highlights. (Try the lemon bars dusted with powdered sugar, or the peanut butter brownie, or the mini caramel Bundt cake—try anything!) The homemade chips sprinkled with Parmesan are impossible to resist. Grilled panini with turkey, bacon, and cheese, or homemade mac and cheese will appeal to kids. Some of the main locations include one in River North at 516 N. Clark St. (© **312/644-8100**), attached to Melman's Maggiano's Italian restaurant; and a location east of Michigan Avenue at 676 N. St. Clair St., at Erie Street (© **312/266-2570**).

1121 N. State St. (at Cedar St.). © **312/787-1969**. High chairs, boosters. Reservations not accepted. Menu items $7–$10. AE, DC, DISC, MC, V. Mon–Thurs 7am–8:30pm; Fri–Sat 7am–9pm; Sun 7am–8pm. Subway/El: Red Line to Clark/Division.

Flapjaw Café BURGERS   This down-home bar and grill is quite a find just off the Mag Mile: a low-key place serving burgers and grilled turkey sandwiches in baskets with fries. The bar-in-the-round with outlying tables and stools has a comfortable atmosphere. Although many young professionals come here for lunch and for a drink after work, it's a bustling, friendly place where kids are welcome. However, because tables are high—most seats are bar stool height—this restaurant is better suited for kids over age 3, who can comfortably sit in a booster. The menu is very simple and straightforward: California-style pizza, grilled sandwiches, salads, soups, and appetizers—all fairly cheap. Sit outside for a nice view of street life around the Loyola University campus.

22 E. Pearson St. © **312/642-4848**. High chairs, boosters. Reservations not accepted. All menu items under $10. AE, DC, DISC, MC, V. Mon–Fri 11am–10pm; Sat 11am–6pm. Subway/El: Red Line to Chicago/State.

foodlife ★★ *Finds* ECLECTIC   Yes, another successful concept courtesy of Lettuce Entertain You's Rich Melman: a food court with a healthy twist. Located on the mezzanine of Water Tower Place, just outside the entrance of the Mity Nice Grill, foodlife consists of a dozen or so kiosks offering both ordinary and exotic specialties—a total of 700 different items. Four hundred seats are spread out cafe-style in a very pleasant environment under realistic boughs of artificial trees festooned with strings of lights in the shapes of grapes and other fruits.

The beauty of a food court, of course, is that it tries to offer something for everybody. At foodlife the burger-and-pizza crowd will be satisfied, but so will vegetarians and diners looking for, say, a low-fat Caesar salad. Diners here can also choose south-of-the-border dishes, an assortment of Asian fare, and veggie-oriented, low-fat fare. Special treats include the Miracle Juice Bar's fresh orange juice and raspberry fruit smoothie, as well as a host of healthy or gooey desserts, and, at a booth called Sacred Grounds, various espresso-based beverages. A lunch or a snack at foodlife is basically inexpensive, but the payment method (each diner receives an electronic card that records each purchase for a total payment upon exit) makes it easy to build up a big tab while holding a personal taste-testing session at each kiosk.

In Water Tower Place, 835 N. Michigan Ave. ☎ 312/335-3663. High chairs, boosters. Reservations not accepted. Most items $5–$10. AE, DC, DISC, MC, V. Breakfast kiosk daily 7:30–10:30am. All other kiosks Sun–Thurs 11am–8pm; Fri–Sat 11am–9pm. Subway/El: Red Line to Chicago/State.

Oak Tree ✦ AMERICAN/BREAKFAST   Tucked away on the sixth floor of the 900 N. Michigan indoor mall (home of Bloomingdale's), Oak Tree isn't exactly high-profile. But it's one of my favorite places for a meal during a day of Magnificent Mile touring. The cafe decor is bright and cheery (with nature-inspired murals to help you momentarily forget that you're inside a mall). If you can, get a table along the windows that look down on Michigan Avenue. Oak Tree's draw is the enormous, varied menu. You'll find something for everyone in the family: a large salad selection, Asian noodles, sandwiches that range from meatball to duck breast, Mexican quesadillas, and even blue-plate specials such as turkey hash or a patty melt. The breakfast menu is just as extensive. Oak Tree can get quite crowded at prime time, with hefty waits, so try to time your visit accordingly.

900 N. Michigan Ave., 6th floor ☎ 312/751-1988. High chairs, boosters. Reservations not accepted. Main courses $7.95–$12. AE, DC, DISC, MC, V. Mon–Fri 7:30am–6:30pm; Sat–Sun 7:30am–5:30pm. Subway/El: Red Line to Chicago/State.

Indulging Your Interest in Baking

While it's not exactly "baking," **Eli's Cheesecake World** does enable dessert fanatics to see the process of baking a Chicago favorite. A visit to the 62,000-square-foot state-of-the-art bakery starts with a sneak peek at Eli's bakers busy at work, and ends with a slice of cheesecake. The bakery also offers a cafe and cheesecake bar, where over 30 different flavors are on sale by the slice each day. The cheesecake you'll see being made is served up at Eli's, the Place for Steak, 215 E. Chicago Ave., at Fairbanks Court (☎ 312/642-1393), a Chicago institution founded 50 years ago by the late Eli Schulman, who opened a neighborhood delicatessen serving central European comfort foods like potato pancakes and liver and onions.

Eli's Cheesecake World, located on the city's northwest side at 6701 W. Forest Preserve, at the corner of Montrose Avenue (☎ 773/736-3417), hosts tours Monday through Friday at noon (although reservations aren't necessary, call to make sure the bakery isn't closed for periodic maintenance). The 40-minute tour costs $3 for adults, $2 for children under 12, and special packages are available for groups of 10 or more. For more information, check out www.elischeesecake.com.

5 River North

Most families visiting Chicago will find themselves heading for dinner in River North at least once during their stay. The city's hot spot for family dining, River North offers an ever-growing, something-for-everyone array of restaurants—from fast food to theme and chain restaurants (plus some of the most fashionable dining destinations, so parents might want to hire a sitter one night and return for "date night"). Whether you seek a quick dog or burger, a casual French meal, or contemporary American fine dining, River North has it all.

EXPENSIVE

Brasserie Jo ★ ALSATIAN/FRENCH   Brasserie Jo, the casual dining destination from partnership Jean Joho (whose upscale Everest restaurant is one of the city's longtime gourmet destinations) and Lettuce Entertain You Enterprises, is a popular spot for convivial meals of robust fare in a Parisian, retro-chic setting. It's big and bustling enough to welcome kids, and once you explain that a croque-monsieur is really a toasted ham and cheese, your kids will find something wonderful on the menu. For the adults, following in the tradition of the classic Alsatian brasserie (meaning "brewery"), Brasserie Jo makes a malty house brew, and diners are welcome for a quick stop-in snack with a glass of wine or a full five-course meal.

You can order a hearty Alsatian *choucroute,* but the menu focuses more on casual French classics: Favorites include onion soup, mussels marinière, *salade niçoise,* croque-monsieur, and steak frites. One house specialty is the "famous shrimp bag," a phyllo pastry filled with shrimp, mushrooms, and herb rice garnished with lobster sauce. Save room for the delightfully decadent crepes *magnifique,* which live up to their name with an amazing alchemy of thin crepes, bananas, and chocolate. Or bypass the dessert menu and indulge in the bountiful "cheese chariot."

59 W. Hubbard St. (between Dearborn and Clark sts.). ⓒ 312/595-0800. www.brasseriejo.com. Kids' menu, high chairs, boosters. Reservations recommended. Main courses $12–$26; kids' menu $7–$9. AE, DC, DISC, MC, V. Mon–Fri 5:30–10pm; Sat 5–11pm; Sun 5–10pm. Subway/El: Red Line to Grand, or Brown Line to Merchandise Mart.

Harry Caray's ★★ AMERICAN/ITALIAN   A shrine to the legendary Cubs play-by-play announcer, this landmark building near the Chicago River is a repository for the staggering collection of baseball memorabilia that Harry amassed, and it covers almost every square inch of the place. Even the bar is a nod to baseball: At 60 feet, 6 inches long, it's the distance from the pitcher's mound to home plate.

But you don't have to be a baseball lover to appreciate Harry's. The dining rooms have an old-Chicago feel that is comfortable and familiar, with high tin ceilings, exposed brick walls, and red-checked tablecloths. It would be easy to lump Harry's with other celebrity restaurants, but as one reviewer pointed out, the food is better than it has to be. The portions are enormous; unless you want leftovers for days, plan to share. Main-course offerings run from traditional items such as pastas with red sauce to chicken Vesuvio, veal, and a variety of seafood choices. Harry's is also a good place to order big plates of meat: dry-aged steaks, lamb, veal, and pork chops. And from the list of side dishes, be sure to order the signature Vesuvio potatoes. The desserts are rich and decadent.

33 W. Kinzie St. (at Dearborn St.). ⓒ 312/828-0966. www.harrycarays.com. Kids' menu, high chairs. Main courses $11–$33; kids' menu around $7. AE, DC, DISC, MC, V. Mon–Sat 11:30am–2:30pm; Mon–Thurs 5–10:30pm; Fri–Sat 5–11pm; Sun noon–4pm (lunch bar only) and 4–10pm. Subway/El: Brown Line to Merchandise Mart, or Red Line to Grand.

MODERATE

Carson's ✿ AMERICAN/BARBECUE   A true Chicago institution, Carson's calls itself "The Place for Ribs," and, boy, is it ever. The barbecue sauce is sweet and tangy, and the ribs are meaty. Included in the $20 price for a full slab of ribs are coleslaw and one of four types of potatoes (the most decadent are au gratin), plus right-out-of-the-oven rolls.

For dinner there's often a wait, but don't despair. In the bar area you'll find a heaping mound of some of the best chopped liver around and plenty of cocktail rye to go with it. (Kids who turn up their noses at chopped liver should start with a kiddie cocktail instead.) When you're seated at your table, tie on your plastic bib—and indulge. In case you don't eat ribs, Carson's also barbecues chicken, salmon, and pork chops, and the restaurant's steaks aren't bad either. But ribs are the house specialty, so make sure that at least someone in your group orders them. (The waitstaff will be shocked if you don't.) If by some remarkable feat you have room left after dinner, the candy-bar sundaes are a scrumptious finale to the meal. Carson's popularity has led to something of a factory mentality among management, which evidently feels the need to herd 'em in and out, but the servers are responsive to requests not to be hurried through the meal.

612 N. Wells St. (at Ontario St.). ✆ 312/280-9200. Kids' menu, high chairs, boosters. Reservations accepted only for groups of 6 or more. Main courses $8.95–$30; kids' menu $6–$14. AE, DC, DISC, MC, V. Mon–Thurs 11am–11pm; Fri 11am–12:30am; Sat noon–12:30am; Sun noon–11pm. Closed Thanksgiving. Subway/El: Red Line to Grand.

Houston's AMERICAN/STEAKHOUSE   Here's a casual steakhouse that's always packed with families. Located next to the Lenox Hotel and Suites, Houston's is cavernous and dark, filled with deep booths lit by overhead fixtures that barely illuminate the tables. The place has a dark-wood-and-brass, 1980s feel to it. (Fittingly so, since it opened here in 1987—today there are 40 Houston's nationwide.) Houston's attracts a mix of tourists, conventioneers, and locals. It's a comfy space, and the booths have the advantage of giving everyone a feeling of privacy. Toasted cheese bread will be a hit with kids, and they'll make chicken fingers and hamburgers to keep the kids happy. For adults, the restaurant offers an extensive list of more than 40 wines collected mostly from California. At dinnertime there's live piano music in the bar.

616 N. Rush St. ✆ 312/649-1121. High chairs, boosters. Reservations not accepted. Main courses $15–$25. AE, DC, DISC, MC, V. Mon–Sat 11am–10pm. Subway/El: Red Line to Grand. Bus: 145, 146, 147, 151.

Leona's ITALIAN/PIZZA   This Chicago-based home-style Italian food chain has a vast menu, good pizza, and budget-friendly prices. With 16 locations and still family-owned and -operated after 52 years, Leona's is a real Chicago restaurant success story. All food is fresh and made from scratch. The River North location features a large, open dining room. Be prepared for huge portions and unusually warm and hospitable service in a very family-friendly setting. The menu (actually, it reads more like a book) runs the gamut and includes ribs, chicken wings, steak sandwiches, burgers, pasta, pizza (deep dish or thin crust), and salads. If that's not enough, Leona's also has a children's menu featuring spaghetti marinara, chicken strips (fried, grilled, or barbecued), 6-inch pizzas, lasagna, fettuccine Alfredo, and more.

646 N. Franklin St. ✆ 312/867-0101. Kids' menu. Main courses $9–$25; kids' menu $5–$8. AE, DC, DISC, MC, V. Mon–Thurs 11:30am–11pm; Fri 11:30am–midnight; Sat noon–midnight; Sun noon–10pm. Subway/El: Brown Line to Merchandise Mart; Red Line to Grand. Bus: 65 or 22.

Maggiano's ✦ ITALIAN   A great pick for large groups, Maggiano's is a shrine to family-style Italian dining. Like many of its fellow Lettuce Entertain You restaurants, Maggiano's feels a bit contrived, with traditional Italian red-checkered tablecloths and old family portraits (which family, we'll never know), designed to create the feel of Little Italy throughout the nine separate dining rooms. Still, heaping plates of pasta meant to be shared make Maggiano's a good choice for a large and budget-conscious family. In fact, everything on the menu is supersize. Steaks are all more than a pound, and most pasta dishes weigh in over 25 ounces. You're expected to share dishes, pass things around, and try a little bit of everything. The menu is vast and features Italian pasta classics such as chicken and spinach manicotti, eggplant Parmesan, and meat or marinara lasagna, plus chicken, veal, steaks (try the Prime New York Steak al Forno Gorgonzola, a strip steak served with caramelized onions and melted Gorgonzola cheese), chops, and seafood. There's no kids' menu, but the kitchen will accommodate with smaller portions. Downstairs, there's a banquet room that accommodates parties of 20 to 200. On holidays Maggiano's has live music.

516 N. Clark St. ✆ **312/644-7700.** High chairs, boosters. Main courses $11–$33. AE, DC, DISC, MC, V. Mon–Thurs 11:30am–10pm; Fri–Sat 11:30am–11pm; Sun noon–10pm. Subway/El: Brown Line to Merchandise Mart; Red Line to Grand. Bus: 65 or 22.

Reza's ✦✦ *Value* MIDDLE EASTERN   Whether your kids are already avid eaters of Middle Eastern food or you want to start exposing them to it, Reza's is a good option. With high ceilings and exposed brick, this warm and family-friendly restaurant is housed in a former microbrewery. Specialties include a deliciously rich chicken in pomegranate sauce, and kids might go for one of a variety of kabobs. Despite the menu's meat-heavy emphasis, there's a full selection of vegetarian options, too. The appetizer combo is a nice option for families; it includes hummus, stuffed grape leaves, tabbouleh, and other standbys nicely presented in a red lacquer bento box. Reza's has another location in Andersonville, at 5255 N. Clark St. (✆ **773/561-1898**), but the River North spot is the most convenient for visitors staying downtown.

432 W. Ontario St. (at Orleans St.). ✆ **312/664-4500.** High chairs, boosters. Main courses $9.95–$17. AE, DC, DISC, MC, V. Daily 11am–midnight. Subway/El: Red Line to Grand.

Scoozi ✦ REGIONAL ITALIAN   Families should plan to visit Scoozi on Sunday evening, when the restaurant gives kids "make your own pizza" time from 4 to 5pm. Chefs show kids how to make a pizza, then pop them in the wood-burning oven. Kids dine on their culinary masterworks, and you get a nice stretch of "adult time" at the table while your little chefs are at work.

Scoozi's sprawling loft space has been its home since 1986, the year it opened and began serving up authentic Italian cooking—a real pioneering effort at the time, complete with focaccia in its breadbaskets. Scoozi's menu is no longer unique, but Chicagoans return for its reliable lineup of Italian flavors. Appetizers include an antipasti bar (favorites are orzo with shrimp and wood-roasted mushrooms); deep-fried calamari with basil, aioli, and arrabbiata sauce (a spicy tomato sauce); or small pizzas, such as one smothered with garlic spinach, oven-roasted tomatoes, and goat cheese. Main courses include *petto di pollo* (grilled chicken breast with baby artichokes, red potatoes, and warm coriander-seed vinaigrette); ravioli baked in a wood oven (smoked chicken, Taleggio cheese with smoked bacon, or artichoke); and *gnocchi con salsa rossa* (homemade potato dumplings in a tomato-basil cream). For dessert, head directly for the tiramisu.

410 W. Huron St. (at Orleans St.). 📞 312/943-5900. Kids' menu, high chairs, boosters. Reservations recommended. Pasta $7.50–$11 lunch and dinner; main courses $8.95–$15 lunch, $9.95–$25 dinner; kids' menu $3.25. AE, DC, DISC, MC, V. Mon–Thurs 5:30–9pm; Fri 5:30–10pm; Sat 5–10pm; Sun 5–9pm. Subway/El: Red Line to Chicago.

INEXPENSIVE

Cafe Iberico ⭐⭐ SPANISH/TAPAS   Families should arrive early to ensure getting a table at this wildly popular tapas joint with a festive atmosphere. I'd recommend this place for older kids and teens with adventurous palates. (Get them to try *pulpo a la gallega*—the best fried octopus around!) Cafe Iberico gets very loud, especially on weekends, and on weekdays, crowds begin pouring in at the end of the workday, so if you arrive around dinnertime, expect a wait. Put a dent in your appetite with a plate of *queso de cabra* (baked goat cheese with fresh tomato-basil sauce). When your waiter returns with the first dish, put in a second order for a round of both hot and cold tapas. Then continue to order as your hunger demands. The waiters are pleasant yet can get a little harried, so it sometimes takes some effort to flag them down. A few standout dishes are the vegetarian Spanish omelet, *patatas bravas* (spicy potatoes with tomato sauce), *pincho de pollo* (chicken brochette with caramelized onions and rice), and *pulpo y la plancha* (grilled octopus with potatoes and olive oil). There are a handful of entrees on the menu, and a few desserts in case you're still not sated.

739 N. LaSalle St. (between Chicago Ave. and Superior St.). 📞 312/573-1510. High chairs. Reservations accepted during the week for parties of 6 or more only. Tapas $2–$7; main courses $7.95–$13. DC, DISC, MC, V. Mon–Thurs 11am–11pm; Fri 11am–1:30am; Sat noon–1:30am; Sun noon–11pm. Subway/El: Red Line to Chicago/State, or Brown Line to Chicago.

Dave & Buster's AMERICAN   Good old-fashioned fun of the coin-operated variety means that you may have to tear your kids away from the games to get them to sit down for dinner. At the Chicago outpost of the Dallas-based mega entertainment and dining chain, you can combine casual dining and an evening's entertainment. (Don't send teens by themselves: Kids must be accompanied by an adult 25 years old or older.) The menu is expansive and features bar food, including pasta, burgers, steak, and ribs. Before you sit down to eat, let your kids burn off energy by getting lost in this neon-lit games emporium. You'll find 1950s-era carnival games, Vegas-style casino games, video games, and virtual reality tests. The main attraction is the glitzy Million Dollar Midway on the second level. Do your kids dream of being an Alpine ski racer or driving the Grand Prix? Video games on the Midway let them simulate the experience. Grown-ups might try a computerized version of blackjack or swing away at the indoor golf simulator, a "virtual" golf driving range that uses laser beams to calculate the ball's flight.

1024 N. Clark St. 📞 312/943-5151. Kids' menu. Main courses $9–$20; kids' menu $3–$8. AE, DC, DISC, MC, V. Mon–Thurs 11am–1am; Fri–Sat 11:30am–2am; Sun 11:30am–midnight. Subway/El: Red Line to Clark/Division. Bus: 22, 70, or 36.

Ed Debevic's ⭐ BURGERS/DINER   "Eat at Ed's" is the call to action at this temple to America's hometown lunch-counter culture. Wherever you sit, in an upholstered banquette or booth or the lunch counter stools, you'll be surrounded by 1950s nostalgia. Tunes such as "Duke of Earl" and other vintage oldies fill the air. Food specialties include pot roast, fountain drinks—and meatloaf. Ed Debevic's calls itself the place "where meatloaf is king." There's no kids' menu, but with the entire menu based on burgers and fries, who needs one? The

1950s-costumed waitstaff cracks gum at you and dishes out rude comments along with the food. And when the jukebox strikes up a song, don't be surprised if your waiter leaps onto the counter (or onto your table, if that's where he happens to be), to dance along. It's all a performance, but it works. One nice bonus is a good view of River North and the skyscrapers of the Loop to the south.

640 N. Wells St. ℂ 312/664-1707. High chairs, boosters. Reservations accepted only for parties of 15 or more. All main courses under $10. AE, DC, DISC, V. Hours: Mon–Thurs 11am–9pm, Fri 11am–11pm, Sat 9am–11pm, Sun 9am–9pm. Subway/El: Brown Line to Franklin.

Gino's East ★★ PIZZA   This famous Chicago pizzeria invites patrons to scrawl all over the graffiti-strewn booths. Waiting in the frigid cold (or sweltering heat) to get into Gino's at its former location just west of the Magnificent Mile used to be a Chicago tourist rite of passage. Now that the restaurant has moved into the vast space formerly occupied by Planet Hollywood, there are no more lines out front.

Many Chicagoans consider Gino's the quintessential deep-dish Chicago-style pizza. True to its reputation, the pizza is heavy (a small cheese pizza is enough for two), so work up an appetite before chowing down here. Specialty pizzas include the supreme, with layers of cheese, sausage, onions, green pepper, and mushrooms; and the vegetarian, with cheese, onions, peppers, asparagus, summer squash, zucchini, and eggplant. Gino's also offers salads, sandwiches, and pastas, but I've never seen anyone order them. If you want to take a pizza home on the plane, call a day in advance and Gino's will pack a special frozen pie for the trip.

633 N. Wells St. (at Ontario St.). ℂ 312/943-1124. Kids' menu, high chairs, boosters. Reservations not accepted. Pizza $8.25–$17; kids' menu around $5. AE, DC, DISC, MC, V. Mon–Thurs 11am–9pm; Fri–Sat 11am–midnight; Sun noon–9pm. Subway/El: Red Line to Chicago/State.

Green Door Tavern BURGERS   The Green Door is a neighborhood refuge and a well-needed respite from the many trendy restaurants in River North. At lunch you'll find the advertising and graphic-design types who work in the neighborhood chowing on burgers in the unpretentious atmosphere. The restaurant's wood-frame building was put up temporarily after the 1871 fire, presumably just before the city ordinance that banned such construction inside the newly designated "fire zone." The place began as a grocery store with living quarters on the second floor, and evolved into a restaurant in 1921. Later a speakeasy was established in a downstairs room no longer open to the public. Apparently the original framing crew went light on the bracing timbers in a few places because the whole building leans to the right. About a decade ago a newly constructed building across from the Green Door was consumed with fire and burned to the ground. Firefighters sprayed the Green Door, earning undying gratitude and an annual honorarium called the Golden Helmet Awards from the management.

There's no kids' menu, but regular menu items should please, including the hickory burger, the triple-decker grilled cheese, and the Texas chili. There are even a veggie burger and a turkey burger, and the menu includes some Cajun fare and pasta. Specials, including the Wednesday meatloaf offering, are posted daily.

678 N. Orleans St. (at Huron St.). ℂ 312/664-5496. High chairs, boosters. Reservations accepted only for parties of 7 or more. Main courses $6.95–$12. MC, V. Mon–Fri 11:30am–2am; Sat 11:30am–3am; Sun noon–9pm. Subway/El: Brown Line to Chicago.

Hard Rock Cafe AMERICAN   Not just an eatery, Hard Rock Cafe is also one of Chicago's main tourist attractions. (Don't expect to find many locals or members of the over-30 age group here.) A regular rock 'n' roll museum, you could easily

---

Finds **Soulful Brunch**

Head to **House of Blues,** 329 N. Dearborn St., at Kinzie Street (📞 312/923-2000), for its popular Sunday gospel brunch featuring live performances from church groups from throughout the Midwest. To guarantee seating, it's a good idea to reserve 2 weeks in advance. Seatings begin at 9:30am and noon.

---

spend hours here pouring over the hundreds of drumsticks, concert photos, gold records, or autographed guitars of your favorite artists, including the likes of Mick Fleetwood and George Harrison. (The most popular pieces are a guitar autographed by the members of Nirvana and a motor scooter used in the 1979 movie *Quadrophenia,* which was based on The Who's album.) The food is pretty standard fare, with fajitas and burgers as specialties, plus a children's menu. But who comes here for the food? The round building has a circular bar decorated in a sports motif, with some nice touches: autographed bats by Ryne Sandberg, Mark Grace, Shawn Dunston, and Frank Thomas, among other ballplayers. Interesting restaurant fact: The original Hard Rock Cafe was founded June 14, 1971, in London by Isaac Tigrett and Peter Morton, the son of Chicago restaurateur Arnold Morton of Morton's steakhouse fame. The Chicago location was opened 12 years later.

63 W. Ontario St. 📞 312/943-2252. Kids' menu, high chairs, boosters. Main courses $8–$15; kids' menu $7. AE, DISC, V. Mon–Thurs 11am–11pm; Fri 11:30am–11:30pm; Sat 11am–midnight; Sun 11am–10pm. Subway/El: Red Line to State/Grand.

Mr. Beef ⭐ *Finds* AMERICAN   Mr. Beef doesn't have much atmosphere or seating room, but it's a much-loved Chicago institution. Squeeze in alongside the lunchtime regulars and enjoy the atmosphere (or lack thereof). Families with small children will be happier getting their sandwiches to go, as lack of space means Mr. Beef is not a high chair–friendly place. Its claim to fame is the classic Italian beef sandwich, the Chicago version of a Philly cheese steak. The Mr. Beef variety is made of sliced beef dipped in jus, piled high on a chewy bun, and topped with sweet or hot peppers. Heavy, filling, and *very* Chicago. Mr. Beef really hops during lunchtime, when dusty construction workers and suit-wearing businessmen crowd in for their meaty fix. While you're chowing down, check out the celebrity photos and newspaper clippings covering the walls and you'll see why this place is considered a local monument.

666 N. Orleans St. (at Erie St.). 📞 312/337-8500. Reservations not accepted. Sandwiches $5.95–$8.50. No credit cards. Mon–Fri 8am–5pm; Sat 10:30am–2pm. Subway/El: Red Line to Grand.

Pizzeria Uno ⭐ *Value* PIZZA   In 1943 Pizzeria Uno invented Chicago-style pizza, and many deep-dish aficionados still refuse to accept any imitations. Uno is now a nationwide chain, but this location is the original. You may eat in the restaurant itself on the basement level or, weather permitting, on the outdoor patio right off the sidewalk. Salads, sandwiches, and a house minestrone are also available, but, hey, the only reason to come here is for the pizza. (And in fact, 90% of the menu is dedicated to deep-dish pizza.)

Uno was so successful that the owners opened **Pizzeria Due** in 1955 in a lovely gray-brick Victorian town house nearby at 619 N. Wabash Ave., at Ontario Street (📞 312/943-2400). The menu is identical at both restaurants, although the space at Pizzeria Due is much larger. *Be forewarned:* This pizzeria serves no pizza before its time. Pizza takes a minimum of 45 minutes to prepare.

29 E. Ohio St. (at Wabash Ave.). ✆ 312/321-1000. High chairs. No reservations accepted Fri–Sat. Pizza $7–$18. AE, DC, DISC, MC, V. Mon–Fri 11:30am–1am; Sat 11:30am–2am; Sun 11:30am–11pm. Subway/El: Red Line to Grand.

Rainforest Cafe AMERICAN   This Minnesota-based chain bills itself as "a wild place to shop and eat." The restaurant strives to create the feel of a rainforest with the sounds of waterfalls, thunder and lightning, and wild animals echoing throughout the place. Check out the floor-to-ceiling aquarium tanks, and duck to avoid the swinging orangutans. The Mexican and Caribbean-inspired menu features salads, sandwiches, and a range of entrees that will please a family of picky eaters. The "chicken-fried chicken" is a bestseller, as is the "mojo bones" rib appetizer. The kids' menu features standard burgers, hot dogs, and mac and cheese. The restaurant also sponsors educational programs designed to bring awareness of the planet's dwindling rainforests.

605 N. Clark St. (at Ohio St.). ✆ 312/787-1501. www.rainforestcafe.com. Kids' menu, high chairs, boosters. Reservations recommended. Main courses $9–$11; kids' menu $6–$8. AE, DC, DISC, V. Mon–Thurs 11am–9:30pm; Fri 11am–10:30pm; Sat 11am–11pm; Sun 11am–9pm. Subway/El: Red Line to State/Grand.

Twisted Spoke ★ Finds DINER   Don't be scared off by the Easy Rider skeleton slowly rotating on a motorcycle atop a tall pole outside the Twisted Spoke: They feed everybody at this laid-back, off-the-beaten-path cafe that caters to the biker crowd but welcomes suburbanites and button-down business folk as well. Co-owners and brothers Cliff and Mitch Einhorn started the Spoke as a "family biker bar" in 1995. The place is filled with antique bike parts and accessories. The food is hearty and well prepared, from the cheese quesadillas to more than a dozen sandwiches, including curry chicken salad, twisted tuna salad, and barbecued chicken. But the Twisted Spoke's mouthwatering burgers are what draw most people here. The "Biker Brunch" features fare that swings wildly from "Real Oats for Real Men" to fruit salad to steak and eggs. It's served Saturday and Sunday from 11am to 3pm. Specials include meatloaf on Monday night, pasta on Wednesday, and fish fry on Friday. Enjoy the view from the great rooftop patio, but clear out while the night is still young, before the bar crowd heads up for bargain-priced beers. The patio overlooks the blue-collar corner of Ogden and Grand avenues and offers a unique cityscape view with the Sears Tower in the distance.

501 N. Ogden Ave. (at Grand Ave.). ✆ 312/666-1500. High chairs, boosters. Reservations recommended for large parties. Main courses $5.25–$8.50. AE, MC, V. Mon–Fri 8am–2am; Sat 11am–3am; Sun 11am–2am. Bus: 65.

Tips Rocking & Rolling at the Golden Arches

The reality of traveling with kids means the occasional fast-food meal can be a real lifesaver. In McDonald's hometown (corporate headquarters is located in west suburban Oak Brook) I would be remiss in not mentioning the second-busiest franchise in the world. Only McDonald's in Moscow claims to be more trafficked than Chicago's **Rock 'n' Roll McDonald's,** located at 600 N. Clark St., at Ohio St. (✆ 312/664-7940). Along with Big Macs, shakes, and fries, you'll find a storehouse of memorabilia and other 1950s and 1960s tchotchkes, including a restored Corvette parked in the dining room and a collection of Beatles mementos. McDonald's has big plans for renovating and expanding this outlet, so call ahead to make sure it's still rocking and rolling while you're in town.

6 Lincoln Park

Singles and upwardly mobile young families inhabit Lincoln Park, the neighborhood roughly defined by North Avenue on the south, Diversey Parkway on the north, the park on the east, and Clybourn Avenue on the west. No surprise, then, that the neighborhood has spawned a dense concentration of some of the city's best restaurants.

EXPENSIVE

Geja's Café ⭐ FONDUE   Are your kids over age 10? Can they sit through a 2-hour meal? If so, they will love Geja's (pronounced Gay-*haz*), an all-fondue restaurant. For some diners, the dark rathskeller decor will be a welcome change from the slick, commercial trattorias and bistros common all over the city. The restaurant has single-handedly preserved the fondue experience in Chicago, providing a fun and welcome break from the ordinary mode of dining.

Choose the Prince Geja's combination dinner, the best Geja's has to offer. The meal begins with a Gruyère fondue appetizer, into which you dip apple wedges and chunks of dark bread. Next, a huge platter arrives, brimming with squares of beef tenderloin, lobster tails, chicken breast, scallops, and jumbo shrimp—all raw—and a caldron of boiling oil to cook them in—the reason why only kids 10 and up are allowed! These delicacies are accompanied by a variety of raw vegetables, and eight different dipping sauces. When the flaming chocolate fondue arrives for dessert, with fresh fruit and pound cake for dipping and marshmallows for roasting, you'll want to beg for mercy. *One word of caution:* You have to work for your fondue—keeping track of how long each piece of meat has been cooking, and taking it out before it burns—so Geja's is not the best choice if you just want to sit back and be pampered.

340 W. Armitage Ave. (between Lincoln Ave. and Clark St.). ℂ 773/281-9101. Reservations accepted every day except late Fri–Sat. 3-course dinners $20–$39. AE, DC, DISC, MC, V. Mon–Thurs 5–10:30pm; Fri 5pm–midnight; Sat 5pm–12:30am; Sun 4:30–10pm. Subway/El: Brown Line to Armitage. Bus: 22.

O'Brien's Restaurant AMERICAN   From the looks of the interior, you'd expect O'Brien's to be a rather ordinary restaurant with that standard "Irish pub" feel—dark wood, brass, and hunter green feature prominently. But outdoors, you'll make an amazing discovery: the best alfresco dining in Old Town. And that's saying something, as you'll find multiple options up and down Wells Street. In good weather the chance to kick back outdoors with your kids can make for a much less stressful dinner—who cares if a few fries wind up on the patio bricks? The birds will thank you for it. The outdoor patio has teakwood furniture, a gazebo bar in the center, and a mural of the owners' country club on a brick wall. Order the dressed-up chips, a house specialty. Rib-eye steak, Dover sole, and whitefish are specialties. The bar has a nice assortment of microbrews. Every night from 7pm until midnight, O'Brien's features piano music.

1528 N. Wells St. (2 blocks south of North Ave.). ℂ 312/787-3131. Kids' menu, high chairs, boosters. Reservations recommended. Main courses $15–$25; kids' menu $5–$8. AE, DC, DISC, MC, V. Daily 11am–2am. Subway/El: Brown Line to Sedgwick.

MODERATE

Goose Island Brewing Company AMERICAN   Some of the best beer in Chicago is manufactured at this comfy, award-winning microbrewery in the Clybourn corridor. (An impressive cast of professional beer critics agrees.) In the course of a year, Goose Island produces about 100 varieties of lagers, ales, stouts, pilsners, and porters that change with the seasons. But why include a beer-oriented

Dining in Lincoln Park & Wrigleyville

Ann Sather **8**
Bourgeois Pig **14**
Buca di Beppo **11**
Byron's Hot Dog Haus **2**
Café Brauer **24**
Charlie's Ale House **18**
El Jardin **6**
Flat Top Grill **29**
Geja's Café **21**
Goose Island Brewing Company **26**
John Barleycorn **16**
John's Place **17**
Kabuki **15**
La Creperie **12**
Leona's Pizzeria **7**
Murphy's Red Hots **9**
Nookies **28**
O'Brien's Restaurant **30**
O'Donovan's **1**
Pat's Pizzeria **10**
Penny's Noodle Shop **5**
Potbelly Sandwich Works **20**
Ranalli's Pizzeria, Libations & Collectibles **23**
Sai Café **25**
Stanley's **22**
Toast **19**
Tuscany **4**
Twin Anchors **27**
Uncommon Grounds **3**
The Wieners Circle **13**

joint in a book for kids? Because the food at the Goose is almost as good as the beer on tap, and a separate, casual dining area attracts plenty of families, especially on the weekends.

The cut-above bar food includes burgers (including a killer, dragon-breath-inducing Stilton burger with roasted garlic), sandwiches (pulled pork, catfish po' boy, chicken Caesar), and some serious salads. Goose Island is also known for its addictive homemade potato chips, fresh-brewed root beer, and orange cream soda. The zero-attitude, come-as-you-are ambience is very refreshing for a lazy afternoon pit stop or a casual lunch or dinner. A second location, at 3535 N. Clark St. in Wrigleyville (© **773/832-9040**), has an enclosed beer garden that welcomes kids.

1800 N. Clybourn Ave. (at Sheffield Ave.). © **312/915-0071**. www.gooseisland.com. Kids' menu, high chairs, boosters. Reservations recommended on weekends. Sandwiches $7.50–$9.95; main courses $11–$17; kids' menu items under $5. AE, DC, DISC, MC, V. Mon–Fri 11:30am–1am; Sat 11am–2am; Sun 11am–1am; main dining room closes at 10pm daily. Subway/El: Red Line to North/Clybourn.

Kabuki JAPANESE   Parents appreciate the laid-back atmosphere at this no-frills sushi restaurant located just off of the busy intersection of Clark and Fullerton. The clientele is mostly Lincoln Park's young professionals, but the atmosphere is welcoming to all. The menu runs the gamut of Japanese foods—sushi, sashimi, tempura, teriyaki, and noodles—in an intimate, 55-seat dining room. Bonsai trees, brush paintings, and window screens decorate a dining room that is dominated by two highly trained sushi chefs from behind their 10-seat sushi bar. Those who want to sample sushi and try a little bit of everything should go for the 11-piece Kabuki combination. Timid beginners may also find a six-piece, cooked sushi platter a low-risk entree into the world of raw fish. For an appetizer, Kabuki recommends the *goma-ae,* a boiled spinach appetizer served cold in a sesame-and-peanut-butter sauce, although your kids might also get a kick out of peeling and eating a pile of salty *edamame* (soybeans cooked in the pod). When Kabuki overflows, you can head to Kabuki II, just a few doors down at 2473 N. Clark. In Wrigleyville visit Kabuki III at 3647 N. Southport (© **773/281-9155**).

2407 N. Clark. © **773/281-3131**. High chairs, boosters. Reservations recommended. Main courses $8–$15. AE, MC, V. Sun–Tues 4:30pm–midnight; Fri–Sat 4:30pm–1pm. Closed Wed. Bus: 22 to Clark or 36 to Broadway.

Sai Café ★ JAPANESE   Here's another good spot to start exposing your kids to the wonders of Japanese cuisine. Despite some upscale sushi bars surfacing in high-profile restaurant districts in the past few years, Lincoln Park's modest Sai Café remains the choice for Lincoln Park residents more interested in food than funky decor. More than 30 varieties of sushi are lovingly prepared and served with élan in this neighborhood setting just off chic Armitage Avenue. And of course, white rice, chicken teriyaki, and shrimp and vegetable tempura are always on the menu, should raw fish prove too daring for your kids. A la carte selections come by the piece or maki-mono style, which pairs anything from tuna and avocado to flying-fish eggs and scallions, and then wraps it all up in rice and a thin sheet of dried seaweed. Combo plates feature different meat, fish, and vegetables that can be dressed in tempura or teriyaki, or served sashimi style. Sai Café also offers a large selection of noodle and rice dishes.

2010 N. Sheffield Ave. (at Armitage Ave.). © **773/472-8080**. High chairs, boosters. Main courses $16–$24 (a la carte sushi $3.75–$6.95 per piece). AE, DC, MC, V. Mon–Thurs 4:30–11pm; Fri–Sat 4:30pm–midnight; Sun 3:30–10pm. Subway: Brown Line to Armitage.

INEXPENSIVE

Bourgeois Pig ★ *Finds* BREAKFAST/SANDWICHES   Eclectic antiques fill this brownstone that's become a mecca for DePaul University students and neighborhood families. Bookshelves are packed with literature, and the atmosphere is cluttered and comfy. The menu makes it clear that the Bourgeois Pig caters to an intellectual crowd: "The Sun Also Rises," "Pilgrim's Progress," and "The Old Man and the Sea" are among the menu's 25 gourmet sandwiches. Kids will enjoy the "build your own sandwich" menu, and staff will accommodate kids' tastes with less-than-gourmet fare such as American cheese. Baked goods, including ginger molasses cookies, are homemade. The Pig always ranks high in surveys for best cup of coffee in Chicago, so don't miss one of the four varieties brewed daily, or one of a mind-bending array of espresso drinks. Juices, shakes, and root beer made here are also great bets. You'll feel comfortable bringing kids in, as there are often a couple sets of parents with strollers parked inside. Treat the kids to an ice cream for dessert.

738 W. Fullerton Pkwy. (at Burling). © 773/883-5282. High chairs, boosters. Main courses under $10. AE, DISC, MC, V. Mon–Thurs 6:30am–11pm; Fri 6:30am–midnight; Sat 8am–midnight; Sun 8am–11pm. Subway/El: Red or Brown Line to Fullerton. Bus: 8, 11, or 74.

Café Brauer ⓖ AMERICAN   A postcard-perfect view of the skyscrapers on North Michigan Avenue, plus Lake Michigan and the greenery of Lincoln Park make this a step above the average microbrewery. Stop here for lunch during a tour of the park, and grab a sandwich, kabob, or flatbread. (Brats and shrimp kabobs are among my favorites.) This pond-side cafe is conveniently near the Lincoln Park Zoo and reopened its doors to the public in 1990 after a major restoration. The beer garden, full of flowers and greenery, is perfectly family-friendly.

2021 Stockton Dr. © 312/742-2480. High chairs, boosters. Main courses under $8. AE, DC, DISC, MC, V. Mon–Sat 11am–8pm, Sun noon–8pm; winter hours for restaurant, 11–5 daily; beer garden Thurs–Sun 11–7. Bus: 151 or 156.

El Jardin MEXICAN   The staff at this sometimes raucous and always fun restaurant loves to cater to kids. Because it's just 3 blocks south of Wrigley Field (that's where the "raucous" comes in), don't show up after a game unless you're prepared for a long wait. At other times you'll be able to walk right in and grab a table in one of the two main dining rooms, the sidewalk cafe, or the backyard garden. The solid Mexican fare should keep both kids and grown-ups happy. Kids might try tacos, enchiladas, burritos, grilled chicken, or carne asada. Little ones can try *sopa de fideo,* a simple noodle soup. Should you have a special occasion to celebrate, the staff will happily trot out a flan decorated with candles. Don't confuse this location with El Jardin Fiesta Cantina Bar, a bar/dance club located a few doors north on Clark Street. On Sunday, try the Fiesta Buffet, served from 11am to 3pm. The buffet includes about 20 items, including soups and egg, beef, chicken, and pork dishes for $9.95.

3335 N. Clark St. © 773/528-6775. High chairs, boosters. Main courses $8–$15. AE, DC, DISC, V. Sun–Thurs 11:30am–11pm; Fri–Sat 11:30am–midnight. Subway/El: Red, Brown or Purple Line to Belmont.

Flat Top Grill ASIAN   This create-your-own-stir-fry restaurant often has lines, but never fear, they move quickly. Kids love creating their own dishes, and if you've never been here before, you might want to follow the suggested recipes on the giant blackboards. Choose from over 80 fresh ingredients including rice, noodles, seafood, chicken, beef, veggies, and sauces—all for one low price. Best yet, the price includes multiple visits to the food line (a lifesaver if your brilliant culinary combination has gone awry). Other locations are at 1000 W. Washington Blvd. (© 312/829-4800) in the Randolph Street Market District, and at 3200 N. Southport Ave. (© 773/665-8100) in Wrigleyville.

319 W. North Ave. © 312/787-7676. www.flattopgrill.com. Kids' menu, high chairs, boosters. Main courses lunch around $9, dinner around $12; kids' stir-fry (under age 11) $5. AE, DC, DISC, MC, V. Sun–Thurs 11am–10pm; Fri–Sat 11am–11pm. Bus: 76.

John Barleycorn AMERICAN/BURGERS Want to get a feel of what it's like to live in a Chicago neighborhood? Stop in to John Barleycorn, which has been a popular neighborhood pub and restaurant since the 1960s. There's a heavy emphasis on food here, so you won't feel like you're taking your kids to a bar. Located in a 19th-century building, the restaurant has that well-worn feel that makes you feel immediately at home. You won't find any pretensions here: Relax with a cold drink and a thick, juicy burger in the outdoor patio. The pub has a storied history, and reputedly served John Dillinger frequently when operating as a speakeasy in the 1920s. A collection of handmade ship models or a quick game of darts should entertain your kids while you're waiting for your food.

658 W. Belden Ave. © 773/348-8899. High chairs, boosters. Reservations not accepted. All main courses under $8. AE, DISC, V. Mon–Fri 3pm–2am; Sat 9am–3am; Sun 9am–2am. Subway/El: Red Line to Fullerton.

John's Place ★★★ AMERICAN This neighborhood favorite combines uncomplicated food with an inviting setting of exposed brick walls and hardwood floors. Families make up a fair share of the crowd at lunch, through the afternoon to early dinner. Although the place wasn't designed to attract kids, it's a natural for the sophisticated 30-something parents who populate the neighborhood and first came to John's while dating. The menu emphasizes vegetarian meals, organic foods, and salads. Some of the highlights of the menu are seafood enchiladas, barbecue-glazed pork tenderloin, and of course, the burgers. The wild line-caught Alaskan salmon, which comes seared as a sandwich at lunchtime, is a knockout. On the weekend, health-conscious eaters will enjoy the free-range Amish chicken eggs served during brunch, and kids are sure to go for pumpkin pancakes and French toast. On a busy afternoon, all 25 of the restaurant's high chairs are put to use.

1200 W. Webster Ave. © 773/525-6670. High chairs, boosters. Kids' menu. Reservations not accepted. All main courses under $8. AE, DISC, V. Tues–Thurs 11am–10pm; Fri 11am–11pm; Sat 8am–11pm; Sun 8am–9pm. Subway/El: Red Line to Fullerton.

La Creperie ★★ *Finds* FRENCH Germain and Sara Roignant have run this intimate gem of a cafe since 1972, never straying from the reasonably priced crepes that draw repeat customers aplenty. (Hey, a crepe is just a pancake rolled up, right kids?) The decor is heavy on '70s era brown, but if you find the main dining room more dark than cozy, head to the back patio (enclosed in winter), which sparkles with strings of white lights. Onion soup, pâté, and escargots are all good starters, but the highlights here are the whole-wheat crepes—each prepared on a special grill that Germain imported from his native Brittany. Single-choice fillings include cheese, tomato, egg, or ham; tasty duets feature chicken and mushroom or broccoli and cheese. Beef bourguignon, coq au vin, or curried chicken are the more adventurous crepe combinations. Noncrepe offerings are few: orange roughy and steak frites. Don't leave without at least sharing one of the dessert crepes, which tuck anything from apples to ice cream within their warm folds. La Creperie is an especially great option if you're taking in a show at one of the nearby off-Loop theaters, such as Briar Street, where the popular Blue Man Group is in residence.

2845 N. Clark St. (½ block north of Diversey Pkwy.). © 773/528-9050. High chairs, boosters. Reservations accepted for groups of 6 or more only. Main courses $5.50–$15. AE, DC, DISC, MC, V. Tues–Fri 11:30am–3:30pm and 5–11pm; Sat 11am–11pm; Sun 11am–9:30pm. Subway/El: Brown Line to Diversey.

Nookies DINER   This "chain" of three restaurants is a Chicago favorite for standard breakfast fare. On weekends you'll find Nookies packed with families and young professionals grabbing pancakes or an omelet after a late night out. This family-owned chain offers breakfast all day, plus soups, salads, and sandwiches. Tables and a lunch counter are available. Nookies has additional branches in Lincoln Park at 2114 N. Halsted St. (✆ **773/327-1400**), and in Lakeview at 3334 N. Halsted St. (✆ **773/248-9888**).

1748 N. Wells St. ✆ **312/337-2454**. High chairs, boosters. Reservations not accepted. All main courses under $8. Cash only. Mon–Sat 6:30am–10pm; Sun 6:30am–9pm. Subway/El: Brown Line to Sedgwick.

Stanley's ★★ AMERICAN   Here's another great neighborhood bar and restaurant that stands in the heart of Lincoln Park, normally the epicenter of the young and the restless, but instead caters to families. Stanley's front room is a bar with several booths, tall tables with old chrome and leather bar stools, satellite- and cable-fed TVs, and a jukebox. The adjacent dining room is an abrupt leap into the family den, decorated with photos, quilts, bowling trophies, and children's drawings. This popular family spot has a special kids' menu with corn dogs and PB&J. On Saturday and Sunday there's an all-you-can-eat brunch buffet, featuring make-your-own omelets, build-your-own Belgian waffles, home-fried potatoes, fried chicken, and mashed potatoes for $11. Daily specials are posted on the chalkboard out front.

1970 N. Lincoln Ave. ✆ **312/642-0007**. Kids' menu, high chairs, boosters. Main courses $8–$15; kids' menu $4. Mon–Tues 5pm–2am; Wed–Fri 11:30am–2am; Sat 11am–3am; Sun 11am–2am. Bus: 11 or 73 to Armitage.

Toast ★ AMERICAN/BREAKFAST   Located in Lincoln Park, Toast is homey yet slightly funky—note the shelf of vintage toasters. Kids are welcome here: The crayons and butcher-block table coverings will keep them busy, and the staff has a reputation for being baby and kid crazy. Breakfast is served all day and includes a twist on the usual diner fare. Pancakes come in all sorts of tempting varieties, from lemon/poppy seed drizzled with honey to the "pancake orgy" of a strawberry, mango, and banana-pecan pancake topped with granola, yogurt, and honey. (Try it: It tastes even better than it looks!). The house specialty is French toast stuffed with mascarpone cheese and strawberry purée. If pancakes equal dessert for you, try one of the omelets or the breakfast burrito. On the side, you can order grilled chicken sausage, apple-wood smoked bacon, or, of course, a stack of toast. Fresh-squeezed orange juice and grapefruit juice are also available. The lunch menu includes a range of creative sandwiches, salads, and wraps. Toast has a second location in at 2046 N. Damen Ave. (✆ **773/772-5600**).

746 W. Webster St. (at Halsted St.). ✆ **773/935-5600**. High chairs, boosters. Reservations not accepted. Breakfast $5–$10. AE, DC, DISC, MC, V. Tues–Fri 7am–4pm; Sat–Sun 8am–4pm. Subway/El: Red Line to Fullerton.

Twin Anchors ★ BARBECUE   Come early (around 5pm—later on, there's more of a bar scene) and experience this Old Town landmark; a fixture since the end of Prohibition, Twin Anchors manages to maintain the flavor of old Chicago. Actually, it also has a flavor of a supper club in northern Wisconsin, which is perhaps why so many transplanted small-town Midwesterners feel comfortable here. It's a friendly, family-owned pub with Frank Sinatra on the jukebox and on the walls. (He apparently hung out here on swings through town in the 1960s.) This totally unpretentious place has a long mahogany bar up front and a modest dining room in back with red Formica-topped tables crowded close. Of course, you don't need anything fancy when the ribs—the fall-off-the-bone variety—come this good. Even non–meat eaters may be swayed if they allow themselves one bite of the enormous slabs of tender baby back pork ribs. (Go for the zesty sauce.) Hamburgers will keep kids happy. Ribs and other entrees come with coleslaw and dark rye bread, plus your choice of baked potato, tasty fries, and the even-better crisp onion rings. For dessert, there's a daily cheesecake selection.

1655 N. Sedgwick St. (1 block north of North Ave.). © 312/266-1616. www.twinanchorsribs.com. Kids' menu, high chairs, boosters. Reservations not accepted. Main courses $9.95–$20; sandwiches $6.75–$8.75; kids' menu around $5. AE, DC, DISC, MC, V. Mon–Thurs 5–11pm; Fri 5pm–midnight; Sat noon–midnight; Sun noon–10:30pm. Subway/El: Brown Line to Sedgwick.

7 Wrigleyville & the North Side

Families visiting the area surrounding Wrigley Field will probably be in the neighborhood for that very reason—Wrigley Field. The area, however, has a long history of being a neighborhood of working-class families. Lately, it's gentrified as developers have built new town houses and apartments, and with that affluence has come a group of new, very popular restaurants spanning a range of culinary offerings and price ranges. Throughout the North Side you'll find a wealth of ethnic restaurants that allow diners to embark on further gastronomic globetrotting.

MODERATE

Buca di Beppo ITALIAN   Always fantasized about being part of a wacky, extended Italian family? You'll feel you've found your home at this Italian-American restaurant (part of a national chain). The restaurant serves humongous family-style dishes in a catacomb-like setting of six cozy rooms. (The decor is eclectic, covered with garage-sale-type mementos gathered by the owners in Italy.) The restaurant is a loud, high-energy place with large groups of diners. Request the "Pope Room," which features pontiff memorabilia and one special thronelike chair at its round table that has room for a pope and his 13 bishops. Portions are huge—one order of chicken cacciatore serves up to five people, pizzas are measured in feet, not inches, and meatballs weigh a half-pound each. Even the smaller portions of pasta serve up to three people.

2941 N. Clark St. © 773/348-7673. High chairs, boosters. Reservations not accepted, but you can call ahead to put your name on the list before you arrive at the restaurant. Main courses $7.95–$21. AE, DC, DISC, MC, V. Mon–Thurs 5–10pm; Fri 4–11pm; Sat 2–11pm; Sun noon–10pm. Subway/El: Brown Line to Wellington. Bus: 8.

INEXPENSIVE

Ann Sather ★★ SWEDISH/AMERICAN/BREAKFAST   A sign hanging by Ann Sather's door bears the following inscription: ONCE ONE OF MANY NEIGHBORHOOD SWEDISH RESTAURANTS, ANN SATHER'S IS THE ONLY ONE THAT REMAINS. Ann Sather is a real Chicago institution, where you can enjoy Swedish meatballs with buttered noodles and brown gravy, or the Swedish sampler of duck breast with lingonberry glaze, meatball, potato-sausage dumpling, sauerkraut, and brown beans. All meals are full dinners, including appetizer, main course, vegetable, potato, and dessert. It's the sticky cinnamon rolls served at breakfast, though, that make addicts out of diners. Weekend brunch here can get frenzied, so get here before 11am, but the people-watching is priceless: a cross-section of gay and straight, young and old.

There are several other branches that serve only breakfast and lunch: a restaurant in Wicker Park, at 1448 N. Milwaukee Ave. (© 773/394-1812), and smaller cafes in Lakeview at 3411 N. Broadway (© 773/305-0024) and 3416 N. Southport Ave. (© 773/404-4475).

929 W. Belmont Ave. (between Clark St. and Sheffield Ave.). © 773/348-2378. High chairs, boosters. Reservations accepted for parties of 6 or more only. Main courses $7–$12. AE, DC, MC, V. Daily 7am–9pm. Free parking with validation. Subway/El: Red Line to Belmont.

O'Donovan's *Finds* AMERICAN   This century-old neighborhood restaurant and jovial pub was sold by the Schulien family in 1999, but thankfully the new owners have kept up the tradition that has thrilled kids for decades: Magicians perform tableside tricks on Saturday evenings. (To avoid the bar-oriented rush, come early, at 5 or 6pm.) Although there's no kids' menu, ordering appetizers for the kids works just as well. For adults, burgers are the thing, although options also include steaks, chops, and seafood. As the night progresses, O'Donovan's draws a good mix of late-20-something blue- and white-collar patrons with a healthy selection of microbrews. On Sunday the expansive buffet features all-you-can-eat scrambled eggs, bacon, sausage, carved ham, roast beef, waffles, and omelets made to order and biscuits and gravy; it costs $7.95.

2100 W. Irving Park Rd. © 773/478-2100. High chairs. Reservations not accepted. Main courses $6–$16. AE, MC, V. Tues–Thurs 4–10pm; Fri–Sat 4–11pm; Sun 10am–3pm. Subway/El: Brown Line to Irving Park. Bus: 11 or 80.

Penny's Noodle Shop ★ *Value* ASIAN/NOODLES   Predating many of Chicago's Pan-Asian noodle shops, Penny's has kept its loyal following even as others have joined the fray. Penny Chiarnopoulous, a Thai native, has assembled a concise menu of delectable dishes, all of them fresh and made to order—and at prices that will make you do a double-take. The two dining rooms are clean and spare. The Thai spring roll, filled with seasoned tofu, cucumber, bean sprouts, and strips of cooked egg, makes a refreshing starter. Of course, noodles unite everything on the menu, so your main decision is choosing among noodles (crispy wide rice, rice vermicelli, Japanese udon, and so on) in a heaping bowl of soup or spread out on a plate. There are several barbecued pork and beef entrees, and plenty of options for vegetarians. The original Penny's, tucked under the El tracks at 3400 N. Sheffield Ave., near Wrigley Field (© **773/281-8222**), is small and often has long waits; you stand a better chance of scoring a table at the Diversey Avenue location (address below) or the one in Wicker Park, at 1542 N. Damen Ave. (© **773/394-0100**).

950 W. Diversey Ave. (at Sheffield St.). © 773/281-8448. High chairs, boosters. Reservations not accepted. Main courses $4.50–$7.95. MC, V. Sun–Thurs 11am–10pm; Fri–Sat 11am–10:30pm. Subway/El: Brown Line to Diversey.

Uncommon Ground ★ *Finds* BREAKFAST/SANDWICHES   A living-room atmosphere created by a wood-burning stove and artwork on the walls that rotates frequently (and is always available for purchase), Uncommon Ground is home to local artists, musicians, and writers. (Five nights a week, you can check out a performance in the back room by a local trying to make the big time— highly recommended for families with teens.) Thankfully for families, the atmosphere is 100% smoke-free. Its menu is heartier and more extensive than most Chicago coffeehouses. Indulge in steaming bowls of latte and hot chocolate and some of the yummy baked goods or choose from the menu, which is heavy on breakfast foods like nutty oatmeal with bananas; the "uncommon" breakfast burrito, a croissant with ham, egg, and cheese; and granola piled with fresh fruit and yogurt. One can't-miss choice is the apple-pecan whole-wheat pancakes with cranberry-honey butter. Lunchtime means sandwiches, hummus platter, and offerings of wine and beer. Pick a prime spot on the window seats, piled with cozy cushions. Teens will get a kick out of the Midwest's alternative press on hand here, from the *Reader* to the *Onion,* for your reading pleasure.

1214 W. Grace St. (at Clark St.). ✆ 773/929-3680. Kids' menu, high chairs, boosters. Main courses $3–$10; kids' menu $2–$5. AE, DC, DISC, MC, V. Sun–Thurs 9am–11pm; Fri–Sat 9am–midnight. Subway/El: Red Line to Addison. Bus: 22.

8 Wicker Park/Bucktown

The booming Wicker Park/Bucktown area followed closely in the race to gentrification on the heels of Lincoln Park and Wrigleyville. First came the artists, photographers, and musicians, followed by armies of yuppies and young families, originally following the cheap rents and real estate, and later chasing the cachet that became attached to the neighborhood. Happily, what's now one of the city's hippest restaurant scenes includes a number of fun options for families. Get yourself to the nexus of activity at the intersection of North, Damen, and Milwaukee avenues, and you won't have to walk more than a couple of blocks in any direction to find a hot spot. (***Note to parents of teens:*** The house featured on MTV's *Real World Chicago* is just south of this intersection, on North Ave., the north side of the street.) Cab fare is within reason from downtown, or you can take the El's Blue Line to Damen.

INEXPENSIVE

Northside Café ★ *Value* AMERICAN/BURGERS   I highly recommend this spot for high-quality cheap eats. Northside cooks up great burgers, sandwiches, and salads, all for under $10. This is strictly neighborhood dining, without attitude and little in the way of decor. The back dining room looks like a rec room circa 1973, complete with a fireplace, pinball machines, and a pool table. In nice weather Northside opens up its large patio for dining, and a sky-lit cover keeps it in use during the winter. You're sure to be entertained people-watching, as Northside attracts all sorts. During the week it's more of a neighborhood hangout, but on the weekends a touristy crowd from Lincoln Park and the suburbs moves in.

1635 N. Damen Ave. (at North and Milwaukee aves.). ✆ 773/384-3555. High chairs, boosters. Reservations not accepted. Menu items $5.95–$11. AE, DC, DISC, MC, V. Sun–Fri 11:30am–2am; Sat 11am–3am. Subway/El: Blue Line to Damen.

Silver Cloud Bar & Grill ★ DINER   How can kids not feel at home here? Silver Cloud is one of few Chicago restaurants I know that has tater tots on the menu (and naturally, every time I eat here, I work my entire meal selection around this "side"). This Bucktown restaurant's motto is FOOD LIKE MOM WOULD MAKE IF SHE WAS GETTING PAID. Although the food isn't extraordinary, it should please kids. The grilled cheese is made with mozzarella, Monterey Jack, and cheddar on Italian bread and served with a bowl of Campbell's tomato soup. Other favorites are chicken potpie, pot roast, and even sloppy joes. Retro desserts include s'mores and root beer floats. Roomy red leather booths are a hit with families. In good weather sit outside (the seating area is on the side street, so you avoid the noise of Damen Ave.). A sign at the bar asks WHY NOT ENJOY A NICE, RIPE CIGAR?—but never fear, families, there's no lighting up until after 10pm. This place is not a tourist hot spot, so enjoy the people-watching—most customers are neighborhood folks. You might try the Sunday brunch, which is especially popular.

1700 N. Damen Ave. (at Wabansia St.). ✆ 773/489-6212. www.silvercloudchicago.com. High chairs, boosters. Reservations accepted. Main courses $6.50–$10 lunch, $6.50–$13 dinner. AE, DC, MC, V. Mon–Thurs 11:30am–11pm; Fri 11:30am–midnight; Sat–Sun 10am–midnight. Subway/El: Blue Line to Damen.

Dining in Wicker Park/Bucktown

Northside Café **2**
Silver Cloud Bar & Grill **1**

9 Only in Chicago

Pizza-loving and hot dog–inhaling kids have it made in Chicago: We've turned them from fast food into art forms. Of course, Chicagoans have their own take on these all-American staples, so to have an authentic taste of Chicago, shun the thin-crust pizza and ketchup as condiment of choice for hot dogs. Try them our way, and I guarantee you'll understand why Chicagoans are passionate about their dogs and pizza.

PIZZA

To the uninitiated: Chicago-style pizza, also known as deep-dish, is thick-crusted and often demands a knife and fork. The thin-crust variety favored in New York is also widely available; a third type, called stuffed, is similar to a pie, with a crust on both top and bottom. Many pizzerias serve both thick and thin, and some make all three kinds. Three of Chicago's best gourmet deep-dish restaurants are **Pizzeria Uno** (p. 129), **Pizzeria Due** (p. 129), and **Gino's East** (p. 128).

In River North **Lou Malnati's Pizzeria** ✿, at 439 N. Wells St. (© **312/828-9800**), bakes both deep-dish and thin-crust pizza and even has a low-fat cheese option. **Edwardo's** is a local pizza chain that serves all three varieties, but with a wheat crust and all-natural ingredients. (Try the tasty spinach pizza, the specialty here.) It has several Chicago locations, including one in the Gold Coast, at 1212 N. Dearborn St., at Division Street (© **312/337-4490**); one in

Printers Row in the South Loop, at 521 S. Dearborn St. (© **312/939-3366**); and one in Lincoln Park, at 2662 N. Halsted St. (© **773/871-3400**). Very near to the Lincoln Park Zoo is **Ranalli's Pizzeria, Libations & Collectibles,** 1925 N. Lincoln Ave. (© **312/642-4700**), with its terrific open-air patio.

In Wrigleyville, just off Belmont Avenue, are **Leona's Pizzeria,** 3215 N. Sheffield Ave. (© **773/327-8861**), and **Pat's Pizzeria,** 3114 N. Sheffield Ave. (© **773/248-0168**), both of which serve all three kinds of pizza. Leona's also has a location in Little Italy, at 1419 W. Taylor St. (© **312/850-2222**), and Pat's has one downtown in the Athletic Club Illinois Center, at 211 N. Stetson Ave. (© **312/946-0220**).

For a unique take on the deep-dish phenomenon, try the "pizza potpie" at **Chicago Pizza & Oven Grinder,** 2121 N. Clark St., steps from Lincoln Park Zoo (© **773/248-2570**); the pizzas are baked in a bowl and then turned over when served, for a distinctive upside-down pizza experience.

HOT DOGS

Chicagoans like to think that they stand head and skewers above the rest of the world when it comes to hot dogs. The facades of Chicago's hot-dog stands, as if by some unwritten convention, are all very colorful, with bright signs of red and yellow, exaggerated lettering, and comic illustrations of the wieners and fries. The classic Chicago hot dog includes a frankfurter by Vienna Beef (a local food processor and hallowed institution), heaps of chopped onions and relish so green it could be pop art, a slather of yellow mustard, pickle spears and fresh tomato wedges, a dash of celery salt, and, for good measure, two or three "sport" peppers, those thumb-shaped holy terrors that turn your mouth into its own bonfire.

Chicago is home to many standout hot-dog stands and shops, such as **Gold Coast Dogs,** 418 N. State St., at Hubbard Street (© **312/527-1222**), 2 blocks off North Michigan Avenue. **Fluky's,** in The Shops at North Bridge mall at 520 N. Michigan Ave. (© **312/245-0702**), is part of a local chain that has been serving great hot dogs since the Great Depression. **Portillo's,** at 100 W. Ontario St. (© **312/587-8910;** www.portillos.com), is another local chain that specializes in hot dogs but also serves excellent pastas and salads. **Murphy's Red Hots,** 1211 W. Belmont Ave. (© **773/935-2882**), is a neighborhoody spot not too far from Wrigley Field. Besides hot dogs, Murphy's serves charbroiled Polish sausages, burgers, and tasty hand-cut fries. **The Wieners Circle,** in Lincoln Park at 2622 N. Clark St. (© **773/477-7444**), is a favorite where rude order-takers are part of the shtick.

But if you ask the locals for their sentimental favorite, we'll most likely steer you to the legendary **Superdawg Drive-In,** 6363 N. Milwaukee (© **773/763-0660**), at the intersection of Milwaukee, Devon, and Nagle avenues. It's impossible to miss: Mr. and Mrs. Superdawg, in Tarzan and Jane tableaux, beckon the masses from the rooftop, their beady eyes pulsing an electric red. Maurie and Florrie Berman haven't changed a thing about their place—the city's last real drive-in, with its Order-Matic ordering system and female carhops on roller skates—since they opened for business in 1948. Their main attraction still arrives in a red 1950s-design enclosed box that declares on one side, YOUR SUPERDAWG LOUNGES INSIDE, CONTENTEDLY CUSHIONED IN SUPERFRIES.

Exploring Chicago with Your Kids

While Chicago has sights that top any world traveler's list (although fewer than New York or London), Chicago offers big family attractions, too. Part of Chicago's kid-friendliness comes from the location of our major museums, which sit within walking distance of beaches and miles of parks. Kids can learn in the morning and run free in the afternoon. Compared to some major cities, outdoor space is easy to find, thanks to miles of unimpeded lakefront. And as every parent knows, being outdoors is a welcome relief when kids need to let off steam.

Although crowds do pack the major museums on weekends and holidays, the crowdedness is not on the level of New York City on a similar day.

Summer is prime time here: Families flock *to* Chicago on the weekends—unlike other urban areas, where families *escape from* the city. When the weather is warm, you'll find that suburbanites, Wisconsinites, Iowans, and families from other surrounding states head to our city to enjoy the cool lake breezes.

Chicago's a no-nonsense Midwestern city, and most establishments are laid-back and open-minded. You won't get the kind of urban snobbery you might experience in other big cities. For the most part, Chicagoans are "nice"—another Midwestern quality—meaning you are more likely to get a sympathetic smile than the evil eye when trying to calm a crying child.

SIGHTSEEING SUGGESTIONS

If You Have 1 Day

Get thee on the water: Take a boat tour of the Chicago River and Lake Michigan. Even if your kids are small, they'll enjoy being on the water, and adults will enjoy learning about our spectacular architecture. (Chicago is a showcase of modern architecture; for more on our best buildings, pick up *Frommer's Chicago.*) Some tours take you up and down the Chicago River, then through locks that release the boat into Lake Michigan. You'll see first-hand that the Chicago River is one of the engineering marvels of our nation; its flow was reversed to move backwards from the lake, not into it, in order to prevent river water from polluting Lake Michigan.

Back on land, head south to the **Museum of Science and Industry,** the classic Chicago kids' attraction that never fails to enthrall. Afterward, head back to the city to dine at a restaurant near Michigan Avenue and the **Magnificent Mile.** Finish off the day with a stroll along the boulevard and up the **lakefront.** Although you won't see the sun set over the lake (remember, the lake is always to the east), the colors can be spectacular anyway. (Interestingly, on the other side of the lake, those in Michigan and Indiana have the opposite view: They never see the sun rise over the lake, only set.)

If You Have 2 Days

Stroll around **the Loop** to see the buildings and the city's extensive

Central Chicago Attractions

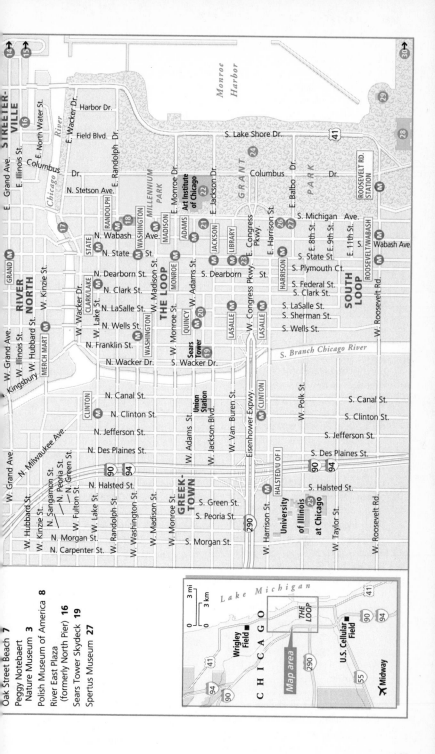

Oak Street Beach **7**
Peggy Notebaert
Nature Museum **3**
Polish Museum of America **8**
River East Plaza
(formerly North Pier) **16**
Sears Tower Skydeck **19**
Spertus Museum **27**

sculpture collection. You can do a self-guided tour or one organized by the **Chicago Architecture Foundation** (the early-skyscraper tour is a good primer). Round out your day with a shopping trip, or even just a window-shopping tour, up the **Magnificent Mile,** and make a trip to the top of the **John Hancock Center.**

In the evening, if the Cubs are in town, take the El uptown and catch a night game at **Wrigley Field.** Dine on hot dogs or bratwurst while you sip a beer and the kids polish off cotton candy and licorice whips.

If You Have 3 Days

If you can add a third day to your stay, explore the Near North Side. Stroll north along Michigan Avenue, starting from the Chicago River. You might want to stop to admire the gothic **Tribune Tower,** just north of the river on the east side of Michigan Avenue. The tower is home to one of the country's media giants, which owns WGN television and radio and the *Chicago Tribune* newspaper.

If your kids are old enough and mobile enough, continue walking north all the way up the Magnificent Mile, until you reach **Lake Shore Drive.** (If you're not in the mood to stroll, catch the no. 151 bus.) Here, you can cross under a pedestrian tunnel to **Oak Street Beach.** Keep walking north until you reach Fullerton Avenue, where you can wander around **Lincoln Park Zoo** and visit the **Farm-in-the-Zoo,** see the famed gorilla house, and check out Chicago's newest addition to its museum roster, the **Peggy Notebaert Nature Museum,** with its spectacular butterfly house.

In the evening, catch a show. You might find a musical playing in one of the **North Loop theater district**'s many venues, or you can check out the kid-pleasing **Blue Man Group** at Briar Street Theatre in Lincoln Park.

If You Have 4 Days or More

On your fourth day, head to an outlying neighborhood or suburb. If your kids are 6 years or older, they might enjoy west suburban **Oak Park,** where special guided Youth Architectural Tours of **The Frank Lloyd Wright Home & Studio** cater to kids 6 to 14.

Many homes in the area were built or influenced by Wright, so if it's a nice day, make sure to take a stroll around the neighborhood. If you have a car, top off the day with a stop at **Peterson's** for their house specialty turtle sundae. See chapter 11 for more information.

If the Weather's Hot

During steamy Midwestern summer days, the best place to be is on the lake. Head for **Navy Pier,** where you can board **Seadog speedboat.** This sleek, bright yellow boat seats 149 passengers and jets across the lake while guides give a narrated tour of facts and tales about Navy Pier, the lakefront, and the skyline.

When you're safely docked again at Navy Pier, you might want to head indoors to the air-conditioned comfort of the **OMNIMAX Theater** at the Museum of Science and Industry, or simply stroll the pier. (Your reward for going all the way to the end of the ¾-mile-long pier is one of the best views of the city.) Those not afraid of heights can take a ride on the 15-story Ferris wheel and enjoy the spectacular view of Chicago's skyline. The pier is always packed with musicians, and inside you'll find shops and restaurants.

If the Weather's Cold

Parents rave about **Garfield Park Conservatory.** The location is slightly off the beaten path in a run-down neighborhood, but there is parking in a lot with security guards.

South Michigan Avenue & Grant Park Attractions

Adler Planetarium & Astronomy Museum **6**
Art Institute of Chicago **2**
Buckingham Fountain **3**
Chicago Cultural Center **1**
Field Museum of Natural History **5**
John G. Shedd Aquarium **4**
National Vietnam Veterans Art Museum **7**

Hyde Park Attractions

DuSable Museum of African-American History **2**
Museum of Science and Industry **5**
Oriental Institute Museum **4**
Robie House **3**
The Smart Museum of Art **1**

Attendance went up 400% here in a single year with the glass sculpture exhibit by artist Dave Chihuly. The jury is still out on if the exposure from that show will have a residual effect on attendance, but chances are, you won't be alone. Inside, check out the Elizabeth Morse Genius Children's Garden, where exhibits show a giant bee pollinating an enormous flower and demonstrate how the sun's rays spark photosynthesis in a plant leaf. A digging area (consisting of a huge pile of dirt and digging toys), waterfall, and slide from the second-story mezzanine (along with the fact that the plants here can be touched) make this a great hands-on adventure for kids.

If You Have a Sitter

If you've managed to arrange for some couple time, book yourself a romantic table for two at one of Chicago's great grown-up restaurants. A sleek, non-kid-friendly spot is **Café des Architectes,** located in the Sofitel, 20 E. Chestnut St., at Rush Street (© **312/324-4000**). The modern and elegant decor combines shades of purple with white leather banquettes. The food is modern French, and the service is solicitous. Specialties include a starter of grilled shrimp over bright purple, beet-infused couscous. One wonderfully unique entree is the melt-in-your-mouth butterfish, caught off the coasts of Portugal and France and flown in daily from Europe. If you're single, head to the **Art Institute** and linger over the Impressionists, then head outdoors to the cafe for a leisurely glass of wine and a sandwich while you watch the world go by on Michigan Avenue.

It wouldn't be Chicago if you didn't get a taste of the blues: In fact, you just might decide that getting the blues is a good thing when you top off your evening at **Buddy Guy's Legends,** 754 S. Wabash Ave., between Balbo and Eighth streets in the South Loop (© **312/427-0333**).

Everyone from Eric Clapton to Muddy Waters has stopped in to jam and listen to the best in blues at this club, owned and operated by Chicago blues legend Buddy Guy. Every January, Guy himself plays a series of shows—if you're in town, don't miss it. Those shows always sell out early, so call in advance. The cover charge ranges from $6 to $15.

1 Sights by Neighborhood

2 Kids' Top 10 Attractions

Adler Planetarium & Astronomy Museum **All ages.** This, the Western Hemisphere's first planetarium, was built by Sears, Roebuck and Co. executive Max Adler, who imported a Zeiss projector from Germany in 1930. Today even the most jaded video-game addict will thrill at the ride into outer space at the world's first StarRider virtual-reality theater, which propels passengers on an exhilarating voyage of discovery into the infinity of space. You participate in the journey by operating controls on the armrests. Six high-resolution video projectors form a seamless image above your head—you'll feel like you're literally floating in space. On Thursday, Friday, and Saturday nights, the theater is open late for SonicVision, a head-trippy digital animation show with an alternative-music soundtrack. The mind-blowing theater is part of the 60,000-square-foot "Sky Pavilion," which wraps itself around the 1920-built planetarium like a high-tech glass visor. Four exhibition galleries, Galileo's cafe (with stunning views of Chicago's skyline), and a gift shop round out the Pavilion's offerings. Of special interest is the planetarium's signature exhibit, **From the Night Sky to the Big Bang,** which traces changing views of the cosmos over 1,000 years and features artifacts from the planetarium's extensive collection of historical astronomical instruments. (*Warning:* Unless your kid is a real astronomy fan, this exhibit can get a bit boring). On the first Friday evening of the month, visitors can view dramatic close-ups of the moon, planets, and distant galaxies through a closed-circuit monitor connected to the planetarium's Doane Observatory telescope.

To find out what to look for in this month's sky, call the Nightwatch 24-Hour Hot Line (© **312/922-STAR**), or check out the planetarium's website.

Families might want to make a point of visiting during **"Far Out Fridays,"** from 5 to 10pm, which feature special activities suited to kids, including telescope viewings and sky shows.

1300 S. Lake Shore Dr. © **312/322-STAR**. Fax 312/322-2257. www.adlerplanetarium.org. Admission (including 1 show) $13 adults, $12 seniors, $11 children 4–17, free for children under 4. Free admission Mon–Tues Sept–Feb only (except the last 2 weeks of Dec). Mon–Fri 9:30am–4:30pm; Sat–Sun 9am–4:30pm; 1st Fri of every month until 10pm; open until 6pm daily Memorial Day to Labor Day. StarRider Theater and Sky Shows at numerous times throughout the day; call © 312/922-STAR for current times. Bus: 12 or 146.

Chicago Children's Museum ☺☺ **All ages.** Parents rave about the Chicago Children's Museum, now in existence for over 20 years. Since it moved to Navy Pier in 1996, the museum has become one of the most popular cultural attractions in the city. The three-story museum has areas especially for preschoolers as well as for children up to age 10. Several permanent exhibits allow kids a maximum of hands-on fun, and there are always creative temporary exhibitions on tap as well. **Dinosaur Expedition** re-creates an expedition to the Sahara, allowing kids to experience camp life, conduct scientific research, and dig for the bones of *Suchomimus,* a Saharan dinosaur recently discovered by Chicago paleontologist Paul Sereno (a full-scale model stands nearby). Another permanent exhibit, **Play It Safe,** addresses possible safety issues in an interactive house and backyard. **WaterWays** allows visitors to learn about the uses and benefits of water resources by constructing dams to direct the flow of water, constructing fountains, and teaming up with others to blast a stream of water 50 feet in the air. **Face to Face: Dealing with Prejudice and Discrimination** is a multimedia display that helps kids identify prejudice and find ways to deal with it. There's also a three-level schooner that children can board for a little climbing, from the crow's nest to the gangplank; **PlayMaze,** a toddler-scale cityscape with everything from a gas station to a city bus that children under 5 can touch and explore; and an arts-and-crafts area where visitors can create original artwork to take home. The museum store is filled with educational and multicultural books, science toys, videos, music, and art supplies.

Navy Pier, 700 E. Grand Ave. ℂ 312/527-1000. www.chichildrensmuseum.org. Admission $7 adults and children, $6 seniors. Free admission Thurs 5–8pm. Tues–Sun 10am–5pm (Thurs until 8pm). Subway/El: Red Line to Grand/State; transfer to city bus or Navy Pier's free trolley bus. Bus: 29, 56, 65, or 66.

The Field Museum of Natural History ★★★   **All ages.** Kids love the Field Museum for its wide-open spaces—we're talking 9 acres of floor space—giant dinos, and hands-on exhibits. Little ones can indulge their inner Indiana Jones by exploring the shadowy tunnels of an Egyptian tomb or feeling the thrill of a passage across the Pacific Ocean in an outrigger canoe. Or explore the African continent by visiting a royal Cameroon palace, witnessing savanna wildlife, and traveling across the Sahara and back to Nigeria. Gleaming gems, giant stuffed elephants, mummies, and Native American artifacts will have your kids enthralled. Scores of permanent and temporary exhibitions—some interactive, but most requiring the old-fashioned skills of observation and imagination—can boggle the mind with their sheer quantity. Some of the diorama-type exhibits have gotten musty over time, but many others have been completely overhauled, with plenty of activities to keep kids interested.

Start with the grand **Stanley Field Hall** (where you enter from either the north or south end). Standing proudly at the north side is the largest, most complete Tyrannosaurus rex fossil ever unearthed. Named **"Sue"** ★★ for the paleontologist who found the dinosaur in 1990 in South Dakota, the specimen was acquired by the museum for a cool $8.4 million following a high-stakes bidding war. The real skull is so heavy that a lighter copy had to be mounted on the skeleton; the actual one is displayed upstairs.

Families should head downstairs for two of the most popular kid-friendly exhibits. The pieces on display in **Inside Ancient Egypt** ✦ were brought to the museum in the early 1900s, after researchers in Saqqara, Egypt, excavated two of the original chambers from the tomb of Unis-ankh, son of the Fifth Dynasty ruler Pharaoh Unis. This *mastaba* (tomb) of Unis-ankh now forms the core of a spellbinding exhibit that realistically depicts scenes from Egyptian funeral, religious, and other social practices. Visitors can explore aspects of the day-to-day world of ancient Egypt, viewing 23 actual mummies and realistic burial scenes, a living marsh environment and canal works, the ancient royal barge, a religious shrine, and a reproduction of a typical marketplace of the period. Many of the

The Field Museum of Natural History

Upper Level

Special Exhibits Gallery–Upper Level

More on Sue

Tibet

Life Over Time

Elizabeth Morse Genius Dinosaur Hall

Fossil Prep Lab

The Sue Store

Life Over Time

Marae Gallery

Pacific Spirits

The Art Lacquer of Japan

Maori Meeting House

Traveling the Pacific

Earth Sciences

Plants of the World

Moving Earth

China

Plants of the World

Hall of Gems

Hall of Jades

GRANGER GALLERY

Main Level

NORTH ENTRANCE

World of Birds

Sue

World of Mammals

Messages from the Wilderness

Nature Walk

Plains and Southwest Indians

Special Exhibit Gallery–Main Level

Lions of Tsavo

Mammals of Asia

Pawnee Earth Lodge

Rice Wildlife Research Station

Africa

Africa Resource Center

North American Indians

Yates Exhibition Center

Mammals of Africa

Bird Habitats

Reptiles & Amphibians

Inside Ancient Egypt

Living Together

Webber Gallery

Animal Biology

What is an Animal?

STANLEY FIELD HALL

Ancient North America and Mesoamerica

The Field Museum Store

Eskimos and Northwest Coast Indians

SOUTH ENTRANCE

Elevator

Information

Special Exhibits Galleries

Stairs

Ground Level

Lecture Hall

Education Department

VENDING MACHINES

WEST ENTRANCE

James Simpson Theater

Kid's Field Trip Store

The Siragusa Center

Man-eater of Mfuwe

Special Exhibits Gallery-Ground Level

Black Box Theater

Bushman

Small Treasures Gallery

Underground Adventure

Food Court

Inside Ancient Egypt

exhibits allow hands-on interaction, and there are special activities for kids, such as making parchment from living papyrus plants.

Next to the Egypt exhibit you'll find **Underground Adventure,** a "total immersion environment" populated by giant robotic earwigs, centipedes, wolf spiders, and other subterranean critters. The Disneyesque exhibit is a big hit with kids, but—annoyingly—requires an extra admission charge ($5 on top of regular admission for adults, $2 for kids). While you're downstairs, plug a dollar bill into one of the old-fashioned wax-molding machines and watch as your very own red T-Rex or green brontosaurus is shaped in front of your eyes. Kids get a thrill out of taking home their very own Field Museum dino.

The "peoples of the world" exhibits are not only mind-opening, they're also great fun. **Traveling the Pacific** is hidden up on the second floor, but it's definitely worth a stop. Hundreds of artifacts from the museum's oceanic collection re-create scenes of island life in the South Pacific. (There's even a full-scale model of a Maori meeting house.) **Africa,** an assemblage of African artifacts and provocative, interactive multimedia presentations, takes viewers to Senegal, to a Cameroon palace, to the savanna and its wildlife, and on a "virtual" journey aboard a slave ship to the Americas. Native Chicagoans will quickly name two more signature highlights: the taxidermied bodies of **Bushman** (a legendary lowland gorilla who made international headlines while at the city's Lincoln Park Zoo) and the **Man-Eating Lions of Tsavo.** (The pair of male lions who munched nearly 140 British railway workers constructing a bridge in East Africa in 1898; their story is featured in the film *The Ghost and the Darkness.*)

The museum hosts special traveling exhibits (recent blockbusters included shows on Cleopatra and the jewels of Russia), as well as numerous lectures, book signings, multiethnic musical and dance performances, storytelling events, and family activity days throughout the year. The Corner Bakery cafe, located just off the main hall, serves fare that's a cut above the usual museum victuals. (To skip the lunchtime lines, pick up one of the premade salads or sandwiches and head for the cash register.) Families also flock to the McDonald's on the lower level. Allow about 3 hours to see it all.

Roosevelt Rd. and Lake Shore Dr. ✆ **312/922-9410** or 312/341-9299 TDD (for hearing-impaired callers). www.fieldmuseum.org. Admission $10 adults; $7 seniors and students with ID; $5 children 3–11; free for teachers, armed-forces personnel in uniform, and children 2 and under. Free admission Mon–Tues mid-Sept to Feb (except the last 2 weeks of Dec). Open daily 9am–5pm. Closed Dec 25 and Jan 1. Bus: 6, 10, 12, 130, or 146.

Hamill Family Play Zoo ★★★   **All ages.** Located within Chicago's largest zoo, the Brookfield Zoo (located in west suburban Brookfield), the Hamill Family Play Zoo lets kids talk to the animals in an up-close and personal way. In fact, the kids' zoo was designed to help kids, from infants to age 10, develop feelings of kinship with the natural world. Children can touch domesticated animals, help care for animals, search for insects under logs, watch zoo keepers prepare animal food, pretend to be a veterinarian, plant seeds, build feeders, and more. You'll find 300 individual animals from 58 species here, and specially trained staff is on hand to help make the most of your visit.

Other Brookfield Zoo exhibits let kids encounter bathing hippos and laugh at the antics of the orangutans. In total, the Brookfield Zoo is spread over 216 acres with 2,700 animals in residence. Kid favorites are Siberian tigers, snow leopards, giraffes, green sea turtles, and baboons. All the animals live in naturalistic environments that allow them to live side-by-side with other inhabitants of their regions (see the Brookfield Zoo review in the "Zoos" section later in this chapter for more information).

Tips **Do-it-yourself Sightseeing**

There comes a time in every parent's life when you decide that trying to force your kids on a guided tour (and trying to enforce good behavior while on that tour) is simply not worth it. If that's the case, an inexpensive and low-pressure way to tour the city is by hopping aboard one of Chicago's El trains or buses. And what kid doesn't love a train or bus ride? Do-it-yourselfers can take their own tour for the cost of subway or bus fare—$1.75, plus 25¢ for a transfer (good for a return trip if you use it within two hours). Here are some of the city's best sightseeing routes:

- **Brown line** (trip duration 20 min.; daily). Ride from the Loop to Belmont Station. You get a bird's-eye view of downtown, gentrified loft districts, and a number of historic neighborhoods. Start at the big El station at Clark and Lake streets and get on the northbound train.

- **No. 151 Sheridan bus** (trip duration 30 min.; daily). Pick up the 151 downtown on Michigan Avenue (the bus stops every two blocks on the avenue) and ride it north to Belmont. You cover Lake Shore Drive and Lincoln Park. If you take the bus south, you travel State Street and wind up at Union Station.

- **No. 146 Marine–Michigan bus** (trip duration 20 min.; daily). This express bus allows you to take in North Michigan Avenue, State Street, and the Museum Campus. Pick up the bus on Sheridan and Diversey going south. (You can also pick up the 146 along Michigan Avenue, although it has fewer stops than the 151.) You see the Harold Washington Library, the Art Institute of Chicago, the Chicago Cultural Center, and the landmark Water Tower.

- **No. 10 Museum of Science and Industry bus** (trip duration 35 min.; weekends year-round, daily in summer and winter holiday season). From North Michigan Avenue at the Water Tower (the stop is in front of Borders Books & Music on Michigan Ave. across from Water Tower Place), ride south to the Museum Campus. You see Grant Park, the Art Institute of Chicago, the University of Chicago, and Chinatown.

First Ave. and 31st St., Brookfield. © 708/485-0263. www.brookfieldzoo.org. Admission to Play Zoo, $3 adults, $2 seniors and children 3–11 (in addition to paying the general Brookfield Zoo admission of $8 adults, $4 seniors and children 3–11). Parking $8. Free admission Tues and Thurs Oct–Mar. Memorial Day to Labor Day daily 9:30am–6pm; fall–spring daily 10am–5pm. To reach the zoo from downtown, take I-290 W. and exit at First Ave. Turn left onto First Ave. and drive 2 miles to the zoo entrance. Subway/El: Blue Line to North Riverside; transfer to bus 304.

John G. Shedd Aquarium ★★★ **All ages.** What do kids love best about the Shedd? The dolphin show! But there's plenty more to see and do here. Thousands of denizens of river, lake, and sea populate the standard aquarium tanks and elaborate new habitats at this marble octagon building. Opened in 1930, the Shedd debuted in auspicious fashion: It boasted the greatest variety of sea life ever exhibited at one institution and was the first inland aquarium to maintain permanent exhibits of both saltwater and freshwater animals.

The first thing you'll see as you enter is the **Caribbean Coral Reef** exhibit. This 90,000-gallon circular tank occupies the Beaux Arts–style central rotunda, entertaining spectators who press up against the glass to ogle divers feeding nurse sharks, barracudas, stingrays, and a hawksbill sea turtle. New technology includes an enhanced sound system and a roving camera connected to video monitors mounted on the tank's periphery, which gives visitors close-ups of the animals inside. It's worth sticking around to catch one of the daily feedings, when a diver swims around the tank and talks into a microphone about the species inside and their eating habits.

The exhibits surrounding the Caribbean coral reef re-create different marine habitats around the world. The best is **Amazon Rising: Seasons of the River,** a 10,000-square-foot exhibit with more than 250 species of animals—including piranhas, birds, sloths, insects, spiders, snakes, caiman lizards, and monkeys—are on display in this re-creation of the Amazon basin.

You'll pay extra to see the other Shedd highlights, but they're quite impressive, so I'd suggest shelling out for at least one, assuming your kids won't run out of gas before then. The 3-million-gallon saltwater **Oceanarium** ★★ is an indoor marine mammal pavilion that re-creates a Pacific Northwest coastal environment and also happens to be the largest of its kind in the world. With its wall of windows revealing the lake outside, the Oceanarium creates a stunning optical illusion of one uninterrupted expanse of sea. As you follow a winding nature trail, you encounter beluga whales, white-sided dolphins, Alaskan sea otters, and harbor seals. A colony of penguins in a separate exhibit area inhabits a naturalistic environment meant to resemble the Falkland Islands in the southern sea off Argentina. You can observe all these sea mammals at play through large underwater viewing windows. On a fixed performance schedule in a large pool flanked by an amphitheater, a crew of friendly trainers puts the dolphins through their paces of leaping dives, breaches, and tail-walking. Check out the Oceanarium schedule as soon as you get to the Shedd; seating space fills up quickly for the shows, so you'll want to get there early. If you're visiting during a summer weekend, you may also want to buy your Oceanarium ticket in advance to make sure you can catch a show that day.

The newest signature exhibit is **Wild Reef—Sharks at Shedd** ★★, a series of 26 interconnected habitats that house a Philippine coral reef patrolled by sharks and other predators. The floor-to-ceiling windows bring the toothy swimmers up close and personal (they even swim over your head in certain spots). The Shedd mounts temporary exhibitions, so call ahead for the latest. A recent feature was Sea Star Quest, with a touch pool that made for the most interactive, kid-friendly exhibit in the Shedd's 74-year history. Look for more of the same as the Shedd strives to give guests a better first-hand understanding of sea creatures.

If you want a quality sit-down meal in a restaurant with a spectacular view of Lake Michigan, check out Soundings, right there inside the aquarium. There's also a family-friendly cafeteria. In total, you'll need about 2 hours to take in all of the Shedd's offerings.

1200 S. Lake Shore Dr. ② **312/939-2438.** www.sheddaquarium.org. All-Access Pass (to all exhibits) $21 adults, $15 seniors and children 3–11; admission to the aquarium and either Oceanarium or Wild Reef $17 adults, $13 seniors and children 3–11; aquarium only, $8 adults, $6 children and seniors. Free admission to aquarium Mon–Tues Oct–Feb (except the last 2 weeks of Dec). Mon–Fri 9am–5pm (until 6pm Memorial Day to Labor Day); Sat–Sun 9am–6pm. Bus: 6 or 146.

The Lakefront ★★★   **All ages.** Chicago was blessed with forefathers with foresight. Thanks to them, the lakefront was declared in 1836 to be public ground "to remain forever open, clear, and free" from construction—that's why you won't find warehouses, docks, and private businesses along our beautiful lakeshore, as you do in many other cities. Instead, join Chicagoans in reveling in 30 miles of sand beaches, green lawns, flower beds, and bicycle paths. More than half of the 2,800 acres of lakefront were created by filling in the lake and building a string of splendid lakeshore parks (from north to south, Lincoln, Grant, Burnham, Jackson, Rainbow, and Calumet). Chicagoans take full advantage of the lakefront to walk, rollerblade, bike, run, swim, picnic, and play volleyball. Most activity takes place around **Oak Street Beach** (just north of the Magnificent Mile) and **North Avenue Beach** (several blocks north of Oak St.). One Chicago mom told me that a favorite activity of her kids is to sit on a bench at the beach and count the dogs as they go by. It's just that simple—kids' entertainment doesn't always have to come at a price.

The Loop Sculpture Tour ★★ **Ages 5 & up.** In the spirit of emphasizing free, flexible, and outdoor activities for kids, I can't fail to note the self-guided tour that lets you navigate through Grant Park and much of the Loop to view some 100 examples of Chicago's monumental public art. With the help of a very comprehensive booklet, *Loop Sculpture Guide* ($3.95 at the gift shop in the Chicago Cultural Center, 78 E. Washington St.), you'll get detailed descriptions of 37 major works, including photographs, plus about 60 other sites located nearby, identified on a foldout map of the Loop. You also can conduct a self-guided tour of the city's public sculpture by following our "Loop Sculpture Tour" map on p. 157.

The single-most-famous sculpture is **Pablo Picasso's *Untitled,*** located in Daley Plaza and constructed out of Cor-Ten steel, the same gracefully rusting material used on the exterior of the Daley Center behind it. Perhaps because it was the buttoned-down Loop's first monumental modern sculpture, its installation in 1967 was met with hoots and heckles, but today "the Picasso" enjoys semiofficial status as the logo of modern Chicago. It is by far the city's most popular photo opportunity among visiting tourists. Kids can view the Picasso from various perspectives and try to decide: Does its mysterious shape look like a woman, a bird, or a dog? At noon on weekdays during warm-weather months, you'll likely find a dance troupe, musical group, or visual-arts exhibition there as part of the city's long-running "Under the Picasso" multicultural program. Call © **312/346-3278** for weekly updates of events.

Millennium Park ★★★ **All ages.** Chicago's latest grand public project is Millennium Park, and it is a doozy. It's not easy to create new icons for a city, but in a few years, I'd venture a guess that some of Millennium Park's installations will come to symbolize Chicago. In fact, I dare you to stand with your toes in the water at the Crown Fountain, surveying the spectacular cityscape of South Michigan Avenue, and not feel an irrepressible urge to uproot your family and move into a condo in downtown Chicago. The park is a strikingly beautiful success, and thank goodness Chicago's donors and government saw fit to overspend the budget by leaps and bounds and go far beyond the deadline for opening to ensure a place like this. It's really an example of what a modern park can be. Compare the Crown Fountain, Millennium Park's interactive fountain, with the grande dame of Chicago fountains, Buckingham Fountain (just to the south in Grant Park), which is lovely but untouchable, and you'll see how far we've come. Even the sculpture is interactive—the "bean" by Anish Kapoor is essentially a gigantic 3-D mirror. Kids and adults are equally attracted to its reflective surface and house-of-mirrors qualities. The Crown Fountain is another kid favorite,

1 *Untitled ("The Picasso"),* Pablo Picasso (1967)

2 *Chicago,* Joan Miro (1981)

3 *Monument with Standing Beast,*
Jean Dubuffet (1984)

4 *Freeform,* Richard Hunt (1993)

5 *Flight of Daedalus and Icarus,*
120 N. LaSalle St., Roger Brown (1990)

6 *Dawn Shadows,* Louise Nevelson (1983)

7 *Loomings* and *Knights and Squires,*
Frank Stella

8 *Batcolumn,* Claes Oldenburg (1977)

9 *The Universe,* Alexander Calder (1974)

10 *Gem of the Lakes,* Raymond Kaskey (1990)

11 *San Marco II,* Ludovico de Luigi (1986)

12 *The Town-Ho's Story,* Frank Stella (1993)

13 *Ruins III,* Nita K. Sutherland (1978)

14 *Flamingo,* Alexander Calder (1974)

15 *Lines in Four Directions,* Sol Lewitt (1985)

16 *The Four Seasons,* Marc Chagall (1974)

17 *Untitled Sounding Sculpture,*
Harry Bertoia (1975)

18 *Cloud Gate,* Anish Kapoor (2004)

19 *Large Interior Form,* Henry Moore (1983)

20 *Celebration of the 200th Anniversary
of the Founding of the Republic,*
Isamu Noguchi (1976)

21 *The Fountain of the Great Lakes,*
Lorado Taft (1913)

with its two 50-foot glass-brick towers facing each other across a black granite plaza, with water cascading down their sides. Faces of Chicagoans are projected through the glass blocks and change at regular intervals—and watch out, because water spews from their mouths when you least expect it. It's public art with a sense of humor. The Jay Pritzker Pavilion, with its Frank Gehry–designed band shell, is a sight to behold, and the BP Pedestrian Bridge, also designed by Gehry, curves and winds its way over Columbus Drive, providing changing views of the cityscape as you walk. Gardens of native plants are just beginning to flourish, and by the next edition of this book, you will surely feel that you are walking through a Midwestern prairie as you stroll the Lurie Garden, with 250 varieties of native perennial plants. All in all, this is a must-see, must-experience park. You can lunch at the **Park Grill** (© **312/521-7275;** www.parkgrillchicago. com; open daily 11am–10:30pm), an eatery overlooking the McCormick Tribune Plaza ice-skating rink. Next door to the grill, Park Café offers take-out salads and sandwiches. Parking is easy, too, with plentiful underground lots at the bargain rate of $10, the best deal in the city.

Michigan Ave., from Randolph Dr. on the north to Monroe Dr. on the south, and west to Columbus Dr. Open 6am–11pm daily. ©312/742-1168. www.millenniumpark.org. El: Blue line to Washington; Red Line to Lake; Brown, Green, Orange or Purple Line to Randolph.

Museum Campus ✶✶✶   **All ages.** The most beautiful collection of museums in any city in the United States lies southeast of Grant Park on Chicago's glistening lakefront. Okay, so I am cheating a little by making "Museum Campus" one single kids' favorite. But the city has connected its great trio of museums (the Field Museum of Natural History, John G. Shedd Aquarium, and the Adler Planetarium & Astronomy Museum) on a landscaped 57-acre campus—thus, "Museum Campus"—so that they feel like one destination. Previously, busy Lake Shore Drive cut off the Field Museum from the aquarium and planetarium. Thanks to an ambitious construction project that was the dream of city leaders for a decade, the northbound lanes of Lake Shore Drive were relocated to the west side of the area. With terraced gardens and broad walkways, the reclaimed parkland makes it easier for pedestrians to visit the museums and has provided new space for picnicking, theater, and museum education activities. Transportation improvements include a trolley from parking lots and the Roosevelt Road El and Metra stops.

To get to the Museum Campus from the Loop, head east across Grant Park from Balbo St. and S. Michigan Ave., trekking along the lakeshore route to the Field Museum, the aquarium, and the planetarium. Or you can make your approach on the path that begins at 11th St. and Michigan Ave. Follow it to the walkway that spans the Metra tracks. Cross Columbus Dr. and then pick up the path that will take you under Lake Shore Dr. and into the Museum Campus. Bus 146 will take you to all 3 of these attractions. Call © **836-7000** (any city or suburban area code) for the stop locations and schedule.

Museum of Science and Industry ✶✶✶   **All ages.** Generations of children recount fond memories of this world-famous museum, the granddaddy of interactive museums, with some 2,000 exhibits. Good news: The museum is still thrilling kids today. Ask anyone who grew up around Chicago and they will reminisce about school field trips to the museum, bringing their cans of soda wrapped in tin foil, and seeing their favorite exhibit—the *U-505* ✶✶ and **Coal Mine** ✶ inevitably top the list of favorites from the past. The *U-505* is a German submarine that was captured in 1944 and brought to the museum 10 years later. In 2004 the U-boat was closed and underwent a restoration process to bring it back to its former glory. When the new 35,000-square-foot exhibit opens in 2005, your kids will undoubtedly join the legions who have been fascinated by the claustrophobic reality of underwater naval life. The full-scale Coal Mine, which dates back to 1934, now incorporates modern mining techniques into the exhibit. Get to these exhibits quickly after the museum opens because they attract amusement-park-length lines during the day.

Kids who love planes, trains, and automobiles shouldn't miss **All Aboard the Silver Streak!,** the museum's Burlington Pioneer Zephyr, the world's first streamlined, diesel-electric, articulated train, which was moved indoors and installed in the museum's three-story underground parking garage. A simulated train station has been installed along the 197-foot-long Zephyr, and visitors can explore the train and its onboard interactive exhibits. **The Great Train Story,** which replaces the museum's 60-year-old model railroad exhibit, takes up 3,500 square feet and depicts the winding rail journey between Chicago and Seattle. Kids can drive a Metra Train (our commuter line to the suburbs), open a drawbridge over the Chicago River, harvest timber in the Cascade Range, and bore a tunnel through the Rocky Mountains. For airplane fans, **Take Flight,** an aviation exhibit, features a full-size 727 airplane that revs up its engines and replays the voice recordings from a San Francisco-to-Chicago flight.

Computer addicts should be entranced by **Networld,** which offers a flashy immersion into the Internet (with plenty of interactive screens). More low-tech—but still fascinating—is the giant walk-through **model of the human heart** ⭐.

Educational exhibits include **Enterprise,** which lets visitors take on the role of CEO for a day as they immerse themselves in the goings-on of a virtual company. **Reusable City** teaches children ecological tips with implements that they might find in their own backyard. **AIDS: The War Within,** is also geared to kids and when it opened a few years ago, it was the first permanent exhibit on the immune system and HIV, the virus that causes AIDS.

And, not to be sexist, but girls (myself included) love **Colleen Moore's Fairy Castle,** a lavishly decorated miniature palace filled with priceless treasures. (Yes, those are real diamonds and pearls in the chandeliers.) The castle is hidden away on the lower level. Younger children up to age 10 love to spend time at the **Idea Factory,** a "learning through play" environment that allows kids to explore scientific principles themselves.

A major attraction at the museum is the **Henry Crown Space Center,** where the story of space exploration, still in its infancy, is documented in copious detail, highlighted by a simulated space-shuttle experience through sight and sound at the center's five-story **OMNIMAX Theater.** The theater offers double features on weekends; call for showtimes.

When you've worked up an appetite, you can visit one of the museum's five restaurants, including a Pizza Hut and an ice cream parlor, and there are also two gift shops. Allow about 3 hours for your visit.

57th St. and Lake Shore Dr. ℭ **800/468-6674** outside the Chicago area, 773/684-1414, or TTY 773/684-3323. www.msichicago.org. Admission to museum only, $9 adults, $7.50 seniors, $5 children 3–11, free for children under 3. Free admission Mon–Tues mid-Sept to Nov and Jan–Feb. Combination museum and OMNIMAX Theater $15 adults, $13 seniors, $10 children 3–11, free for children under 3 on an adult's lap. Mon–Sat 9:30am–4pm; Sun 11am–4pm (until 5:30pm daily Memorial Day to Labor Day). Closed Dec 25. Bus: 6 or Metra Electric to 57th St. and Lake Park Ave.

Navy Pier ⭐   **All ages.** After you've spent a couple of fun-filled hours at the Chicago Children's Museum, check out Navy Pier—Chicago's top tourist attraction. Built during World War I, this 3,000-foot-long pier has been a ballroom, a training center for Navy pilots during World War II, and a satellite campus of

Museum of Science and Industry

Main Floor

Legend:
- ◆ Elevator
- ▦ Stairs
- ℗ Dining area
- ⓘ Information

AIDS: The War Within **16**
All Aboard the Silver Streak **7**
The Brain **15**
Coal Mine **2**
Colleen Moore's Fairy Castle **11**
Enterprise **3**
The Great Train Story **4**
The Heart **14**
Henry Crown Space Center **9**
Model of the human heart **14**
Networld **5**
Omnimax Theater **8**
Reusable City **12**
727 Airplane **13**
Take Flight **13**
U-505 Submarine **10**
Whispering Gallery **6**
Yesterday's Main Street **1**

the University of Illinois. But any military aura is long gone, now that the place has been transformed into a bustling tourist mecca. A combination of carnival, food court, and boat dock, the pier makes a fun place to stroll (if you don't mind crowds), but you'll have to walk all the way to the end to get the best views of the city.

Midway down the pier are the Crystal Gardens, with 70 full-size palm trees, dancing fountains, and other flora in a glass-enclosed atrium; a white-canopied open-air Skyline Stage that hosts concerts, dance performances, and film screenings; a carousel; and a 15-story Ferris wheel that's a replica of the original that debuted at Chicago's 1893 World's Fair. The 50 acres of pier and lakefront property also are home to the aforementioned Chicago Children's Museum (p. 150), a 3-D **IMAX theater** (✆ 312/595-0090), a small ice-skating rink, and the Chicago Shakespeare Theater (p. 245). Naturally, there are a handful of rather bland shops and pushcart vendors. Dining options include a food court, an outpost of Lincoln Park's popular Charlie's Ale House, and the white-tablecloth seafood restaurant Riva. You'll also find a beer garden with live music; Joe's Be-Bop Cafe & Jazz Emporium (run by Joe and Wayne Segal of Jazz Showcase fame), a Southern-style BBQ restaurant with live music nightly; and Bubba Gump Shrimp Co. & Market, a casual family seafood joint.

The **Smith Museum of Stained Glass Windows** sounds dull, but is actually a remarkable installation of more than 150 stained-glass windows set in illuminated display cases. Occupying an 800-foot-long expanse on the ground floor of Navy Pier, the museum features works by Frank Lloyd Wright, Louis Sullivan, John LaFarge, and Louis Comfort Tiffany, and is divided into four themes: Victorian religious windows, Victorian secular windows, designs of the Prairie School, and contemporary designs.

Slumbering at Chicago's Museums

A trend has swept our museums, and that trend is . . . sleeping. Two Chicago museums offer scheduled sleepovers, a trend that promises to continue. Word is that the Museum of Science and Industry is considering adding a sleepover to the public as well. This may well happen, so call the education department (✆ 773/684-9844) if that's of interest. Whether or not you will actually get any sleep is up in the air, but it's sure to be a memorable experience.

Dozin' with the Dinos at the **Field Museum** allows kids to roam the halls, take part in workshops and tours, or explore a mummy's tomb by flashlight. With an adult in tow, children ages 5 to 12 can bring a sleeping bag and bed down with the dinos. The event costs $47 per person, including a snack and breakfast, and takes place twice a year—once during the summer months, and once during the holiday season, usually in late November. Call ✆ 312/665-7400 for reservations for the next sleepover.

The slightly threatening-sounding **Sleeping with the Fish** evening at the **Shedd Aquarium** is an annual event that takes place on a Friday in September, usually from 6:30pm to 9am. The event costs $45 per person. Call ✆ 312/939-2438 for more information.

Tips Free Museum Admission Days

Plan your time in Chicago carefully and you can save yourself admission fees to the city's major museums. Admission to special exhibitions and films are often extra on free days.

Sunday: DuSable Museum of African-American History

Monday: All of the following are free on Monday from September through February, except for the last 2 weeks of December: Adler Planetarium, Field Museum of Natural History, and John G. Shedd Aquarium (Oceanarium admission extra).

Tuesday: Adler Planetarium (Sept–Feb except for the last 2 weeks of Dec), Art Institute of Chicago, Field Museum of Natural History (Sept–Feb, except for the last 2 weeks of Dec), International Museum of Surgical Science, Museum of Contemporary Art (5–8pm only), Museum of Science and Industry (Sept–Feb except for the last 2 weeks of Dec), Shedd Aquarium (Sept–Feb, except the last 2 weeks of Dec; Oceanarium admission extra).

Thursday: Chicago Children's Museum (5–8pm only).

Friday: Spertus Museum.

Always Free: Chicago Cultural Center, David and Alfred Smart Museum of Art, Garfield Park Conservatory, Jane Addams Hull-House Museum, Lincoln Park Conservatory, Lincoln Park Zoo, Martin D'Arcy Gallery of Art, Mexican Fine Arts Center Museum, Museum of Contemporary Photography, Newberry Library.

Navy Pier hosts a variety of conventions and trade shows, from tennis to flower and garden shows. There's something for everyone, but the commercialism of the place might be too much for some people. If that's the case for you, take the ½-mile stroll to the end of the pier, east of the ballroom, where you can find a little respite and enjoy the wind, the waves, and the city view, which is the real delight of a place like this. Or unwind in **Olive Park,** a small sylvan haven with a sliver of beach that lies just to the north of Navy Pier.

You'll find, moored along the south dock, more than half a dozen different sailing vessels, including a couple of dinner cruise ships, the pristine white-masted tall ship _Windy_ (ask about the special "Pirate" sails), and the 70-foot speedboats _Seadog I, II,_ and _III._ In the summer months, water taxis speed between Navy Pier and other Chicago sights. For more specifics on sightseeing and dinner cruises, see "Lake & River Cruises," later in this chapter.

600 E. Grand Ave. (at Lake Michigan). ℂ **800/595-PIER** (outside 312 area code) or 312/595-PIER. www. navypier.com. Free admission. Summer Sun–Thurs 10am–10pm, Fri–Sat 10am–midnight; fall–spring Mon–Sat 10am–10pm, Sun 10am–7pm. Bus: 29, 65, 66, 120, or 121. Parking rates start at $11 for the 1st hr. and go up to $19 for up to 8 hr. However, the lots fill quickly. Free trolley buses make stops on Grand Ave. and Illinois St. from State St. Subway/El: Red Line to Grand/State; transfer to city bus or board a free pier trolley bus.

3 Best Views

Sweeping views of the city from north to south are one of the main attractions of the many **boat tours** that leave from Navy Pier. Hop aboard and get the lay of the land from a waterborne vantage point. It's the best way to see how the city sweeps from Museum Campus in the south, to the Loop, across the Chicago River, and up through the Magnificent Mile, then onto the condo buildings that populate the lakefront moving north to the suburbs. See "Kid-Friendly Tours," later in this chapter, for a full listing of boat tour options.

The Hancock Observatory ★★ **All ages.** Kids can play "count the rooftop pools" from the 1,000-foot high observation deck as they look down (way down) on the residential neighborhoods below. For my money, the Hancock Center offers the best views in town. Why? You're located right on the Magnificent Mile, offering a close view of the city from the observatory on the 94th floor. (Most people don't agree with me, however, because over 1.5 million people go up the Sears Tower each year.) Although it's not as famous as the Sears Tower, for many local residents, the Hancock remains the archetypal Chicago skyscraper, with its bold, tapered shape and exterior steel cross-bracing design. The building rises to a total height of 1,107 feet above Michigan Avenue—1,456 feet if you count its twin 349-foot antennas. The view from the top of Chicago's third-tallest building is enough to satisfy, and some high-tech additions to the experience include "talking telescopes" with sound effects and narration in four languages, history walls illustrating the growth of the city, and the Skywalk open-air viewing deck—a "screened porch" that allows visitors to feel the rush of the wind at 1,000 feet. It's a sky-high step outside. Kids can check out the building's infrastructure on computers and locate 80 Chicago attractions on virtual-reality television screens.

The Hancock Observatory delivers an excellent panorama of the city and an intimate view over nearby Lake Michigan and the various shoreline residential areas. On a clear day you can see portions of the three states surrounding this corner of Illinois (Michigan, Indiana, and Wisconsin), for a radius of 40 to 50 miles. The view up the North Side is particularly dramatic, stretching from the nearby Oak Street and North Avenue beaches, along the green strip of Lincoln Park, to the line of high-rises you can trace up the shoreline until they suddenly halt just below the boundary of the northern suburbs. A high-speed elevator carries passengers to the observatory in 40 seconds, and the entrance and observatory are accessible for people with disabilities.

"Big John," as it's referred to by some locals, also has a sleek restaurant, **The Signature Room at the 95th,** with an adjoining lounge. (For about the same cost as the observatory, you can take in the views with libation in hand). During the day plenty of tourists make the place kid-friendly; at night it's more adult-oriented. In the afternoon it's not very crowded, so don't be afraid bring the family for a drink.

94th floor of the John Hancock Center, 875 N. Michigan Ave. (enter on Delaware St.). ℭ **888/887-9596** or 312/751-3681. Fax 312/751-3675. www.hancock-observatory.com. Admission $9.50 adults, $7.50 seniors, $6 children 5–12, free for children under 5. Daily 9am–11pm. Bus: 145, 146, 147, or 151. Subway/El: Red Line to Chicago/State.

⌒ *Tips* **Walker's Warning**

Chicago is a great city to explore on foot, but I must warn people against trying to cross Lake Shore Drive on foot. People have been seriously injured and even killed attempting to dodge the traffic on the drive. Look for the pedestrian underpasses at Chicago Avenue, Oak Street, and North Avenue, among other locations.

Moments **A Great View**

After a quick visit to the Lincoln Park Zoo or the Peggy Notebaert Nature Museum, take a quick stroll on Fullerton Avenue to the bridge that runs over the lagoon (just before you get to Lake Shore Dr.). Standing on the south side of Fullerton Avenue, you'll have a great view of the Chicago skyline and Lincoln Park—and an excellent backdrop for family souvenir photos. This path can get very crowded on summer weekends, so I suggest trying this photo op during the week.

Navy Pier   **All ages.** Because Navy Pier juts 3,000 feet into Lake Michigan, the view from the end of the pier looking toward the city is fabulous—the next best thing to seeing the Chicago skyline by boat. And, if you like heights, hop aboard the Ferris wheel and get a 15-story-high vantage point. Go early in the morning to see the sun rise, the rays gleaming off the glass Mies van der Rohe buildings lining Lake Shore Drive. Surrounded by Lake Michigan, lush gardens, and sculpture, the view from the Navy Pier is one of the best in the city. See the review in the previous section for more details about the other attractions at Navy Pier.

600 E. Grand Ave. (at Lake Michigan). © 800/595-PIER (outside 312 area code), or 312/595-PIER. www. navypier.com.

North Avenue Beach   **All ages.** One of the most famous views of Chicago (and one that you'll find in many guidebooks as a featured photo) is taken on the lakefront bike path, looking south to the John Hancock Center. To get a photo of your family in this picture-perfect scene, walk north on Lake Shore Drive to the tunnel at North Avenue that leads under Lake Shore Drive to North Avenue Beach. Once on the lakefront path, turn south toward the city, and you will have your photo opportunity. (Just watch out for cyclists, skaters, runners, and dog walkers if it's a nice summer day!) See "Enjoying the 'Third Coast': Chicago's Beaches," in chapter 8 for more information.

Lake Shore Dr. at North Ave. © 312/742-PLAY for Chicago Park District and beach information.

Sears Tower Skydeck ★ *Overrated*   **All ages.** When you stand on a perch this high and view the trains, river traffic, and expressways streaming with cars, you can teach your kids the meaning of the term "transportation hub." Sears Tower is one of Chicago's most popular attractions. Since its debut in 1973, the Sears Tower's lock on the crown of "world's tallest building" has been a source of civic pride for the city. Sadly, the building's namesake, Sears, sold the building and moved to cheaper suburban offices in 1992. Another blow to morale came when Petronas Towers in Kuala Lumpur, Malaysia, went up and laid claim to the title of world's tallest buildings. (The Sears Tower has since put up a 22-ft. antenna in an attempt to win back the title.) Tallest-building posturing aside, this is still a great place to orient your family to the city, but I wouldn't put it on the top of must-see sights for any family with limited time or limited patience for crowds.

The view from the 103rd-floor Skydeck is everything you'd expect it to be— once you get there. Unfortunately, you're usually stuck in a very long, very noisy line, so by the time you make it to the top, your patience could be as thin as the atmosphere up there. *One suggestion:* I once went up the tower at night on a weeknight, a couple of hours before closing (in summertime, it stays open until 10pm). We had the observation deck practically to ourselves. If that's too late for

---

Moments **Photo Op**

For a great photo op, walk on Randolph Street toward the lake in the morning. That's when the sun, rising in the east over the lake, hits the string of high-rises that line South Michigan Avenue—giving you the perfect backdrop for an only-in-Chicago picture.

---

your kids, try the late afternoon, when crowds have thinned. On a clear day, visibility extends up to 50 miles, and you can catch glimpses of the surrounding states. Despite the fact that it's called a "skydeck," you can't actually walk outside (though I can't understand why you'd want to—but that's just my fear of heights speaking!). The 70-second high-speed elevator trip will feel like a thrill ride for some, but it's a nightmare for anyone with even mild claustrophobia. Recent upgrades to the Skydeck include multimedia exhibits on Chicago history and **Knee High Chicago,** an exhibit for kids. Allow 1 to 2 hours, depending on the length of the line.

233 S. Wacker Dr. (enter on Jackson Blvd.). © 312/875-9696. www.the-skydeck.com. Admission $9.95 adults, $7.95 seniors, $6.95 children 3–12, free for children under 3. May–Sept daily 10am–10pm; Oct–Apr daily 10am–8pm. Subway/El: Brown, Purple, or Orange Line to Quincy; Red or Blue Line to Jackson; then walk a few blocks west. Bus: 1, 7, 126, 146, 151, or 156.

4 More Chicago Museums

Chicago has plenty of museums that make every effort to turn a bored child into a stimulated one. Many of the city's museums are leaders in the "please touch me" school of interactive exhibitions, with buttons and lights and levers and sounds and bright colors, and activities for kids at special exhibitions.

Art Institute of Chicago ★★★ **All ages.** Chicago's pride and joy is a warm, welcoming museum—one that's never too stuffy to embrace kids. You know this is a museum with a winning sense of whimsy when at the holidays, the famous lion sculptures that guard its entrance sport Santa hats.

The Art Institute goes the extra mile to help kids get through a few hours here without even a hint of boredom. The Kraft Education Center on the lower level features interactive exhibits for children and has a list of "gallery games" that encourage kids to "seek and find" to make visiting the museum more fun. Special exhibitions are designed for kids with accompanying hands-on programs. Kids might be taught by a visiting children's book illustrator, for example, and then learn how to make their own books. A highlight tour for kids runs on Saturday. The center is open during regular museum hours and family programs are free with museum admission.

In other parts of the museum, kids will be entranced by the **Thorne Miniature Rooms,** filled with tiny reproductions of furnished interiors from European and American history (heaven for a dollhouse fanatic). Another popular attraction is the original **Trading Room of the old Chicago Stock Exchange,** salvaged when the Adler and Sullivan Stock Exchange building was demolished in 1972. One parent says her boys love the great hall of European arms and armor dating from the 15th to 19th centuries. Composed of more than 1,500 objects, including armor, horse equipment, swords, daggers, pole arms, and maces, it's one of the most important assemblages of its kind in the country.

(If you do head down here, don't miss Marc Chagall's stunning stained-glass windows at the end of the gallery.)

If you have older kids, you'll find an array of works to satiate any interest: Japanese *ukiyo-e* prints, ancient Egyptian bronzes and Greek vases, 19th-century British photography, masterpieces by most of the greatest names in 20th-century sculpture, or modern American textiles. No matter how many times you visit, there are always new works to be seen and special shows that draw in even more crowds.

For a good general overview of the museum's collection, take the free "Highlights of the Art Institute" tour, offered at 2pm on Saturday, Sunday, and Tuesday. Those with limited time and kids with limited patience for tours should head straight to the museum's renowned collection of Impressionist art (including one of the world's largest collections of Monet paintings), one of the more highly trafficked areas of the museum. Among the treasures here you'll find Seurat's pointillist masterpiece *Sunday Afternoon on the Island of La Grande Jatte.* Your second must-see area is the galleries of European and American contemporary art, ranging from paintings, sculptures, and mixed-media works from Pablo Picasso, Henri Matisse, and Salvador Dalí through Willem de Kooning, Jackson Pollock, and Andy Warhol. Visitors are sometimes surprised when they discover many of the icons that hang here. (Grant Wood's *American Gothic* and Edward Hopper's *Nighthawks* are two that bring double takes from many visitors.)

If you want to steer clear of the crowds, you'll find more breathing room in the galleries of Indian, Himalayan, and Southeast Asian art. Other recommended exhibits are the collection of delicate mid-19th-century glass paperweights in the museum's famous Arthur Rubloff collection.

The museum also has a cafeteria and an elegant full-service restaurant, a picturesque courtyard cafe with a jazz quintet on Tuesday evenings in the summer (open June–Sept and highly recommended for families), and a large shop. There is a busy schedule of lectures, films, and other special presentations, as well as guided tours, to enhance your viewing of the art.

111 S. Michigan Ave. (at Adams St.). ℭ 312/443-3600. www.artic.edu. Suggested admission $10 adults; $6 seniors, children, and students with ID. Additional cost for special exhibitions. Free admission Tues. Mon–Fri 10:30am–4:30pm (Tues until 8pm); Sat–Sun 10am–5pm. Closed Thanksgiving and Dec 25. Subway/El: Green, Brown, Purple, or Orange Line to Adams; Red Line to Monroe/State or Jackson/State. Bus: 3, 4, 60, 145, 147, or 151.

Tips Touring the Art Institute

Keeping track of your kids in the crowds that flood the Art Institute during its peak days might reduce your enjoyment of your favorite masterpieces.

Your best bet is to avoid the craziest times: Many people don't realize the museum is open on Monday, so the galleries are relatively subdued. Wednesday is a close second. Tuesday tends to draw the masses because the Art Institute is free and open late (until 8pm). Try to arrive when the doors open in the morning or else during the lunchtime lull. *Another tip:* If the Michigan Avenue entrance is crowded, head around to the entrance on the Columbus Drive side, which is usually less congested and is more convenient to the Grant Park underground parking garage. There's also a small gift shop near the Columbus Drive entrance that you might want to check out if the main shop is too bustling.

Chicago Archicenter **Ages 13 & up.** Chicago's architecture is one of the city's main claims to fame, and a quick swing through this center will help you understand why. Run by the well-regarded Chicago Architecture Foundation, it's conveniently located across the street from the Art Institute. Still trying to figure out the difference between Prairie School and postmodern? Stop in here for a lesson. Exhibits include a scale model of downtown Chicago, profiles of the people and buildings that shaped the city's look, and a searchable database with pictures and information on many of Chicago's best-known skyscrapers. "Architecture ambassadors" are on hand to provide information on tours run by the foundation (see "Chicago Architecture Foundation Tours," p. 189). Two galleries feature changing exhibits about ongoing Chicago design projects—so you can see firsthand how local architecture continues to evolve. There's also an excellent gift shop filled with architecture-focused books, decorative accessories, and gifts. Allow a half-hour, more if you want to browse in the store.

224 S. Michigan Ave. (*C*) 312/922-3432. www.architecture.org. Free admission. Exhibits open daily 9:30am–4pm. Shop and tour desk open Mon–Sat 9am–6:30pm; Sun 9am–6pm. Subway/El: Brown, Green, Orange, or Purple Line to Adams; Red Line to Jackson. Bus: 3, 4, 145, 147, or 151.

Chicago Cultural Center ★ *Finds* **Ages 3 & up.** Free family programs are the main attraction of this landmark building, built in 1897 as the city's public library and transformed into a showplace for visual and performing arts in 1991. Its basic Beaux Arts exterior conceals a sumptuous interior of rare marble, fine hardwood, stained glass, polished brass, and mosaics of Favrile glass, colored stone, and mother-of-pearl inlaid in white marble. The crowning centerpiece is Preston Bradley Hall's majestic Tiffany dome, said to be the largest of its kind in the world.

The building also houses one of the Chicago Office of Tourism's visitor centers, which makes it a good place to kick-start your visit. If you stop in to pick up tourist information and take a quick look around, your visit won't take longer than half an hour. But the Cultural Center also hosts an array of art exhibitions, concerts, films, lectures, and other special events (many free), which might convince you to extend your time here. Programs might include African drumming, a recital by a mezzo-soprano from the Lyric Opera, or readings by Chicago playwrights. A long-standing tradition is the 12:15pm Dame Myra Hess Memorial classical concert every Wednesday in the Preston Bradley Hall. Other ongoing programs include a monthly cultural festival—which highlights a different city or country over a weekend with art, theater, and film.

Guided architectural tours of the Cultural Center are offered Wednesday, Friday, and Saturday at 1:15pm. For information, call (*C*) **312/744-8032.**

78 E. Washington St. (*C*) 312/744-6630, or 312/FINE-ART for weekly events. Fax 312/744-2089. www.city ofchicago.org/exploringchicago. Free admission. Mon–Thurs 10am–7pm; Fri 10am–6pm; Sat 10am–5pm; Sun 11am–5pm. Closed holidays. Subway/El: Brown, Green, Orange, or Purple Line to Randolph; Red Line to Washington/State. Bus: 3, 4, 20, 56, 60, 145, 146, 147, 151, or 157.

Chicago Fed Visitors Center It's not worth a special trip (unless you're a huge Alan Greenspan fan), but the Visitors Center at the Federal Reserve Bank of Chicago makes for a surprisingly kid-friendly stop if you're touring the Loop's other attractions. Offering more than just the standard history-of-banking exhibits, the center has kid-friendly features such as a giant cube that holds a million dollars, and an exhibit that lets kids try to detect counterfeit bills. And yes, there's even a section where visitors can pretend to be Alan Greenspan for a moment, and learn how changes in interest rates affect the economy. Free guided tours are offered weekdays at 1pm. Allow a half-hour.

230 S. LaSalle St (at Quincy St.). ✆ **312/322-2400.** www.chicagofed.org. Free admission. Mon–Fri 9am–4:30pm, except federal holidays. Subway/El: Brown Line to Quincy/Wells. Bus: 134, 135, or 156.

Chicago Historical Society ⚲★ **Ages 7 & up.** Located at the southwestern tip of Lincoln Park, the Historical Society is one of Chicago's oldest cultural institutions (founded in 1856), but one that has successfully brought its exhibits into the 21st century. More updating is underway and will continue through 2005. The good news is that the renovations are intended to create more hands-on, family-friendly exhibits. During the work, exhibits will remain open, but call ahead to check the status.

Inside the Historical Society's lovely redbrick and glass-walled building, you'll find a fascinating display of objects, artifacts, artworks, and other items in galleries that are both beautifully executed and easy to navigate. (It's also just a Frisbee toss from North Ave. Beach, the best beach in the city, and across the street from the Gold Coast's most elite addresses.) Kids can climb aboard the 160-year-old Pioneer, Chicago's first locomotive, and visit the Hands-On Gallery, where they can step into an early fur trader's cabin. An Illinois Pioneer Life gallery features daily craft demonstrations.

Casual visitors can get a good overview of the highlights in about an hour; history buffs will need more time. The must-see permanent exhibit is **A House Divided: America in the Age of Lincoln,** which explores the institution of slavery in America and the devastation of the Civil War. (Items on display include the bed that Lincoln died in and an original copy of the 13th amendment abolishing slavery, signed by Honest Abe himself.) Another highlight is the CHS's costume collection, which includes suits worn by George Washington and John Adams, articles of clothing belonging to Abraham and Mary Todd Lincoln, and, of more current vintage, one of Michael Jordan's costumes and numerous gowns by contemporary fashion designers. Other worthy stops are the Charles F. Murphy architectural study center, featuring one of the nation's largest collections of architectural working drawings; the decorative and industrial-arts collection, including stained-glass designs by Frank Lloyd Wright and Louis Sullivan; and **We the People,** a permanent exhibit on the founding of the United States.

The Historical Society sponsors lectures, symposia, and seminars; film screenings; family programs; historical reenactments and performances by local theater companies; and music concerts on the beautiful plaza overlooking Lincoln Park. On the ground floor of the museum, past the gift shop, is Big Shoulders Cafe, entered through a flora- and fauna-decorated terra-cotta arch removed from the old Stockyard Bank and reassembled here. The museum's website is worth checking out before your visit, especially the impressive online "exhibit" on the Great Chicago Fire. After your visit, head a few blocks east to North Avenue Beach, the best beach in the city, or wander the neighboring residential street of the exclusive Gold Coast. Allow 1 to 2 hours.

1601 N. Clark St. (at North Ave.). ✆ **312/642-4600.** www.chicagohistory.org. Admission $5 adults, $3 seniors and students, $1 children 6–12, free for children under 6. Free admission on Mon. Mon–Sat 9:30am–4:30pm; Sun noon–5pm. Research center Tues–Sat 10am–4:30pm. Bus: 11, 22, 36, 72, 151, or 156.

Chicago Public Library/Harold Washington Library Center **Ages 2 & up.** The Harold Washington Library Center is named in memory of Chicago's first and only African-American mayor, who died of a heart attack in 1987 at the beginning of his second term in office. This massive redbrick neoclassical edifice—occupying an entire city block at State Street and Congress Parkway—is the largest public library in the world. There's a stunning 52-foot glass-domed winter garden on the top floor. On the second floor is another treasure: the vast **Thomas Hughes Children's Library,** housing more than 100,000 volumes. The library offers an interesting array of events and art exhibitions worth checking out, and is an excellent resting spot for families touring the Loop. A 385-seat auditorium is the setting for a unique mix of dance and music performances, author talks, and children's programs, including readings by librarians, puppet shows, and visits from book characters. (For example, kids might meet "Angelina Ballerina" and make crowns with her.) The library also has a cafe adjacent to the ninth-floor winter garden, and a coffeehouse and used-book store on the ground floor. Allow 1 hour.

400 S. State St. ⓒ 312/747-4300. www.chipublib.org. Free admission. Mon–Thurs 9am–7pm; Fri–Sat 9am–5pm; Sun 1–5pm. Closed holidays. Subway/El: Red Line to Jackson/State; Brown Line to Van Buren/ Library. Bus: 2, 6, 11, 29, 36, 62, 145, 146, 147, or 151.

City Gallery   **All ages.** Along with the pumping station across the street, the Chicago Water Tower is one of only a handful of buildings to survive the Great Chicago Fire of 1871. It has long been a revered symbol of the city's resilience and fortitude, although today—more than 130 years after it first rose to a once-mighty height of 154 feet—the Water Tower is dwarfed by the high-rise shopping centers and hotels of North Michigan Avenue. The Gothic-style limestone building now has been reinvented as an art gallery. While this may be a welcome and inventive use of the structure, it's actually an idea that first cropped up in 1948 but was never acted upon. The spiffed-up interior is intimate and sunny, and it's a refreshing pit stop of culture on your way to the Water Tower shopping center or pumping-station tourist information center across the street. Exhibits have included works by Chicago-based photographer Victor Skrebneski. Allow a half-hour.

806 N. Michigan Ave. (between Chicago Ave. and Pearson St.). ⓒ 312/742-0808. Free admission. Mon–Sat 10am–6:30pm; Sun 10am–5pm. Bus: 3, 145, 146, 147, or 151.

DuSable Museum of African-American History   **Ages 5 & up.** The DuSable Museum is a repository of the history, art, and artifacts pertaining to the African-American experience and culture. Named for Chicago's first permanent settler, Jean Baptiste Point du Sable, a French-Canadian of Haitian descent, it is admirable not so much for its collections and exhibits as for the inspiring story behind its existence. Founded in 1961 with a $10 charter and minimal capital, the museum began in the home of Dr. Margaret Burroughs, an art teacher at the city's Du Sable High School. In 1973, as a result of a community-based campaign, the museum took up residence in its present building (a former parks administration facility and police lockup) on the eastern edge of Washington Park. With no major endowment to speak of, the DuSable Museum has managed to accumulate a respectable collection of more than 13,000 artifacts, books, photographs, art objects, and memorabilia. Its collection of paintings, drawings, and sculpture by African-American and African artists is excellent.

In 1993 the DuSable Museum added a 25,000-square-foot wing named in honor of the city's first and only African-American mayor, Harold Washington. The permanent exhibit on Washington contains memorabilia and personal effects, and surveys important episodes in his political career. More recent is a permanent exhibit called **Blacks in Aviation,** which celebrates the achievements of the legendary Tuskegee Airmen and features such items as the flight jacket of Major Robert H. Lawrence, the nation's first African-American astronaut.

Moments **Summer Solstice**

If you're here in mid-June, don't miss the Museum of Contemporary Art's annual **Summer Solstice** celebration (📞 **312/280-2660**), a 24-hour festival of contemporary art and music. It's a mind-blowing mix of cutting-edge entertainment and family-focused fun (with plenty of hands-on activities for kids). The event is free, and it takes place every June 21.

Youth programming and workshops are scheduled year-round, including jazz and blues series and children's film series. The Arts and Crafts Festival, going strong for over 30 years, is held in June and July; call or visit the website for details. The museum also has a gift shop, a research library, and an extensive program of community-related events, all which are presented in a 466-seat auditorium.

740 E. 56th Place. 📞 **773/947-0600**. www.dusablemuseum.org. Admission $3 adults, $2 students and seniors, $1 children 6–12, free for children under 6. Free admission Sun. Mon–Sat 10am–5pm; Sun noon–5pm. Closed Thanksgiving, Dec 25, and Jan 1. Subway/El: Metra Electric train to 57th St. and Lake Park Ave., then a short cab ride. Bus: 6.

Historic Pullman ★★ **Ages 7 & up.** Railway magnate George Pullman was a fabulously wealthy industrialist, and he fancied himself more enlightened than his 19th-century peers. So when it came time to build a new headquarters for his Pullman Palace Car Company, he dreamed of something far more grand than the standard factory surrounded by tenements. Instead, he built a model community for his workers, a place where they could live in houses with indoor plumbing and abundant natural light—amenities almost unheard of for industrial workers in the 1880s. Pullman didn't do all this from the goodness of his heart; he hoped that the town named after him would attract the most skilled workers (who would, not coincidentally, be so happy here that they wouldn't go on strike). As one of the first "factory towns," Pullman caused an international sensation and was seen as a model for other companies. The happy workers that Pullman envisioned, however, did not entirely cooperate, going on strike in 1894, frustrated by the company's control over every aspect of their lives.

Today the Pullman district makes a fascinating stop for families with kids interested in history or architecture. Although many of the homes are private residences, a number of public buildings still stand (including the lavish Hotel Florence, the imposing Clock Tower, and the two-story colonnaded Market Hall). A fire damaged some buildings in the late 1990s, but Pullman has thankfully been recognized as a unique historic site, and much-needed repairs are underway. You can walk through on your own (stop by the visitor center for a map), or take a guided tour at 12:30 or 1:30pm on the first Sunday of the month, from May to October ($4 adults, $3.50 seniors, $2.50 students).

11141 S. Cottage Grove Ave. 📞 **773/785-8901**. www.pullmanil.org. Tues–Sun 11am–3pm. Train: Metra Electric line to Pullman (111th St.), turn right on Cottage Grove Ave. and walk 1 block to the visitor center.

International Museum of Surgical Science *Finds* **Ages 12 & up.** This museum is not for the faint of stomach. (Although I lived three doors down from this museum for 7 years, I was afraid to set foot inside—maybe it was the real skeletons they put in the windows every Halloween that scared me off?) Run by the International College of Surgeons, the museum is housed in a historic 1917 Gold Coast mansion designed by the noted architect Howard Van Doren

Shaw, who modeled it after Le Petit Trianon at Versailles. Displayed throughout its four floors are surgical instruments, paintings, and sculpture depicting the history of surgery and healing practices in Eastern and Western civilizations. The exhibits are old-fashioned (no interactive computer displays here!) but that's part of the museum's odd appeal.

You'll look at your doctor in a whole new way after viewing the trepanned skulls excavated from an ancient tomb in Peru. The accompanying tools were used to bore holes in patients' skulls, a horrific practice thought to release the evil spirits causing their illnesses. (Some skulls show signs of new bone growth, meaning that some lucky headache-sufferers actually survived this low-tech surgery.) There are also battlefield amputation kits, a working iron-lung machine in the polio exhibit, and oddities such as a stethoscope designed to be transported inside a top hat. Other attractions include an apothecary shop and dentist's office (ca. 1900), re-created in a historic street exhibit, and the hyperbolically christened "Hall of Immortals," a sculpture gallery depicting 12 historic figures in medicine, from Hippocrates to Madame Curie.

1524 N. Lake Shore Dr. (between Burton Place and North Ave.). © 312/642-6502. www.imss.org. Admission $6 adults, $3 seniors and students. Free admission Tues. Tues–Sat 10am–4pm; Sun 10am–4pm May–Sept. Bus: 151.

Intuit: The Center for Intuitive and Outsider Art   Ages 3 & up. Chicago

is home to an active community of collectors of so-called outsider art, a term attached to a group of unknown, unconventional artists who do their own artwork without any formal training or connection to the mainstream art world. Often called folk or self-taught artists, their work is highly personal and idiosyncratic, and they work in a range of media, from bottle caps to immense canvases. Intuit was founded in 1991 to bring attention to these artists through exhibitions and educational lectures. Housed in the warehouse district northwest of the Loop, with two galleries and a performance area, Intuit is slowly gaining a higher profile on the city's art scene. The museum offers a regular lecture series, and if you time your visit right, you might be here for one of the center's tours of a private local art collection. Intuit doesn't offer special programs for kids, but events like quilt sales featuring quilts of the African-American improvised tradition, or graffiti art, should satisfy them.

756 N. Milwaukee Ave. (at Chicago and Ogden aves.). © 312/243-9088. www.outsider.art.org. Free admission. Wed–Sat noon–5pm. Subway/El: Blue Line to Chicago. Bus: 56 or 66.

Jane Addams Hull-House Museum   Ages 8 & up. In 1889 a young woman

named Jane Addams bought an old mansion on Halsted Street that had been built in 1856 as a "country home" but was now surrounded by the shanties of the immigrant poor. Here Addams and her co-worker, Ellen Gates Starr, launched the American settlement-house movement with the establishment of Hull House, an institution that endured on this site in Chicago until 1963. (It continues today as a decentralized social-service agency known as Hull House Association.) Orphans found a home here, and immigrants received health care, job training, and English lessons. In 1963 all but two of the settlement's 13 buildings, along with the entire residential neighborhood in its immediate vicinity, were demolished to make room for the new University of Illinois at Chicago campus, which now owns the museum buildings. Of the original settlement, what remains today are the Hull-House Museum (the mansion itself) and the residents' dining hall, snuggled among the ultramodern, poured-concrete buildings of the university campus. Inside are the original furnishings, Jane Addams's office, and numerous settlement maps and photographs. Rotating exhibits re-create the history of the settlement and the work of its residents, showing how Addams was able to help transform the dismal streets around her into stable inner-city environments. Allow a half-hour.

University of Illinois at Chicago, 800 S. Halsted St. (at Polk St.). ℂ 312/413-5353. www.uic.edu/jaddams/hull. Free admission. Tues–Fri 10am–4pm; Sun noon–4pm. Subway/El: Blue Line to Halsted/University of Illinois. Bus: 8.

Martin D'Arcy Museum of Art   Ages 5 & up. A treasure trove of medieval, Renaissance, and baroque art, the Martin D'Arcy Museum of Art covers the years A.D. 1100 to 1700. All the rich symbolism of Catholicism through the baroque era is embodied in such works as a gem-encrusted silver and ebony sculpture of Christ's scourging, a head of John the Baptist on a silver platter, golden chalices, rosary beads carved with biblical scenes, and many other highly ornamented ritual objects.

Loyola University, 6525 N. Sheridan Rd. ℂ 773/508-2679. Free admission. Tues–Sat noon–4pm. Closed Aug. Subway/El: Red Line to Loyola. Bus: 151.

Mexican Fine Arts Center Museum ⭐   All ages. Chicago's vibrant Pilsen neighborhood, just southwest of the Loop, is home to one of the nation's largest Mexican-American communities. Ethnic pride emanates from every doorstep, *taqueria,* and bakery and the multitude of colorful murals splashed across building exteriors and alleyways. But this museum, the largest Latino cultural institution in the country, may be the neighborhood's most prized possession. That's quite an accomplishment, given that the Mexican Fine Arts Center Museum was founded in 1987 by a passel of public schoolteachers who pooled $900 to get it started.

The museum is very family-oriented, offering a deluge of educational workshops for kids and parents: It's truly a living museum. There are wonderful exhibits to be sure, showcasing Mexican and Mexican-American visual and performing artists, and often drawing on the museum's permanent collection of more than 2,400 works. But it's the visiting artists, festival programming, and community participation where the museum really shines. Its Day of the Dead celebration, which runs for about 8 weeks beginning in September, is one of the most ambitious in the country. The Del Corazon Mexican Performing Arts Festival, held in the spring, features programs by local and international artists here and around town. And the Sor Juana Festival, presented in the fall, honors Mexican writer and pioneering feminist Sor Juana Ines de la Cruz with photography and painting exhibits, music and theater performances, and poetry readings by Latina women.

The museum also has a splendid gift shop, and it stages a holiday market, featuring gift items from Mexico, on the first weekend in December. Allow 1 hour.

1852 W. 19th St. (a few blocks west of Ashland Ave.). ℂ 312/738-1503. www.mfacmchicago.org. Free admission. Tues–Sun 10am–5pm. Subway/El: Blue Line to 18th St. Bus: 9.

Museum of Broadcast Communications   Ages 3 & up. This museum, formerly housed in the basement of the Chicago Cultural Center, closed its doors in 2004 and plans to reopen in 2006 in a new, 50,000-square-foot home on State Street at Kinzie Avenue. The Museum of Broadcast Communications claims to be one of only three broadcast museums in the nation. Its new home will include expanded archives and exhibit galleries, seminars and public events, a radio and television studio, a gift shop, and a cafe. Stay tuned for more, as they say in the business.

400 N. State St. (at Kinzie), Suite 240. ℂ 312/245-8200. www.mbcnet.org.

Museum of Contemporary Art   **Ages 5 & up.** The MCA is the largest contemporary-art museum in the country, emphasizing experimentation in a variety of media—painting, sculpture, photography, video and film, dance, music, and performance. To be honest, some of the works are challenging enough for adults, much less kids, but kids might get into some of the touring shows, which have included Roy Lichtenstein, Cindy Sherman, and Chuck Close.

Sitting on a front-row piece of property between the lake and the historic Water Tower, the classically styled building, clad in aluminum panels, is a subdued, almost-somber presence, and the steep rise of stairs leading to the entrance is monumental yet a bit daunting. But don't let the gloomy exterior get you down; the interior spaces are more vibrant, with a sun-drenched two-story central corridor, elliptical staircases, and three floors of exhibition space.

You can see the MCA's highlights in about an hour, although art lovers will want more time to wander (especially if a high-profile exhibit is in town). Your first stop should be the handsome barrel-vaulted galleries on the top floor, dedicated to pieces from the permanent collection. For visitors who'd like a little guidance for making sense of the rather challenging works found at a contemporary-art museum, there is an audio tour for rent, as well as a free daily tour (1 and 6pm Tues; 1pm Wed–Fri; 11am, noon, 1 and 2pm Sat–Sun). In addition to a range of special activities and educational programming, including films, performances, and a lecture series in a 300-seat theater, the museum features Puck's at the MCA, a cafe operated by Wolfgang Puck of Spago restaurant fame, with seating that overlooks a 1-acre terraced sculpture garden. The museum store, Culturecounter, has one-of-a-kind gift items that make it worth a stop even if you don't visit the museum. Allow 1 to 2 hours.

220 E. Chicago Ave. (1 block east of Michigan Ave.). © **312/280-2660.** Fax 312/397-4095. www. mcachicago.org. Admission $10 adults, $6 seniors and students with ID, free for children 12 and under. Free admission on Tues 5–8pm. Tues 10am–8pm; Wed–Sun 10am–5pm. Subway/El: Red Line to Chicago/State. Bus: 3, 10, 66, 145, 146, or 151.

Museum of Contemporary Photography   **Ages 8 & up.** Columbia College's photography museum sometimes has shows that kids find appealing (one show featured fairy-tale based photography aimed at preteens; another featured photos of twins)—so call or check out the website for current shows. Ensconced in a ground-floor space at the college, a progressive arts- and media-oriented institution that boasts the country's largest undergraduate film department and a highly respected photojournalism-slanted photography department, the Museum of Contemporary Photography is the only museum in the Midwest of its ilk. As the name indicates, it exhibits, collects, and promotes modern photography, with a special focus on American works from 1959 to the present. Rotating exhibitions showcase images by both nationally recognized and "undiscovered" regional artists. Related lectures and special programs are scheduled during the year.

600 S. Michigan Ave. © **312/663-5554.** Fax 312/344-8067. www.mocp.org. Free admission. Mon–Wed and Fri 10am–5pm; Thurs 10am–8pm; Sat noon–5pm. Subway/El: Red Line to Harrison. Bus: 6, 146, or 151.

National Vietnam Veterans Art Museum *(Finds)* **Ages 12 & up.** Junior high kids and older can emerge from this unique museum with a better understanding of the Vietnam War and the lives touched by this experience. This museum houses one of the most stirring art collections anywhere—and the only one of its kind in the world—telling the story of the men who fought in Vietnam. Since the war, many of the veterans made art as personal therapy, never expecting to show it to anyone, but in 1981 a small group of them began showing their works together in Chicago and in touring exhibitions. The collection has grown to more than 700 paintings, drawings, photographs, and sculptures from all over the country and other countries, including Vietnam. Titles such as *We Regret to Inform You, Blood Spots on a Rice Paddy,* and *The Wound* should give you an idea of the power of the images in this unique legacy to the war. Housed in a former warehouse in the Prairie Avenue district south of the Loop, the museum is modern and well organized. An installation that's suspended from the ceiling, **Above & Beyond** ⭐, comprises more than 58,000 dog tags with the names of the men and women who died in the war—the emotional effect is similar to that of the Wall in Washington, D.C. The complex also houses a small theater, a cafe open for breakfast and lunch, a gift shop, and an outdoor plaza with a flagpole that has deliberately been left leaning because that's how veterans saw them in combat. Allow 1 hour.

1801 S. Indiana Ave. (at 18th St.). 🕐 312/326-0270. www.nvvam.org. Admission $6 adults, $5 seniors and students with ID. Tues–Fri 11am–6pm; Sat 10am–5pm; Sun noon–5pm. Closed major holidays. Bus: 3 or 4.

Newberry Library   Ages 12 & up. Got a bookworm in the family? The Newberry Library is a bibliophile's dream. Established in 1887 at the bequest of the Chicago merchant and financier Walter Loomis Newberry, the noncirculating research library today contains many rare books and manuscripts (such as Shakespeare's first folio and Jefferson's copy of *The Federalist Papers*). Although most of the library is off-limits to kids under 16, the library does hold children's story hours throughout the year. It also houses a vast depository of published resources for those who are seriously delving into American and European history and literature, as well as other aspects of the humanities from the late Middle Ages onward. The library is also a major destination for genealogists digging at their roots, and its holdings are now open for the use of the public for free (over the age of 16 with a photo ID). The collections, many items of which are displayed during an ongoing series of public exhibitions, include more than 1.5 million volumes and 75,000 maps, housed in a comely five-story granite building, designed in the Spanish-Romanesque style by Henry Ives Cobb and built in 1893. For an overview, take a free 1-hour tour Thursday at 3pm or Saturday at 10:30am. The library also operates a fine bookstore. One popular annual event that older kids might enjoy is the "Bughouse Square" debates. Held across the street in Washington Square Park, the debates re-create the fiery soapbox orations of the left-wing agitators in the 1930s and 1940s. Chicago favorite son Studs Terkel, the Pulitzer Prize–winning oral historian, often emcees the hullabaloo. Allow a half-hour.

60 W. Walton St. (at Dearborn Pkwy.). 🕐 **312/943-9090** or 312/255-3700 for programs. www.newberry.org. Reading room Tues–Thurs 10am–6pm; Fri–Sat 9am–5pm. Subway/El: Red Line to Chicago/State. Bus: 22, 36, 125, 145, 146, 147, or 151. Validated parking available at Clark and Chestnut sts.

Oriental Institute Museum ⭐ *Finds*   **Ages 10 & up.** Don't skip this museum because of its slightly intimidating name. Kids love the Egyptian artifacts here (including toys and clothes from ancient Egyptian children). Located near the midpoint of the University of Chicago campus, just north of the Memorial Chapel, the Oriental Institute houses one of the world's major collections of Near Eastern art. Although most of the galleries have been renovated within the last few years, this is still a very traditional museum: lots of glass cases, very few interactive exhibits (that's why I recommend it only for older kids). It won't take you long to see the highlights here—but a few impressive pieces make it worth a stop for history and art buffs.

Your first stop should be the **Egyptian Gallery** ★★, which showcases the finest objects among the 35,000 artifacts from the Nile Valley held by the museum. At the center of the new gallery stands a monumental 17-foot solid-quartzite **statue of King Tutankhamen,** the boy king who ruled Egypt from about 1335 to 1324 B.C. The largest Egyptian sculpture in the Western Hemisphere (tipping the scales at 6 tons), the Oriental Institute excavated it in 1930. The surrounding exhibits, which document the life and beliefs of Egyptians from 5000 B.C. to the 8th century A.D., have a wonderfully accessible approach that emphasizes themes, not chronology. Among them: mummification (there are 14 mummies on display—five people and nine animals, including hawks, an ibis, a shrew, and a baby crocodile), kingship, society, writing (including a deed for the sale of a house, a copy of the *Book of the Dead,* and a schoolboy's homework), family, art, tools and technology, occupations, popular religion, medicine, the gods, food, games, clothing, and jewelry. Kids will be especially interested in two fragile objects used by Egyptian children: papyrus documents and a child's linen tunic from 1550 B.C.

The institute also houses important collections of artifacts from civilizations that once flourished in what are now Iran and Iraq. The highlight of the **Mesopotamian Gallery** ★ is a massive, 16-foot-tall sculpture of a winged bull with a human head, which once stood in the palace of Assyrian King Sargon II. The gallery also contains some of the earliest man-made tools ever excavated, along with many other pieces that have become one-of-akin since the looting of the National Museum in Baghdad in 2003. The Persian Gallery displays some 1,000 objects dating from the Archaic Susiana period (ca. 6800 B.C.) to the Islamic period (ca. A.D. 1000). Other galleries are filled with artifacts from Sumer, ancient Palestine, Israel, Anatolia, and Nubia.

The gift shop at the Oriental Institute, called the Suq, stocks many unique items, including reproductions of pieces in the museum's collection. Allow 1 hour.

1155 E. 58th St. (at University Ave.). © 773/702-9514. www.oi.uchicago.edu. Free admission; suggested donation $5 adults, $2 children. Tues and Thurs–Sat 10am–4pm; Wed 10am–8:30pm; Sun noon–4pm. Bus: 6 or Metra Electric train to 57th St. and Lake Park Ave.

Peace Museum   **Ages 8 & up.** If you're making a trip to the Garfield Park Conservatory, here's a second stop in the neighborhood. Located in the Garfield Park Gold Dome, the Peace Museum presents four exhibits a year and keeps on permanent display such 20th-century artifacts as manuscripts by Joan Baez, Civil Rights–era photos, and a John Lennon guitar. The museum claims to be the first and only of its kind, founded in 1981 by an artist-activist and a U.S. ambassador to UNICEF, and dedicated to exploring the impact of war and peace through the arts. Here's a little trivia for you: The rock group U2 named one of its albums, *The Unforgettable Fire,* for an exhibition of drawings by survivors of Hiroshima and Nagasaki that Bono and the boys viewed at this museum.

Garfield Park Gold Dome, 100 N. Central Park Ave. (2 blocks south of Garfield Park Conservatory). © 773/638-6450. www.peacemuseum.org. Admission $3.50 adults; $2 seniors, students, and children. Thurs–Sat 11am–4pm. Subway/El: Green Line to Conservatory/Central Park Dr.

Polish Museum of America   **Ages 6 & up.** One million people of Polish ancestry live in Chicago, giving the city the largest Polish population outside of Warsaw. So it's no surprise that Chicago is the site of the Polish Museum of America, located in the neighborhood where many of the first immigrants settled. This museum has one of the most important collections of Polish art and historical materials outside Poland (it is also the largest museum in the United States devoted exclusively to an ethnic group). The museum's programs include rotating exhibitions, films, lectures, and concerts, and a permanent exhibit about Pope John Paul II. There is also a library with a large Polish-language collection, and archives where visitors can research genealogical history (call in advance if you want to look through those records). Parents should request a "seek and find" booklet with questions for kids (and get a free Polish Museum pen, too).

984 N. Milwaukee Ave. (at Augusta Blvd.). 𝄞 773/384-3352. www.pma.prcua.org. Suggested donation $3 adults, $2 students, $1 children. Fri–Wed 11am–4pm. Subway/El: Blue Line to Division.

The Smart Museum of Art ⭐ **Ages 5 & up.** The University of Chicago's fine-arts museum looks rather modest, but it packs a lot of talent into a compact space. Its permanent collection of more than 7,000 paintings and sculptures spans Western and Eastern civilizations and ranges from classical antiquity to the present day. Bona fide treasures include ancient Greek vases, Chinese bronzes, and old-master paintings; Frank Lloyd Wright furniture; Tiffany glass; sculptures by Degas, Matisse, and Rodin; and 20th-century paintings and sculptures by Mark Rothko, Arthur Dove, Mexican muralist Diego Rivera, Henry Moore, and Chicago sculptor Richard Hunt. Built in 1974, the contemporary building doesn't really fit in with the Gothic style of other campus buildings, but its sculpture garden and outdoor seating are available for families, who are welcome to picnic on the lawn. The museum is reaching out to families through Art Afternoons, held Wednesday from noon to 3pm, when families can try a hands-on art activity. It's available for a small fee; check the website or call ahead to confirm. The museum also has a gift shop and a cafe.

5550 S. Greenwood Ave. (at E. 55th St.). 𝄞 773/702-0200. www.smartmuseum.uchicago.edu. Free admission; donations welcome. Tues–Wed and Fri 10am–4pm; Thurs 10am–8pm; Sat–Sun 11am–5pm. Closed holidays. Bus: 6.

Spertus Museum **Ages 5 & up.** The Spertus Museum, an extension of the Spertus Institute of Jewish Studies, showcases intricately crafted and historic Jewish ceremonial objects, textiles, coins, paintings, and sculpture, tracing 5,000 years of Jewish heritage. Kids enjoy the Artifact Center, with 12 authentic archaeological dig sites and tools that let future archaeologists discover replicas of artifacts (such as pottery) under the sand. (Reserved for school groups in the mornings, but it's open to the public in the afternoon). Though small in scale, the **Zell Holocaust Memorial** exhibit is particularly moving, featuring a video montage of Holocaust victims with a Chicago connection and a display of related artifacts and documents. The institute's Asher Library boasts one of the largest collections of Jewish books, periodicals, videos, and music in the country. The Bariff Shop for Judaica carries a large selection of art, books, music, videos, and contemporary and traditional Jewish ceremonial gifts. Allow 1 hour.

618 S. Michigan Ave. 𝄞 312/322-1747. www.spertus.edu. Admission $5 adults; $3 seniors, students, and children; $10 maximum family rate. Free admission Fri. Sun–Wed 10am–5pm; Thurs 10am–7pm; Fri 10am–3pm. Subway/El: Red Line to Harrison; Brown, Purple, Orange, or Green Line to Adams. Bus: 3, 4, 6, 145, 147, or 151. Validated parking in nearby lots.

Swedish-American Museum Center ⭐ **Ages 4 & up.** Chicago parents recommend a visit to this storefront museum, which chronicles the Swedish immigrant contribution to American life. The museum is a hub of activity, with cultural lectures, concerts, and classes and folk dancing geared to Swedish Americans, some

For Train Lovers

Chicago and trains go together like, well, kids and trains. From little red streetcars to thundering steam trains, two area museums are the places to ride the rails—and maybe even learn a bit about history.

At the **Fox River Trolley Museum** (www.foxtrolley.org; © 847/697-4676) in west suburban South Elgin, hop a trolley and ride a real electric railway that first opened on July 4, 1896. The 3-mile ride takes you along the banks of the scenic Fox River. The Aurora, Elgin, and Fox River Electric Co. Interurban Line once connected communities along the Fox River, including Carpentersville, Elgin, Aurora, and Yorkville. The railway was abandoned to passenger traffic in 1935, and in 1972 the museum purchased part of the line. At the museum you can check out antique trolleys from 1891 to 1952. The museum's most popular annual event is the Pumpkin Trolley, run on two weekends in October. Ride the trolley to the museum's pumpkin patch, pick your own, and head back to the museum for a picnic lunch and a visit to the museum store.

The museum is located at 361 S. LaFox St. (Illinois Rte. 31) in South Elgin, about 40 miles west of Chicago. Fares are $3.50 for adults, $2 for seniors, and $2 for children 2 to 11. The museum is open Mother's Day through November 4 on Sunday from 11am to 5pm, and June 30 to September 1 on Saturday from 11am to 5pm. To get there, take I-90 or U.S. Route 20 west to Elgin, and exit on Illinois Route 31 southbound. To make it an all-train day, take the Metra commuter train to Elgin on the Milwaukee District West Line. Then take Pace bus no. 801 to State Street, South Elgin, and walk 3 blocks south to the museum (or take a taxi from the Elgin train station).

America's largest railway museum is the **Illinois Railway Museum** (www.irm.org) located in Union, about 60 miles northwest of Chicago.

of whom still live in the surrounding Andersonville neighborhood. The **Children's Museum of Immigration** is located on the third floor, where Swedish craft demonstrations and classes, as well as language classes, are offered. Geared toward kindergarteners through sixth graders, the museum lets kids experience the journey from the Old World. They can step inside an authentic Swedish farmhouse, board a steamship for America, and begin a new life in a log cabin. A modern-day refugee's raft connects children to today's immigration story.

The permanent exhibits on display draw on a small collection of art and artifacts dating to the mass immigration of Swedes to Chicago 2 centuries ago. Temporary exhibitions (usually Swedish folk art) are mounted four times a year. There's also a nice gift shop that offers Orrefors glassware; books on Swedish folk art, decorating, and cooking; children's toys; and holiday knickknacks. Strolling down this stretch of Clark Street, where Swedish bakeries and gourmet-food stores are interspersed with an attractive mix of restaurants, bars, cafes, and theater companies, is the best reason for stopping in here.

5211 N. Clark St. (near Foster Ave.). © 773/728-8111. www.museum@samac.org. Suggested donation $4 adults, $2 seniors and students, $1 children. Tues–Fri 10am–4pm; Sat–Sun 11am–4pm. Subway/El: Red Line to Bryn Mawr, then walk several blocks west to Clark. Bus: 22.

With 120 acres and 400 engines and cars, sprawling rail lines criss-cross the property. (Be sure to look both ways before crossing any tracks!) The museum has a 5-mile rail line, where you'll find steam, diesel, and heavy electric trains chugging along, and a mile-long streetcar loop. On the weekend you can jump on a steam or diesel train from the museum's East Union depot (built around a station dating from 1851) and take a 40-minute round-trip ride to Kishwaukee Grove, passing prairie and farm-land. Whether you get on a steam locomotive with its hissing brakes and billowing steam, a diesel dating from the 1950s, or an Electroliner, which ran between Chicago and Milwaukee until 1963 and is powered by over-head wires, you're in for a thrill. Smaller trains depart from the 50th Avenue rapid transit station built in 1910 and removed from Cicero.

A streetcar line encircles the museum grounds so you can hop on and off at different "barns" that house everything from red cabooses to lux-urious private passenger cars from the late 1800s. Call ✆ **800/BIG-RAIL** or 815/923-4000 in advance to find out which trains are operating. Diesels operate most weekends and holidays, but steam trains only run about 12 times a season. Electric cars run daily.

The museum is open from April through October. Grounds are open from 9am to 6pm, and trains run on weekends from 10:30am to 5pm, and weekdays from 10am to 4pm. Rides cost $6 to $10 (depending on the trains running) for adults, and $4 to $8 for children, with family maximums of $20 to $40. To get there, take I-90 to U.S. Route 20. Take the Marengo exit and drive northwest on Route 20 to Union Road. Go north on Union Road.

5 Best Rides

The best ride in the city is the "El," with boat tours of the river and lake a close sec-ond (see "Kid-Friendly Tours" later in this chapter). Other rides are tucked away in Chicago's top attractions: Don't miss the endangered-species merry-go-round at Lincoln Park Zoo and the Ferris wheel and carousel at Navy Pier. Not enough excitement for you? Thrill seekers should head directly to an amusement park.

Six Flags Great America   **All ages.** One of the Midwest's biggest theme/amusement parks is located midway between Chicago and Milwaukee on I-94 in Gurnee, Illinois. The park has more than 100 rides and attractions and is a favorite of roller-coaster devotees. There are a whopping 10 of them here, including the nausea-inducing Déjà vu, where riders fly forwards and backwards over a twisting, looping inverted steel track, and Superman, where you speed along hanging headfirst (with your legs dangling). Other don't-miss rides for the strong of stomach include the Iron Wolf, where you do corkscrew turns and 360-degree loops while standing up, and the American Eagle, a classic wooden coaster. Because this is a place that caters to families, you'll also find plenty to appeal to the young set. The Looney Tunes National Park is full of kiddie rides with a cartoon theme; other worthwhile stops include the double-decker carousel and bumper cars. Six Flags also has live shows, IMAX movies, and restaurants. If you take the trouble to get out here from the city, allow a full day.

I-94 at Rte. 132 E., Gurnee. ℂ 847/249-4636. www.sixflags.com. Admission (including unlimited rides, shows, and attractions) $42 adults, $30 seniors and children over 54 in. tall, free for children 3 and under. Open daily May 10am–7pm; June–Aug 10am–10pm; weekends only in Sept 10am–7pm. Parking $10. Take I-94 or I-294 W. to Rte. 132 (Grand Ave.). Approximate driving time from Chicago city limits is 45 min.

6 Historic Houses

An extensive tour of the neighborhood surrounding the Frank Lloyd Wright Home and Studio leaves from the **Ginkgo Tree Bookshop,** 951 Chicago Ave. (ℂ **708/848-1606**), on weekends from 10:30am to 4pm (tour times are somewhat more limited Nov–Feb). This tour lasts 1 hour and costs $9 for adults and $7 for seniors and children 7 to 18, and is free for children under 7. If you can't make it to Oak Park on the weekend, you can follow a self-guided map and audiocassette tour of the historic district (recorded in English, French, Spanish,

The (Frank Lloyd) Wright Stuff

Oak Park has the highest concentration of houses or buildings anywhere designed and built by Wright, probably the most influential figure in American architectural history. People come here to marvel at the work of a man who saw his life as a twofold mission: to wage a single-handed battle against the ornamental excesses of architecture, Victorian in particular, and to create in its place a new form that would be at the same time functional, appropriate to its natural setting, and stimulating to the imagination.

Not everyone who comes to Oak Park shares Wright's architectural philosophy. But scholars and enthusiasts admire Wright for being consistently true to his own vision, out of which emerged a unique and genuinely American architectural statement. The reason for Wright's success could stem from the fact that he himself was a living exemplar of a quintessential American type. In a deep sense, he embodied the ideal of the self-made and self-sufficient individual who had survived, even thrived, in the frontier society—qualities that he expressed in his almost-puritanical insistence that each spatial or structural form in his buildings serve some useful purpose. But he was also an aesthete in Emersonian fashion, deriving his idea of beauty from natural environments, where apparent simplicity often belies a subtle complexity.

The three principal ingredients of a tour of Wright-designed structures in Oak Park are the **Frank Lloyd Wright Home & Studio tour,** the **Unity Temple tour,** and a **walking tour**—guided or self-guided—to view the exteriors of homes throughout the neighborhood that were built by the architect. Oak Park has, in all, 25 homes and buildings by Wright, constructed between the years 1892 and 1913, which constitute the core output of his Prairie School period. Visiting another 50 dwellings of architectural interest by Wright's contemporaries, scattered throughout this community and neighboring River Forest, is also worthwhile.

Oak Park Attractions

Frank Lloyd Wright Home and Studio **1**

Ginkgo Tree Bookshop **2**

Oak Park Visitors Center **3**

Unity Temple **4**

> ⌒Tips **The Wright Plus Tour**
>
> Die-hard fans of the architect will want to plan to be in town the third Saturday in May for the annual Wright Plus Tour, during which the public can tour several Frank Lloyd Wright–designed homes and several other notable Oak Park buildings, in both the Prairie School and the Victorian styles, in addition to Wright's home and studio and the Unity Temple. The tour includes 10 buildings in all. Tickets go on sale March 1 and can sell out within 6 weeks. Call ℂ **708/848-1976** (Frank Lloyd Wright Home & Studio) for details and ticket information.

German, Japanese, and Italian). Available at the Ginkgo Tree Bookshop from 10am to 3:30pm, the self-guided tour costs $9 for adults and $7 for seniors and children. In addition to Wright's work, you will see that of several of his disciples, as well as some very charming examples of the Victorian styling that he so disdained. A more detailed map selling for $3 at the bookshop, *Architectural Guide Map of Oak Park and River Forest,* includes text and photos of all 80 sites of interest in Oak Park and neighboring River Forest.

The Frank Lloyd Wright Home & Studio ★★★ **Ages 3 & up.** For the first 20 years of Wright's career, this remarkable complex served first and foremost as the sanctuary from which Wright was to design and execute more than 130 of an extraordinary output of 430 completed buildings. During this highly fertile period, the house was Wright's showcase and laboratory, but it also embraces many idiosyncratic features molded to his own needs rather than those of a client. The home began as a simple shingled cottage that Wright built for his bride in 1889 at the age of 22, but it became a work in progress, as Wright remodeled it constantly over the years. With its many add-ons—including a barrel-vaulted children's playroom and a studio with an octagonal balcony suspended by chains—the place has a certain whimsy that others might have found less livable. This, however, was not an architect's masterpiece, but the master's home, and every room in it can be savored for the view it reflects of the workings of a remarkable mind. The Home and Studio Foundation has restored the residence and studio to its 1909 vintage—the year Wright left the house.

The special guided Junior Architecture Tour presents the home through the eyes of the six Wright children who grew up here. (One of those children later invented Lincoln Logs.) Tours, which are for kids age 6 to 14, are led the fourth Saturday of the month from January to November and last 45 minutes. What's most special is that the tours are given by the Preservation Trust's Junior Interpreters, specially trained 5th- through 10th-grade students. Tour cost is $3.

951 Chicago Ave. ℂ **708/848-1976.** www.wrightplus.org. Admission $9 adults, $7 seniors and children 7–18, free for children under 7. Combined admission for Home & Studio tour and guided or self-guided historic district tour (see below) $15 adults, $11 seniors and children 7–18. Admission to home and studio is by guided tour only; tours depart from the Ginkgo Tree Bookshop Mon–Fri 11am, 1pm, and 3pm; Sat–Sun every 20 min. 11am–3:30pm. Facilities for people with disabilities are limited; please call in advance.

Robie House ★★ **Ages 7 & up.** One of Frank Lloyd Wright's finest works, the Robie House is considered among the masterpieces of 20th-century American architecture. The open layout, linear geometry of form, and craftsmanship are typical of Wright's Prairie School design. Completed in 1909 for inventor Frederick Robie, a bicycle and motorcycle manufacturer, the home is also notable for its exquisite leaded- and stained-glass doors and windows. It's also among the last of his Prairie School–style homes: During its construction, Wright abandoned both his family and his Oak Park practice to follow other pursuits, most prominently the realization of his Taliesin home and studio in Spring Green, Wisconsin. Docents from Oak Park's Frank Lloyd Wright Home and Studio Foundation lead tours here, even though the house is undergoing a massive, 10-year restoration (the house will be open throughout the process, but your photos might include plenty of scaffolding). A Wright specialty bookshop is located in the building's former three-car garage—which was highly unusual for the time in which it was built. Although I've noted that this is for ages 7 and up, older children and teens will appreciate Robie House most. Allow 2 hours.

5757 S. Woodlawn Ave. (at 58th St.). ⓒ **773/834-1847.** Admission $9 adults, $7 seniors and children 7–18. Mon–Fri tours at 11am, 1pm, and 3pm; Sat–Sun every ½ hr. 11am–3:30pm. Bookshop open daily 10am–5pm. Bus: 6 or Metra Electric train to 57th St. and Lake Park Ave.

Unity Temple ⟨ Ⓕ ⟩   **Ages 5 & up.** After fire destroyed its church around 1900, a Unitarian Universalist congregation asked one of its members, Frank Lloyd Wright, to design an affordable replacement. Using poured concrete with metal reinforcements—a necessity, owing to the small budget of $40,000 allocated for the project—Wright created a building that on the outside seems as forbidding as a mausoleum but that on the inside contains in its detailing the entire architectural alphabet of the Prairie School that has since made Wright's name immortal. Following the example of H. H. Richardson (of Glessner House fame; see below), Wright placed the building's main entrance on the side, behind an enclosure—a feature often employed in his houses as well—to create a sense of privacy and intimacy. Front entrances were too anonymous for these two architects. Wright complained, furthermore, that other architectural conventions of the church idiom, such as the nave in the Gothic-style cathedral across from the future site of Unity Temple, were overpowering. Of that particular church, he commented that he didn't feel a part of it.

Yet his own vision in this regard was somewhat confused and contradictory. He wanted Unity Temple to be "democratic." But perhaps Wright was unable to subdue his own personal hubris and hauteur in the creative process, for the ultimate effect of his chapel, and much of the building's interior, is very grand and imperial. Unity Temple is no simple meetinghouse in the tradition of Calvinist iconoclasm. Instead, its principal chapel looks like the chamber of the Roman Senate. Even so, the interior, with its unpredictable geometric arrangements and its decor reminiscent of Native American art, is no less beautiful.

Wright used color sparingly within Unity Temple, but the pale, natural effects that he achieved are owed in part to his decision to add pigment to the plaster rather than use paint. Wright's use of wood for trim and other decorative touches is still exciting to behold; his sensitivity to grain and tone and placement

---

⟨ Finds More Frank Lloyd Wright Homes

In addition to Robie House, several of Wright's earlier works, still privately owned, dot the streets of Hyde Park, such as the **Heller House,** 5132 S. Woodlawn Ave. (1897); the **Blossom House,** 1332 E. 49th St. (1882); and the **McArthur House,** 4852 S. Kenwood Ave. (1892). These homes are not open to the public but can be admired from the sidewalk.

The Pride of Prairie Avenue

Prairie Avenue, south of the Loop, was the city's first "Gold Coast," and its most famous address is **Glessner House,** a must-see for anyone interested in architectural history. The only surviving Chicago building designed by Boston architect Henry Hobson Richardson, it represented a dramatic shift from traditional Victorian architecture when it was built in 1886 (and inspired a young Frank Lloyd Wright).

The imposing granite exterior gives the home a forbidding air. (Railway magnate George Pullman, who lived nearby, complained, "I do not know what I have ever done to have that thing staring me in the face every time I go out my door."). But step inside and the home turns out to be a welcoming, cozy retreat, filled with Arts and Crafts furniture and decorative arts.

Visits to Glessner House are by guided tour only. Tours are given Wednesday to Sunday at 1, 2, and 3pm year-round (except major holidays). Tours are first-come, first-served, with no advance reservations except for groups of 10 or more. It's located at 1800 S. Prairie Ave. (© 312/326-1480; www.glessnerhouse.org). Admission is $9 for adults, $8 for students and seniors, and $4 for children 5 to 12. Bus: 1, 3, or 4 from Michigan Avenue at Jackson Boulevard (Get off at 18th St.).

was akin to that of an exceptionally gifted woodworker. Wright was a true hands-on, can-do person; he knew the materials he chose to use as intimately as the artisans who carried out his plans. And his stunning, almost-minimalist use of form is what still sets him apart as a relevant and brilliant artist. Other details to which the docent guide will call your attention, as you complete a circuit of the temple, are the great fireplace, the pulpit, the skylights, and the clerestory (gallery) windows. Suffice it to say, Unity Temple—only one of Wright's masterpieces—is counted among the 10 greatest American architectural achievements. For small kids, a brief peek into the temple on a walk around the neighborhood (after touring the Frank Lloyd Wright Home & Studio, for example) is best; teens will appreciate the architecture more.

875 Lake St. © 708/383-8873. www.unitytemple-utrf.org. Self-guided tours $6 adults; $4 seniors, children 5–12, and students with ID. 45-min. guided tours Sat–Sun on the hour 1–3pm at no extra charge. Mon–Fri 10:30am–4:30pm; Sat–Sun 1–4pm. Church events can alter the schedule; call in advance.

7 Zoos

Brookfield Zoo ★★★ **All ages.** Brookfield is the Chicago area's largest zoo. In contrast to the rather efficient Lincoln Park Zoo, Brookfield is spacious and spreads out over 216 acres with 2,700 animal residents—camels, dolphins, giraffes, baboons, wolves, tigers, green sea turtles, Siberian tigers, snow leopards, and more—living in naturalistic environments that put them side by side with other inhabitants of their regions. These creative indoor and outdoor settings— filled with activities to keep kids interested—are what set Brookfield apart. One of the newest exhibits, **The Living Coast,** explores the western coast of Chile and Peru and includes everything from a tank of plate-size moon jellies to a rocky shore where Humboldt penguins swim and nest as Inca terns and gray gulls fly freely overhead. Other impressive exhibits include **The Swamp,** which re-creates the bioregions of a Southern cypress swamp and an Illinois river scene and discusses what people can do to protect wetlands, and **Habitat Africa!,** a multiple ecosystem exhibit-in-progress that eventually will encompass 30 acres—about the size of the entire Lincoln Park Zoo. The thrills here aren't always high concept: Some of my favorite exhibits are the Australia House, where fruit bats flit around your head, and Tropic World, where you wander at treetop level with monkeys. The dolphins at the **Seven Seas Panorama** put on an amazing show that has been a Brookfield Zoo fixture for years. If you go on a weekend, buy tickets to the dolphin show at least a couple of hours ahead of time because they tend to sell out quickly.

First Ave. and 31st St., Brookfield. ✆ 708/485-0263. www.brookfieldzoo.org. Regular admission $8 adults, $4 seniors and children 3–11, free for children under 3. Free admission Tues and Thurs Oct–Mar. Summer daily 9:30am–6pm; fall–spring daily 10am–5pm. Take the Stevenson (I-55) and Eisenhower (I-290) expressways 14 miles west of the Loop. Bus: 304 or 311.

Lincoln Park Pritzker Children's Zoo & Farm-in-the-Zoo ★ *Value* **All ages.** After gazing upon the animals from afar in the rest of the Lincoln Park Zoo, kids can come here for some hands-on experience. Kids have the opportunity to touch many of the animals, including hedgehogs, rabbits, and iguanas, under the supervision of zookeepers. There's also a very popular glass-walled animal nursery, where zoo docents and keepers care for the babies of more exotic species—often, this means gorillas and chimpanzees—who are ill, born weak, or rejected by their mothers. The adjacent outdoor portion of the Children's Zoo houses owls, otters, and other small critters in winding, natural habitats. The Children's Zoo also features an annex called **Conservation Station,** with interactive exhibits and workshop activities focusing on wildlife and environmental preservation.

The Farm-in-the-Zoo is a working reproduction of a Midwestern farm, complete with a white-picket-fenced barnyard. You can see live demonstrations of butter churning and weaving. Thanks to the chicken coops, and stalls filled with livestock, including cows, sheep, and pigs, even the aroma is authentic. Inside the Main Barn (filled with interactive exhibits), the main attraction is the huge John Deere tractor that kids can climb up into and pretend to drive. Allow 1 hour.

2200 N. Cannon Dr. ✆ 312/742-2000. Free admission. Daily 9am–4:30pm. Bus: 151 or 156.

Lincoln Park Zoo ★★★ *Value* **All ages.** One of Chicago's don't-miss attractions for kids, Lincoln Park Zoo occupies a scant 35 acres, and its landmark Georgian Revival brick buildings and modern structures sit among gently rolling pathways, verdant lawns, and a kaleidoscopic profusion of flower gardens. It's so compact that a tour of the various habitats takes all of 2 or 3 hours—a convenience factor even more enticing when you consider that the nation's oldest zoo (it was founded in 1868) stays open 365 days a year and is one of the last free zoos in the country. Lincoln Park Zoo has held a special place in the hearts of Chicagoans since the days of Bushman, the mighty lowland gorilla who captivated the world in the 1930s and 1940s and now suffers the ignominious fate of a stuffed exhibit at the Field Museum of Natural History. The late Marlon Perkins, legendary host of the *Mutual of Omaha's Wild Kingdom* TV series, got his start here as the zoo's director, and filmed a pioneering TV show called *Zoo Parade* (*Wild Kingdom*'s predecessor) in the basement of the old Reptile House.

The zoo has taken on an ambitious modernization, renovating and expanding exhibits to reflect natural habitats. For years, the star attraction has been the

Lincoln Park Zoo

DINING ◆

Big Cats Café **7**
Café Brauer **19**
Elephant Café **1**
Ice Cream
  Shoppe **18**
Landmark Café **6**
Park Place Café **15**

SHOPPING ✳

Fitz's General
  Store **22**
Safari Shop **11**
Wild Things! shop **8**

ANIMAL ATTRACTIONS ●

Antelope & Zebra Area **20**
Ameritech Endangered Species
  Carousel **13**
Bear & Wolf Habitat **2**
Bird House **3**
Birds of Prey Exhibit **4**
Children's Zoo **9**
Farm-in-the-Zoo **21**
Lester E. Fisher Great Ape House **20**
Lion House **12**
Penguin & Seabird House **5**
Primate House **14**
Sea Lion Pool **10**
Small Mammal–Reptile House **17**
Swan Pond **16**

lowland gorillas at the **Great Ape House** ✿, which was completely rebuilt in 2004. The zoo has had remarkable success in breeding both gorillas and chimpanzees, and watching these ape families is mesmerizing. **Regenstein African Journey** ✿✿ is home to elephants, giraffes, rhinos, and other large mammals; large glass-enclosed tanks allow visitors to go face-to-face with swimming pygmy hippos and (not for the faint of heart) a rocky ledge filled with hissing cockroaches from Madagascar.

The **Small Mammal–Reptile House** is a state-of-the-art facility, housing 200 species and featuring a glass-enclosed walk-through ecosystem simulating river, savanna, and forest habitats. The popular **Sea Lion Pool,** situated in the center of the zoo and home to harbor seals, gray seals, and California sea lions, features an underwater viewing area spanning 70 feet and an amphitheater.

The Park Place Café food court is located in a historic building that originally was Chicago's first aquarium. And the Mahon Theobold Pavilion features a sprawling indoor gift shop and a unique rooftop eatery called Big Cats Café that opens at 8am (1 hr. before the exhibits do) and serves fresh-baked muffins and scones, focaccia sandwiches, salads, and flatbreads. *Tip:* For best animal viewing, go on a temperate weather day—in really hot weather, the animals tend to be lethargic (like human beings, I guess!). Allow 2 to 3 hours.

2200 N. Cannon Dr. (near Lake Shore Dr. at Fullerton Pkwy.). ✆ **312/742-2000.** www.lpzoo.com. Free admission. Buildings open daily 10am–5pm (until 6:30pm Sat–Sun Memorial Day to Labor Day); grounds open 9am–6pm (until 7pm Memorial Day to Labor Day and until 5pm Nov 1–Mar 31). Free trolley service from area CTA stations and parking garages on Sat–Sun and holidays 10am–6pm Memorial Day to Labor Day; visit the zoo's website for route information and schedule.

8 Gardens & Conservatories

Garfield Park Conservatory ✿ **All ages.** Designed by the great landscape architect Jens Jensen in 1907, Garfield Park Conservatory is one of the largest gardens under glass in the world at 2 acres in size. And it's open 365 days a year from 9am to 5pm, with free admission. Surprisingly, it took a blockbuster exhibit by glass artist Dave Chihuly a few years ago for many Chicagoans to "discover" the conservatory.

Chicago parents give the conservatory a thumbs-up for the special kids' area, which features a slide, climbing equipment, and a big pile of dirt (and digging tools), all within an environment that feels downright tropical. Educational displays such as plants, pods, and insects and staff members who work with kids ensure that some learning gets done along with digging. Unfortunately, the conservatory is surrounded by a rather blighted neighborhood with a high crime rate. I advise driving there and forgoing public transportation. Allow 1 hour.

300 N. Central Park Ave. ✆ **312/746-5100.** Free admission. Daily 9am–5pm. Free parking in an adjacent lot.

Lincoln Park Conservatory ✿ **All ages.** Just beyond the zoo's northeast border is a lovely botanical garden housed in a soaring glass-domed structure. Inside are four great halls filled with thousands of plants that, unless you're an avid horticulturist, will take you perhaps a half-hour to explore. The Palm House features giant palms and rubber trees (including a 50-ft. fiddle leaf rubber tree dating from 1891), the Fernery nurtures plants that grow close to the forest floor, and the Tropical House is a shiny symphony of flowering trees, vines, and bamboo. The fourth environment is the Show House, where seasonal flower shows are held.

Even better than the plants inside, however, might be what lies outside the front doors. The expansive lawn with its French garden and lovely fountain on the conservatory's south side is one of the best places in town for an informal picnic (especially nice if you're visiting the zoo and want to avoid the congestion at its food concession venues). Allow a half-hour.

Fullerton Ave. (at Stockton Dr.). ☏ 312/742-7736. Free admission. Daily 9am–5pm. Bus: 73, 151, or 156.

9 Nature Centers

Morton Arboretum   **Ages 5 & up.** Should your visit to Chicago coincide with Arbor Day, here's the place to celebrate: More than 3,000 kinds of trees, shrubs, and vines grow on the 1,700-acre site in west suburban Lisle. The place has been spruced up lately (sorry for the pun), with improvements to many of the facilities' buildings. Special areas include the Illinois Tree Trails' woodlands, meadows, and marshes; an area with sugar maples (colorful in the fall); a crabapple orchard (splendid when the trees are in full bloom); and a prairie with tall grasses and flowers that blossom in summer and fall. The arboretum also features trees from other countries. Most of the 13 miles of trails are covered with wood chips, so they are not stroller-friendly. If your kids are young, it's best to see the landscape by car along 11 miles of one-way roads or take a bus tour. One-hour tram tours depart at noon and 1:15pm Wednesday, Saturday, and Sunday from May to October. Cost for the tram is $4 per seat, and $3 for children ages 3 to 12. Stop by the visitor center for additional information. Light meals are available in the Ginkgo Restaurant, sandwiches and soups are served in the coffee shop, and there's a picnic area near a small lake.

4100 Illinois Hwy. 53 (at Interstate 88, the East-West Tollway), Lisle. ☏ 630/719-2400. www.mortonarb.org. Admission: $5 adults, $4 seniors, $2 children 3–12, children 2 and under are free. Reduced admission fees on Wed. Nov–Mar daily 7am–5pm; Apr–Oct daily 7am–7pm. Visitor center daily 9am–5pm; Gingko Tree restaurant daily 11am–3pm; coffee shop daily 9am–5pm. Free parking. Subway/El: Metra train stops at Lisle, 1½ miles away; cabs available.

Peggy Notebaert Nature Museum ★★   **All ages.** Built on an ancient sand dune—once the shoreline of Lake Michigan—Chicago's newest museum bills itself as "an environmental museum for the 21st century." Most of the exhibits here are hands-on, making this a good stop for kids. Shaded by huge cottonwoods and maples, the sand-colored exterior with its horizontal lines composed of interlocking trapezoids itself resembles a sand dune. Rooftop-level walkways give strollers a view of birds and other urban wildlife below. Paths wind through gardens planted with native Midwestern wildflowers and grasses, and trace the shore of the newly restored North Pond. Inside, large windows throughout create a dialogue between the outdoor environment and the indoor exhibits designed to illuminate it. The 73,000-square-foot facility features plenty of exhibits on nature and the interaction between human activities and the environment.

Throughout, the focus is on interactivity, done with imagination and intelligence. Don't miss the **Butterfly Haven** ★, a greenhouse habitat where about 25 Midwestern species of butterflies and moths carry on their complex life cycles. Wander through as a riot of color flutters all around you. Another top exhibit is **City Science,** a 3,000-square-foot, two-story "house" with functional rooms where visitors can view the pipes and ducts that connect our homes with power sources miles away. **Water Lab** is a model river system demonstrating the uses and abuses that a waterway undergoes as it meanders from rural to urban environments. It's probably safe to say that the **Children's Gallery** is the only place in town where kids can clamber in and out of a model ground-squirrel town or explore a beaver lodge from the inside.

The sunny Butterfly Cafe offers fresh, healthful meals cafeteria-style. In summer get there early to enjoy coffee and a muffin—and the lovely surroundings—with joggers and other locals. Allow 1 hour.

Fullerton Ave. and Cannon Dr. ✆ 773/755-5100. www.chias.org. Admission $7 adults, $5 seniors and students, $4 children ages 3–12, children under 3 free. Free admission Thurs. Mon–Fri 9am–4:30pm; Sat–Sun 10am–5pm. Closed Thanksgiving, Dec 25, and Jan 1. Free trolley service from area CTA stations and parking garages on Sat–Sun and holidays 10am–6pm Memorial Day to Labor Day; visit the museum website for route information and schedule.

10 Kid-Friendly Tours

If you want someone else to organize your sightseeing, by bus or by boat, you're in luck: Chicago has a number of experienced companies that provide just about any kind of itinerary you can imagine.

ORIENTATION TOURS

Chicago Trolley & Double Decker Company   All ages. Chicago Trolley Company offers guided tours on a fleet of rubber-wheeled "San Francisco–style" trolleys that stop at a number of popular spots around the city, including Navy Pier, the Grant Park museums, the Museum of Science and Industry, Lincoln Park Zoo, and the cluster of theme restaurants in River North. If you can bear the touristy-ness of it all, you'll find that the tours are fun and informative, especially if you get a good driver. You can stay on for the full 1½-hour ride or get on and off at each stop. The trolleys operate year-round, but in the winter you won't need to bundle the kids in snowsuits: The vehicles are enclosed and heated in the chilliest months. The same company also operates the Chicago Double Decker Company, which has a fleet of London-style, red, two-story buses. The buses follow the same route as the trolleys; if you buy an all-day pass, you can hop from bus to trolley at any point. You can buy tickets online or at any of the stops.

✆ 773/648-5000. www.chicagotrolley.com. All-day hop-on, hop-off pass $20 adults, $17 seniors, $10 children 3–10. Family package (2 adults, 2 children) $54. Daily 9am–5pm (until 6:30 Apr–Oct).

Gray Line   Ages 8 & up. Part of a company that offers bus tours worldwide, Gray Line Chicago offers professional tours in well-appointed buses. Most tours run 3 to 4 hours, so this is recommended only for kids who will sit for that long. Tours include lunch and feature highlights of downtown or various neighborhoods; some tours also include a cruise on Lake Michigan or a visit to the Sears Tower Skydeck. You'll also find some more intellectual offerings, including Chicago and the Civil War and Literary Chicago.

27 E. Monroe St., Suite 515. ✆ 800/621-4153 or 312/251-3107. www.grayline.com. Tours cost $35–$60.

CHICAGO ARCHITECTURE FOUNDATION TOURS

Chicago is the first city of architecture, and the **Chicago Architecture Foundation (CAF),** 224 S. Michigan Ave. (✆ **312/922-3432,** or 312/922-TOUR for recorded information; www.architecture.org), offers first-rate guided programs, led by nearly 400 trained and enthusiastic docents. The foundation offers walking, bike, boat, and bus tours to more than 60 architectural sites and environments in and around Chicago. The foundation also has another tour center in the John Hancock Center, 875 N. Michigan Ave. Below is a sampling of the tours the foundation offers.

BY BOAT

Perhaps the CAF's most popular tour is its 1½-hour **Architecture River Cruise,** which glides along both the north and the south branches of the Chicago River.

Although you can see the same 50 or so buildings that the cruise covers on your own by foot, traveling by water lets you enjoy the buildings from a unique perspective. The excellent docents also provide interesting historical details, as well as some fun facts (For example: David Letterman once called the busts of the nation's retailing legends that face the Merchandise Mart the "Pez Hall of Fame"). The cruise points out both landmark buildings, such as the Gothic 1925 Tribune Tower, and contemporary ones, including the late-1980s NBC Tower, constructed in wedding-cake style in homage to the city's old zoning codes mandating that sunlight reach down to the street.

The docents generally do a good job of making the cruise enjoyable for visitors with all levels of architectural knowledge. In addition to pointing out famous buildings—Marina City, the Civic Opera House, the Sears Tower, to name a few—they approach the sites thematically, explaining, for example, how Chicagoans' use of and attitudes toward the river have changed in the past 2 centuries.

Tickets are $23 per person weekdays, $25 on weekends and holidays, and are scheduled hourly every day June through October from 11am to 3pm (weekends only in May and Nov). The trips are extremely popular, so purchase tickets in advance through Ticketmaster (② **312/902-1500;** www.ticketmaster.com), or avoid the service charge and buy your tickets at one of the foundation's tour centers, 224 S. Michigan Ave. or the John Hancock Center, or from the boat launch on the southeast corner of Michigan Avenue and Wacker Drive. Although it's an expensive tour, I still highly recommend it, especially if you're at all interested in architecture—it's by far the best tour in the city, on land or on water. The cruises leave from the southeast side of the Michigan Avenue bridge, on the river level. If your kids are small, and you just want a "fun" cruise on the water, you'd be better off opting for a cruise with Wendella Sightseeing Boats (see the "Lake and River Cruises" section below), where kids' tickets are only $9.

BY BUS

Reservations are required for all bus tours, although walk-ins are welcome if there's space.

The **"Chicago Architecture Highlights by Bus"** is a 3½-hour tour offered Wednesday, Saturday, and Sunday at 9:30am (Apr–Nov). The route covers the Loop, Hyde Park, and the Gold Coast, plus several other historic districts. The tour includes a visit to the interior of Frank Lloyd Wright's Robie House. Tickets are $30 per person; tours depart from the Chicago Archicenter at 224 S. Michigan Ave.

Some of the tours are pretty long and involved for your average kid (such as the 4-hr. bus tour of Frank Lloyd Wright sites in Oak Park), but check the website or

---

Tips Oak Park Bus Tours

Parents with teens interested in the Frank Lloyd Wright phenomenon might want to try the **Chicago Architecture Foundation's** 4-hour bus tour of Wright sights in Oak Park, offered once a month on Saturday from May to October ($35). The tour includes walks through three neighborhoods and commentary on more than 25 houses—but does not take visitors inside Wright's home and studio. A separate 4-hour bus tour takes Wright fans inside the master's home and Oak Park's Unity Temple ($40). Both tours leave from the Archicenter, 224 S. Michigan Ave. Reservations are required; call ② **312/922-3432,** ext. 240.

(Finds   **The Wright Stuff in the Gold Coast**

Architecture junkies also might want to inquire about house tours of the **Charnley-Persky House** (© 312/915-0105 or 312/573-1365), designed by Frank Lloyd Wright and Louis Sullivan in 1891. The house is located in the Gold Coast at 1365 N. Astor St. and would make a nice highlight to an informal walking tour of the area. One-hour tours are offered on Wednesday at noon (free) and Saturday from April through November at 10am and 1pm ($5); reservations are not accepted.

---

call for the latest and greatest offerings. For example, a one-time summer tour called "A View from the Road" offered a tour of Chicago's roadside attractions. The tour included a lunch stop at the famed Superdawg drive-in with commentary by its owner and designer, and visits to the original Ray Kroc McDonald's in Des Plaines and the Leaning Tower YMCA in Niles (yes, it's a replica of the Leaning Tower of Pisa!). Other special theme bus tours have included Chicago movie palaces and historic churches. Like I said, you never know, so give them a call.

ON FOOT

If you prefer exploring on your own two feet, the CAF offers a variety of guided walking tours. For first-time visitors, I highly recommend two tours that give an excellent introduction to the dramatic architecture of the Loop: **Historic Skyscrapers,** which covers buildings built between 1880 and 1940, including the Rookery and the Chicago Board of Trade, and **Modern Skyscrapers,** which includes modern masterpieces by Mies van der Rohe and postmodern works by contemporary architects. The 2-hour tours cost $12 each ($20 for both) for adults and $9 each ($15 for both) for seniors and students. The tours are offered daily and depart from the Archicenter at 224 S. Michigan Ave. Call © 312/922-TOUR for exact tour times.

The CAF also offers more than 50 **neighborhood tours,** including the Gold Coast, River North, Grant Park, Old Town, the Jackson Boulevard Historic District, and even the Lincoln Park Zoo. Most cost $5 to $10 and last a couple of hours. Call © 312/922-TOUR for details. (See the "Special-Interest Tours" section below for details on neighborhood tours offered by organizations other than the CAF.)

LAKE & RIVER CRUISES

Getting out on the lake is a great way to take in Chicago's incredible skyline from a new vantage point. Don't forget that you're always going to be at the mercy of the weather if you book in advance: I've taken sightseeing cruises in the rain—luckily, most boats have plenty of covered areas for this reason. But when the weather cooperates, the sight of sunlight glinting off the city's skyscrapers never fails to thrill.

Chicago from the Lake   All ages. This company runs 90-minute architectural river cruises and lake and river historical cruises that explore the development of the city. Complimentary coffee (Starbucks, no less), lemonade, cookies, and muffins are served. For tickets, call or stop by the company's ticket office, located on the lower level on the east end of River East Plaza. Advance reservations are recommended.

Departing from Ogden Slip adjacent to River East Plaza (formerly North Pier) at the end of E. Illinois St. © 312/527-2002. www.chicagoline.com. Tickets $26 adults, $24 seniors, $14 children 7–18, free for children under 7. Daily May–Oct.

MetroDucks Tours **All ages.** These amphibious transports go on land and water—originally they were designed to bring troops and supplies ashore during World War II. You'll start with a one-hour land tour of the Loop, Michigan Avenue, Grant Park, and the Museum Campus. Next, your duck rolls into the water—kids love the change from car to boat—and transports you on a 30-minute tour of Chicago from the lake.

Departing from the Rock 'n' Roll McDonald's at 600 N. Clark St. (at Ohio St.). © **800/298-1506.** www.metroducks.com. Tickets $20 adults, $18 seniors and active military personnel, $10 children 12 and under, $1 children 3 and under. Tours daily 10am–4pm.

Mystic Blue Cruises **All ages.** A more casual alternative to fancy dinner cruises, this is promoted as a "fun" ship (that means DJs at night, although you'll also be treated to some live entertainment no matter when you sail). Daily lunch and dinner excursions are available, as well as midnight voyages on weekends. The same company offers more formal (and expensive) cruises aboard the Odyssey (see next review), and motorboat rides on the 70-passenger Seadog (see below), if you really want to feel the water in your face.

Departing from Navy Pier. © **877/299-7783.** www.mysticbluecruises.com. Lunch cruises $28–32, dinner $58–61, midday cruise $22, moonlight cruise $26. Cruises run year-round.

Odyssey Cruises **All ages.** The most upscale dinner cruise on the lake offers daily lunch and dinner cruises during the warm months, plus brunch on weekends and moonlight cruises. All ages are welcome, but at $130 for dinner per person (and kids pay full price for dinner), I'd make this a special occasion and hire a babysitter. At lunch and brunch, however, kids are charged only half the regular price, making it feasible, especially for older kids.

Departing from Navy Pier. © **888/636-7737.** www.odysseycruises.com. Lunch cruises $54, dinner $130, brunch $63. Cruises run year-round but scale back in frequency during the colder months.

Seadog Ventures **All ages.** Got a speed demon in your family? The Speed-boat Lake Tour on the Seadog departs from Navy Pier for a heart-pumping 30-minute tour. The turbo-charged engines roar and music cranks as you speed along the shores of Lake Michigan up to the Museum Campus and back along the Magnificent Mile. You'll love every minute of the fresh lake air blowing in your face. Hang on!

Departing from Navy Pier. © **888/636-7737.** www.seadogcruises.com. Tickets $10–$16. Cruises run daily from May 1–Sept. 30.

Shoreline Sightseeing **All ages.** Shoreline schedules 30-minute lake cruises called Skyline Boat Tours, every half-hour from its three dock locations: the Shedd Aquarium, Navy Pier, and Buckingham Fountain in Grant Park. It's a great way to get a quick primer about famous landmarks and a panoramic view of the city skyline in a short time. Shoreline has also gotten in on the popularity of architecture tours by offering its own version, narrated by an architectural guide (with higher prices than their regular tours). A water taxi also runs every half-hour from Navy Pier to both the Sears Tower and the Shedd Aquarium. One-way tickets for the water taxi are $6 for adults, $5 for seniors, and $3 for children under 12; all-day passes cost $12 for adults and $6 for children.

Departing from Navy Pier, Shedd Aquarium, and Buckingham Fountain in Grant Park. © **312/222-9328.** www.shorelinesightseeing.com. Tickets $10 adults, $9 seniors, $5 children under 12. Cruises run daily from May 1–Sept. 30.

The Spirit of Chicago **Ages 12 & up.** This luxury yacht offers a variety of wining and dining harbor cruises, from a lunch buffet to the Moonlight Dance

Party. Children are allowed, with some restrictions; otherwise, book a sitter and hit one of the cruises. However, this can be a fairly pricey night out if you go for the whole dinner package.

Departing from Navy Pier. ⟨ 866/211-3804. www.spiritcruises.com. Lunch cruises $35–$45, dinner (seated) $75–$95, sunset and midnight cruises $32. Ask about children's rates. Daily year-round.

Wendella Sightseeing Boats   All ages. Wendella is the granddaddy of all sightseeing operators in Chicago. Started in 1935, it's run by the original owner's son, Bob Borgstrom, whose own two sons serve as captains. You won't find a more authoritative source on the Chicago River than Borgstrom.

Wendella operates a 1-hour water tour along the Chicago River, and a 1½-hour tour along the river and out onto Lake Michigan (One of the highlights for kids is passing through the locks that separate the river from the lake). Boats run from late April to early October. The 2-hour sunset tour runs Memorial Day to Labor Day starting at 7:45pm. Scheduling for cruises depends on the season and the weather, but cruises usually leave every hour during the summer.

Departing from Michigan Ave. and Wacker Dr. (on the north side of the river at the Wrigley Building). ⟨ 312/337-1446. www.wendellaboats.com. Tickets $18 adults, $16 seniors, $9 children under 12. Daily Apr–Oct.

Windy   Ages 8 & up. One of the more breathtaking scenes on the lake is watching this tall ship approach the docks at Navy Pier. The 148-foot-long, four-masted schooner (and its new sister ship, the *Windy II*) sets sail for 90-minute cruises two to five times a day, both day and evening. Of course, the boats are at the whims of the wind, so every cruise charts a different course. Passengers are welcome to help raise and trim the sails and occasionally take turns at the ship's helm (with the captain standing close by). Ask about "Pirate" cruises for the kids. The boats are not accessible for people with disabilities.

Departing from Navy Pier. ⟨ 312/595-5555. Tickets $25 adults, $15 seniors and children under 12. Tickets go on sale 1 hr. before the 1st sail of the day at the boat's ticket office, on the dock at Navy Pier. Reservations (except for groups) are not accepted. Call for sailing times.

CARRIAGE RIDES

Noble Horse (⟨ 312/266-7878) maintains the largest fleet of antique horse carriages, stationed around the old Water Tower Square, at the northwest corner of Chicago and Michigan avenues. Each of the drivers, outfitted in black tie and top hat, has his own variation on the basic Magnificent Mile itinerary (and can also do tours of the lakefront, river, Lincoln Park, and Buckingham Fountain). The charge is $30 for each half-hour. The coaches run year-round, with convertible coaches in the warm months and enclosed carriages furnished with wool blankets in winter. There are several other carriage operators, all of whom pick up riders in the vicinity.

SPECIAL-INTEREST TOURS

NEIGHBORHOOD TOURS   It's a bit of a cliché to say that Chicago is a city of neighborhoods, but if you want to see what really makes Chicago special, that's where you have to go. And if you're a bit intimidated by public transportation and getting around a less tourist-friendly area of the city, an escorted tour is the perfect way to see places you'd otherwise miss. Sponsored by the Department of Cultural Affairs, **Chicago Neighborhood Tours** (⟨ 312/742-1190; www.chgocitytours.com) are 4- to 5-hour narrated bus excursions to about a dozen diverse communities throughout the city. Embarking from the Chicago Cultural Center, 77 E. Randolph St., every Saturday (not on major holidays and not during Jan, generally, so call first), the tours visit different neighborhoods, from

Chinatown and historic Bronzeville on the South Side to the ethnic enclaves of Devon Avenue and Uptown on the North Side. Neighborhood representatives serve as guides and greeters along the way as tour participants visit area landmarks, murals, museums, and shopping districts. Tickets (including a light snack) are $25 for adults and $20 for seniors, students, and children 8 to 18. Several specialty tours have recently been added to the mix, including Literary Chicago; the Great Chicago Fire; Roots of Blues, Gospel & Jazz; Threads of Ireland; Jewish Legacy; and an Ethnic Cemetery tour. These tours, which generally run 4 to 6 hours and include lunch, are more expensive ($50 adults, $45 seniors and children).

The Chicago Historical Society offers a handful of walking tours every summer of the **Gold Coast, Old Town,** and **Lincoln Park** neighborhoods. Led by CHS docents, they average about four per month from June through August. Day and evening tours are available, and a few specialty walking tours usually are offered as well. Tours are $10 per tour or $25 for a preregistered combination of any three tours. Registration is recommended but not required. Tours depart from the CHS museum at Clark Street and North Avenue, and light refreshments are served immediately afterward. Call ✆ **312/642-4600** for updates.

Groups can arrange tours of Chicago's **"Black Metropolis,"** the name given to a South Side area of Bronzeville, where African Americans created a flourishing business-and-artistic community after World War II. Contact **Tour Black Chicago** (✆ **773/684-9034;** www.tourblackchicago.com) for more information.

GANGSTER TOURS   **Untouchable Tours,** or so-called "gangster tours," 10924 S. Prospect Ave., Chicago, IL 60643 (✆ **773/881-1195;** www.gangster tour.com), is the only bus tour that takes you to all of the city's old hoodlum hangouts from the Prohibition era. The focus is definitely more on entertainment (guides with names like "Al Dente" and "Ice Pick" appear in costume and role-play their way through the tour) than a seriously historic take on the era. But the bus trip gives you a pretty thorough overview of the city, in addition to the gangster hot spots. You'll see the site of O'Bannion's flower shop, the site of the St. Valentine's Day massacre, and much more. The tour is pretty tame, but if you have impressionable young ones, use your discretion; kids over age 8 should be fine. The cost is $24 for adults, $18 for children. Tours, which depart from the southeast corner of Clark and Ohio streets, run Monday to Wednesday at 10am; Thursday at 10am and 1pm; Friday at 10am, 1pm, and 7:30pm; Saturday at 10am, 1pm, and 5pm; and Sunday at 10am and 1pm.

GHOST TOURS   Another offbeat way to experience the real "spirit" of Chicago is to take a narrated **supernatural bus tour** of cemeteries, murder sites, Indian burial grounds, haunted pubs, and other spooky places. Richard Crowe, who bills himself as a "professional ghost hunter," spins out ghost stories, legends, and lore on the 4-hour trip, held both day and night (afraid of the dark?). I'd only take teens on these tours due to touchy subject matter and the rather expensive price; use your discretion. Tickets are $35 per person, and the tour begins at **Goose Island Restaurant,** 1800 N. Clybourn Ave. (a short walk from the North/Clybourn El station on the Red Line). Two-hour **supernatural boat excursions** are available for $24 per person in July and August through Labor Day weekend, and board at 10:30pm from the Mercury boat dock, at Michigan Avenue and Wacker Drive. Reservations are required for each tour; call ✆ **708/499-0300** or visit www.ghosttours.com. As you might imagine, Crowe's tours get especially popular around Halloween, so you'll definitely want to reserve well ahead of time if that's when you want to go.

CEMETERY TOURS   Don't be scared away by the creepy connotations. Some of Chicago's cemeteries are as pretty as parks, and they offer a variety of intriguing monuments that offer insight into the city's history.

One of the best area cemeteries is **Graceland,** which stretches along Clark Street in the Swedish neighborhood of Andersonville. The land between Irving Park Road and Montrose Avenue, running for about a mile along Clark Street, is occupied exclusively by cemeteries—primarily Graceland. Here you can view the tombs and monuments of many Chicago notables. When Graceland was laid out in 1860, public parks as such did not exist. The elaborate burial grounds that were constructed in many large American cities around this same time had the dual purpose of relieving the congestion of the municipal cemeteries closer to town and providing pastoral recreational settings for the Sunday outings of the living. Indeed, cemeteries like Graceland were the precursors of such great municipal green spaces as Lincoln Park. Much of Lincoln Park, in fact, had been a public cemetery since Chicago's earliest times. Many who once rested there were reinterred in Graceland when the plans for building Lincoln Park went forward.

The Chicago Architecture Foundation (📞 **312/922-3432**) offers walking tours of Graceland on selected Sundays during August, September, and October. The tour costs $10 per person and lasts about 2 hours. Among the points of interest you will discover as you meander the paths of these 121 beautifully landscaped acres are the Ryerson and Getty tombs, famous architectural monuments designed by Louis Sullivan. Sullivan himself rests here in the company of several of his most distinguished colleagues: Daniel Burnham, Ludwig Mies van der Rohe, and Howard Van Doren Shaw, an establishment architect whose summer home in Lake Forest, called Ragdale, now operates as a writers' and artists' colony. Some of Chicago's giants of industry and commerce are also buried at Graceland, including Potter Palmer, Marshall Field, and George Pullman. An ambiguous reference in the *WPA Guide to Illinois* (Pantheon Books, 1983), reprinted without revisions, records that Graceland also contains the grave of Chicago's first white civilian settler, John Kinzie. (The racial adjective is a reminder that Chicago's very first settler was a black man named Jean Baptiste Point du Sable.) The Chicago Architecture Foundation offers tours of some other cemeteries, as well, including the Oak Woods Cemetery, Rosehill Cemetery, and the suburban Lake Forest Cemetery. Call for details. **Oak Woods,** located just south of Hyde Park on the city's south side, is the final resting place for many of Chicago's most famous African-American figures, including Jesse Owens, Ida B. Wells, and the late Mayor Harold Washington. Also buried here are nuclear physicist Enrico Fermi, who helped give birth to the atomic age while at the University of Chicago, and legendary trial lawyer Clarence Darrow.

7

Neighborhood Strolls

The best way to get a feel for Chicago is to stroll its streets. Every block brings interesting window-shopping, people-watching, or snippets of conversation that are sure to keep you and the wee ones entertained. The orderly configuration of Chicago's streets and the excellent public transportation system make walking a breeze—when you get tired, you can hop on a bus or the El without having to veer too far off your course.

This chapter provides brief walks that will give you a snapshot of the city's most frequented neighborhoods.

1 Near North/Magnificent Mile

North Michigan Avenue is known as the Magnificent Mile, from the bridge spanning the Chicago River on the south end to Oak Street on the northern tip. Many of the city's best hotels, shops, and restaurants are to be found on and around elegant Michigan Avenue. But never fear: Michigan Avenue offers excellent family shopping, too. Scattered among the shops owned by Gucci, Salvatore Ferragamo, and Cartier are more kid-friendly stops such as American Girl Place and Niketown. You and your kids will feel right at home making your way up this storied avenue. Strolling the entire mile will take you half a day, since you'll want to stop frequently. Of course, if you're determined to avoid the shops, you can do it in less than an hour—but who'd want to?

Start at the **Riverwalk** that goes along the north side of the Chicago River. Walk down the steps that lead off the Michigan Avenue Bridge. You can walk for a short distance and see the plaza of the NBC Tower, as well as some of the newest condominium and town house developments along the river. Backtrack and continue north on Michigan Avenue. You'll run right into the **Chicago Tribune Tower.** The tower is notable for its signature array of stones jutting out from the exterior.

The collection was started shortly after the building's completion in 1925 by the newspaper's notoriously despotic publisher Robert R. McCormick, who gathered them during his world travels. *Tribune* correspondents then began supplying stone souvenirs encountered on assignment. Each one now bears the name of the structure and country whence it came. There are 138 stones in all, including chunks and shards from the Great Wall of China, the Taj Mahal, the White House, the Arc de Triomphe, the Berlin Wall, the Roman Colosseum, London's Houses of Parliament, the Great Pyramid of Cheops in Giza, Egypt, and the original tomb of Abraham Lincoln in Springfield. Send your kids on a scavenger hunt to see how many they can find. *Hint:* Inside the *Tribune's* lobby, there's a brochure telling you where they are.

Chicago Neighborhoods

Turn to chapter 3 for more descriptions of Chicago neighborhoods. Also see p. 53 for a map of the neighborhoods.

Walk This Way: Chicago's Underground Pedway

Rainy day? Snowy? So windy you're afraid your kids will blow away? Take a break and cruise around Chicago's Loop through the not-so-secret underground **Pedway.** The city started building tunnels to connect subway stations in the early 1950s, and today the underground system of tunnels covers 23 blocks that are fun for kids to explore. You'll find stores, restaurants, and other businesses. Don't worry—if you ever get lost, just look for an exit and go up to street level to get your bearings (and you can pick up a map at the Chicago Cultural Center).

A good spot to enter the Pedway is the State Street subway station, between Randolph and Washington streets. On the stretch west of State Street, you'll find a newsstand selling snacks and fresh fruits, a barbershop, a Starbucks, a big gift store, and a food court. Beneath the Chicago Cultural Center, your children can look through the window at a radio station that broadcasts books for the blind. Farther along, at the Athletic Club, kids can see a seven-story climbing wall and watch office workers working out at lunchtime. The eastern section is the most elegant—it travels under several hotels and has a shopping concourse.

Continue north along Michigan Avenue. When you reach Chicago Avenue, just ahead of you is the **Chicago Water Tower** (not to be confused with a mall of the same name, located kitty-corner from the real tower). Michigan Avenue's best-known landmark is dwarfed by high-rises today but still gleams like a fairytale castle. Surrounded by lawns and park benches, the tower is illuminated at night, and street musicians often play here. Chicagoans are proud of their talisman, one of the few buildings to survive the Great Fire of 1871. (And it serves a real purpose by covering an ugly, 138-ft.-high standpipe used in connection with pumping water from Lake Michigan.) The gothic-style limestone building now houses an art gallery and is a refreshing cultural pit stop. Across the street the pumping station has been transformed into a tourist information center.

To conclude your walk up Michigan Avenue, step across the street to **Ghirardelli's** (located on DeWitt, half a block west of Michigan Ave.) and grab an ice cream cone. If you walk up 1 more block north, you can enjoy your ice cream in the shaded, ivy-covered courtyard of **Fourth Presbyterian Church,** located at Chestnut Street and Michigan Avenue—a tranquil spot just steps from the bustle of Michigan Avenue.

2 The Loop

South Michigan Avenue is less congested than its northerly branch, the Magnificent Mile. Down here you can amble along and take in a couple of Chicago's famous museums and two parks, including Millennium Park, which was completed in 2004, and is expected to become Chicago's second-largest tourist draw after Navy Pier. South Michigan Avenue can be strolled in an hour or two, but if you stop to check out building lobbies and have lunch, it can be a half-day event. Because this walk focuses on architecture, it's best for older children and teens.

Cross the Chicago River on the Michigan Avenue Bridge and walk south, into the Loop business district. On this easterly fringe of the Loop lie some of

Chicago's top cultural institutions and parks. Continue south, past Lake and Randolph streets. On your left, you will see a clearing: This is the new **Millennium Park,** located on the north end of Grant Park along Michigan Avenue. Admire the dramatic new music pavilion designed by Frank Gehry, and check out the large public art displays. At the corner of Michigan and Randolph is a huge Beaux Arts–style building, called the **Chicago Cultural Center.** Built in 1897 as the city's public library, the Cultural Center is now your home base for tourist information. Go in, pick up all the information you need, and while you're at it, check out the building's stunning interior. Free tours guide visitors up a sweeping staircase of white Italian marble to admire what is, for my money, the most stunning interior in Chicago. At the top of the staircase is a majestic Tiffany dome, believed to be the world's largest. You'll also discover mosaics of Favrile glass, colored stone, and mother-of-pearl inlaid in white marble.

As you stroll south from the Cultural Center, you're seeing "Michigan Avenue Cliff," a particularly impressive great wall of buildings that stretches south to Congress Parkway (location of the Auditorium Building). It's a visual treat for architecture lovers and novices alike.

Abutting the park on the south, facing Adams Avenue, is the **Art Institute.** Save the tour for another time—for now, climb the steps and visit the stone lions. Watch the other people who are sitting on the steps people-watching. If you need a break, stop in the outdoor cafe. Parents can get a glass of wine while the kids enjoy a lemonade.

Further south on the avenue is the **Fine Arts Building,** constructed in 1885 as a showroom for Studebaker carriages, and converted into an arts center in 1917. The building offers two theaters, offices, shops, and studios for musicians, artists, and writers. Frank Lloyd Wright, sculptor Lorado Taft, and L. Frank Baum, author of *The Wonderful Wizard of Oz,* had offices here. Located throughout the building are a number of interesting studios and musical-instrument shops. Take a quick walk through the marble-and-wood lobby, which suggests something monastic and cloisterlike, or visit the top floor to see the spectacular murals (and to get there, you'll be fortunate to ride in an old-fashioned elevator manned by a real, live operator!).

Last stop on our south Michigan Avenue tour is the **Auditorium Building.** This wonder of architecture was designed and built in 1889 by Louis Sullivan and Dankmar Adler. At the time, it was the heaviest (110,000 tons) and most massive modern building on earth, the most fireproof building ever constructed, and the tallest building in Chicago. It was also the first large-scale building to be electrically lighted, and its theater was the first in the country to install air-conditioning. The lobby fronting Michigan Avenue has faux ornamental marble columns, molded ceilings, mosaic floors, and Mexican onyx walls. If this inspires you and

---

Tips Sorting Out the Post Office

While you're near the Loop, treat your kids to a look at the inner workings of the **Chicago Main Post Office,** 433 W. Harrison (© **312/983-7550**), and see for yourselves what happens to the letters you send. The 90-minute tour includes the sorting process, a look at the latest automated equipment, and an enormous stamp collection. The tour is suggested for ages 10 and older and reservations are required; call the number above to arrange a time. Admission is free.

your kids, take the elevator to the 10th-floor library reading room and have a look at what was once the city's first top-floor dining room. Soak in the decorative details and show your kids that they just don't make them like this anymore—the barrel-vaulted, muraled ceiling and marvelous views of Grand Park and the lake will make architecture fans out of novices.

3 The Gold Coast

Walking north on **Lake Shore Drive** from North Michigan Avenue, you will enter a neighborhood known as the Gold Coast. The neighborhood runs from about Oak Street on the south to North Avenue on the north and includes some of Chicago's most desirable real estate and historic architecture. This is the classic "old money" neighborhood of Chicago, where many of the city's wealthiest citizens built homes after the 1871 fire. Sadly, most of the mansions that once lined Lake Shore Drive have been torn down and high-rises put in their stead, but you can see the remnants of Chicago's storied past in the three mansions still standing near Lake Shore Drive's intersection with Goethe Street. This hour-long stroll is suitable for the whole family and can be combined with a foray into Lincoln Park to make a day's worth of activities.

To get a feel for the neighborhood, walk up Lake Shore Drive to **Schiller Street.** Turn left and walk 1 block to **Astor Place.** Turn right onto Astor and enjoy the amble past stately mansions and beautiful brownstones. (Just a block or two further west, State and Dearborn sts. also feature homes fit for magazine covers.) Once you reach **North Avenue,** you'll see a redbrick mansion on your left. This is the home of Cardinal Francis George, Catholic archbishop of Chicago, and is owned by the Catholic archdiocese of Chicago. Ask your kids to count the chimneys—I bet they'll lose track.

You can continue on into **Lincoln Park,** or turn back south. If you go south, walk 1 block west to State Street and follow that to Division Street. From there going south, you will find a thriving zone of restaurants, bars, and nightclubs, many featuring sidewalk seating—all the better to view the beautiful people that frequent the area.

4 Old Town

This residential neighborhood is best known as the home of the Second City comedy troupe for the past 30-plus years. This formerly hippie haven of the 1960s and 1970s has gentrified as Cabrini Green (located on the far southern border of Old Town), America's most notorious housing project, has fallen to the wrecking ball. The northern part of Old Town, particularly that located north of North Avenue and west of Wells Street, has a lovely residential neighborhood, and on any given day, you will see plenty of strollers and parents with kids in tow. I'd allow a couple of hours to stroll through the neighborhood, including time to linger in the shops.

To get the flavor of Old Town, start at the intersection of Wells Street and North Avenue. On the northwest corner is **Pipers Alley,** a shopping complex containing a large cinema, Starbucks, restaurants, and shops. Directly to the north is **Second City.** Walk north up Wells Street. Small retail shops, florists, cafes, bread stores, and more line the street. When you reach the intersection with Lincoln Avenue, turn back and head south down the opposite side of the street. Cross North Avenue going south. Kids will be magnetically attracted to the colorful fish swimming around the front windows of **Old Town Aquarium,** a shop located on the west side of the street at 1538 N. Wells St.

Chicago & the Great Black Migration

From 1915 to 1960 hundreds of thousands of black Southerners poured into Chicago, trying to escape segregation and seeking economic freedom and opportunity. The so-called "Great Black Migration" radically transformed Chicago, both politically and culturally, from an Irish-run city of recent European immigrants into one in which no group had a majority and in which no politician—white or black—could ever take the black vote for granted. Unfortunately, the sudden change gave rise to many of the social and economic disparities that still plague the city, but it also promoted an environment in which many black men and women could rise from poverty to prominence.

Between 1910 and 1920 Chicago's black population almost tripled, going from 44,000 to 109,000; between 1920 and 1930, it more than doubled, to 234,000. The Great Depression slowed the migration to a crawl, with 278,000 blacks residing here in 1940. But the boom resumed when World War II revived the economy, causing the black population to skyrocket to 492,000 between 1940 and 1950. The postwar expansion and the decline of Southern sharecropping caused the black population to nearly double again, to 813,000, by 1960.

Although jobs in the factories, steel mills, and stockyards paid much better than those in the cotton fields, Chicago was not the paradise that many blacks envisioned. Segregation was almost as bad here as it was down South, and most blacks were confined to a narrow "Black Belt" of overcrowded apartment buildings on the South Side. But the new migrants made the best of their situation, and for a time in the 1930s and 1940s, the Black Belt—dubbed "Bronzeville" or the "Black Metropolis" by the community's boosters—thrived as a cultural, musical, religious, and educational mecca, much as New York's Harlem did in the 1920s. As journalist and Great Migration historian Nicholas Lemann writes in *The Promised Land: The Great Black Migration and How It Changed America,* "Chicago was a city where a black person could be somebody."

Some of the Southern migrants who made names for themselves in Chicago included black separatist and Nation of Islam founder Elijah Muhammed; Robert S. Abbott, publisher of the powerful *Chicago Defender* newspaper, who launched a "Great Northern Drive" to bring blacks to the city in 1917; Ida B. Wells, the crusading journalist who headed an antilynching campaign; William Dawson, for many years the only black congressman; New Orleans–born jazz pioneers Jelly Roll Morton, King Oliver, and Louis Armstrong; *Native Son* author Richard Wright; John H. Johnson, publisher of *Ebony* and *Jet* magazines and one of Chicago's wealthiest residents; blues musicians Willie Dixon,

5 Lincoln Park

Chicago's most popular residential neighborhood is fashionable Lincoln Park. Stretching from North Avenue to Diversey Parkway, it's bordered on the east by the huge park of the same name, which is home to two major museums and one

Muddy Waters, and Howlin' Wolf; Thomas A. Dorsey, the "father" of gospel music, and his greatest disciple, singer Mahalia Jackson; Robert Taylor, head of the Chicago Housing Authority, after whom the CHA's most notorious buildings are named; and Ralph Metcalfe, the Olympic-gold-medalist sprinter who turned to politics once he got to Chicago, eventually succeeding Dawson in Congress.

When open housing legislation enabled blacks to live in any neighborhood, the flight of many Bronzeville residents to less crowded areas took its toll on the remaining community. Through the 1950s almost a third of the housing became vacant, and by the 1960s the great social experiment of urban renewal through wholesale land clearance and the creation of large tracts of public housing gutted this once thriving neighborhood.

In recent years, however, community and civic leaders appear committed to restoring the neighborhood to a semblance of its former glory. Landmark status has been secured for several historic buildings in Bronzeville, including the **Liberty Life/Supreme Insurance Company,** 3501 S. King Dr., the first African-American-owned insurance company in the northern United States, and the **Eighth Regiment Armory,** which, when completed in 1915, was the only armory in the United States controlled by an African-American regiment. The former home of the legendary **Chess Records** at 2120 S. Michigan Ave.—where Howlin' Wolf, Chuck Berry, and Bo Diddley gave birth to the blues and helped define rock 'n' roll—now houses a museum and music education center, **Blues Heaven Foundation** (✆ **312/808-1286**), set up by Willie Dixon's widow, Marie Dixon, with financial assistance from rock musician John Mellencamp. Entertainer Lou Rawls, who grew up at 45th Street and King Drive (formerly South Pkwy.), is building the **Lou Rawls Theater and Cultural Center** at the famous crossroads of 47th Street and King Drive, where Chicago's fabled Regal Theater once stood and hosted performances by such legends as Count Basie, Duke Ellington, and Ella Fitzgerald. Along Dr. Martin Luther King, Jr., Drive, between 24th and 35th streets, several **public art installations** now celebrate Bronzeville's heritage as well. The most poignant of them is sculptor Alison Saar's **Great Northern Migration bronze monument,** at King and 26th, depicting a suitcase-toting African-American traveler standing atop a mound of worn shoe soles.

For tours of Bronzeville, contact the Chicago Office of Tourism's **Chicago Neighborhood Tours** at ✆ **312/742-1190; Tour Black Chicago** at ✆ **312/332-2323;** or the **Black Metropolis Convention and Tourism Council** at ✆ **773/548-2579.**

of the nation's oldest zoos (established in 1868). You'll find it easy to spend a whole day and evening in Lincoln Park and the surrounding neighborhood. Thanks to the museums, zoo, and beach, plus shopping and restaurants in the surrounding neighborhood, there's something for all ages.

To explore the park, start at the **Chicago Historical Society,** located at Clark Street and North Avenue. You can pick up a walking path behind the building and pass through a pedestrian tunnel that takes you underneath a busy street and into the heart of the park. You'll have company on the wide gravel path—joggers, bikers, and dog walkers make good use of this route. Veer right coming out of the tunnel and walk past the baseball fields to the pedestrian bridge. If you cross the bridge going over Lake Shore Drive, you'll wind up on **North Avenue Beach,** Chicago's busiest beach. In the summer this is beach-volleyball central. Take your shoes off, dig your toes in the sand, and check out Lake Michigan's water temperature. (*Warning:* It will be cold, even in Aug!) Your kids might want to explore the beach house, designed like a real boat, and you can pick up some ice cream and cool drinks inside.

Now that you've seen the park, it's time to check out the neighborhood of the same name. The trapezoid formed by **Clark Street, Armitage Avenue, Halsted Street,** and **Diversey Parkway** contains many of Chicago's most happening bars, restaurants, retail stores, music clubs, and off-Loop theaters. One manageable area to explore on foot is the Armitage Avenue area, which starts at the intersection of Halsted Street and Armitage Avenue. Strolling west on Armitage Avenue, you'll find a string of charming boutiques, featuring shoes and clothing for kids and adults, outdoor outfitters, home decor, and more. Should you choose to go north on Halsted from Armitage Avenue, you'll find more shops, including GapKids and other chain stores. Going south from Halsted on Armitage, you will find restaurants and the nationally acclaimed theater, **Steppenwolf Theatre Company.**

6 Andersonville

This formerly Scandinavian neighborhood stretches several blocks along North Clark Street immediately north of Foster Avenue. Today, a burgeoning community of gays and lesbians makes Andersonville their home, and immigrant groups have moved in. You might want to have lunch at **Ann Sather** at 5207 N. Clark St. (p. 138) and walk the meal off by strolling up and down Clark Street for an hour or two.

Clark Street going north from Foster is a very walkable small stretch that includes the **Swedish-American Museum Center** (p. 177), a pair of Scandinavian delis, a Swedish bakery, and two good Swedish restaurants. Since the wave of Scandinavian immigrants ended over 100 years ago, new immigrants have moved in. You'll find excellent Middle Eastern restaurants, including a northern branch of **Reza's** (p. 126), and delis with barrels of olives, figs, and other Middle Eastern delicacies. Make sure to stop at **Women & Children First** (p. 227), a wonderful bookstore for kids (and women). Stop for a bite at stroller-friendly **Kopi Café,** where you can get a mean mango smoothie, or at Ann Sather, where you can get gooey fresh-baked cinnamon rolls (plus free advice for moms from the very motherly owner).

7 Bucktown/Wicker Park

Home to the third-largest concentration of artists in the country, this neighborhood is rapidly gentrifying. Over the past century the area has hosted waves of German, Polish, and, most recently, Spanish-speaking immigrants (not to mention writer Nelson Algren). Heading north on Damen Avenue, you'll pass hot new restaurants, stores featuring the latest in alternative culture, and loft-dwelling yuppies surfing the gentrification wave that's washing over this still-somewhat-gritty neighborhood.

The go-go gentrification of the Wicker Park/Bucktown area has been followed by not only a rash of restaurants and bars, but also retailers with an artsy bent reflecting the neighborhood's bohemian spirit. Mixed in with old neighborhood businesses, such as discount furniture stores and religious-icon purveyors, is a proliferation of antique-furniture shops, too-cool-for-school clothing boutiques, and eclectic galleries and gift emporiums. Teenagers will love this walk—in 2001 the neighborhood was the location for MTV's *The Real World: Chicago,* so if your kids have watched the show, either originally or in its plentiful reruns, they might recognize many of the area's restaurants and bars.

To get a feel for the neighborhood's artsy vibe, stroll up and down Damen Avenue, starting from the intersection with North Avenue. Head south for the best concentration of restaurants and shops. One notable kids' store along your path is the children's clothing store **The Red Balloon Company,** 2060 N. Damen (p. 234). When you're ready for a break, stop at **Silver Cloud Bar & Grill,** 1700 N. Damen, for grilled cheese and tomato soup (p. 140), or pop across the street to **Northside Café,** 1635 N. Damen, for a burger or a beverage on the huge outdoor patio (p. 140).

For the Active Family

With its wide blue lake and emerald string of parks, Chicago is one big playground for kids. The city's ample green space means it's easy to get out and be active. Whether your kids like water-based sports or activities on solid ground, you'll probably be able to find it here.

A handy resource for those interested in the sporting life is **Windy City Sports** (© 312/421-1551; www.windy citysportsmag.com), a free monthly publication that you'll find at many retail shops, grocery stores, and bars and cafes.

1 Enjoying the "Third Coast": Chicago's Beaches

Public beaches line Lake Michigan all the way up north into the suburbs and Wisconsin, and southeast through Indiana and into Michigan. The most well known is **Oak Street Beach** ✦; its location at the northern tip of the Magnificent Mile creates some interesting sights as sun worshippers sporting swimsuits and carting coolers make their way down Michigan Avenue. The most popular is **North Avenue Beach,** about 6 blocks farther north, which has developed into a volleyball hot spot and recently rebuilt its landmark steamship-shaped beach house and added a Venice Beach–style gym; this is where the Lincoln Park singles come to play, check each other out, and fly by on bikes and in-line skates. Even though families might be outnumbered by singles, the atmosphere is open and easy, and you won't feel out of place in the least. The beach has a **Bike & Roll** shop (© 773/327-2706) for renting bicycles, a chess pavilion, and Stefani's Castaway Restaurant for sandwiches. The beach is the place to be during the annual Air and Water Show, which takes place along the waterfront in August.

For more seclusion, try **Ohio Street Beach,** an intimate sliver of sand in tiny Olive Park, just north of Navy Pier, which, incredibly enough, remains largely ignored despite its central location. If you have a car, head up to **Montrose Beach,** a beautiful unsung treasure about midway between North Avenue Beach and Hollywood-Ardmore Beach (with plenty of free parking). Long popular with the city's Hispanic community, it has an expanse of beach mostly uninterrupted by piers or jetties, and a huge adjacent park with soccer fields and one big hill great for kite flying—even a small bait shop where anglers can go before heading for a nearby long pier designated for fishing. Teens can find a pickup game of volleyball here during the warmer months. **Hollywood-Ardmore Beach** (officially Kathy Osterman Beach), at the northern end of Lake Shore Drive, is a lovely crescent that's less congested and has steadily become more popular with gays who've moved up the lakefront from the Belmont Rocks, a longtime hangout.

If you've brought the family pooch along, you might want to take him for a dip at the **doggie beach** south of Addison Street, at about Hawthorne and Lake

Shore Drive—although this minute spot aggravates some dog owners because it's situated in a harbor where the water is somewhat fouled by gas and oil from nearby boats. *Tip:* Try the south end of North Avenue Beach in early morning, before it opens to the public for the day. (Also consider that, in off season, all beaches are fair game for dogs.)

Beaches are officially open with a full retinue of lifeguards on duty beginning about June 20, but swimmers can wade into the chilly water from Memorial Day to Labor Day. Only the bravest souls venture into the water before July, when the temperature creeps up enough to make swimming an attractive proposition. Please take note that not the entire lakefront is beach, and don't go doing anything stupid such as diving off the rocks. Be extremely careful with your kids. The lake has drop-offs at points along the shore, and kids can easily get into deeper water than they bargained for. Lake Michigan can develop large waves, too, so exercise the same caution you would at the ocean.

Oak Street, North Avenue, Loyola, Osterman, Montrose, South Shore, and Rainbow beaches are wheelchair- and stroller-friendly—they offer specially designed mats that create a path over the sand to the water. For questions about the 29 miles of beaches and parks along Lake Michigan, call the park district's lakefront region office at © **312/747-2474.**

2 Green Chicago: City Parks

Thanks to architect Daniel Burnham and his coterie of visionary civic planners—who drafted the revolutionary 1909 Plan of Chicago in the aftermath of the Great Chicago Fire of 1871—the city boasts a wide-open lakefront park system unrivaled by most major metropolises. Downtown Chicago has two extensive downtown parks: Grant Park on the southern end of Michigan Avenue, and Lincoln Park, starting at North Avenue.

GRANT PARK ★★★
Modeled after the gardens at Versailles, Grant Park is Chicago's front yard, composed of giant lawns segmented by *allées* of trees, plantings, and paths, and pieced together by major roadways and a network of railroad tracks. Covering the greens is a variety of public recreational and cultural facilities (although these are few in number and nicely spread out, a legacy of mail-order magnate Aaron Montgomery Ward's *fin de siècle* campaign to limit municipal buildings in the park). Incredibly, the entire expanse was created from sandbars, landfill, and Chicago Fire debris; the original shoreline extended all the way to Michigan Avenue. Grant Park is the major venue for festivals in the city, but although it's beautiful, it has fewer attractions for families than Lincoln Park (see review below).

The immense **Buckingham Fountain,** accessible along Congress Parkway, is the baroque centerpiece of the park, composed of pink Georgia marble and patterned after—but twice the size of—the Latona Fountain at Versailles, with adjoining esplanades beautified by rose gardens in season. Throughout the late spring and summer, the fountain spurts columns of water up to 165 feet in the air, illuminated after dark by a whirl of colored lights, and building toward a grand finale before it shuts down for the night at 11pm. New concession areas and restrooms have also been opened on the plaza.

A popular summer series of outdoor classical music concerts is staged at the **Petrillo Music Shell,** at Jackson Boulevard and Columbus Drive, by the Grant Park Symphony Orchestra and Chorus. If construction goes according to plan, the symphony will be performing in the new Millennium Park at the north end

Grant Park

(*Fun Fact* **Did You Know?**

Buckingham Fountain's jets and electric light displays are actually controlled by a computer 700 miles away in Atlanta.

---

of Grant Park, in a band shell designed by superstar architect Frank Gehry. The music festival, which includes performances Wednesday through Sunday evenings over a 10-week period, bills itself as the nation's only remaining free, municipally funded outdoor classical music festival. For a schedule of concert times and dates, contact the **Grant Park Music Festival** (© 312/742-7638). Other favorite annual events are the free outdoor blues festival (in June) and the jazz festival (Labor Day). **Taste of Chicago** (© 312/744-3315), purportedly the largest food festival in the world (the city estimates its annual attendance at around 3.5 million), takes place every summer for 10 days around the July 4th holiday. Local restaurants serve up more ribs, pizza, hot dogs, and beer than you'd ever want to see, let alone eat. (See chapter 2 for a comprehensive listing of summer events in Grant Park.)

Scattered about the park are a number of sculptures and monuments, including a heroic sculpture of two Native Americans on horseback entitled *The Spearman and the Bowman* (at Congress Pkwy. and Michigan Ave.), which has become the park's trademark since it was installed in 1928, as well as likenesses of Copernicus, Columbus, and Lincoln *(The Seated Lincoln),* the latter by the great American sculptor Augustus Saint-Gaudens, located on Congress Parkway between Michigan Avenue and Columbus Drive. On the western edge of the park, at Adams Street, is the **Art Institute** (p. 166), and at the southern tip in the newly redesigned Museum Campus are **The Field Museum of Natural History** (p. 151), the **Adler Planetarium** (p. 150), and the **Shedd Aquarium** (p. 154). At the north end of the park, adjacent to the nascent Millennium Park, is Daley Bicentennial Park, featuring an outdoor sports plaza with a dozen lighted tennis courts, a rink for ice-skating in the winter and 'blading or roller-skating in the summer, and a field house.

331 E. Randolph St. © 312/742-7648. Subway/El: Brown Line to the Loop. Bus: 3, 4, 6, 60, 146, or 151.

LAKE SHORE PARK

Located just behind the Museum of Contemporary Art, this park offers a view of the lake and packs some good facilities into a small space. You'll find baseball diamonds, a fitness center, a gym for basketball, an outdoor running track, and tennis courts. Again, although it's tiny, this little green space is a big find for families staying in the heart of the city.

808 N. Lake Shore Dr. (at Chicago Ave., 3 blocks east of Michigan Ave.). © 312/742-PLAY. Bus: 151.

LINCOLN PARK ★★★

Straight and narrow Lincoln Park begins at North Avenue and follows the shoreline of Lake Michigan northward 6 miles to Ardmore Avenue (not far from the East Asian enclave radiating from Argyle Ave. and quaint Andersonville), making it the city's largest park. Within its elongated 1,200 acres are a world-class zoo, a half-dozen bathing beaches, a botanical conservatory, two excellent museums, a golf course, and the usual meadows, formal gardens, sporting fields, and tennis courts typical of urban parks. Attractions in the park include the **Chicago Historical Society** (p. 169), **Lincoln Park Zoo** (p. 185), **Lincoln Park Conservatory** (p. 187), and **Peggy Notebaert Nature Museum** (p. 188).

Lincoln Park

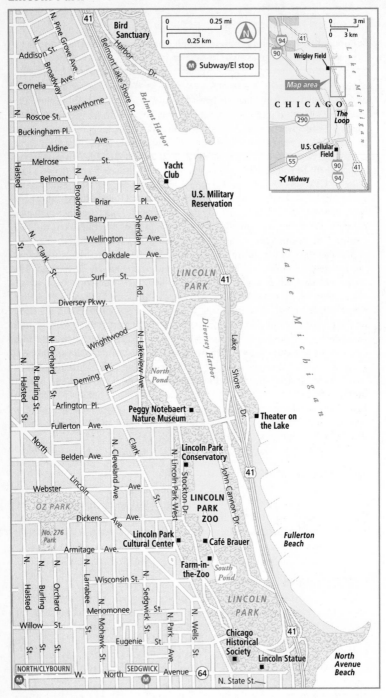

Bird Sanctuary

Harbor
Belmont Lake Shore Dr.
Dr.
Belmont Harbor

0   0.25 mi
0   0.25 km

Ⓜ Subway/El stop

Addison St.
N. Pine Grove Ave.
Broadway Ave.
Cornelia
Hawthorne
Roscoe St.
Buckingham Pl.
Ave.
Aldine
St.
Melrose
Belmont   N.   Ave.
Halsted
N. Broadway
Briar   Ave.
N. Pl.
Barry   Ave.
Sheridan
Wellington   Ave.
Oakdale   Ave.
N. Clark St.
Surf   St.
Rd.
Diversey Pkwy.

Yacht Club

U.S. Military Reservation

LINCOLN PARK

41

Lake Michigan

Wrigley Field
CHICAGO
The Loop
U.S. Cellular Field
Midway

Diversey Harbor

N. Orchard St.
Wrightwood
Deming
N. Lakeview Ave.
Pl.
N.
Arlington Pl.
North Pond

N. Burling St.
N. Halsted St.
Fullerton   Ave.
North
Belden   Ave.
Clark
N. Cleveland Ave.
Lincoln
Webster
Ave.
Stockton Dr.
N. Lincoln Park West
St.
OZ PARK
Dickens   Ave.
No. 276 Park
Armitage   Ave.
N. Orchard St.
N. Burling
N. Larrabee St.
Wisconsin St.
Sedgwick St.
N. Park Ave.
Halsted
Menomonee
N. Mohawk St.
N. Wells St.
Willow   St.
Eugenie   St.
NORTH/CLYBOURN
SEDGWICK
W.   North   Avenue
64
N. State St.

Peggy Notebaert Nature Museum

Theater on the Lake

Lincoln Park Conservatory

John Cannon Dr.
Lake Shore Dr.
41

LINCOLN PARK ZOO

Fullerton Beach

Lincoln Park Cultural Center

Café Brauer

Farm-in-the-Zoo

South Pond

LINCOLN PARK

Chicago Historical Society

Lincoln Statue

North Avenue Beach

Lake Michigan

The park's lakes, trails, and pathways make it ideal for biking, hiking, picnicking, and enjoying nature. Baseball, softball, and soccer fields, and basketball and tennis courts are concentrated mainly around the South Field, Waveland, and Montrose sections. You'll find archery and a 9-hole golf course in the Waveland area. Minigolf and a driving range are located near Diversey Harbor. Families can rent paddleboats and explore the South Pond from a little dock in front of Café Brauer, located on the northwest side of lovely South Pond ($9 per half-hr., $15 per hr.). You can also rent boats from the boathouse on North Pond. Boat rentals are available from May through September.

Families with small children won't want to miss the **Farm-in-the-Zoo** (p. 185), located on the southern end of South Pond. Five barns house cows, chickens, horses, goats, and other livestock. Kids can get a farmhand's-eye view of butter churning, milking, and other farm activities throughout the day.

The **statue of the standing Abraham Lincoln** (just north of the North Ave. and State St. intersection) in the park that bears his name is one of two in Chicago by Augustus Saint-Gaudens. (*The Seated Lincoln* is in Grant Park.) Saint-Gaudens also did the Bates Fountain near the conservatory. The statue marks the southern boundary of the park.

A one-time Chicago dining institution near the zoo, **Café Brauer** (p. 135) reopened its doors to the public in 1990. Operating a cafe and ice cream parlor on the ground floor, and a ballroom called the Great Hall on the second floor that's flanked by two curving loggias, the return of the Brauer restores some of the elegant atmosphere that characterized the park around 1900, when this landmark building was erected. (If you visit on a weekend, chances are good that caterers will be setting up for a wedding in the Great Hall, but they'll usually let you in to sneak a peek.) I've heard from park district employees that, while touring the restoration, the son of the building's late architect, Dwight Perkins, was moved to tears. Perkins was one of the leaders of Chicago's Prairie School architecture movement, and Brauer is undeniably his masterwork. Best of all, though, is the picture-postcard view from the adjacent bridge spanning the pond of the John Hancock Center and neighboring skyscrapers beyond Lincoln Park's treetops.

If you're looking for an evening's entertainment, check out the **Theater on the Lake,** Fullerton Avenue, for open-air theater with a relaxed setting. For information, call © **312/742-7994.**

Bounded by Lake Shore Dr. from North Ave. to Bryn Mawr Ave. © **312/742-7726.** The park's visitor center is located in the Lincoln Park Cultural Center, 2045 N. Lincoln Park W. Park open daily from dawn until dusk. Visitor center open year-round Mon–Thurs 9am–9pm; Fri 11am–7pm; Sat 8am–4pm; Sun 11am–5pm. Bus: 22, 145, 146, 147, 151, or 156.

Moments A Great View

After a visit to the Lincoln Park Zoo or the Peggy Notebaert Nature Museum, take a quick stroll on Fullerton Avenue to the bridge that runs over the lagoon (just before you get to Lake Shore Dr.). Standing on the south side of Fullerton Avenue, you'll have a great view of the Chicago skyline and Lincoln Park—an excellent backdrop for family souvenir photos. This path can get very crowded on summer weekends, so I suggest trying this photo op during the week.

MILLENNIUM PARK ★★★

At the north end of Grant Park along Michigan Avenue is the city's newest urban showpiece. The architectural highlight of the park is the Frank Gehry–designed Pritzker Music Pavilion, home of the free summer music concerts performed by the Grant Park Symphony Orchestra. Another popular attraction is the huge elliptical sculpture by British artist Anish Kapoor, his first public work in the U.S. Once you see the sculpture, officially titled *Cloudgate,* you'll see why most Chicagoans affectionately call it "The Bean." For much more on the park, see p. 156 in chapter 6.

PING TOM MEMORIAL PARK

Families touring Chinatown should make a point of stopping at this wonderfully themed playground and park. Brightly colored swing sets, rubberized surfacing, and signs in Mandarin and English are surrounded by grounds landscaped with plants indigenous to China, such as bamboo. The park shelter is of Chinese design. It's all part of the Chicago Park District's new efforts to make parks attractive to both kids and adults, and appropriate to their neighborhood. You'll find the park at 300 W. 19th St.

300 W. 19th St. ✆ **312/742-PLAY.** Subway/El: Orange Line to Cermak.

WASHINGTON SQUARE PARK

This little park, built on 3 acres, may have been named after New York's Washington Square Park, which is located in a similarly elegant neighborhood. Although small in size, its location is wonderful, just west of the Magnificent Mile. If you need a place for your kids to run free after a day of shopping or touring, this park will give them some open space and immerse you in a "neighborhood" area, not far from busy Michigan Avenue.

The park has had its ups and downs, following the fortunes of the neighborhood. Surrounded by fine residences and churches in the late 1800s, the neighborhood fell upon harder times in the 1910s and many mansions were converted into flophouses. The park earned the nickname "Bughouse Square." Like Speakers' Corner in London's Hyde Park, Washington Square became a popular spot for soapbox orators. Artists, writers, political radicals, and hobos pontificated, read poetry, and ranted and raved.

In the late 1990s, the park district, city, and neighborhood organizations restored the park by reconstructing a historic Victorian fountain and installing period lighting, fencing, and new plantings. Today the park is surrounded by historic mansions, new condo buildings, and **Newberry Library** (p. 175).

901 N. Clark St. (at Delaware St.). ✆ **312/742-PLAY.** Bus: 11.

3 Playgrounds in the City Center

Chicago has a network of 552 city parks—most of which have playgrounds. To find information on a neighborhood park, go to **www.chicagoparkdistrict.com** or call ✆ **312/742-PLAY** for a list of parks and their facilities.

One of the most centrally located children's playgrounds is at **Daley Bicentennial Plaza in Grant Park,** at 337 E. Randolph St. The recently refurbished playground is set in the shadow of downtown skyscrapers at Randolph Street and Lake Shore Drive, which has fine views of the skyline and the lake. Kids will find all-new equipment for climbing, playing, and interacting, including swing sets and more, on a safe, rubberized surface. In addition to the play area, the plaza also offers a fitness center, locker rooms, and tennis courts, plus ice-skating in the winter. (For more on the skating rink, see "Sports & Games," below.)

Another heavily used playground is **Seneca Playlot Park,** 228 E. Chicago Ave., located just west of Chicago's venerable pumping station on Michigan Avenue. Seneca Park features both a lawn with shaded walkways and a play lot with a standard swing set, slide, and more. It's small, and could use a little updating, but Seneca provides a quiet oasis near the bustling Magnificent Mile. On the lawn sit two recent sculptures by nationally recognized artists: *Ben,* a bronze horse by sculptor Debra Butterfield, and *Farmer's Dream,* an abstract piece by sculptor Richard Hunt. The heavily used play lot is named for Eli Schulman (1910–88), a well-known restaurateur who founded Eli's, the Place for Steak, and who was active in promoting recreational activities for children. The park itself takes its name from adjacent Seneca Street, named for the Iroquois tribe of upstate New York.

4 Sports & Games

BASEBALL

Chicago's Park District offers baseball in many of its 552 parks; one diamond that's easily accessible and in a central location is **Lincoln Park.** The baseball fields are located on the southern tip, just north of the Chicago Historical Society. Even if a game is underway, you'll find some room to throw a ball back and forth with your child. For more information on baseball in city parks, visit www.chicagoparkdistrict.com.

Chicago parents who want to get kids involved in baseball should contact **Little League.** Kids ages 5 to 12 can participate. Teams change every year, so the best way to find one near you is to visit www.littleleague.org. Click on the "Finding a Local League" link to start your search for a team for your child.

Comiskey Park, 333 W. 35th St. (© **312/674-1000;** www.whitesox.mlb.com), does a great job getting kids excited about baseball. Before every Chicago White Sox home game, White Sox Training Center coaches conduct a baseball clinic. Kids can practice in the batting cages, at the base-running drill, and in the practice pitching areas. It's all free of charge. Enter Comiskey Park at Gate 3 or ask a Guest Services Representative how to get there. FUNdamentals, as the program is called, opens the gates about 1½ hours before game time and stays open for 1½ hours after the game starts. (If you're hungry after your pregame workout, stop by the Pepsi Kids Corner near Section 100 for kids' concessions like peanut-butter-and-jelly sandwiches, plus other kid favorites. Near Section 101, you'll find a kids' gift shop, featuring kids' souvenirs and apparel.)

If it's a little batting practice you're seeking, head for the batting cages **Sluggers,** located near Wrigley Field at 3540 N. Clark St. (© **773/248-0055**). This neighborhood sports bar is super–kid-friendly. It offers dozens of TV screens bringing in games via satellite, a fitting backdrop for you and your kids to test your skill in the batting cages. The upstairs batting cages approximate both softball and baseball pitches; there's also Pop-a-Shot and high-ball (a basketball-type game played on a trampoline), and an arcade. In the northern suburbs, try **Skokie Sports Park,** 3459 Oakton (© **847/674-1500**). The cages are open from April through October, Sunday to Thursday from 8am to 10pm, and Friday and Saturday from 8am to 11pm.

BASKETBALL

One of Chicago's better public parks to catch (or watch) a game of hoops is **Blackhawk Park,** located at 2318 N. Lavergne Ave. in the Irving Park neighborhood

(© 773/746-5014). A basketball court and baseball and softball fields dot the grounds of this family-friendly park. Basketball programs are offered for ages 5 and up. You'll also find an outdoor playground and spray pool and an indoor swimming pool. Park hours are Monday through Friday from 8am to 9pm and Saturday and Sunday from 9am to 5pm. Also recommended for their excellent kids' basketball programs are **Oz Park,** at 2021 N. Burling in the Lincoln Park neighborhood; **Portage Park,** 4100 N. Long Ave. on the northwest side; and **Independence Park,** at 3945 Springfield Ave. in the Irving Park neighborhood.

You can walk in to any **YMCA of Metropolitan Chicago** and use the gym to play basketball for a small fee. The most centrally located YMCA in the downtown area is New City YMCA, located at 1515 N. Halsted, at Clybourn (© **312/ 440-7272**). For more information, see www.ymcachgo.org.

BIKING

Biking is a great way to see the city, particularly the lakefront, along which there's a bike path that extends for more than 18 miles. The stretch between Navy Pier and North Avenue Beach gets extremely crowded in the summer (you're jostling for space with in-line skaters, joggers, and dawdling pedestrians). If you're looking for more wide-open spaces, I recommend biking south from Navy Pier— once you're past the Museum Campus, traffic on the trail is light, and you can cruise all the way to Hyde Park. If you want a more leisurely tour with good people-watching potential, head north (through the crowds) and be patient—once you pass Belmont Harbor, the traffic lets up somewhat. It's possible to ride all the way to Hollywood Beach, where the lakefront trail ends—a great workout.

To rent bikes, try **Bike & Roll,** which has locations at Navy Pier (© **312/ 595-9600**) and North Avenue Beach (© **773/327-7206**). Open from 8am to 8pm May through October (weather permitting), Bike & Roll stocks mountain and touring bikes, kids' bikes, kids' seats and trailers for any kids too young for a bike, strollers, and—most fun of all—quadcycles, which are four-wheeled contraptions equipped with a steering wheel and canopy that can accommodate four or five people. Rates for bikes are $9.75 an hour, $39 a day, with helmets, pads, and locks included. Quadcycles rent for $20 per hour.

Both the park district (© **312/742-PLAY**) and the **Chicagoland Bicycle Federation** (© **312/42-PEDAL;** www.chibikefed.org) offer free maps that detail popular biking routes. The latter, which is the preeminent organization for cyclists in Chicago, also sells a much larger, more extensive map for $6.95 that shows routes within a seven-county area. They sponsor a number of bike rides throughout the year, including the highly enjoyable **Boulevard Lakefront Tour,** held in mid-September, which follows the historic circle of boulevards that had their genesis in the Chicago Plan of 1909. It starts in Hyde Park at the University of Chicago campus.

A word of caution: Locking your bike anywhere you go is a no-brainer. More important, though, is never heading anywhere on the city's streets without first strapping on a helmet. Chicago Mayor Richard M. Daley is an avid cyclist himself and has tirelessly promoted the addition of designated bike lanes along many main thoroughfares. But, that said, most cabbies and drivers tend to ignore them. Bike with extreme caution on city streets (you can get a ticket for biking on the sidewalks), and stick to the lakefront path if you're not an expert rider.

BOWLING

What better way to bond as a family than an evening of gutter-dusting? Two popular hangouts mix teens, serious league bowlers, and families in an irresistible recipe for fun. At **Diversey River Bowl,** 2211 W. Diversey Ave. (© **773/227-5800**), tunes spun by a DJ (from an eclectic 300-CD collection) will get your feet tapping as you lace your bowling shoes. You'll find plenty of 20-somethings here on weekends, many of whom play in leagues. Prepare for a wait: It can be an hour. The festive atmosphere is complemented by a collection of bowling pins signed by "bowling greats" such as Dolly Parton and Eddie Vedder. Lanes are open Monday through Friday from noon to 2am; on Saturday and Sunday, leagues are usually scheduled, but there are always open lanes reserved for non-league bowlers. Cost is $19 per hour per lane Monday through Thursday, and $32 per hour per lane on Friday and Saturday. Shoe rental is $3.

Another option is **Waveland Bowl,** 3700 N. Western Ave. (© **773/472-5900**). Open 24/7, Waveland has 40 lanes and gets pretty loud when busy. Even though the place is huge, expect to wait your turn.

When in the suburbs, **Brunswick Zone** is your best bet and birthday-party central. One plus for families is the video games. The company has lanes in sub-urban Algonquin, Carol Stream, Deerfield, Deer Park, Glendale Heights, Kanka-kee, Mount Prospect Naperville, Niles, Oak Lawn, Palatine, Roselle, Waukegan/Lakehurst, and Woodridge. For phone numbers or to make online reservations, visit **www.brunswickbowling.com**.

CLIMBING

Sorry to point out the obvious, but Chicago has no hills, much less mountains. (When I was in a training group for the Chicago Marathon, we did our hill training by running up the corkscrew ramp in the John Hancock Center park-ing garage—that's how serious Chicago's hill shortage is!) Your best option for climbing in the city is "Mount Chicago," located at the **Lakeshore Athletic Club** (© **312/616-9000**). Billed as "the world's highest indoor climbing wall," the man-made wall rises 110 feet. Kids ages 5 and up can climb on Saturday after 2pm and all day Sunday. You don't have to be a member to use the wall. Cost for kids is $15 for an orientation class. Kids' classes and private lessons are available; classes take place Sunday mornings from 9 to 10am for 6 consecutive weekends and require preregistration. Even if you don't have previous experi-ence, adults, too, can venture onto the wall through an orientation and safety class (all while wearing a protective harness, of course). The club is private but is open to guests of any hotel for $20 a day and to guests at the nearby Fairmont Hotel and Hyatt Regency Chicago for $15 a day. It's located at 211 N. Stetson, 1 block east of North Michigan Avenue at Lake Street. To get there, take any bus that serves Michigan Avenue.

Chicago residents who want to enroll their kids in classes might investigate the indoor rock climbing at **Lakeshore Academy,** located at 937 W. Chestnut, near the intersection of Halsted and Chicago (© **312/563-9400;** www.lake shoreacademy.com). Membership is $100 per year and lasts until the same term 1 year later, and classes are organized by age group for kids from age 5 to 16. "Hidden Peak," as the climbing area is called, is a great way to discover the chal-lenge of indoor rock climbing. Staffed with experienced and friendly people, Hidden Peak offers tons of user-friendly programs for kids (and adults). *Tip:* A fun option for a birthday party is climbing parties, held for kids age 6 and up, that cost $40 per instructor and $10 per child. Lakeshore Academy gives these parties over a 2-hour period on Saturday and Sunday evenings, or Sunday morn-ings. Check out the website for more information.

FISHING

The Chicago Park District runs fishing programs for kids; for the latest details, check out **www.chicagoparkdistrict.com**. One program, "Fish N Kids," offers rods, reels, bait, and instruction for four daily 45-minute sessions at all Chicago Park District lagoons and at four lakefront locations. The Sam Romano Youth Fishing Derby (named for a charter boat captain who loved fishing and kids), which runs all summer, is open to kids ages 8 to 15. Kids enter their catches in a category: rock bass, panfish, catfish, and carp. Twenty kids in each category win prizes of new fishing equipment.

Want to do battle with the scrappy coho salmon, or tie into a tackle-testing, arm-aching 20-pound chinook? Salmon fishing has been popular on Lake Michigan since Pacific species were introduced in the 1970s. Gather a group of six (to split the cost of $395 for 5 hr. of fishing) and be prepared to start at dawn. You can find a charter boat through the **Chicago Sportfishing Association** (© 312/922-1100), with boats available in both Burnham and Diversey harbors.

Lake perch are another popular Lake Michigan fish—they won't give you the fight that salmon do, but they are fun to catch and good to eat. (Pan-fried is the way to go.) They are plentiful from May to August. Jumbo perch weigh in at 1 pound and are caught with ultralight spinning tackle or hand lines rigged with multiple hooks. Check sporting-goods stores for equipment and bait. The local anglers' favorite spot is Montrose Harbor Pier, east of Lake Shore Drive at Wilson Avenue. Harbor fishing is allowed in designated areas of Belmont, Montrose, Diversey, DuSable, Monroe, Burnham, 59th Street, and Jackson Inner and Jackson Outer harbors. To find out more, call **Chicago Park District** harbor information at © 312/747-7527.

GOLF

Chicago has an impressive number of golf options within the city limits. The Chicago Park District offers six courses, three driving ranges, and three learning centers. Don't let a little cold weather stop you: As further evidence of the hardiness of Chicagoans, the golf courses closed only 1 day in 2001, when there was a blizzard. (Yes, you can golf in Chicago year-round, even on Christmas Day!) For tee times and information, call © 312/245-0909. Most recommended for kids is the **Diversey Driving Range** (© 312/742-7929), located in Lincoln Park just north of Diversey Harbor; it's a fun way to get outside after dinner on a summer evening. This two-level range attracts all levels, from show-off scratch golfers to shanking beginners. The price is right ($11 for a bucket of 50 balls), and the setting is pretty much perfect.

One of the most popular golf courses operated by the Chicago Park District is the 9-hole **Sydney Marovitz Course,** 3600 N. Lake Shore Dr., at Waveland Avenue. Many Chicagoans refer to it simply as "Waveland." Thanks to its picturesque lakefront location, it's always busy on weekends, so make a reservation well in advance, and don't expect a quick round—this is where beginners come to practice. Another good bet, and one that's usually less crowded, is the 18-hole course in **Jackson Park** at 63rd St. and Stoney Island Avenue. These city-run courses are open from mid-April through November. For information on greens fees, locations, and hours, call the **Chicago Park District** golf office (© 312/245-0909), or go to www.cpdgolf.com.

If you're planning on visiting the suburbs and want to play a round on one of the many plush and pricey suburban courses, visit the website of the Chicago District Golf Association at www.cdga.org.

No Horsing Around

Let me be frank: Horseback riding in downtown Chicago is impossible. About the closest you can get is a horse-and-buggy ride. Carriages depart from the southwest corner of Michigan Avenue and Pearson Street (next to the Water Tower). For $30 for a half-hour ride (for up to four people), it's a picturesque way to take in the city's sights. The rides are operated by The Noble Horse, which owns the only remaining stable in downtown Chicago, from a 1917 brick building at 1410 N. Orleans Ave. For group tours or other information, call **The Noble Horse** at © **312/266-7878**.

In the northern suburbs, **Skokie Sports Park,** 3459 Oakton (© **847/674-1500**), offers an 18-hole around-the-world-themed miniature golf course, a 9-hole miniature golf course for the smallest tots, a two-tiered driving range, and junior golf lessons. The Traveler's Quest miniature golf course, geared toward older kids and adults, lets you putt around the Eiffel Tower and over the waterfall near Easter Island. Check out the African water hole (in which you putt into the hippo's mouth), the Japanese garden with lanterns offering sizable hazards, and the Great Wall of China. The park is open April through October Sunday through Thursday from 8am to 10pm, Friday and Saturday until 11pm.

In nearby Lincolnwood, **Bunny Hutch Novelty Golf and Games,** 3550 W. Devon Ave. (© **847/679-9434**), offers miniature golf, batting cages, a video arcade, and an ice cream parlor. It's a 50-year-old operation that's open daily from 10am to midnight from early March through late October.

ICE SKATING

Whether you and your kids are executing graceful toe loops or merely stumbling across the rink, you can hit the ice in the heart of Chicago's Loop. The city's premier skating destination is the **McCormick Tribune Ice Rink** at Millennium Park, 55 N. Michigan Ave., located at the intersection of Michigan Avenue and Monroe Street. The location is unbeatable. You'll skate in the shadows of grand skyscrapers and within view of the lake. The rink is open daily from 9am to 9pm, November to March. Admission is free, and skate rentals are $5. Try going on a weeknight when the city lights sparkle over you, and grab a hot chocolate from a vending machine to warm up before hitting the ice.

Year-round skating and ice-skating lessons are available at the only city-run indoor ice arena at **McFetridge Sports Complex,** located in the Lakeview neighborhood at 3845 N. California Ave., at Irving Park Road (© **773/742-7585**). Open skating sessions in the indoor rink are held Wednesday and Friday afternoons from 3:30 to 5pm, and Saturday and Sunday from 4:30 to 6pm. Skates can be rented for $2.50 a pair; the rink fee is $3 for adults, $2.75 for teens 14 to 17, and $2.25 for kids 13 and under. The rink is huge and can be very crowded on weekends. You might want to take advantage of the free skating lessons, available on Monday from 5:15 to 5:55pm.

IN-LINE SKATING

In-line skaters have been taking over Chicago's sidewalks, streets, and bike paths since the early 1990s. Numerous rental places have popped up, and several sporting-goods shops that sell in-line skates also rent them. The rentals generally include helmets and pads. **Bike & Roll,** with locations at Navy Pier (© **312/595-9600**) and North Avenue Beach (© **773/327-7206**), charges $8.75 an hour or $34 a day (you can have the skates 8am–8pm). A second rental spot is **Londo Mondo,** 1100 N. Dearborn St. (© **312/751-2794**), on the Gold Coast, renting blades for $7 an hour or $20 a day.

The best route to skate, of course, is the lakefront trail that leads from Lincoln Park down to Oak Street Beach. Beware, though, that those same miles of trail are claimed by avid cyclists—and I've seen plenty of collisions between 'bladers and bikers. Approach Chicago lakefront traffic as carefully as you would a major expressway!

SAILING

It seems a shame just to sit on the beach and watch all those beautiful sailboats gliding across the lake. Go on, get out there. The **Chicago Sailing Club,** in Belmont Harbor (© **773/871-SAIL;** www.chicagosailingclub.com), rents J-22 and J-30 boats from 9am to sunset, weather permitting, May through October. A J-22 holds four or five people. Rates for a J-22 range from $35 to $55 an hour ($10 extra for a skipper). A J-30 accommodates up to 10 people and can sail at night. Rates are $70 to $90 per hour, plus $20 per hour for a skipper. If you want to take the boat out without a skipper, you need to demonstrate your skills first (and pay an additional $10 checkout fee). Those who'd rather sit back and relax while a pro does the sailing can charter a boat here as well. Reservations are recommended.

SWIMMING

The Chicago Park District maintains about 30 indoor pools for lap swimming and general splashing around, but none are particularly convenient to downtown. If you are a resident, you should check out your local park (to find out where parks are located, see www.chicagoparkdistrict.com). Some neighborhoods have incredible facilities that are safe and clean. For example, **Portage Park,** located on Chicago's northwest side at 4100 Long Ave. (© **773/685-7235**), has a stunning outdoor Olympic-size pool, a diving board with three levels and its own dive pool, and a kids' pool with a water playhouse, waterfalls, and more. It's absolutely wonderful, and it's free. The neighborhood is populated by Hispanic and eastern European immigrants and tons of kids jam the pool every summer weekend. Another great park for swimming is **Blackhawk Park,** located at 2318 N. Lavergne Ave. in the Irving Park neighborhood (© **773/746-5014**). You'll find an outdoor spray pool and an indoor swimming pool. Pool hours vary according to age: Youth swim is at 3pm, teen swim at 5pm, and family swim at 7pm.

Still, my advice to visitors would be to skip the park district pools, because many are located in off-the-beaten-track neighborhoods. As a visitor, your best bet for summer swimming is **Lake Michigan,** where beaches are open for swimmers Memorial Day through Labor Day from 9am to 9:30pm in areas watched over by lifeguards (no swimming off the rocks, please). It's a safe place to swim and a uniquely "Chicago" experience. How often do you and your kids get the chance to take a dip in a Great Lake? Watch the news for beach closings, which happen occasionally, as the water is tested daily for bacteria. If you're a serious lap swimmer, you'll find company along the wall beginning at Ohio Street Beach, located slightly northwest of Navy Pier. The Chicago Triathlon Club marks a course here each summer with a buoy at both the ¼- and ½-mile marks. This popular swimming route follows the shoreline in a straight line. The water is fairly shallow. For more information, call the park district's beach and pool office (© **312/742-PLAY**).

The Chicago Park District manages 31 beaches along 24 miles of lakefront. Amenities vary, but most have a comfort station or a beach house and food vendors selling hot dogs, burgers, and soda. The two beaches I can recommend without hesitation are **Oak Street Beach** and **North Avenue Beach.** Both also feature a broader menu for dining: The Oak Street Beachstro (p. 117) offers gourmet salads, beef tenderloin, grilled salmon, and Key lime pie; the restaurant in the beach house at North Avenue Beach offers Jamaican jerk chicken and specialty ice cream.

For more information, call the park district's beach and pool office at © **312/ 747-0832.**

TENNIS

The best—and cheapest—tennis in the city is found at **Waveland Courts,** located on Lake Shore Drive at Addison. For $4 per hour, you can play on these public courts. It's first-come, first-served, so get there early—the park is open from 6am to 11pm. Pay before you play at the trailer located close to the Addison entrance. Tennis buffs report that the availability of courts is pretty good in the morning. League play takes place in the evenings, and it's difficult to get a court. Any nontennis players in your family can play golf, which is also available here.

If it's lessons you're seeking, head for **McFetridge Sports Complex,** 3845 N. California Ave. (© **773/478-2609**). Students here report that the tennis pros are great, lessons are good, and the price is right: An 8-week-long group lesson starts at about $35 for 4-year-olds or $40 for teens (no single lessons are available). The complex offers lessons and tournaments for kids. You can also pay for court time here just to play on your own, but book ahead, especially in winter. In the summer you'll have no problem booking an indoor court.

5 Indoor Playgrounds

The only city-run indoor playground is free, highly recommended, and located in **Garfield Park Conservatory;** see p. 187 for a full description.

The national chain **Gymboree** offers a series of classes for kids from newborn to age 4 in a playscape with slides, inflatable logs, colorful mats, and all kinds of things to jump on and crawl inside. A Gymboree teacher leads the way with activities and songs. Visitors can call ahead to request space in one of the classes; most local parents sign up for a full series. In Chicago the sole location is at 3158 N. Lincoln Ave. (© **773/296-4550;** www.gymboree.com). You'll also find branches in suburban Wilmette, Skokie, Northbrook, and Wheaton.

Odyssey Fun World (www.odysseyfunworld.com), in west suburban Naperville and Tinley Park, features 250 video games and rides, plus a Little Tykes playground, a four-level soft playland (for kids 12 and under), a roller-coaster simulator, a cafe, a rock-climbing-wall thrill ride, paintball, and some outdoor attractions, including 36 holes of adventure golf, go-cart tracks, and batting cages. Each activity has a fee, and games require tokens (usually 25¢ each, less if bought in quantity); admission to the soft playground is $6.95. Other rides vary from $2 to $5. Locations are at 19111 S. Oak Park Ave., Tinley Park (© **708/429-3800**), and 3440 Odyssey Court, Naperville (© **630/416-2222**).

6 Classes & Workshops

Chicago Children's Museum   A plethora of wonderful classes is available at the museum. The array might include wintertime decorating of fleece scarves that kids can wear, making glitzy bookmarks, designing quilt squares of kids' favorite books, or dancing out storybook classics such as *The Gingerbread Man.* Classes are available for all ages. They change often, so see the "Activities" section of the website, www.chichildrensmuseum.org.

At Navy Pier, 700 E. Grand Ave. (© 312/527-1000. www.chichildrensmuseum.org. Class fee included in museum admission fee ($7 adults and children, $6 seniors). Subway/El: Red Line to Grand/State; transfer to city bus or Navy Pier's free trolley bus. Bus: 29, 56, 65, or 66.

The Field Museum of Natural History   From fossil-hunting field trips to hands-on seminars on the mythology and crafts of the Incas, to an immersive workshop in video storytelling, the Field Museum offers workshops year-round for families. For more information, see the "Education" section of www.fmnh.org or call (© **312/665-7400.**

Roosevelt Rd. and Lake Shore Dr. (© 312/922-9410 or 312/341-9299 TDD (for hearing-impaired callers). www.fmnh.org. Bus: 6, 10, 12, 130, or 146.

Lill Street Art Center   This center for working artists offers a huge array of classes for kids from 2 years old and up, involving pottery, watercolors, singing, and more. If you want to drop in, you can browse the studios, where the kids can see the artists at work.

1021 W. Lill, 3 blocks north of Fullerton St. in the DePaul University area. (© 773/477-6185. www.lillstreet. com. 10-week-long kids' courses start at $140 (single lessons not available). Gallery hours Tues–Sat 11am–6pm; Sun noon–5pm. Subway/El: Red Line to Fullerton.

Museum of Science and Industry   Who knows how many current chemists, biologists, and real-life rocket scientists were once inspired by this museum? Get your young Einstein involved in the wonders of science with "Saturday Science Clubs," where kids can engage in hands-on science and technology activities. Participants are encouraged to work together to investigate scientific issues and develop problem-solving skills. Club activities cover subjects such as chemistry, physics, flight, electric circuitry, and forensics. Morning science clubs run from 9:30am to noon. Afternoon clubs run from 1 to 3:30pm. Workshops are for kids grades six to nine. For current offerings, see the "Education" section of the website www.msichicago.org, or call (© **773/684-7844,** ext. 2687.

57th St. and Lake Shore Dr. (© 800/468-6674 outside the Chicago area, 773/684-1414, or TTY 773/684-3323. www.msichicago.org. Bus: 6, 10, 55, 151, or 156.

Old Town School of Folk Music   Chicago's premier music education center offers kids' classes in music, dance, art, and theater as well as private lessons. Children's courses last 8 or 16 weeks, and are 45 minutes to 1 hour in length. Visitors, however, can get a taste of the fun by trying out a class. You can show up the day of the class and pay $13 to attend that day. (Art classes are excluded.) Drop-in opportunities include the Wiggle Worms class, a music-and-movement class that Chicago parents say is the absolute most fun class in the city for small children (about 6 months–3 years).

Teen classes are just for students ages 11 to 18, and are offered during afterschool and weekend hours. All classes meet once a week, and most are 80 minutes in length, in a relaxed group atmosphere of 8 to 12 students. Most teen music classes cost about $90 for 8 weeks of classes; theater classes run 16 weeks. Starlight: Teen Open Mic at the Old Town School takes the stage from 7 to 10pm on the second Friday of every month. Call for information or to be added to the Teen Open Mic mailing list. This new monthly event is a showcase for musicians, actors, and audience members at the 909 W. Armitage Ave. location.

4544 N. Lincoln Ave. (© 773/728-6000. www.oldtownschool.org. Subway/El: Brown Line to Western.

Shopping with Your Kids

When I talked to other Chicago parents about shopping with their kids, they often joked, "The best shopping experience is *no* shopping experience!" True, shopping with kids can be a strain, and maybe this chapter is better titled "Shopping *for* Your Kids." To keep kids interested during your shopping expeditions, I've included some stores that wouldn't necessarily be considered children's stores but which kids find fascinating—stores that sell thousands of different buttons, for example.

For more on shopping for adults in Chicago, pick up a copy of *Frommer's Chicago*. This chapter concentrates on the Magnificent Mile, State Street, and several trendy neighborhoods, where you'll find one-of-a-kind shops and boutiques that make shopping such an adventure. It also includes a sampling of retailers organized by merchandise category.

1 The Shopping Scene

SHOPPING HOURS & SALES TAXES

As a general rule, stores are open Monday through Saturday from 10am to 6 or 7pm, and Sunday from noon to 6pm. Neighborhood stores tend to keep later hours, with some remaining open until 8pm Monday through Saturday and until 6pm on Sunday. Many stores are open later on Thursday, and almost all have extended hours during the holiday season. Nearly all the stores in the Loop are open for daytime shopping only, generally Monday through Saturday from 9 or 10am to no later than 6pm. (The few remaining big downtown department stores have some evening hours; see below.) Many Loop stores not on State Street are closed Saturday; on Sunday the Loop—except for a few restaurants, theaters, and cultural attractions—is shut down pretty tight.

You might do a double take after checking the total on your purchase: At 8.75%, the state and local sales taxes on nonfood items is one of the steepest in the country.

SHOPPING DISTRICTS
THE MAGNIFICENT MILE

The nickname "Magnificent Mile" refers to the roughly mile-long stretch of North Michigan Avenue between Oak Street and the Chicago River. As Chicago's top shopping destination, the Magnificent Mile is magnificent not because of the sightseeing or the architecture: The stores are the thing. The density of first-rate shopping is, quite simply, unmatched anywhere. Even jaded shoppers from other worldly capitals are delighted at the ease and convenience of the stores concentrated here. Taking into account that tony Oak Street is just around a corner (again, if you want to hit Hermès and Prada, I must refer you to *Frommer's Chicago*), the overall area is a little like New York's Fifth Avenue and Beverly Hills's Rodeo Drive rolled into one. Whether your passion is Bulgari jewelry, Prada suits, or Ferragamo footwear, you'll find it on this stretch of concrete. Window-shoppers and people-watchers also will find plenty to amuse themselves. This is the city's liveliest corridor: The sidewalks are packed in the summer and on weekends with hordes of shoppers strolling up and down the avenue and pausing to enjoy the many street performers who enliven this strip. Holidays on Michigan Avenue are a magical time, as the city knocks itself out with lights and music and a spectacular Christmas tree in the John Hancock Center plaza.

But don't think you're seeing everything by walking down the street. Michigan Avenue is home to several indoor, high-rise malls, where plenty more boutiques and restaurants are tucked away. The face of one of Chicago's most prestigious addresses has been dramatically transformed over the past quarter-century since the first mall—Water Tower Place—went up on the north end of the street. Several more malls and large-scale, hotel-retail projects have followed. As the rush for square footage escalated beginning in the late 1980s, many city residents lamented the metamorphosis of the street from a rather intimate and graceful promenade of 1920s buildings to a glitzy canyon of retail theater. Eager to get in on the action, national and international retailers—from middle-brow discounters to high-brow couture purveyors—have continued to look for front-row locations to squeeze into.

For the ultimate Mag Mile shopping adventure, start at one end of North Michigan Avenue and try to work your way to the other. In this section are listed some of the best-known kid-related shops on the avenue and on nearby side streets.

NORTH MICHIGAN AVENUE & THE MAGNIFICENT MALLS

North Michigan Avenue is lined with shops and includes four of the aforementioned vertical malls—each a major shopping destination in its own right. These indoor malls offer shopping on multiple levels.

WATER TOWER PLACE   Chicago's first—and still busiest—vertical mall is Water Tower Place, a block-size, marble-sheathed building at 835 N. Michigan Ave. (© **312/440-3165;** www.shopWaterTower.com), between East Pearson and East Chestnut streets. The mall's seven floors contain about 100 stores that reportedly account for roughly half of all the retail trade transacted along the Magnificent Mile. The mall also houses a dozen different cafes and restaurants.

Water Tower was the first big indoor mall to open downtown (in 1975), and 20 years ago its glass elevators and shiny gold trim gave the place a glamorous air. These days, after some recent renovations, the spiffed-up mall remains popular, but doesn't have much to distinguish it from any other upscale shopping center. Water Tower is a magnet for suburban teenagers (just like your mall back home!) and can get quite crowded during the summer tourist season. Most of its stores are part of national chains (Gap, Victoria's Secret, and the like). But there are a few shops that make it worth a stop, including hip young designs from the British store and young teen magnet **French Connection** (fifth floor; © **312/932-9460**) and wearable women's clothing at **Eileen Fisher** (second floor; © **312/943-9190**). The department stores anchoring the mall include the Mag Mile outpost of the Loop's famed **Marshall Field's** (floors one to eight; © **312/335-7700;** p. 228) and a **Lord & Taylor** (floors one to seven; © **312/787-7400;** p. 228). One of the mall's best features is the innovative **foodlife** food court, which contains more than a dozen stations, from burgers and pizza to Mexican and Moroccan, plus the **Mity Nice Grill** (© **312/335-4745**), a faux-1940s diner. Two movie complexes contain eight screens. Of note to kids are **Accent Chicago** (© **312/944-1354**) for T-shirts, pizza pans, logo sports gear, and other souvenirs that say "Chicago"; **Number One Blue**

Magnificent Mile Shopping

E. Bellevue Pl.

Lake Michigan

E. Oak St.

E. Walton St.

900 North Michigan Shops

E. Delaware Pl.

John Hancock Center

E. Chestnut St.

Water Tower Place

W. Chestnut St.

Old Water Tower

E. Pearson St.

Museum of Contemporary Art

W. Chicago Ave.

CHICAGO

E. Chicago Ave.

W. Superior St.

E. Superior St.

W. Huron St.

Chicago Place

E. Huron St.

W. Erie St.

E. Erie St.

N. W. Erie St.

W. Ontario St.

E. Ontario St.

STREETER-VILLE

W. Ohio St.

E. Ohio St.

W. Grand Ave.

GRAND

E. Grand Ave.

To Navy Pier →

Westfield North Bridge

E. Illinois St.

RIVER NORTH

W. Illinois St.

W. Hubbard St.

Wrigley Building

E. North Water St.

W. Kinzie St.

Chicago River

- Subway/El stop

CHICAGO

Wrigley Field ■

THE LOOP

U.S. Cellular Field ■

✈ Midway

Map area

American Girl Place **11**
Barbara's Bookstore **14**
Blue Chicago Store **18**
Borders **10**
Chicago Place **13**
Children in Paradise Bookstore **4**
GapKids and babyGap **17**
Ghirardelli Chocolate Shop **8**
Jazz Record Mart **19**
John Hancock Center **7**

Madison and Friends **1**
Neiman-Marcus **12**
Niketown **15**
900 North Michigan Avenue **5**
Penny's from Heaven **6**
Sony **16**
Tender Buttons **2**
Urban Outfitters **3**
Water Tower Place **9**
Westfield Shops at North Bridge **20**

Engine (📞 312/335-9302), the only toy store on North Michigan Avenue with all things dedicated to Thomas the Tank Engine (wooden train sets, apparel, books, videos, and accessories); and **Gamers Paradise** (📞 312/587-0077), with its large collection of board games, card games, video games, and more. The mall is home to **Abercrombie & Fitch** (p. 229), **GapKids** (p. 230), **Limited Too, Claire's Boutique, Jacadi** (p. 230), **Campus Colors,** with Chicago's largest selection of collegiate wear, and **Gymboree** (p. 230).

900 NORTH MICHIGAN AVE.   The most upscale of the Magnificent Mile's three vertical malls, 900 North Michigan (📞 312/915-3916) is often called the "Bloomingdale's building" for its most prominent tenant. The mall avoids the tumult of Water Tower Place by appealing to a more upscale shopper, while still generating the vitality essential to a satisfying shopping spree. In addition to about 70 stores are a few good restaurants and a nice salon on the lower level.

Young teens will make a beeline for the ground-level outpost of **Club Monaco** (📞 312/787-8757), with minimalist casual-chic clothes at affordable prices. On the second floor, **J. Crew** (📞 312/751-2739) offers sweaters, slacks, hats, belts, and other clothing featuring the scrubbed-clean look, popular with young teens to adults. You'll also want to check out the fifth floor, home to **Galt Toys** (p. 237), and **Mini Me** (p. 230), which features great kids' clothing.

The mall's bathrooms are large, clean, and well equipped with infant changing areas; you'll find them on the second and fifth levels. *An added treat:* Shoppers are serenaded by live piano music on weekends from noon to 5pm on the second level. You'll also find kid-friendly restaurants, including **Tucci Benucch,** a casual Italian restaurant that has a kids' menu, coloring sheets, and crayons; and **Oak Tree,** a bustling place on the sixth floor that welcomes families.

CHICAGO PLACE   Inaugurated in 1991 at 700 N. Michigan Ave., Chicago Place (📞 312/266-7710) has been looking for an identity ever since. The mall is mainly notable as the home of **Saks Fifth Avenue** (📞 312/944-6500; p. 229). You won't find much for kids here, except a **Talbots Kids** (p. 232) for those seeking out the preppy look, and a food court on the eighth floor that features cheap eats. You'll find the usual mall favorites (McDonald's, Subway, Taco Bell), but healthier dishes are available at **Pita Pavilion** (Mediterranean). Kids love the crispy french fries at the **Great Steak & Potato Company** and the hot dogs at **Chicago Dog & Grill.** Grab one of the tables near the gigantic windows for a great Michigan Avenue view.

WESTFIELD NORTH BRIDGE   The best concentration of kids' stores on the Mag Mile is located in this mall at 520 N. Michigan Ave. The third floor is devoted to children's shops, the best of which is **The Lego Store** (📞 312/494-0760). Look for the replicas of Chicago landmarks built out of those distinctive colored-plastic blocks, and be prepared to stay awhile: Kids can easily spend an hour here. Other stores of interest to kids are **Benetton Kids** (p. 230), **Chicago Harley-Davidson, The Children's Place, Jordan Marie, Oilily** (p. 231), and **Sanrio.**

The anchor of the mall is a four-story **Nordstrom** (📞 312/379-4300). The mall includes the first Chicago location for **A/X Armani Exchange** (📞 312/467-5702), Giorgio Armani's younger and more affordable line that's a big hit with teens. There's a large food court on the fourth level with local standouts like **Potbelly Sandwich Works** (p. 113). Other eating options near the North Bridge mall include **Big Bowl** (p. 120), **ESPN Zone** (p. 120), **California Pizza Kitchen** (p. 121), and a host of fast-food outlets on the fourth floor.

The Red Balloon Company 1

Sweet Thang 3

The T-Shirt Deli 2

STATE STREET & THE LOOP

State Street was Chicago's first great shopping district. Between the time the first stores were established in 1852 and World War I, seven of the largest and most lavish department stores in the world were competing for shoppers' loyalties along a half-mile stretch between Randolph Street and Congress Parkway. The area has now been eclipsed by Michigan Avenue, and State Street is lined with discount stores and fast-food outlets. But it's still worth visiting for the two grand old department stores that remain: **Marshall Field & Co.,** 111 N. State St., at Randolph Street (© 312/781-1000; p. 228); and **Carson Pirie Scott & Co.,** a few blocks south, at 1 S. State St., at the corner of Madison Street (© 312/641-7000; p. 227). Both buildings are city landmarks and attractions in themselves. Architecturally speaking, the Louis Sullivan–designed Carson's is the more celebrated of the two; however, Field's State Street store remains one of the world's largest, occupying an entire city block and featuring the largest Tiffany glass mosaic dome in the United States. If you're in Chicago between Thanksgiving and New Year's, a visit to Marshall Field's to see the holiday windows and to have lunch under the Great Tree in the Walnut Room is in keeping with local tradition.

Although State Street has not recaptured the glamour of decades past, it manages to draw crowds of loyal customers from the Loop's office towers and Chicagoans turned off by Michigan Avenue's snob factor. There's no better example of the street's revival than the 2001 opening of a new **Sears** store (© 312/373-6000) at the corner of State and Madison streets. A large **Old Navy** store (p. 231) at Washington and State streets (© 312/551-0522) also brings in the crowds— check out the kids' wares, which are cheap and hip.

Just off State Street, heading east on Randolph Street, is the **Gallery 37 Store,** 66 E. Randolph St. (© 312/251-0371; www.gallery37.org). The store sells goods made by Chicago youth ages 14 to 21 who are participants in the Gallery 37 arts training program. The not-for-profit pairs young artists with experienced artists. Proceeds from the sales of the paintings, jewelry, ceramics, decorated furniture, textiles, and sculptures benefit the program.

RIVER NORTH

River North, the area west of the Magnificent Mile and north of the Chicago River, is Chicago's primary art gallery district. Other interesting shops, concentrated on Wells Street from Kinzie Street to Chicago Avenue, include home furnishings and collectibles, and are probably of most interest to adults. The neighborhood even has a mall of its own—**The Shops at the Mart** (© 312/527-7990)—in the Merchandise Mart, at Wells and Kinzie streets, with a standard collection of chain stores. The rest of the Merchandise Mart, the world's largest commercial building, houses mostly interior design showrooms, which are open only to professional designers. If you want to get a sense of the whole massive complex, take a public tour, which is usually offered on Friday at 1pm ($10; © 312/527-7762). The rest of the River North area is ripe for gallery-hopping but doesn't have many shops to interest kids, unless they have a mature understanding of art, so check out *Frommer's Chicago* if you have an interest in that area.

(**Tips** **Point Zero**

If the quick change from north to south in the Loop confuses you, keep in mind that in Chicago, point zero for the purpose of address numbering is the intersection of State and Madison streets.

LINCOLN PARK

I highly recommend shopping for kids in Lincoln Park. Sidewalks are crowded with parents and strollers on a weekend afternoon. This North Side neighborhood has a variety of unique specialty shops that make it easy to browse through this leafy, picturesque community. Many of the shops on Michigan Avenue are branches of national chains and offer few surprises, but the shops and boutiques in Lincoln Park tend to be locally owned and offer unique and interesting wares. Shops are located on the primary commercial arteries running through the area, including Armitage Avenue, Webster Avenue, Halsted Street, Clark Street, and Lincoln Avenue.

For kids, the highest concentration of stores is found on **Armitage Avenue** and **Halsted Street,** which form one of the finest 19th-century neighborhood commercial streetscapes remaining in Chicago. The district contains an excellent cross section of residential and commercial building types significant in the development of such streets, including small residential buildings and larger, multistory mixed-use buildings, and is especially noteworthy for the profusion of pressed-metal decoration, including bays, cornices, and corner turrets, on many of the buildings. Together, the district's buildings form an important streetscape that exemplifies the importance of neighborhood shopping streets to the history of Chicago.

Armitage Avenue has emerged as a shopping destination in its own right, thanks to an influx of wealthy young professionals who have settled into historic townhomes on the neighboring tree-lined streets. The shops and boutiques here, which sell everything from artisan-made apparel to interesting, offbeat gifts, are geared toward a sophisticated, well-heeled shopper, and make for great browsing. As you stroll the area, you'll get some sense of its strong community spirit, with neighbors greeting each other and catching up on street corners. Most of the shops are concentrated between Halsted Street and Clybourn Avenue. To give you a sampling of the number of children's boutiques in this area, clothing stores alone include **The Second Child, Active Kids, GapKids,** and **LMNOP.** All are covered in detail under "Fashion," later in this chapter.

LAKEVIEW

Shoppers will find elements of both prosperous Lincoln Park and alternative-ish Wicker Park when they're wandering along Lakeview's principal commercial avenues. One strip worth a stroll—and one that's popular with the stroller set—is the gentrifying retail row along Southport Avenue, a few blocks west of Wrigley Field. With the **Music Box Theater** at 3733 N. Southport Ave., north of Addison Street, as its anchor, the area has an interesting mix of quirky and artsy merchants and restaurateurs. Start at Southport and Roscoe streets and walk north to find a string of hip kids' clothing and toy boutiques, including **Sweet Pea,** 3447 N. Southport (© 773/281-4426), and **Elizabeth Marie,** 3453 N. Southport (© 773/525-4100). Nearby, on Ashland Avenue, you'll find **Bebe Elegante,** 3338 N. Ashland (© 773/477-2323), and on Lincoln Avenue, **Building Blocks Toy Store,** 3306 N. Lincoln (© 773/525-6200).

BELMONT AVENUE & CLARK STREET   Radiating from the intersection of Belmont Avenue and Clark Street is a string of shops catering to rebellious kids on tour from their homes in the 'burbs. (The Dunkin' Donuts on the corner is often referred to as "Punkin' Donuts" in their honor.) If you have preteens or young teens, they will be fascinated by the youth culture, the street life—and the shops.

Alley, 858 W. Belmont Ave., at Clark Street (© 773/525-3180), is an "alternative shopping complex" selling everything from plaster gargoyles to racks of leather jackets. It has separate shops specializing in condoms, cigars, and bondage wear.

All the latest men's (and some women's) fashion—from names such as Fresh Jive, Fuct, and Diesel—can be found under the same roof at the multiroom scene housing the **Aero** and **Untitled** shops, 2707 N. Clark St. (© 773/404-9225). Whether you're into tight, fitted fashion or the layered, droopy-pants look, it's here. **Tragically Hip,** a storefront women's boutique at 931 W. Belmont Ave. (© 773/549-1500), next to the Belmont El train stop, has outlasted many other similar purveyors of cutting-edge women's apparel.

Get plugged into what the kids are reading at **Chicago Comics,** 3244 N. Clark St. (© 773/528-1983), the industry's 1998 pick for best comics shop in the country. Besides the usual superhero titles, the shop stocks the Midwest's largest selection of alternative comics. You'll also find lots of back stock and European and Japanese comics, along with underground books and 'zines.

WICKER PARK/BUCKTOWN

The go-go gentrification of the Wicker Park/Bucktown area has been followed by not only a rash of restaurants and bars, but also retailers with an artsy bent reflecting the neighborhood's bohemian spirit. Mixed in with old neighborhood businesses, such as discount furniture stores and religious-icon purveyors, is a proliferation of antique-furniture shops, too-cool-for-school clothing boutiques, and eclectic galleries and gift emporiums. Although the neighborhood focus is art, collectibles, and hip adult clothing, you'll find a few kids' stores, including **The Red Balloon Company,** 2060 N. Damen (© 773/489-9800; p. 234. For a new twist on custom clothing, stop by **The T-Shirt Deli,** 1739 N. Damen Ave. (© 773/276-6266), where you and your kids can order up your own personalized T-shirt creation. Choose from hundreds of vintage logos, add your own lettering, and your shirt will be printed while you wait (and to thrill your kids, the shirt is packaged up in a paper bag with a side of potato chips).

2 Shopping A to Z

As you might expect, Chicago has shops selling just about anything your kids could want or need, be it functional or ornamental, whimsical or exotic. The following list only scratches the surface, but it will give you an idea of the range of merchandise available.

ARTS & CRAFTS

Pearl Art and Craft Supplies   Graphic designers, artists, and arts and crafts aficionados flock to Pearl for every art supply known on earth. If you need to pick up supplies for a rainy-day project, you'll love Pearl. 255 W. Chicago Ave. (at Franklin St.). © 312/915-0200. www.pearlpaint.com. Subway/El: Brown Line to Chicago.

Tender Buttons *Finds*   Here's a perfect little break while shopping on the Magnificent Mile—a store filled floor to ceiling with thousands of buttons. From simple white buttons selling for 50¢ to antique gold buttons selling for hundreds of dollars, your kids will marvel over the colors and styles. If you're looking to replace missing buttons, no matter how unusual, or are trying to find just the perfect accent to update an existing jacket, this little store is just the place. 946 N. Rush (at Oak St.). © 312/337-7033. Subway/El: Red Line to Chicago/State.

BOOKS

Barbara's Bookstore   This haven for small, independent press titles also has extensive selections of everything current. In addition, it has a well-stocked children's section, with sitting areas for the tots to peruse the books. If you enjoy author readings, call the store to see if your visit coincides with that of one of your favorite writers. There are a total of six branches including a small tourist-targeted shop at Navy Pier, 700 E. Grand Ave. (📞 **312/222-0890**). 201 E. Huron St. (just east of Michigan Ave.). 📞 **312/926-2665**. Subway/El: Red Line to Chicago.

Barnes & Noble   This two-level store comes complete with a cafe, in case you get the munchies while perusing the miles of books. Check out postings for readings, book groups, and other special events. The children's section offers easy access to picture books, first readers, and young-adult books, plus cozy reading nooks. There's another store in Lincoln Park, at 659 W. Diversey Ave., 1 block west of Clark Street (📞 **773/871-9004**), and one at 1441 W. Webster Ave., at Clybourn Avenue (📞 **773/871-3610**). 1130 N. State St. (at Elm St.). 📞 **312/280-8155**. Subway/El: Red Line to Clark/Division.

Borders   You couldn't ask for a better location, right across from Water Tower Place. Head to the lower level for the kids' section, which features a particularly impressive collection of picture books. There are carpeted platforms for sitting and perusing. This place is like a mini–department store, with books, magazines, CDs, and computer software spread over four floors, and a cafe with a view overlooking the Mag Mile. There are also author readings, book signings, and other special events. There's also a Borders in the Loop at 150 N. State St., at Randolph Street (📞 **312/606-0750**), and one in Lincoln Park at 2817 N. Clark St., at Diversey Avenue (📞 **773/935-3909**). 830 N. Michigan Ave. (at Pearson St.). 📞 **312/573-0564**. Subway/El: Red Line to Chicago.

Children in Paradise Bookstore *(Finds)*   Chicago's largest children's bookstore is a must-see for parents with young readers. For little ones, check out the storytelling on Tuesday and Wednesday. On Saturday you'll find special events, including sidewalk chalk drawing and visits from book characters and authors. Highly qualified staff makes this store a joy to visit. After you've stocked up on reading material, head north on Rush Street to grab burgers at Johnny Rockets. 909 N. Rush St. (between Delaware Place and Walton St.). 📞 **312/951-5437**. www.chicagochildrensbooks.com. Subway/El: Red Line to Chicago.

Women & Children First   This feminist and children's bookstore holds the best selection in the city of titles for, by, and about women. Co-owner Linda Bubon holds a children's storybook hour every Wednesday at 10:30am; several book groups meet regularly as well, including one for mothers and daughters. The store also hosts frequent readings by the likes of Gloria Steinem, Amy Tan, Alice Walker, and Naomi Wolf. 5233 N. Clark St. (between Foster and Bryn Mawr aves.). 📞 **773/769-9299**. Subway/El: Red Line to Berwyn.

DEPARTMENT STORES

Bloomingdale's   The first Midwestern branch of the famed New York department store, Bloomingdale's is on par in terms of size and selection with Marshall Field's Water Tower store. The fifth floor features kids' clothing. 900 N. Michigan Ave. (at Walton St.). 📞 **312/440-4460**. Subway/El: Red Line to Chicago.

Carson Pirie Scott & Co.   This venerable Chicago institution that was almost wiped out by the Chicago Fire has made a recent bid to capture the corporate, if not the carriage, trade. Carson's has added a number of more upscale apparel lines, plus a trendy housewares department, to appeal to the moneyed crowd that works in the Loop. On the seventh floor you'll find children's clothing and stuffed animals. 1 S. State St. (at Madison St.). ℂ 312/641-7000. Subway/El: Red Line to Monroe.

Lord & Taylor   Lord & Taylor, one of two large department stores in Water Tower Place (see also Marshall Field's, below), carries about what you'd expect: cosmetics, accessories, and women's, men's, and children's clothing. Head for the second floor for children's apparel. The formerly crowded first floor has gotten an upscale makeover, but its offerings remain fairly affordable. The store's star department is most definitely shoes; the selection is fairly broad, and something's usually on sale. Water Tower Place, 835 N. Michigan Ave. ℂ 312/787-7400. Subway/El: Red Line to Chicago.

Marshall Field's   Although it's been sold more than once to out-of-towners, Chicagoans still consider Marshall Field's their "hometown" department store. The flagship store, which covers an entire block on State Street, is second in size only to Macy's in New York City. A number of exclusive "miniboutiques" are scattered throughout the overwhelming space, including the first Yves Saint Laurent Rive Gauche accessories department in the U.S., beauty stations where you can get a manicure and pick up products made exclusively for Field's, the first American boutique from German sportswear designer Olsen Europe, and a gourmet-food department developed by celebrity chef Charlie Trotter. Field's is the only U.S. department store to carry the full Designers Guild home collection, an eye-catching line of linens and accessories from British color maven Tricia Guild. The enormous shoe department is another highlight, with everything from killer high heels (at killer prices) to slippers and casual sandals. For children, head to the fifth floor for toys and clothing.

The breadth is what makes this store impressive; shoppers can find a rainbow of shirts for under $20, a floor or so away from the 28 Shop, the Field's homage to designer fashion. For a sophisticated take on the latest trends at a more affordable price, look for clothes from Field's own label, 111 State.

The Water Tower store—the Water Tower Place mall's primary anchor—is a scaled-down but respectable version of the State Street store. Its eight floors are actually much more manageable than the enormous flagship, and its merchandise selection is still vast (although this branch tends to focus on the more expensive brands). Look for children's wear on the eighth floor. The mall location is at 835 N. Michigan Ave., at Pearson St. (ℂ 312/335-7700); take the Red Line to Chicago Avenue. 111 N. State St. (at Randolph St.). ℂ 312/781-1000. www.marshallfields.com. Subway/El: Red Line to Washington.

Neiman Marcus   Yes, you'll pay top dollar for designer names here—after all, the store must live up to its "Needless Mark-ups" moniker—but Neiman's has a broader price range than many of its critics care to admit. It also has some mighty good sales. The four-story store, a beautiful environment in its own right, also sells cosmetics, shoes, furs, fine and fashion jewelry, and menswear and children's wear. On the top floor is the children's department, plus a fun gourmet-food department and a pretty home-accessories area. Neiman's has two restaurants: one relaxed, the other a little more formal. 737 N. Michigan Ave. (between Superior St. and Chicago Ave.). ℂ 312/642-5900. Subway/El: Red Line to Chicago Ave.

Nordstrom   The most recent arrival on the Chicago department store scene, Nordstrom has upped the stakes with its spacious, airy design and trendy touches (wheatgrass growing by the escalators, funky music playing on the stereo system). Kids' clothing is found on the third floor, with a nice selection of clothing and gifts for infants through teens. The selection of children's shoes is extensive. In the cosmetics department, you'll find a wide array of smaller labels and an "open sell" environment (meaning you're encouraged to try on makeup without a salesperson hovering over you). In keeping with the store's famed focus on service, a concierge can check your coat, call a cab, or make restaurant reservations. If you need a lift, Cafe Nordstrom offers a shopping break, with salads and sandwiches. Set up cafeteria-style, the restaurant also features a Kid's Cafe. The bathrooms, one on each level, contain infant-changing areas and women's lounges equipped with upholstered chairs where you can comfortably and semi-privately nurse an infant. Westfield North Bridge Mall, 55 E. Grand Ave. (at Rush St.). ℂ 312/464-1515. www.nordstrom.com. Subway/El: Red Line to Grand.

Saks Fifth Avenue   Saks Fifth Avenue might be best known for its designer collections—Valentino, Chloe, and Giorgio Armani, to name a few—but the store also does a decent job of buying more casual and less-expensive merchandise. Check out, for example, Saks's own Real Clothes or The Works women's lines. Plus, the store has very good large-size and petite women's apparel departments. The children's department has a variety of casual and dress clothes, as well as a few stuffed animals. The men's department is located in a separate building across Michigan Avenue. Don't forget to visit the cosmetics department, where Saks is known, in particular, for its varied fragrance selection. Chicago Place, 700 N. Michigan Ave. (at Superior St.). ℂ 312/944-6500. Subway/El: Red Line to Chicago/State.

DOLLS & DOLLHOUSES

Think Small   If your child dreams of building (in other words, dreams of having mom and dad build) a dollhouse, you'll find everything you need here. Sometimes the path of least resistance is best: In that case, check out the ready-made dollhouses that are available for purchase. You can also buy the dolls and furniture that will reside in the house. For those ambitious enough to build their child's dream house themselves, the store offers workshops on Wednesday, Thursday, Saturday, and Sunday. You can drop in, but it might be a good idea to call ahead before you go. The fee is $75, and includes the use of tools and paintbrushes, paper goods, wood glue, and cleaning materials. 3209 N. Clark St. (at W. Belmont St.). ℂ 773/477-1920. Subway/El: Red Line to Belmont.

FASHION

Abercrombie & Fitch   The cool "uniform" of preference for middle school kids is anything Abercrombie. Clothes here are pricey but well made, and if you break down and just buy a T-shirt, it shouldn't break your budget. Water Tower Place, 849 Michigan Ave. ℂ 312/274-9859. www.abercrombie.com. Subway/El: Red Line to Chicago/State.

Active Kids *(Finds* This offshoot of the popular outdoor and sporting goods store Active Endeavors (p. 234) specializes in clothes for kids living the outdoorsy life—or who just look like they are. Patagonia and other big-name outdoor outfitters are featured among the clothing for infants through size 16. 838 W. Armitage Ave. (at North Dayton St.). ℂ 773/281-2002. Subway/El: Red Line to Sheffield.

Alcala's   Do your kids dream of the open range? Here's just the spot to help them look the part. Cowboy hats, boots, shirts, jeans, and chaps for miniature cowpokes are the focus at Alcala's. And to prove that you're never too young to start appreciating the Wild West, soft leather booties get even the littlest cowpokes off to the right start. 1733 W. Chicago Ave. (at Wood St.). ✆ 312/226-0152. www.alcalas.com. Subway/El: Red Line to Sheffield.

Anthropologie   Eclectic and funky clothes that appeal to the young teen set (sorry, females only) and a mix of new and vintage home furnishings and accessories that appeal to Mom make this store a delight to browse. 1120 N. State St. ✆ 312/255-1848. www.anthropologie.com. Subway/El: Red Line to Clark/Division.

Benetton Kids   Pricey but prone to frequent sales, Benetton's children's collection is colorful and fun, with great knits—just like the grown-up version of the store. The design is sporty rather than frilly and streamlined rather than fussy, for kids from infant through age 12. The Shops at North Bridge, 520 N. Michigan Ave. ✆ 312/494-9161. Subway/El: Red Line to Grand/State.

GapKids and babyGap   Classic and fun, although definitely not avant-garde, Gap produces reliable clothes and accessories for kids. Inventory turns quickly here, so it's easy to pick up a few things on sale. The store has five locations in Chicago. The largest store is located at 555 N. Michigan Ave., where you'll find a large kids' and baby section on the lower level. (1) 555 N. Michigan Ave. (at E. Ohio St.). ✆ 312/335-1896. Subway/El: Red Line to Grand/State. (2) Water Tower Place, 835 N. Michigan Ave. ✆ 312/255-8883. Subway/El: Red Line to Chicago/State. (3) 2108 N. Halsted (at W. Webster St.). ✆ 773/549-2065. Subway/El: Red Line to Sheffield. (4) 3033 N. Broadway Ave. (at W. Wellington St.). ✆ 773/929-4085. Subway/El: Brown Line to Diversey. (5) 3155 N. Lincoln Ave. (at W. Barry St.). ✆ 773/883-9050. Subway/El: Brown Line to Wellington.

Gymboree   Bright primary colors and strong patterns are the trademark of Gymboree clothing. You'll find items here for infants up to age 7. The chain also runs play centers (see "Indoor Playgrounds," in chapter 8). Water Tower Place, 835 N. Michigan Ave. ✆ 312/649-9074. www.gymboree.com. Subway/El: Red Line to Chicago/State.

Jacadi   An upscale Parisian clothing company with beautiful (and pricey) clothing for infants through age 12. Rich colors and pastels in cottons and knits are the focus here. Water Tower Place, 835 N. Michigan Ave. ✆ 312/337-9600. www.jacadi usa.com. Subway/El: Red Line to Chicago/State.

LMNOP   Nothing ordinary about the children's clothing you'll find here, for ages newborn to 6 years. 2574 N. Lincoln Ave. (at Sheffield Ave.). ✆ 773/975-4055. Subway/El: Red or Brown Line to Fullerton.

Madison and Friends   When Chicago parents with a money's-no-object attitude go shopping for special-occasion clothing for kids, they make a beeline for Madison and Friends. The selection is top-of-the-line, the inventory large and unique. You'll find baby-size leather jackets and yoga pants for toddlers. A separate back room caters to older kids and 'tweens—with a staggering array of jeans. You can find clothing here for kids from newborn through size 16. 940 N. Rush St. (at Oak St.). ✆ 312/642-6403. www.madisonandfriends.com. Subway/El: Red Line to Chicago.

Mini Me   This store specializes in European-style clothing for girls from infant through age 10 and boys up to size 4. In the mall at 900 N. Michigan Ave. ✆ 312/988-4011. Subway/El: Red Line to Chicago/State.

Psycho Baby   The definitive sign that Bucktown is completely gentrified? The opening of this everything-for-baby shop. The prices might cause you to do a double take ($60 for shoes that your child will outgrow in 3 months?), but the creative selection and fun vibe make it a great store for browsing. 2911 N. Broadway (between Diversey Pkwy. and Belmont Ave.). ✆ 773/665-7400. Subway/El: Brown Line to Diversey.

Oilily   Even if you don't mix plaids and florals on a daily basis (a trademark of this designer), just one of Oilily's distinctive and colorful items can perk up a wardrobe from infant to size 12. Clothes are the focus, but some accessories like quilts and backpacks are also offered. To keep kids happy while you shop, rolling wooden chairs and blocks are on hand. The Shops at North Bridge, 520 N. Michigan Ave. ℂ 312/527-5747. Subway/El: Red Line to State/Grand.

Old Navy *(Value)*   The lower-priced relative of Gap carries an extensive collection of kids' clothes, from infants and up. Sales here are fantastic—and frequent.

Tips **From Chicago with Love**

Need to bring some Chicago gifts home for friends and family? With more national chain stores hitting town, it's getting harder to find distinctive, only-in-Chicago souvenirs. Here are some unique ideas:

- The **Archicenter Shop,** at 224 S. Michigan Ave. (ℂ 312/922-3432), sells some of the coolest gifts in town. This bright, sleek shop is part of the Chicago Architecture Foundation, so everything in stock—including toys, photography books, tour guides, and stationery—has a definite sense of style. Whether you're in the market for a $900 reproduction of a vase from Frank Lloyd Wright's Robie House or a more affordable black-and-white photo of the city skyline, it's well worth stopping in.
- The *Chicago Tribune* store, at 435 N. Michigan Ave. (ℂ 312/222-3080), has your standard tourist selection ("Chicago" emblazoned on everything from shirts to shot glasses). But this is also a good place to pick up Cubs memorabilia (the Tribune Company owns the team), along with books from some of the city's top journalists. You can also order reproductions of the *Tribune*'s front page or color prints of photos from the newspaper's archives.
- **Sportmart,** at 620 N. LaSalle St. (ℂ 312/337-6151), is where you'll find jerseys and hats from Chicago's other pro sports teams. The victorious Jordan years might be behind us, but his shirts still sell well here.
- The ultimate Chicago tasty treats are Frango Mints from **Marshall Field's.** Although they now come in a variety of flavors, stick with the original: melt-in-your-mouth chocolate mixed with mint. Once you're hooked, you might find yourself returning to Chicago more often to stock up.
- **City of Chicago Store,** located in the Water Works Visitor Center, right off of Michigan Avenue at 163 E. Pearson St. (ℂ 312/742-8811), is a convenient stop for Chicago-related souvenirs and gifts, including truly one-of-a-kind pieces of retired municipal equipment (although the parking meters we've seen for sale here might be a little difficult to stuff into your suitcase).
- **The Savvy Traveller,** located at 310 S. Michigan Ave., at Van Buren Street (ℂ 312/913-9800), is where smart travelers buy their Frommer's guidebooks. This Loop specialty store carries just about everything a traveler might need, from maps to rain gear to games that keep the kids occupied on long car trips.

Clothes are trendy and stylish. The collection for boys is great, a refreshing change for moms who are frustrated with the ho-hum choices available at most stores. The store has three Chicago locations. The biggest and best is the State Street location. (1) 35 N. State St. (at E. Washington St.). ☏ 312/551-0523. Subway: Brown, Purple, Green, or Orange Line to Randolph/Wabash and walk 1 block south and 1 block west; or Red Line to Washington/State. (2) 1596 W. Kingsbury (at North Ave.). ☏ 312/397-0624. Subway/El: Red Line to Clybourn. (3) 1730 W. Fullerton Ave. (at N. Clybourn Ave.). ☏ 773/871-0613. Subway/El: Red Line to Fullerton.

The Second Child *Value*   This consignment store offers children's clothing for infants through size 14, plus toys, furniture, and equipment for kids (and maternity clothes if you've got another on the way). Yes, the merchandise is secondhand, but thanks to the store's location in a tony Lincoln Park neighborhood, it's *upscale* secondhand. You'll find name brands and excellent quality. The store ensures that its collection of furniture and equipment meets current safety standards. Lock your stroller just outside the building and take the stairs up. 954 W. Armitage (just east of N. Sheffield Ave.). ☏ 773/883-0880. www.2ndchild.com. Subway/El: Red Line to Sheffield.

Talbots Kids   Just what you'd expect from Talbots—well-made, classic clothes for kids with a decidedly preppy flair. You'll find everything from basics to party clothes here, all with that neatly pressed look. Chicago Place, 700 N. Michigan Ave. ☏ 312/943-0255. www.talbots.com. Subway/El: Red Line to Chicago/State.

Urban Outfitters   Fun, funky and offbeat clothing and accessories, from bean-bag chairs to trendy clothing and glittery nail polish, sure to please young teens. There's a second location in Lincoln Park, at 2352 N. Clark St. (☏ 773/549-1711). 935 N. Rush St. (at Walton St.). ☏ 312/640-1919. www.urbanoutfitters.com. Subway/El: Red Line to Chicago/State.

GAMES & HOBBY SHOPS

Ash's Magic Shop   Mr. Ash, a real-life magician with a love of his craft, stocks his shop with tricks, jokes, books, and videos that will make you believe in magic, too. 4955 N. Western Ave. (at W. Argyle). ☏ 773/271-4030. Subway/El: Brown Line to Western.

Fantasy Headquarters   Although this store is meant for adults (if you need a Halloween costume to end all Halloween costumes, this is the place), I dare you not to have fun with your kids here. This sprawling costume shop covers an entire city block and is devoted to make-believe. The store stocks more than a million items, including 800 styles of masks (priced $1–$200) and all the accessories and makeup needed to complete any costume. Make sure you check out the full-service wig salon. 4065 N. Milwaukee Ave. (west of Cicero Ave.). ☏ 773/777-0222. Subway/El: Blue Line to Irving Park.

Uncle Fun *Finds*   Uncle Fun and his staff travel the world to bring home bobbing head figurines, accordions, and stink bombs from all corners of the earth—for the sole purpose of tickling your fancy. Bins and cubbyholes are stuffed full of the standard joke toys (rubber-chicken key chains and chattering wind-up teeth), but you'll also find every conceivable modern pop-culture artifact, from Jackson Five buttons to demon-on-wheels *Speed Racer*'s Mach-Five model car. 1338 W. Belmont Ave. (near Southport Ave.). ☏ 773/477-8223. www.unclefunchicago.com. Subway/El: Red or Brown Line to Belmont.

MUSIC

Beat Parlor   If the idea of hanging out with local DJs appeals to your kids, then Beat Parlor is your place. In the city where house music was born, Howard Bailey's Bucktown shop sells lots of it, plus plenty of hip-hop and local DJs' mix tapes, on CD and vinyl. The store's two turntables are always in use by cutters checking out new merchandise. 1653 N. Damen Ave. © 773/395-CUTS. Subway/El: Blue Line to Damen.

Blue Chicago Store *(Finds* Here's one that's near and dear to my blues-loving heart—a store that's dedicated to teaching kids about the blues. America's orig-inal contribution to the world of music, and the basis for jazz and rock 'n' roll, is alive and thriving in Chicago. Treat your kids to a stop here, pick up some books, and maybe even plan to attend the Saturday night dance-a-thons that are open to all ages. 534 N. Clark (at W. Grand Ave.). © 312/661-1003. www.bluechicago.com. Subway/El: Red Line to State/Grand.

Dusty Groove America In April 1996, using a rickety old PC, Rick Wojcik and John Schauer founded an online record store, www.dustygroove.com. Since then, the operation has expanded in both cyberspace and the real world. Dusty Groove covers a lot of ground, selling soul, funk, jazz, Brazilian, lounge, Latin, and hip-hop music on new and used vinyl and all new CDs. For the most part, all selections are either rare or imported, or both. 1120 N. Ashland Ave. © 773/342-5800. Subway/El: Blue Line to Division.

Guitar Center When your kids are, oh, somewhere around age 12 and decide it's time to start their own garage band, you'll need to find the one store that can satisfy their needs. Guitar Center is it: Your kids can check out the keyboards, music software, recording equipment, dance music gear, drums, amplifiers, basses, acoustic guitars, accessories, and vintage instruments. 2633 N. Halsted (at Diversey). © 773/248-2808. www.guitarcenter.com. Subway/El: Brown Line to Wellington.

Jazz Record Mart *(Finds* This is possibly the best jazz record store in the coun-try. It's so cool, even your disenchanted teenager will love it, despite himself. The first of four rooms houses the "Killer Rack," a display of albums that the store's owners consider essential to any jazz collection. In addition to jazz, there are bins filled with blues, Latin, and "New Music;" the albums in the record rooms are filed alphabetically and by category (vocals, big band, and so on), and there are a cou-ple of turntables to help you spend wisely. Jazz Record Mart also features a stage, with seating for 50, where local and national artists coming through town enter-tain with in-store performances. 444 N. Wabash Ave. (at Grand Ave.). © 312/222-1467. Subway/El: Red Line to Grand.

Little Strummer Located in the Old Town School of Folk Music, which offers music classes for children, this compact store stocks every kind of mini-instrument imaginable, from accordions and guitars to wind chimes and music boxes. There's also a good selection of music-related games and kids' CDs. 909 W. Armitage Ave. (at Halsted St.). © 773/751-3410. Subway/El: Brown Line to Armitage.

New Sound Gospel Chicago is the birthplace of gospel music, but when Lee Johnson opened New Sound Gospel 20 years ago, few people were selling it. That has all changed, thanks to the recent resurgence in gospel led by Kirk Franklin, whose platinum albums have crossed over into mainstream success. All the major labels now have gospel music divisions, and the rising tide has helped store owners like Johnson, who has since opened a second location at 10723 S. Halsted St. (© 773/785-8001). Both brim with records, CDs, and tapes, from gospel's greatest legend, Mahalia Jackson, to groups with names such as Gospel Gangstaz. 5958 W. Lake St. © 773/261-1115. Subway/El: Green Line to Austin.

Reckless Records The best all-around record store for music that the cool kids listen to, Reckless Records wins Brownie points for its friendly and helpful staff. You'll find new and used CDs and albums in a variety of genres (psychedelic and progressive rock, punk, soul, and jazz) here, along with 'zines and a small collection of DVDs. There's also a location in Wicker Park, at 1532 N. Milwaukee Ave. ((*C* 773/235-3727). 3157 N. Broadway (at Belmont Ave.). *C* 773/404-5080. Subway/El: Red or Brown Line to Belmont.

SHOES

Carrara Children's Shoes   Hard-to-fit foot? Head to Carrara, where sizes span a huge range, as does the inventory of styles. The focus is on Italian footwear for kids, from infant to size 9 (yes, that's size 9 in men's and women's terms). Anything from slippers to snow boots to sneakers is fair game here. Pick up some socks and tights on your way to the register. 2506 N. Clark St. (at W. Deming Place). *C* 773/529-9955. Subway/El: Red or Brown Line to Fullerton. Bus: 22 or 36.

Fleet Feet Sports *Finds*   This store, owned by a former banker who decided to follow his love of running to create a new business, is a wonderful place to buy shoes for little athletes. Although running is the forte here, you can buy all types of athletic shoes. The staff is made up of athletes who can relate when you complain about your sore Achilles—and better yet, they can find a pair of shoes that will help. You'll even get a chance to hop on a treadmill to get your running gait videotaped. The staff will assess your style and bring you a variety of shoes to try. (*Note:* Don't ask to try on a pair of shoes simply because you like the color. That request is sure to get you a disapproving look!) There's a second location in the Lincoln Square neighborhood, at 4555 N. Lincoln (*C* 773/271-3338). 210 W. North Ave. (at Wells St., in the Pipers Alley complex). *C* 312/587-3338. www.fleetfeetchicago.com. Subway/El: Brown Line to Sedgwick.

Piggy Toes   European makers are featured in this boutique's selection of shoes, sandals, and boots, plus hats, socks, tights, and other accessories. Shoe sizes for infants through children's size 6. 2205 N. Halsted (at W. Belden Ave.). *C* 773/281-5583. www.ptoes.com. Subway: Brown Line to Armitage.

Steve Madden *Value*   Funky and inexpensive, Steve Madden specializes in the platform, chunky-heel style shoe. Your teenage daughter probably covets Steve Maddens already. Boys' styles are appearing in the store as well, although it's still female-dominated territory. Most styles start at size 5. When a sale is on, you can sometimes pick up a pair for as little as $15. Water Tower Place, 845 N. Michigan Ave. *C* 312/440-1590. www.stevemadden.com. Subway/El: Red Line to Chicago/State.

SHOWER & BABY GIFTS

The Red Balloon Company *Finds*   This creative little shop in the trendy Wicker Park neighborhood offers casual clothes for infants through age 8, hand-painted furniture, linens, and books. It's a great place to find a special gift. Children's classic books such as *The Red Balloon, The Lonely Doll,* and *Mike Mulligan and His Steam Shovel* are displayed atop decoupaged bedroom furnishings. There are lots of vintage-inspired items, too, including Pinecone Hill reversible blankets, caps, and burp cloths. The store features antiques and one-of-a-kind pieces. If there's a furniture item you want made, just ask the staff—some items can be custommade. 2060 N. Damen Ave. (at W. Armitage Ave.). *C* 773/489-9800. www.theredballoon.com. Subway/El: Blue Line to Damen.

SPORTS STUFF

Active Endeavors *Finds*   Everything you need for the outdoor life can be found right here, from camping gear to running shoes, plus everyday sporty apparel. For the low-down on the kids' version of this store, which features outdoor clothing,

Tips **Pop on In**

Across the street from Niketown, you'll probably see a line of people trailing out from the **Garrett Popcorn Shop**, 670 N. Michigan Ave. ((C) **312/944-2630**), a 50-year-old landmark. Join the locals in line and pick up some caramel corn for a quick sugar rush.

see the review of Active Kids on p. 229. 853 W. Armitage Ave. (between Sheffield Ave. and Halsted St.). (C) **773/281-8100**. Subway/El: Brown Line to Armitage.

Kozy's Cyclery   A Chicago favorite, this third-generation family-owned business has been selling and servicing bikes for 56 years. You'll find name brands, a vast collection of accessories, and store personnel with opinions you can trust. If you're a Chicago resident, you can count on complete servicing for your bikes, and the staff will connect you with all kinds of cycling resources. Check out Kozy's online catalog (www.kozy.com), complete with photos, to get an idea of what the shop carries. (For out-of-towners, shipping is available.) The store has four locations. (1) 601 S. LaSalle (at W. Harrison St.). (C) **312/360-0020**. Subway/El: Blue Line to LaSalle. (2) 1451 W. Webster (at N. Clybourn Ave.). (C) **773/528-2700**. Subway/El: Brown Line to Armitage. (3) 3712 N. Halsted (at W. Waveland Ave.). (C) **773/281-2263**. (4) 219 W. Erie. (C) **312/266-1700**. Subway/El: Red Line to Addison.

Niketown *Overrated*   When Niketown opened some 10 years ago, it was truly something new: A store that felt more like a funky sports museum than a place hawking running shoes. In the days when Michael Jordan was the city's reigning deity, Niketown was the place to bask in his glory. These days Niketown is no longer unique to Chicago (it's sprung up in cities from Atlanta to Honolulu), and the store's celebration of athletes can't cover up the fact that the ultimate goal is to sell expensive shoes. But the crowds keep streaming in—and snatching up products pitched by Niketown's new patron saint, Tiger Woods. 669 N. Michigan Ave. (C) **312/642-6363**. Subway/El: Red Line to Grand.

Sportmart   The largest sporting-goods store in the city, the flagship store of this chain offers seven floors of merchandise, from running apparel to camping gear. Sports fans will be in heaven in the first- and fifth-floor team merchandise departments, where Cubs, Bulls, and Sox jerseys abound. Cement handprints of local sports celebs dot the outside of the building; step inside to check out the prints from Michael Jordan and White Sox slugger Frank Thomas. 620 N. LaSalle St. (at Ontario St.). (C) **312/337-6151**. Subway/El: Red Line to Grand.

STROLLERS, CRIBS & FURNITURE

Bellini   Outfitting your dream nursery? Head to this high-end boutique for furniture with Italian design and a distinctly contemporary flair. (And even if some prices are a bit out of your budget stratosphere, you'll at least find inspiration.) Cribs, changing tables, armoires, and rocking chairs are on offer, plus items to achieve just the right decor. Clothing and accessories for baby top off the selection here. 2100 N. Southport. (C) **773/880-8840**. www.bellini.com. Subway/El: Brown Line to Fullerton.

Cella for Baby   If you're planning to visit the North Shore and are outfitting your first nursery and find yourself overwhelmed by stores, brands, and friends' recommendations, here's a place to find a little clarity. Cella's buyers have sorted through all of the baby paraphernalia on the market and stocks what they have decided are "the best" items available in the market. The large showroom is packed with nursery furniture, cribs, strollers, car seats, lamps, books, toys, bedding, feeding and personal care items, and clothing (from preemie to 4-toddler). Anything from all-terrain baby joggers to handmade layette items are covered here. 188 E. Westminster Rd., Lake Forest. Ⓒ 847/604-8522. www.cellaforbaby.com.

The Right Start   Gadgets for babies and toddlers and sanity-saving devices such as bouncers, swings, and exersaucers are the focus here. If Junior is suddenly up and walking and you need to baby-proof your home, this store is your source for gates, electrical-outlet covers, and cabinet locks. It's a chain, but you can't beat the convenience of being able to buy so many gadgets in one location. 2121 N. Clybourn Ave. (at N. Wayne St. in the Market Square Shopping Center). Ⓒ 773/296-4420. www.therightstart.com. Subway/El: Brown Line to Armitage.

SWEETS FOR THE SWEET

Bittersweet   Run by Judy Contino, one of the city's top pastry chefs and bakers of all things sweet and sinful, this Lakeview cafe and shop is sought out by brides-to-be and trained palates who have a yen for gourmet cakes, cookies, tarts, and ladyfingers. The rich chocolate mousse cake, a specialty of the house, is out of this world. 1114 W. Belmont Ave. Ⓒ 773/929-1100. Subway/El: Red Line to Belmont.

Ghirardelli Chocolate Shop & Soda Fountain   This Midwest outpost of the famed San Francisco chocolatier, just half a block off the Mag Mile, gets swamped in the summer, but they've got their soda-fountain assembly line down to a science. In addition to the incredible hot fudge sundaes, there's a veritable mudslide of chocolate bars, hot-cocoa drink mixes, and chocolate-covered espresso beans to tempt your sweet tooth. 830 N. Michigan Ave. Ⓒ 312/337-9330. Subway/El: Red Line to Chicago.

Margie's Candies *Value*   This family-run candy and ice cream shop hasn't changed much since it opened in 1921. It still offers some of the city's finest handmade fudge, whether it comes in a box or melted over a banana split served in a clamshell dish. The store is known for its turtles—chocolate-covered pecan and caramel clusters—and may be the only place in the city still selling rock candy on wooden sticks. 1960 N. Western Ave. (just north of Armitage Ave.). Ⓒ 773/384-1035. Subway/El: Blue Line to Western.

Sweet Thang   When bopping around Wicker Park's boutiques and quirky shops, don't miss Bernard Runo's Euro-style cafe for a tasty treat to tide you over. Runo, a classically trained pastry chef who has worked in the kitchens of the city's best hotels and learned his trade in France, imports most of the ingredients for his croissants, cookies, tarts, and other pastries from across the pond. The cafe has a laid-back atmosphere, with red distressed walls covered with abstract art and Parisian-style tables and chairs that are set outside in warm weather. 1921 W. North Ave. Ⓒ 773/772-4166. Subway/El: Blue Line to Damen.

Vosges Haut-Chocolat *Finds*   Some of the works of chocolatier Katrina Markoff might be a reach for kids (such as wasabi-flavored truffles), but chocolate bars and the best toffee I've ever tasted are a hit no matter what the age range. Markoff studied at Le Cordon Bleu in Paris and honed her skills throughout Europe and Asia. Her exotic gourmet truffles—with fabulous names such as absinthe, mint julep, wink of the rabbit, woolloomooloo, and ambrosia—are made from premium Belgian chocolate and infused with rare spices, seasonings, and flowers from around the world. The store—which looks more like a modern art gallery than a chocolatier—includes a gourmet-hot-chocolate bar, where you're welcome to sit and sip. 520 N. Michigan Ave. (in Westfield North Bridge Shopping Center). © 312/644-9450. Subway/El: Red Line to Grand.

THEME STORES

American Girl Place   One of Chicago's hottest family destinations, this three-story doll emporium attracts hordes of young girls (and parents with credit cards at the ready) hooked on the popular mail-order doll company's line of historic character dolls. A stage show brings stories from the American Girl books to life, and the store's cafe is a nice spot for a special mother-daughter lunch or afternoon tea. All of the American Girl dolls from different eras of U.S. history, plus their many accessories, are for sale here. Dioramas for each doll change with the seasons. A cafe serves food mentioned in the books—and your doll can dine with you. Breakfast, lunch, tea, and dinner seatings are available 7 days a week. You can also see the musical review *Circle of Friends: An American Girl Musical* at the in-store theater. The show (recommended for ages 6 and up) lasts 1 hour and 15 minutes and costs $26. There's a new 35-minute show for the younger set called *Bitty Bear's Matinee: The Family Tree* ($15 for kids ages 3 and up, and $7.50 for kids under age 3). Reservations are needed for the theater and cafe (well in advance). Check the website for a full lineup of special events, from lessons on how to cook like a pro to visits with American Girl book authors. American Girl also does birthday parties. For $26 per person, you get a two-course meal, chocolate-vanilla cake and pink peppermint ice cream, a birthday certificate, and goody bags. They'll even provide invitations and thank-you notes. Bathrooms are spacious and clean, and one has a changing table. You'll need 1 to 2 hours to explore the store. If you include the cafe and theater, this can be a full-day activity. (For a review of the American Girl Place Cafe, see p. 116). 111 E. Chicago Ave. © 877/AG-PLACE or 312/943-9400. www.americangirlplace.com. Subway/ El: Red Line to Chicago/State.

Sony Gallery of Consumer Electronics   The latest high-tech gadgets are displayed in a museum-like setting at this multilevel store. The home office with Web TV, Vaio laptops, and more will rivet adults while kids spend time in the PlayStation play area, also on the first level. On the second floor, check out the newest wide-screen Trinitrons, Walkmen, minidisk players, and stereo components. The first floor has a 15-foot Chicago diorama with working camcorders that you can use set up all around it. 663 N. Michigan Ave. © 312/943-3334. Subway/El: Red Line to State/Grand.

TOYS

Dorby Magoo & Co. *(Finds*   What's not to love about a toy store that's laid out like your own home? Kids feel an immediate welcome as they look for toys in the bedroom or books in the library. There's even a living room, den, kitchen, and bathroom. Birthday parties can be scheduled for the dining room and back yard area (complete with Astroturf "grass" and a ceiling painted to look like the sky). Each section is labeled with an age range, from infants on up, to make gift shopping easy, and there's a stellar collection of arts-and-crafts projects. You'll also find bins of cheap classics like superballs and plastic rings. Gag gifts, like fake prechewed gum and whoopee cushions, are also in abundance. 2744 N. Lincoln Ave. (at W. Diversey St.). © 773/935-2663. Subway/El: Brown Line to Diversey.

Galt Toys   This shop offers its own brand of toys, which are known for their craftsmanship, quality, and design. The staff is especially helpful when you're desperately seeking, say, a few toys to keep a toddler entertained on your flight home. There's a full selection of Baby Einstein DVDs, books, and other products, as well as Chicco brand plastic toys and much, much more. In the mall at 900 N. Michigan Ave. ℭ 312/440-9550. www.galttoys.com. Subway/El: Red Line to Chicago/State.

Kite Harbor   On breezy days when the wind is just right off of Lake Michigan, stop in to Kite Harbor to pick up a colorful kite. (There are the standard kid-size kites, all the way up to spectacular jumbo kites for the ambitious—or experienced.) The shop stocks all sorts of flying objects, from boomerangs to whirligigs, and even juggling sets. 109 N. Marion St., Oak Park ℭ 708/848-4907. Subway/El: Green Line to Harlem.

LEGO Store   You'll marvel at replicas of Chicago landmarks, made entirely of LEGOs. Special-edition sets for young builders who want to create huge animals and people are often featured, too. A LEGO Construction Zone just outside of the store lets kids design and build in their own play area with a life-size racecar built from LEGO bricks; LEGO walls; and tables. The play zone is open daily from 11am to 5:30pm. The Shops at North Bridge, 520 N. Michigan Ave. ℭ 312/494-0760. www.lego.com. Subway: Red Line to Grand/State.

Saturday's Child   This store sells everything from wagons, tricycles, and scooters to blocks, books, wooden toys, and puppets. The clever toys here range from rubber snakes and frogs to sidewalk chalk and kids' large-face wristwatches. Cooperative and creative play is the focus here—not a high-tech gadget or computer game in sight. Real old-fashioned toys and picture books, Folkmanis puppets, arts and crafts supplies, and puzzles and games are stocked here. 2146 N. Halsted St. (south of Webster Ave.). ℭ 773/525-8697. www.childtoystore.com. Subway/El: Brown Line to Armitage.

Toys and Treasures   Tired of mass-market toys? Check out this boutique for children that offers toys for infants up to kids age 10, baby and kids clothes up to size 6, plus books, art supplies, and stuffed animals. Many of the toys are handmade and have an educational and developmental bent. The store stocks a few lines of infant clothes that are made by local women. The owner, Bea, has a talent for matching the kid to the toy, so be sure to ask her advice! 5311 N. Clark St. (at Berwyn Ave.). ℭ 773/769-5311. Subway/El: Red Line to Berwyn.

Toyscape   Don't walk in here expecting to buy a GI Joe or a PlayStation. This shrine to anticommercialism sells only old-fashioned toys that let kids exercise their imagination. Wooden toys, musical instruments, and puppets are all in stock. The environment is friendly, and the store hosts special events during the year. One perennial favorite is "Bunnies on Parade," held in April, when kids are invited to put on some ears or bunny suits and parade around and in front of the store. 2911 N. Broadway (between Diversey Pkwy. and Belmont Ave.). ℭ 773/665-7400. www.toyscapecatalog.com. Subway/El: Brown Line to Diversey.

Toys et cetera   Next time you're visiting the Museum of Science and Industry, make the short trek into Hyde Park to visit this special toy store. Although it's known for its excellent website, you'll have more fun at the real store. The space is small but packed with educational puzzles and games, and toys, toys, toys. (Check out the wide assortment of dolls.) Dress-up clothes and an arts-and-crafts area round out the store. 5211-A S. Harper (in Harper Court Shopping Center) in Hyde Park. ℭ 773/324-6039. www.toysetcetera.com. Bus: 4.

Entertainment for the Whole Family

For most families, showbiz central in Chicago is the North Loop theater district. Until a couple of years ago, the district had a down-on-its-luck, brother-can-you-spare-a-dime atmosphere—not the kind of place you wanted to be after dark with tots in tow. Happily, the district has undergone something of a renaissance, particularly along State and Randolph streets. Many of the city's major theater venues have been restored to their former glory. This is good news for parents, as many of those glorious old theaters host the traveling Broadway productions that attract families.

Chicago is a regular stop on the big-name entertainment circuit, whether it's the national tour of Broadway shows such as *Rent* and *Cabaret* or pop music acts such as U2 or Bruce Springsteen (both of whom sell out multiple nights at stadiums when they come to town). High-profile shows such as Disney's *Aida* and Mel Brooks's stage version of *The Producers* had their first runs here before moving on to New York.

While Chicago's off-Loop theaters, such as Steppenwolf Theatre, have built their reputations on a gritty style of acting (and a repertoire geared to adults), Chicago has plenty of theater companies that are less avant-garde and more attuned to the younger set. Even the city's blues community sees the wisdom of bringing the next generation into the fold, with special nights that are smoke- and alcohol-free. In the classical realm, the Chicago Symphony supports a youth symphony. Even Chicago's opera companies make an effort to reach out to kids—so don't limit yourself!

FINDING OUT WHAT'S ON Check out *Chicago Parent Magazine* (② 708/386-5555; www.chicago parent.com) for calendars of upcoming cultural events targeted to kids. You can usually pick up free copies of the magazine at public libraries, bookstores, toy stores, and kids' clothing stores. The City of Chicago has cultural listings on its website at **www. cityofchicago.org/tourism**. For theater, you can't beat **www.chicagoplays. com**, the website for the League of Chicago Theatres. The site links you to more than 130 Chicago-area theaters, and provides an online database of all current and upcoming productions, updated weekly. (They are also categorized so you can look up "children's theater.") The league's Hot Tix website (**www.hottix.org**) has twice-daily posts offering half-price tickets at the seven Chicago-area Hot Tix locations.

Chicago Dance and Music Alliance's website, **www.chicagoperformances. org**, provides listings on performances in these categories: Cultural Center, Ravinia, Grant Park, Dame Myra Hess Memorial Concerts, Jazz, Children's, and Dance. The website also provides a calendar where you can search for events by date.

For up-to-date entertainment listings, check the local newspapers and magazines, particularly the "Friday" and "Weekend Plus" sections of the

Entertainment in the Loop & Magnificent Mile

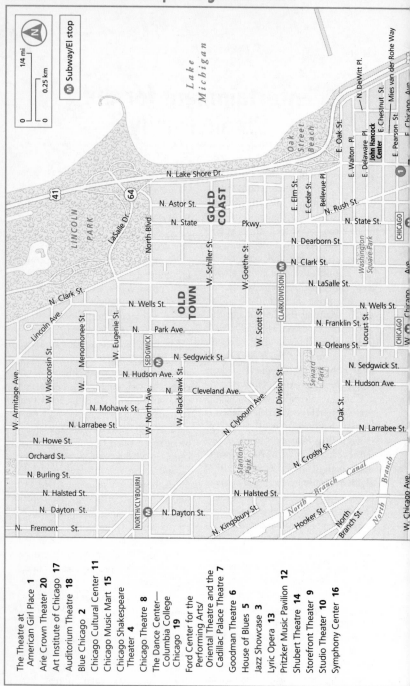

M Subway/El stop

Lake Michigan

N. Lake Shore Dr.

LINCOLN PARK

GOLD COAST

OLD TOWN

Oak Street Beach

John Hancock Center

The Theatre at American Girl Place **1**
Arie Crown Theater **20**
Art Institute of Chicago **17**
Auditorium Theatre **18**
Blue Chicago **2**
Chicago Cultural Center **11**
Chicago Music Mart **15**
Chicago Shakespeare Theater **4**
Chicago Theatre **8**
The Dance Center—Columbia College Chicago **19**
Ford Center for the Performing Arts/Oriental Theatre and the Cadillac Palace Theatre **7**
Goodman Theatre **6**
House of Blues **5**
Jazz Showcase **3**
Lyric Opera **13**
Pritzker Music Pavilion **12**
Shubert Theatre **14**
Storefront Theater **9**
Studio Theater **10**
Symphony Center **16**

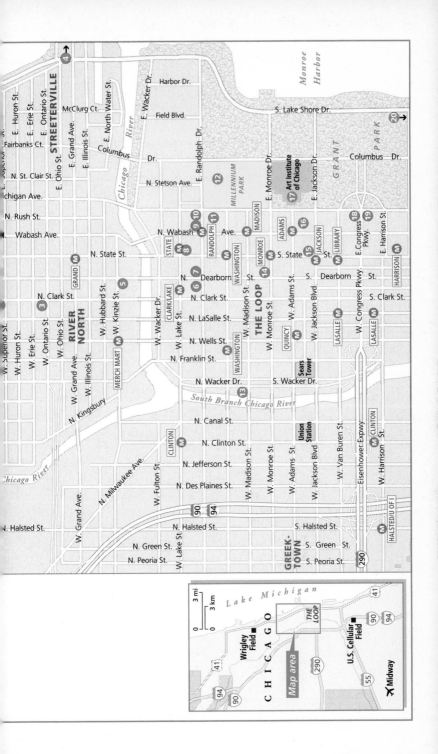

Entertainment in Lincoln Park & Wrigleyville

Apollo Theater **4**
Athenaeum Theatre **2**
Briar Street Theatre **3**
Theater on the Lake **5**
Mercury Theater **1**

Lake _M i c h i g a n_

North Avenue Beach

LINCOLN PARK

■ Chicago Historical Society

ⓜ Subway/El stop

Ⓝ

0.25 mi
0.25 km

N. Burton Pl.
N. State St.
N. Dearborn St.
N. Clark St.
N. La Salle St.

Ⓜ 5

Lake Shore Dr.

John Cannon Dr.

Diversey Harbor

South Pond

LINCOLN PARK ZOO

Stockton Dr.
N. Lincoln Park West

N. Lakeview Ave.

Clark St.

N. Cleveland Ave.

Wrightwood Pl.
Deming Pl.
Arlington Pl.

N. Orchard St.

N. Burling St.
N. Halsted St.

Ⓜ 4

LINCOLN PARK

Ave.

Lincoln Ave.

North Ave.

OZ PARK

No. 276 Park

Armitage Ave.

Wisconsin St.

Menomonee St.

N. Wells St.

64

N. Park Ave.
Eugenie St.

N. Sedgwick St.

Ⓜ SEDGWICK

Cleveland Ave.

N. Mohawk St.
N. Larrabee St.

Schiller St.

OLD TOWN

N. Orchard St.
N. Burling St.
N. Halsted St.

Halsted St.

Avenue

Ⓜ NORTH/CLYBOURN

N. Dayton St.
N. Fremont St.
N. Bissell St.
N. Sheffield Ave.

Wisconsin St.
Wisconsin St.

Willow St.

North Ave.

Weed St.

Ⓜ FULLERTON

DePaul University

ARMITAGE
Ⓜ ARMITAGE

St.

Belden Ave.

Webster Ave.

Trebes Park

Dickens Ave.

Clifton St.

Magnolia Ave.

Clybourn

Marcey St.

Kingsbury St.

North

Chicago River

West

Turning Basin

64

Lakewood Ave.

Fullerton Ave.

N. Racine Ave.

Montana St.

Schubert Ave.
Wrightwood Ave.

Wayne Ave.

N. Southport Ave.

Altgeld St.

N. Greenview Ave.

N. Ashland Ave.

North Ave.

North Branch

Cortland St.

Elston Ave.

Kennedy Expwy.

90 94

Ave.

Noble

N. Greenview
N. Bosworth
N. Ashland

N. Wood St.

two dailies, the *Chicago Tribune* and the *Chicago Sun-Times;* the *Chicago Reader* and *New City,* two free weekly tabloids with extensive listings; and the monthly *Chicago* magazine. The *Tribune's* entertainment-oriented website, **www.metromix.com**, is an excellent source for reviews of cultural events, and the *Reader's* website, **www.chireader.com**, is known for having one of the most complete weekly listings of cultural happenings. The local Citysearch website, **www.chicago.citysearch.com**, is also an excellent source of information, with lots of opinionated reviews.

GETTING TICKETS

Why pay full price? **Hot Tix** (www.hottix.org) offers half-price tickets on the day of the show to more than 125 theaters throughout the Chicago area (on Fri, you can also purchase tickets for weekend performances). Tickets are sold Sunday through Thursday for the day of performance. You must buy the tickets in person at a Hot Tix outlet; the main Hot Tix box office is located at 78 W. Randolph St., just east of Clark Street. If the show you've got

your heart set on doesn't have half-price tickets available, never fear: Hot Tix is also a Ticketmaster outlet selling full-price tickets to all Ticketmaster events. A second, smaller Hot Tix outlet is located in the heart of the city's shopping district, in the old pumping station at Michigan and Chicago avenues. Recently renamed the **Chicago Water Works Visitor Center,** its entrance is on Pearson Street, across from the Water Tower Place mall. It's open daily from 7:30am to 7pm. The Hot Tix website (www.hottix.org) lists what's on sale for that day beginning at 10am.

In addition, a few theaters offer last-minute discounts on their leftover seats. Steppenwolf Theatre Company often has half-price tickets on the day of a performance; call or stop by the box office 1 hour before showtime. The "Tix at Six" program at the Goodman Theatre offers half-price, day-of-show tickets; many of them are excellent seats that have been returned by subscribers. Tickets go on sale at the box office at 6pm for evening performances and at noon for matinees.

Tips Scoring the Elusive Ticket

Will Junior be crushed if you miss the traveling Broadway show he's been dreaming about seeing? Here are some tips for coming out a hero in your kids' eyes by getting tickets when demand is high:

- Hard-core Chicago theatergoers say the best way to score tickets is to **head right for the box office,** even for a hot show. (This is how I got tickets to *The Producers*—on the day of the show—when it was previewed in Chicago!) Don't phone. This way, you avoid those additional fees—and you will probably get better seats than you would by phone.
- **Use Hot Tix.** In New York plentiful half-price tickets usually means the show is a loser. In Chicago the League of Chicago Theatres expects all its members to offer tickets to its Hot Tix program, whether the show is a hit or flop.
- **Catch shows while they're still in previews.** Tickets are less expensive and more plentiful. If you want to see the cast in ideal form, get tickets for the final preview, which might coincide with the press opening.

1 The Big Venues

Arie Crown Theater   Musicals and pop acts are the focus here; a renovation has improved what were terrible acoustics (Elton John once interrupted a performance to complain about the sound), but this is still a massive, somewhat impersonal hall. 2301 S. Lake Shore Dr., in the McCormick Place convention center at 23rd St. and Lake Shore Dr. ℰ 312/791-6190. Bus: 3 or 4.

Auditorium Theatre   This beautiful theater is a certified national landmark, too. Built in 1889 by Louis Sullivan and Dankmar Adler, the grand hall hosts mostly musicals and dance performances. Even if you don't catch a show here, stop by for a tour. The occasional show will appeal to kids, from *Riverdance* to the Joffrey Ballet of Chicago's *The Nutcracker.* 50 E. Congress Pkwy., between Michigan and Wabash aves. ℰ 312/922-2110. www.auditoriumtheatre.org. Subway/El: Brown, Green, Orange, or Purple Line to Library/Van Buren, or Red Line to Jackson. Bus: 145, 147, or 151.

Briar Street Theatre   The Briar Street Theatre has been turned into the "Blue Man Theater" since fall 1997. The New York City performance phenomenon known as **Blue Man Group** has transformed the 625-seat theater, beginning with the lobby, which is now a jumble of tubes and wires and things approximating computer innards. The show—which mixes percussion, performance art, mime, and rock 'n' roll—has become an immensely popular permanent fixture on the Chicago theater scene. The three strangely endearing performers, whose faces and heads are covered in latex and blue paint, know how to get the audience involved. Your first decision: Do you want the "splatter" or the "nonsplatter" seats? (The former necessitates the donning of a plastic sheet.) I dare you to find a kid who doesn't get a kick out of seeing the Blue Men stuff their faces (literally) with marshmallows. Of all the long-running hits in Chicago, this is the one to beat—and the best kid-pleaser in town. This show is often a sellout, so call for tickets in advance. 3133 N. Halsted St. (at Briar St.). ℰ 773/348-4000. Tickets $46–$56. Subway/El: Red or Brown Line to Belmont.

Chicago Cultural Center _Value_   Built in 1897, the Cultural Center's mandate has always been to provide the people of Chicago with access to the arts. Fortunately for families, children's shows are a major thrust of their programming, especially on Saturday and sometimes Sunday. The center puts on workshops and performances for children several times a month and major festivals four times a year. Concerts featuring Thai music or dance programs depicting the history and architecture of Chicago are just a few of the types of programs you might find. Your children can become familiar with many performing-arts genres and with the artists themselves. Best of all, it's free. 78 E. Washington St. ℰ 312/346-3278. Free tickets. Subway: Red or Brown Line to Randolph and State.

Chicago Shakespeare Theater on Navy Pier   Normally I wouldn't recommend that parents take kids to a performance of Shakespeare, especially with audiences as dedicated as those who attend this theater. However, this company does a great job of making Shakespeare accessible to kids with Family Saturdays, an annual winter/spring offering that brings abbreviated versions of the Bard's work to life (the 2004 selection was a 75-min. abridgement of *Comedy of Errors*). This group's home on Navy Pier is a visually stunning, state-of-the-art jewel. The centerpiece of the glass-box complex, which rises seven stories, is a 525-seat courtyard-style theater patterned loosely after the Swan Theater in Stratford-upon-Avon. The complex also houses a 180-seat studio theater, an English-style pub, and lobbies with commanding views of Lake Michigan and the Chicago

> ### *Tips* Going to the show by El or bus
>
> You have several public transportation options when stepping out on a budget. Bus and El (train/subway) rides cost $1.75 plus 25¢ for transfers. For more information on Chicago's public transportation system, see Chapter 3.
>
> - **Chicago Theatre:** Green, purple, orange, or brown line El to State and Lake, or State Street bus (no. 2, 6, 10, 11, 29, 36, 44, 62, or 146) to corner of State and Lake.
> - **Ford Center for the Performing Arts:** Green, purple, orange, or brown line El to Randolph, or State Street bus (no. 2, 6, 10, 11, 29, 36, 44, 62, or 146) to corner of Randolph and State.
> - **Goodman Theatre:** Green, purple, orange, or brown line El to Randolph, or State Street bus (no. 2, 6, 11, 29, 36, 44, 62, or 146) to corner of State and Randolph, and walk one block west to Dearborn.
> - **Shubert Theatre:** Red line El to Monroe, or State Street bus (no. 2, 6, 10, 11, 29, 36, 44, 62, or 146) to corner of Monroe and State.
> - **Steppenwolf Theatre Company:** Red line El to North and Clybourne, or bus no. 33 or 41 to corner of North and Halsted.
> - **Lyric Opera of Chicago:** Metra train to Northwestern station, or take the green, purple, brown, or orange line El to Washington. Take the Madison Street bus (no. 14, 20, 56, 131, or 157) to the corner of Madison and Wacker.
> - **Petrillo Music Shell:** Green, purple, brown, or orange line El to Adams, or the Michigan Avenue bus (no. 3, 4, 60, 145, 147, or 151) to the corner of Michigan and Jackson.
> - **Symphony Center:** Green, purple, brown, or orange line El to Adams, or the Michigan Avenue bus (no. 3, 4, 60, 145, 147, or 151) to the corner of Michigan and Jackson.

skyline. The main theater presents three plays a year—almost always by the Bard—with founder and artistic director Barbara Gaines usually directing one of the shows. 800 E. Grand Ave. ✆ 312/642-2273. www.chicagoshakes.com. Tickets $40–$62. Guaranteed parking in attached garage at 40% discount. Subway/El: Red Line to Grand, then bus 29 to Navy Pier.

Chicago Theatre   This 1920s music palace has been reborn as an all-purpose entertainment venue, hosting everything from pop acts and magicians to stand-up comedy. The theater also hosted a long run of *Joseph and the Technicolor Dreamcoat* starring Donny Osmond. 175 N. State St. (at Lake St.). ✆ 312/443-1130. Subway/El: Red Line to Lake/State; Brown or Orange Line to Clark/Lake.

Ford Center for the Performing Arts/Oriental Theatre and the Cadillac Palace Theatre   Late 1990s renovations of these opulent theaters inevitably required corporate sponsorship—in this case, from car companies—transforming them into the Cadillac Palace and the awkwardly named Ford Center for the Performing Arts/Oriental Theatre. Both book major touring shows and are well worth a visit for arts buffs. The Oriental's fantastical Asian look includes elaborate carvings almost everywhere you look; dragons, elephants, and griffins peer down at the audience from the gilded ceiling. The Palace features a profusion of Italian marble surfaces and columns, gold-leaf accents a la Versailles, huge decorative mirrors, and crystal chandeliers. Oriental Theatre: 24 W. Randolph St. © 312/782-2004. Palace Theatre: 151 W. Randolph St. © 312/384-1510. Subway/El: Brown Line to Randolph.

Goodman Theatre   Chicago kids (and their parents) come back year after year for the Goodman's annual production of *A Christmas Carol,* a Chicago holiday tradition. The show runs from mid-November to the end of December. Book well in advance; the run always sells out. It's a great way for families to experience the Goodman's state-of-the-art theater complex in the heart of Chicago's revitalized downtown theater district. The project was a total gut rehab of the historic Harris and Selwyn theaters, a pair of former rococo movie houses. None of the historic bric-a-brac was retained; the new building has a very modern, minimalist feel (the side of the building glows with different colors in the evenings). The centerpiece—the 830-seat Albert Ivar Goodman Theatre—is a brand-new limestone-and-glass stucutre. Connected to the main theater is another addition, a cylindrical, glass-walled building housing retail operations, the 400-seat Owen Theatre, and Italian restaurant Petterino's. The Goodman is the dean of legitimate theaters in Chicago, producing both original productions and familiar standards, including everything from Shakespeare to musicals. Productions at the Goodman are always solid; you may not see anything revolutionary, but you'll get some of the best actors in the city.

During the season, the Goodman presents a Family Theatre Series, written and performed for children, so call or check online for this season's offerings. 170 N. Dearborn St. © 312/443-3800. www.goodman-theatre.org. Tickets $30–$50 main stage, $10–$40 studio. Subway/El: Red Line to Washington/State or Lake/State; Brown or Orange Line to Clark/Lake.

North Shore Center for the Performing Arts in Skokie   This north suburban theater is home to the well-respected Northlight Theater, the Skokie Valley Symphony Orchestra, and a series of touring acts, including comics, dance troupes, and children's programs. 9501 Skokie Blvd., Skokie. © 847/673-6300. To reach the theater, take the Edens Expwy. and exit at Old Orchard Rd.; go right onto Old Orchard; make a right onto Skokie Blvd. The theater is at the intersection of Skokie Blvd. and Golf Rd.

Rosemont Theatre   A major venue for traveling shows, this is a top suburban stop for musicals and concerts. *Radio City Christmas Spectacular Starring the Rockettes* and *Bear and the Big Blue House* are recent offerings that have appealed to kids of a wide age range. 5400 River Rd. in Rosemont, near O'Hare Airport. © 847/671-5100.

Shubert Theatre   Built in 1906 as a home for vaudeville, today the Shubert books mostly big-name musicals and sometimes comedy performers. A lot of the musicals are great family fare, so you may well find yourself here. If you get

---

Tips **Finding a Better Seat**

Most of Chicago's grand old theaters have balconies that go way, way up toward the ceiling—and if you're stuck in the cheap seats, you'll be straining to see what's happening onstage. Although theaters are very strict about checking tickets when you arrive, the ushers relax during intermission. So scope out empty seats during the first act, and then move down to better (and much pricier) spots for the rest of the show.

Tips **If You Have a Sitter: The Music Scene**

Chicago is home to the world's most popular and widely heard style of blues and is an important venue for jazz. So book a sitter, grab some dinner, then head for one of these standout clubs. Just remember, it's going to be a late night: many music venues don't get hopping until after 11pm. Plan to arrive between 9 and 10pm. to allow time to get seats in the club, have a drink, and relax before the show. Most clubs continue to pulse until the wee hours, depending on what's happening on stage.

First, how to catch the blues:

Celebrate the women of blues at **Blue Chicago,** 736 and 536 N. Clark St., River North (✆ **312/642-6261**), which showcases top female talent. The cover charge is $5 to $8.

B.L.U.E.S., 2519 N. Halsted St. between Wrightwood and Fullerton avenues, Lincoln Park (✆ **773/528-1012**), satisfies the most ardent fans with live music 365 days a year, since 1979. The dark, narrow club places patrons up close to performers. As at Kingston Mines (described later in this box), expect to spend the evening standing. The cover is $4 to $12.

If Chicago is the body and soul of blues music, then **Buddy Guy's Legends,** 754 S. Wabash Ave. between Balbo and 8th streets, South Loop (✆ **312/427-0333**), is its heart. Everyone from Eric Clapton to Muddy Waters has stopped in to jam and listen to the best in blues at this club owned and operated by blues legend Buddy Guy. Every January, Guy plays a series of shows that sell out early. The cover charge is $6 to $8.

Keep an eye out for Jake and Elwood at the **House of Blues,** 329 N. Dearborn St. at Kinzie Street, River North (✆ **312/923-2000**). Dan Ackroyd, also known as Elwood, is an owner. The hotel, restaurant, bar, and concert venue books a wide variety of acts and stages a popular Sunday gospel brunch for about $35. The cover varies from about $8 to $50 for a big name.

Kingston Mines, 2548 N. Halsted St. between Wrightwood and Fullerton avenues, Lincoln Park (✆ **773/477-4646**), has two stages' worth of blues greats. It may not be up to par with Buddy Guy's, but

balcony seats, be aware that you are going to be way, way up. The view is still good, but if you have any fear of heights (or want to see expressions on the performers' faces), you might want to try for tickets on the main floor. 22 W. Monroe St. ✆ 312/977-1700. Subway/El: Red Line to Washington.

Storefront Theater   Every kind of lively art, from theater, dance, performance art, chamber opera, puppetry, and cabaret to staged readings, finds a home here. Located in the Gallery 37 Center for the Arts, in the heart of the Loop's revitalized theater district, this state-of-the-art black box theater is providing a forum for Chicago's best artists to show off their accomplishments. 66 E. Randolph St. ✆ 312/742-8497. Subway/El: Brown Line to Randolph.

it's certain to satisfy your craving for down-home blues. Performances last until 4 a.m. on Saturdays. The cover charge is $8 to $12.

If you prefer to jazz up the night:

Live jazz is performed virtually around the clock, mostly by nationally known musicians, at **Andy's Jazz Club,** 11 E. Hubbard St. between State Street and Wabash Avenue, River North (✆ **312/642-6805**). This loud, grungy hangout for serious jazz fans offers three-hour sets at lunch on weekdays and music throughout the evening all week. The kitchen stays open late; pizza and burgers are decent. Depending on the day of the week and the time, you arrive, the cover charge is $5 to 10.

Green Dolphin Street, 2200 N. Ashland Ave. at Webster Avenue, Lincoln Park (✆ **773/395-0066**), is a retro supper club that's slick—and pricey. Stylish patrons in their 30s to 50s enjoy seafood and contemporary American cuisine from a celebrated kitchen and then head to an adjacent room that accommodates 200 people for live jazz. The music ranges from headliners, such as Wynton Marsalis, to experimental artists, plus Latin jazz and big band music. Main courses range from $25 and up.

Known for great jazz in a historical setting, **Green Mill,** 4802 N. Broadway at Lawrence Avenue, near Andersonville (✆ **773/878-5552**), was established in 1907 and frequented by infamous mobster Al Capone. You hear Latin jazz, big band jazz, jazz piano, and more. On Tuesday and Thursday nights, jitterbugging hipsters swarm to the club for Prohibition-era swing and big band music. On Sunday, the club hosts Chicago's best-known poetry slam. The cover ranges from being free to $8.

Joe Segal, founder of **Jazz Showcase,** 59 W. Grand Ave. at Clark Street, River North (✆ **312/670-2473**), books some of the hottest names in the business. With two performances each night (open to audiences of all ages) and a 4 p.m. Sunday matinee, this club is ushering in the next generation of fans. The cover charge is $20.

If you're in the mood for bubbly, **Pops for Champagne,** 2934 N. Sheffield Ave. at Oakdale Avenue, Lincoln Park (✆ **773/472-1000**), offers more than 100 labels, plus live jazz combos. The cozy fireplace and dim lighting make this a hot spot for couples seeking a romantic night out. The cover ranges from free to $10.

Studio Theater *Value*   When you pop in to the Chicago Cultural Center, you might find yourself seeing a show here, at an intimate stage. The theater is used as an incubator space, giving Chicago's best off-Loop theater companies the opportunity to share their work with downtown audiences. The Department of Cultural Affairs provides the space for free to encourage the growth of new creative talent. Ticket prices are kept low or admission is free for select events to allow everyone the chance to enjoy some of Chicago's best theater. 77 E. Randolph St. ✆ **312/744-6630.** Subway/El: Brown, Green, Orange, or Purple Line to Randolph, or Red Line to Washington/State. Bus: 3, 4, 20, 56, 60, 127, 131, 145, 146, 147, 151, or 157.

Symphony Center Symphony Center is the building that encompasses Orchestra Hall, home of the Chicago Symphony Orchestra. Expanded and renovated a few years back, the building now includes a six-story sky-lit arcade, recital spaces, and the fine-dining restaurant Rhapsody. While the CSO is the main attraction (and it's off-limits to kids under 12), the Symphony Center hosts a family matinee series, plus a series of piano recitals, classical and chamber music concerts, and the occasional jazz or pop artist. 220 S. Michigan Ave., between Adams St. and Jackson Blvd. ℂ 312/294-3000. Subway/El: Red Line to Washington/State. Bus: 3, 4, 20, 56, 60, 127, 145, 146, 147, 151, or 157.

The Theatre at American Girl Place *Circle of Friends: An American Girl Musical* at the in-store theater is a musical revue ($26) for ages 6 and up that lasts 1 hour and 15 minutes. Inspired by the American Girls stories, the musical features young girls in the roles of seven brave characters who teach girls about believing in your strengths and following your heart. At the heart of American Girls is a popular series of books about living in different places and eras of American history, from Colonial Williamsburg to World War II. Besides providing a history lesson, young readers can discover similarities between their own lives and the lives of these girls. There's also a new show for younger kids, *Bitty Bear's Matinee: The Family Tree,* that's just 35 minutes long, priced at $15 for kids ages 3 and up, and $7.50 for kids under age 3. You'll need reservations for either show. 111 E. Chicago Ave. ℂ 877/AG-PLACE. www.americangirlplace.com. Subway/El: Red Line to Chicago/State.

2 Seasonal Events

Chicago Human Rhythm Project *(Finds* **Ages 6 & up.** This group performs an annual tap-dance festival that was created in 1990 and brings together tap and percussive dancers from all over the world. It's an impressive sight (and sound). Dancers spend a month in Chicago, taking a series of workshops and outreach programs. It all culminates in a stirring week of performances in late July at the Athenaeum Theatre, 2936 N. Southport Ave. (at Lincoln Ave.). Office: 1920 Lincoln Ave. ℂ 312/587-8370. www.chicagotap.com. Tickets $20. Subway/El: Brown Line to Wellington.

A Christmas Carol **Ages 6 & up.** This beloved Chicago holiday tradition took on a new look in 2001 when the Goodman Theatre moved into its new home and unveiled a completely redesigned set. The new production of *A Christmas Carol,* with expenses of more than $1 million, was darker and more operatic—along the lines of a Tim Burton take on the old classic. Kids love it, parents love it, and theater buffs loved the fact that the Goodman didn't turn the show, admittedly one of the darker Christmas stories ever penned, into a sugarcoated Broadway event. In fact, the show is even better for being more of a serious play and ghost story—it makes the ending even more uplifting. The show runs every year from the third weekend in November until just before Christmas. 170 N. Dearborn St. ℂ 312/443-3800. www.goodman-theatre.org. Tickets $30–$50. Subway/El: Red Line to Washington/State or Lake/State; Brown or Orange Line to Clark/Lake.

Dance Chicago *(Value* **Ages 5 & up.** In addition to Chicago Human Rhythm Project (reviewed above), the Athenaeum also hosts the annual Dance Chicago, a highly engaging month-long festival showcasing the talents of up-and-coming contemporary-dance companies and choreographers. It usually takes place in October or November. In recent years the programs have included jazz, hip-hop, tap, ballroom, tango, salsa, swing, and more. A kids' show called *Dance for Kids,*

Tips **A Do-It-Yourself** *Messiah*

Fancy yourself an ecclesiastical crooner? Should you be in town over the Christmas holidays, don't skip the LaSalle Talman **Do-It-Yourself** *Messiah,* an extraordinarily popular and rousing rendition of the Handel classic. Now staged at the opulent Civic Opera House (although for years, Orchestra Hall provided the setting), the program enlists audience members as part of a 3,500-voice chorus, who are accompanied by a volunteer orchestra and four professional soloists. Even if you and your kids don't join in the singing, just sitting in the audience and absorbing the roof-raising aural power that fills the theater guarantees goose bumps. This is a hot, hot, hot ticket, so check in November for registrations at www.lasallebank.com/messiah.

Too! usually runs every Saturday afternoon at a cost of $12 for adults and $5 for kids ages 4 and up. (To attend the evening programs, kids need to be age 5 or older.) The kids' program features numerous dance companies, both youth and professional, whose work is geared to families. At the Athenaeum Theatre, 2936 N. Southport Ave. (at Lincoln Ave.). ✆ 773/935-6860. www.dancechicago.com. Tickets $5–$25. Subway/El: Brown Line to Wellington.

Grant Park Music Festival   **All ages.** A great Chicago event takes place from late June through August: the series of free outdoor classical music concerts given by the Grant Park Symphony and Chorus, as well as a number of visiting artists. They perform in the Frank Gehry–designed Pritzker Music Pavilion in Millennium Park (with the surrounding Loop skyscrapers creating an impressive backdrop). Featuring Gehry's signature sinuous lines, the pavilion is surrounded by dramatic ribbons of curved steel. The Grant Park Symphony not only looks better than ever, it sounds great, too, thanks to a state-of-the-art sound system. The Grant Park Music Festival has been a Chicago tradition since 1931, when Mayor A. J. Cermak suggested free concerts to lift Chicagoans' spirits. Concerts are held Wednesday through Sunday, with most performances beginning at 7:30pm. Bring a blanket if you plan to sit on the lawn; seats in the band shell are reserved for subscribers, but unclaimed seats are offered to the public about 15 minutes before the concert begins. It's a great way for families to enjoy music together. If you sit in the back, your kids will find plenty of company—it looks like a veritable playground of kids back there. Selections might include Broadway favorites, Bernstein, Mozart, Brahms, Cole Porter, and Gershwin. Pritzker Music Pavilion, at the cover of Michigan Ave. and Randolph St. ✆ 312/742-4763. www.grant parkmusicfestival.com. Subway/El: Red Line to Washington/State or Brown, Orange or Green Lines to Randolph/Wabash.

The Nutcracker   **Ages 8 & up.** When the Joffrey Ballet of Chicago moved here several years ago, it brought along a new holiday tradition: its annual production of *The Nutcracker.* The ballet is performed at the beautiful Auditorium Theatre for 3 weeks in December. It's simply the best version in town, with a live orchestra helping to bring Tchaikovsky's holiday tale to life. Office: 70 E. Lake St. ✆ 312/739-0120. www.joffrey.com. Tickets $34–$74. Auditorium Theatre, 50 E. Congress Pkwy. Bus: 145, 147, or 151. Subway/El: Brown, Green, Orange, or Purple Line to Library/Van Buren, or Red Line to Jackson.

Ravinia Festival *Finds*   **All ages.** Ravinia, summer home of the Chicago Symphony Orchestra in suburban Highland Park, is a Chicago summer tradition.

The festival strives to be family-friendly by maintaining low ticket prices and inviting patrons to pack their own picnics and sit on the lawn. There's even a series of **Kraft Kids Concerts** that reach out to the next generation of music lovers. In the past the series has featured the Ravinia Festival Jazz Mentors with the Muntu Dance Theatre of Chicago, Ravinia Festival Orchestra, Chicago Human Rhythm Project, the Apollo Chorus, River North Dance Chicago, the Joffrey Ballet and more. Held about eight times each summer, the kids' concerts usually begin at 11am on Saturday and have a discounted price of $5 to $8 for reserved seats (in the Pavilion) and $3 for lawn tickets. My advice? Bring a picnic lunch and stake out a spot on the lawn (with the added bonus that your kids can run and burn off excess energy).

If your kids are a bit older, they would enjoy hanging on the lawn during the regular season, which runs from mid-June to Labor Day and includes far more than classical concerts: You can also catch pop acts, dance performances, operatic arias, and blues concerts. Tickets are sold to both the covered pavilion, where you get a reserved seat and a view of the stage, and the lawn, which is the real joy of Ravinia: sitting under the stars and a canopy of leafy branches while listening to music and indulging in an elaborate picnic. (It's a local tradition to try to outdo everyone else by bringing candelabras and fine china.) Whether it's Mozart or Lyle Lovett, the setting is magical every time. The wide lawn to the left of the stage is a popular place for families to spread out.

Dining options available at the park range from the fine-dining restaurant **Mirabelle** (© 847/432-7550 for reservations) to prepacked picnic spreads from the **Gatehouse,** featuring gourmet items to go. Lawn catering is also available for parties of 20 or more. But what most cognoscenti do is pack a picnic of delectables and eat on the lawn. Do arrive early if you're coming for a pop act because the lawn can get packed. For about $8, you can rent a pair of lawn chairs and a table. If you're wondering about the weather conditions at concert time, dial Ravinia's Weather Line (© 847/433-5010). Green Bay and Lake-Cook roads, Highland Park. © 847/266-5100 or 312/RAVINIA. www.ravinia.org. Tickets: pavilion $15–$50, lawn $10. Most concerts are held in the evening. Catch the Ravinia bus at the following locations: Marshall Field's (State and Randolph sts.); the Palmer House Hilton (Monroe St. entrance); Westin River North, 320 N. Dearborn St. (the Clark St. side); The Drake hotel (Walton St. and Michigan Ave.); Harbor House (3200 N. Lake Shore Dr.); Sheridan and Hollywood; Sheridan and Devon; or the Davis St. Station in Evanston. Round-trip tickets are $12. Many of the major hotels also charter buses during the season. You can also catch the 5:50pm commuter train, which leaves from the North Western Station near the Loop at Madison and Canal sts. The train stops in Highland Park directly at the festival; the "Ravinia Special" round-trip fare is $4.

Ringling Bros. and Barnum & Bailey Circus   **Ages 6 & up.** Come one, come all to this massive circus, which stops in Chicago every fall for several weeks beginning in November. Three rings of glitzy, over-the-top entertainment are in store, from trapeze artists to the horses, tigers, elephants, and crocodiles who make up some of the 200 human and animal performers. There's nothing subtle about this show—in fact, smaller kids might be overwhelmed by the sheer size of the United Center, plus the flashing lights and eardrum-blasting music. Still, at least once in your life, it's worth it to see this darn impressive "greatest show on earth." United Center, 1901 W. Madison St. © 312/559-1212. www.ringling.com. Tickets $11–$75. Bus: 9 or 20.

SummerDance   **Ages 5 & up.** Now entering its sixth year, the annual Chicago SummerDance Festival usually runs from late June through August in Grant Park. Presented by the Chicago Department of Cultural Affairs, the festival features

1-hour dance lessons to taped music, followed by dancing to live orchestras, every Thursday, Friday, and Saturday evening from 6 to 9:30pm and Sunday afternoons from 2 to 5pm, weather permitting. The festival also presents folk dance from Scandinavia, Israel, Ireland, Scotland, Wales, and others at various venues throughout the city. Grant Park, 601 S. Michigan (between Harrison and Balbo, across from Columbia College). For complete information on what's scheduled, call the Chicago Department of Cultural Affairs at (©) 312/744-6630. Free admission. Subway/El: Red Line to Jackson.

3 Theater

Chicago Playworks for Families and Young Audiences (Value) **Ages 3 & up.** How can the 35,000 kids and adults who flock to see this company's performances each year be wrong? Founded in 1925 as Goodman Children's Theatre, Chicago Playworks later became part of DePaul University and is one of the first important children's theaters in the United States. The company presents three shows per season, which runs from October through April. Located in the historic Merle Reskin Theatre, built in 1910 as the Blackstone Theater, kids can cozy up in plush red seats and marvel at the sparkling chandeliers and grand scale of the surroundings. If you're a Chicago resident, you might want to try the season tickets, which entitle you to two free admission tickets to the Chicago Children's Museum at Navy Pier. Ask about the Ice Cream Social package, offered three times a year, which gets you into an after-show ice cream bar and features discussion and an autograph session with the cast at the nearby Hilton Chicago. Shows run from October to May, usually Tuesday and Thursday at 10am and Saturday at 2pm. Merle Reskin Theatre, 60 E. Balbo Dr. (©) 312/922-1999. http://theatreschool.depaul.edu. Tickets $8 and up. Subway/El: Red Line to Jackson.

The Children's Theater Fantasy Orchard   Ages 3 & up. Performing in the Mercury Theater, a small, modern theater in Lakeview's hot Southport Avenue area, Children's Theater Fantasy Orchard presents fairy and folk tales from around the world. Founded in 1990, the company now performs for 30,000 kids annually. Some 30 actors and technicians come up with new productions each year. In doing so, the company tries to depict universal struggles and truths as they stoke kids' imaginations. In 2003 the schedule included *Three Cinderella Stories,* featuring African, Asian, and Spanish Cinderellas. At Mercury Theater, 3745 N. Southport. (©) 773/325-1700. www.kidtheater.com. Tickets $10 for adults, $5 for kids. Subway/El: Brown Line to Southport.

Emerald City Theatre Company   Ages 2 & up. From Tarzan and Jane to Dr. Seuss classics, this relative newcomer to the kids' theater scene produces shows for kids ages 2 and up. The company is currently performing at the Apollo Theater, a modern theater with 400 seats—although that has changed from time to time throughout the years. Emerald City Theatre Company was

---

Calling a Cab

Taxis are easy to hail in the Loop, on the Magnificent Mile and the Gold Coast, in River North, and in Lincoln Park, but if you go much beyond these key areas, you might need to call a cab. Try one of these cab companies:

- **Flash Cab** ((©) 773/561-1444)
- **Yellow Cab** ((©) 312/TAXI-CAB or 312/829-4222)
- **Checker Cab** ((©) 312/CHECKER or 312/243-2537)

254 CHAPTER 10 · ENTERTAINMENT FOR THE WHOLE FAMILY

Tips A Brief Primer on Theater Etiquette for Kids

A night at the theater used to mean dressing formally and sitting stiffly. Although casual dress and equally casual manners have replaced much of the formality of a night at the theater, some rules of etiquette still prevail. Before heading to a show with your kids, you might want to talk through the following basic guidelines:

- Don't use cameras or video cameras in the theater. Taping is prohibited by law.
- Don't talk during a performance; it's distracting for other patrons who have paid a pretty penny for their seat (most shows cost well over $50 a ticket these days).
- Turn off beepers and cellphones. Most theaters will remind patrons of this rule before the curtain rises, as it seems inevitable that someone will forget, and that one ring will ruin everyone's enjoyment (and possibly, the actors' concentration!).
- Rustling candy wrappers can be as much of a nuisance as a ringing cellphone. If you or your kids must eat candy, unwrap it before the show starts.
- Dress comfortably, but within bounds. You can anticipate seeing theatergoers dressed up for a blockbuster musical and dressed down for a storefront repertory, so dress accordingly. While Chicago is a relaxed Midwestern city, sweatshirts and jeans are too casual for the theater. For men, a nice sweater or collared shirt with slacks or jeans will work almost everywhere, and similar attire for women (sweaters, dress pants or a skirt) is always appropriate.
- Make sure kids are fed before the show—squirming kids with growling stomachs do not make for a pleasant theater-watching experience for anyone, the kids especially.
- No need to tip the ushers. Acknowledging their help with a thank you or a pleasant nod or smile is all that's required. However, if you manage to battle your way to the bar during intermission, the beleaguered bartender will appreciate your tip.
- Take special care to be on time. Chicago theaters tend to be punctual, and tardy patrons usually must wait to be seated until the conclusion of the scene or musical number in progress. Arriving late for the opera can be especially troublesome. With acts lasting for over an hour, you'll be sitting outside watching the performance on a television—not a good use of your entertainment dollar.

founded in 1996, and recent shows have included *The Sorcerer's Apprentice, Cinderella, The Wizard of Oz,* and *Where the Wild Things Are.* Each season, Emerald City produces four shows, some of which are original works written for the company. Many Chicago kids had their first theater experience with Emerald City (named in honor of *The Wonderful Wizard of Oz,* written by Frank L. Baum while he lived in Chicago). At the Apollo Theater, 2540 N. Lincoln. Office: 2936 N. Southport.

© **773/935-6100.** www.emeraldcitytheatre.com. Tickets $8 for children 2–12, $10 for ages 13 and up. Subway/El: Red or Brown Line to Fullerton.

Lifeline Theatre KidSeries   Ages 2 & up. Lifeline Theatre—the grown-up version—has a faithful following who anticipates its creative stage adaptations of literary classics such as *Jane Eyre.* Its KidSeries plays are original adaptations of favorite children's books, and often include music written especially for them. These shows, which are presented on Saturday and Sunday afternoons, are great for even the youngest kids. Recent performances have included *Giggle Giggle Quack,* about a farmer who goes on vacation and the duck who takes charge of the barnyard, and *Sophie's Masterpiece,* a tale about a spider with hidden artistic talents. After each performance, actors come out to the lobby to meet kids, give autographs, and answer questions. The theater is small—100 seats—and is located in the Rogers Park neighborhood. Look for metered parking on Morse Avenue or free parking 3 blocks north of the theater at the corner of Glenwood and Estes avenues in the Trilogy, Inc. lot. 6912 N. Glenwood Ave. *©* **773/761-4477.** www.lifelinetheatre.com. Tickets $9. Subway/El: Bus 147 to Sheridan and Arthur; transfer to bus 155 to Glenwood.

Medieval Times   Ages 6 & up. Does jousting count as "theater"? This dinner-and-tournament show features knights competing in games, swordplay, jousting, and pyrotechnics. Sound familiar? You may have caught the act in the Jim Carrey film *The Cable Guy.* (Naturally, Jim Carrey got a bit too involved in the show, but in real life, kids shouldn't expect to find themselves wearing armor and riding horses.) It's pure kitsch, but if you can get off your high horse (so to speak) you might find yourself sucked in to the "drama." Besides, kids dig it. Guests dine on a four-course "medieval" banquet served by staff posing as "serving wenches." Performances take place on weekends, and during the holidays, Thursday nights are sometimes added. 2001 Roselle Rd. at I-90, Schaumburg. *©* **847/843-3900.** Tickets $50 for adults, $36 for children 12 and under. Matinee rates might be available, so call for showtimes and ticket prices.

4 Concerts

Blue Chicago *Finds*   **Ages 8 & up.** A blues club for families? Yes, it's true—from 8pm to midnight on Saturday, the basement of the Blue Chicago store becomes a venue geared to families, featuring the music of the Gloria Shannon Blues Band. In fact, "Down in the Basement" is the only venue in Chicago that offers a regular live blues show for all ages. No alcohol is served and no smoking is allowed.

Blue Chicago pays homage to female blues belters with a strong lineup of the best women vocalists around. The 1940s-style brick-walled room, decorated with original artwork of Chicago blues vignettes, is open Monday through Saturday, with music beginning at 9pm. Admission allows you to club-hop between this venue and a second location, open Tuesday through Sunday, down the street at 536 N. Clark St. Next door, at 534 N. Clark, is the Blue Chicago Store, which sells blues-related clothing, merchandise, and artwork. 736 N. Clark St. (between Chicago Ave. and Superior St.). *©* **312/642-6261.** www.bluechicago.com. Tickets $5 for adults, free for children 12 and under. Subway/El: Red or Brown Line to Chicago.

Chicago Children's Choir   Ages 6 & up. Two self-produced concerts are performed each year, in May and December, by this multiracial, multicultural choral music education program. Venues change, so call for information. This is not just any kids' choir: In the past, the choir performed with Bobby McFerrin at the Chicago Theatre. Founded in 1956, the choir trains nearly 3,000 young singers a year. The choir runs 61 in-school choruses in 40 Chicago elementary schools and five after-school Neighborhood Choirs. The showpiece is the 125-voice Concert Choir, which includes Treble and Chamber ensembles, Madrigals, and a Show Choir. Office: Chicago Cultural Center, 78 E. Washington, 5th floor. © **312/849-8300.** www.ccchoir.org. Tickets $27–$47.

Chicago Music Mart at DePaul Center   All ages. Spark the interest of the budding musician in your family at the "Mart," where instrument stores abound, and kids are welcome to test out the instruments. At lunchtime, "Tunes at Noon" presents free concerts on weekdays, indoors in winter and outdoors in summer, featuring high school bands, choral groups, or young performers playing everything from classical to jazz. 333 S. State St. © **312/362-6700.** Subway/El: Red Line to Jackson.

Chicago Opera Theater   Ages 8 & up. As the "other" opera company in town, Chicago Opera Theater doesn't get all the big names, but it does make opera accessible to a wider audience with an emphasis on American composers and performers who sing in English. It also helps that tickets are less expensive and more plentiful than those for the Lyric Opera. The opera has a wonderful educational outreach program that features one opera per season (a short one, usually!) that is performed by and for children. Call well in advance for tickets to the next performance, as they always sell out. Back in 2002 the opera made a splash with its performance of *Brundibár,* a 30-minute opera first performed in 1942 at the Jewish boys' orphanage in Prague for which it was written. By the time of the premiere, the composer, conductor, and director had all been sent to Terezin, a Nazi concentration camp. The opera is a story of good triumphing over evil, and each performance was followed by a discussion with performers. The production was designed by famed author and artist Maurice Sendak. No matter what the bill, the talent and production values are top-notch. 205 E. Randolph Dr. © **312/704-8414.** www.chicagooperatheater.org. Tickets $30–$97 adults, children half price. Subway/El: Red Line to Washington/State.

Chicago Symphony Orchestra   Ages 6 & up. The CSO does a nice job of outreach to young ones with the Kraft Family Matinee series, which exposes kids to the storytelling of music through classics. In the past, performances have included "special guests" such as Woofgang and Meowzart, who appear at performances of *Stomp Your Foot!,* and Underground Railway Theater puppeteers at performances of *The Firebird.* The series runs on select Saturdays at 11am and 12:30pm. Concerts are performed by members of the Chicago Symphony Orchestra and guest artists. Another kid favorite is the annual Halloween concert for ages 5 to 17. Kids are invited to wear costumes to the concert. Highlights include seeing Grainger Hall transformed into a haunted house, and participating in face painting and storytelling—and orchestra members dress in costumes, too.

Another option for kids is the Chicago Youth Symphony Orchestra, which performs at Orchestra Hall (© **312/939-2207;** www.cyso.org). Founded in 1946, the orchestra is comprised of a senior-level group of 105 top high school musicians in the Chicagoland area. Recognized as one of the nation's best youth orchestras, the CYSO performs in November and May.

If your children are over age 12, they are welcome to attend a regular performance of the CSO, currently led by music director Daniel Barenboim (who will be leaving at the end of the 2006 season), and among the best in the world—a legacy of the late maestro Sir Georg Solti, who captured a record-breaking 31 Grammy awards for his CSO recordings and showcased the orchestra at other major musical capitals during frequent international tours. In addition to classical music, the "Symphony Center Presents" series has included some of the top jazz, world beat, Latin, and cabaret artists in the world in recent years. Although they're in high demand, good seats often become available on concert day. Call Symphony Center or stop by the box office to check availability.

Summertime visitors have an opportunity to hear a CSO performance at the delightful **Ravinia Festival** (p. 251) in suburban Highland Park, led by music director Christoph Eschenbach.

The **Civic Orchestra of Chicago,** the training orchestra of the Chicago Symphony since 1919, is also highly regarded and presents free programs at Orchestra Hall. The **Chicago Symphony Chorus** also performs there. Orchestra Hall, in Symphony Center, 220 S. Michigan Ave. ✆ 312/294-3000. www.chicagosymphony.org. Tickets $10–$90; box seats $165. Subway/El: Red Line to Jackson.

House of Blues   **Ages 8 & up.** Gospel as well as blues originated in Chicago, and the House of Blues's popular Sunday gospel brunch, offering a Southern-style buffet, brings a different Chicago gospel choir to the stage each week; the three weekly "services" often sell out, so get tickets in advance. Kids will delight in the funky decor at the club, part of a nightclub, restaurant, and hotel complex that has breathed new life into Marina City. The largest outpost in the growing House of Blues chain, this 55,000-square-foot complex, extravagantly decorated with 600 pieces from owner Isaac Tigrett's collection of Mississippi Delta folk art, isn't really a blues club as much as a showcase for rock, R&B, zydeco, reggae, and everything else. 329 N. Dearborn St. (at Kinzie St.). ✆ 312/923-2000 for general information, 312/923-2020 for concert information. www.hob.com. Ticket prices vary depending on the act. Subway/El: Red Line to Grand.

Jazz Showcase   **Ages 8 & up.** The Segals make an effort to cultivate new generations of jazz lovers: The club admits all ages (children under 12 are free), has a nonsmoking policy, and offers a Sunday 4pm matinee show that won't keep the kids up late. Spanning more than 50 years and several locations, founder Joe Segal has become synonymous with jazz in Chicago. His son, Wayne, has taken over the business, but this latest venue in the River North restaurant-and-entertainment district is the spiffiest yet, a spacious and handsome room with sharp black-and-white photographs of jazz greats, many of whom have passed through Segal's clubs. There are two shows a night, and reservations are recommended when a big-name headliner is featured. Such well-regarded musicians as McCoy Tyner, Clark Terry, Maynard Ferguson, and Ahmad Jamal have made appearances in recent years.

The Segals' latest outpost is the new **Joe's Be-bop Cafe and Jazz Emporium** at Navy Pier, 600 E. Grand Ave. (✆ **312/595-5299**), a Southern-style BBQ restaurant with live music nightly. 59 W. Grand St. (at Clark St.). ✆ **312/670-2473**. Tickets $20–$25. Subway/El: Red Line to Grand.

Lyric Opera of Chicago   **Ages 12 & up.** A major American opera company, the Lyric attracts top-notch singers from all over the world. Naturally, this is not the place for toddlers, but if you have kids in seventh through twelfth grades, you might want to expose them to opera through the company's student matinees. Kids should be prepared for performances to run approximately 90 minutes. Just soaking in the ambience at the glamorous and opulent opera house is

---

(*Tips*   **Chuckling the Night Away at a Comedy Club**

If you've got a sitter, or if your kids are in their teens, you might want to explore Chicago's comic side. From the storied Second City company to scrappier, up-and-coming troupes, Chicago is a training ground for the nation's best comedians. If you are going to bring your teenagers to a club, it's advisable to call ahead to check out the show's content. The box office personnel should be able to warn you if the show will be too racy for your kids.

The Second City, 1616 N. Wells St. at North Avenue, Lincoln Park (© 312/337-3992; www.secondcity.com), packs a comic punch line—with a pedigree. Dan Ackroyd, Alan Alda, Alan Arkin, Ed Asner, John Belushi, John Candy, Don Castellaneta (also known as "Homer Simpson"), Chris Farley, Shelley Long, Elaine May, Tim Meadows, Bill Murray, Brian Doyle-Murray, Mike Nichols, Gilda Radner, Joan Rivers, Martin Short, George Wendt . . . whew! The list goes on and on, but you get the point: The alumni of Second City—Chicago's comic breeding ground—read like a laundry list of great American comedic talent. Some of the alums hail from the Toronto branch, but they're all part of this improv factory, one of the most prolific training grounds in American theater history. You rarely see a bad show here. Tickets are easy to get, and shows change frequently—and no doubt you'll be seeing at least one rising star. You can choose between two sketch comedy productions on the main stage and ETC (et cetera), a smaller venue. The cover charge runs $8 to $16.

A block away at **Zanies Comedy Club,** 1548 N. Wells St. between North Avenue and Schiller Street (© 312/337-4027), high-caliber comedians treat sold-out houses to the best in standup. The cover charge is $18 to $20, with a two-drink minimum.

Improv Olympics, 3541 N. Clark St. at Addison Street, Wrigleyville (© 773-880-0199), engages the audience as the talented cast solicits suggestions and creates original performances. The show is free on Wednesday; otherwise you pay a $5 to $14 cover charge.

---

quite an experience (even if you leave at intermission!). The handsome, 3,563-seat Art Deco Civic Opera House is the second-largest opera house in the country, built in 1929. Add to that the magnificence of the Lyric Opera Orchestra and chorus, the amazing sets and costumes, and the beautiful voices, and it's an experience your kids won't soon forget. Kids are encouraged to dress up for the occasion, and proper etiquette is expected. Ticket prices are $5 for the upper balcony, $10 for the first balcony, $13 for the second section of the main floor, and $16 for box seats and the front section of the main floor.

If you can't snag tickets or if you visit during the opera's off-season in February and March, you can still check out the theater by taking a tour (© 312/827-5685). Civic Opera House, at Madison St. and Wacker Dr. © 312/332-2244. Fax 312/332-8120. www.lyric opera.org. Tickets $29–$139. Subway/El: Brown Line to Washington.

Old Town School of Folk Music *Finds*   **All ages.** Country, folk, bluegrass, Latin, Celtic—the Old Town School of Folk Music covers a spectrum of indigenous musical forms. A full schedule of classes, concerts, and special events are geared to children ages 6 months to teen years. (For more on dropping in for a class, see chapter 8.) The school is best known as a training center offering a slate of music classes, but it also hosts everyone from the legendary Pete Seeger to bluegrass phenom Alison Krauss. The school's home, in a former 1930s library, is the world's largest facility dedicated to the preservation and presentation of traditional and contemporary folk music. The Old Town School also houses an art gallery showcasing exhibitions of works by local, national, and international artists; a music store offering an exquisite selection of instruments, sheet music, and hard-to-find recordings; and a cafe. The school hosts an annual Chicago Folk and Roots Festival in July in Wells Park at Lincoln and Montrose, with stage performances and an activity-and-craft tent for kids. Headliners are name-brand performers such as Patti Smith. The school maintains another retail store and a schedule of children's classes at its first location, 909 W. Armitage Ave. 4544 N. Lincoln Ave. (between Wilson and Montrose aves.). (C) **773/728-6000.** www.oldtownschool.org. Tickets $10–$25. Subway/El: Blue Line to Western.

5 Movies

Chicago has its share of multiplex theaters that feature kid fare. The **AMC River East,** located at 322 E. Illinois, east of Columbus Drive ((C) **312/596-0333**), is Chicago's newest and largest movie complex and features stadium seating and digital sound in all auditoriums. (When the theater opened, it literally doubled the number of first-run-movie screens downtown). Other major downtown cinemas include **600 N. Michigan Theaters,** at that address ((C) **312/255-9340**), **Esquire 6,** 58 E. Oak ((C) **312/280-0101**), and **Pipers Alley 4,** 1608 N. Wells ((C) **312/642-6890**).

One IMAX and one OMNIMAX theater surround you with sights and sounds. Cineplex Odeon's **IMAX Theater on Navy Pier** ((C) **312/595-5629**), shows not only traditional IMAX films on its six-story, 80-foot-wide screen, but also 3-D movies. The **OMNIMAX Theater** at the Museum of Science and Industry, 57th Street and Lake Shore Drive ((C) **773/684-1414;** www. msichicago.org), usually presents movies in conjunction with exhibits. The theater also has an Omnilaser Fantasy light show featuring rock music and costs the same as a movie. To ensure tickets, reserve in advance—even if you have a ticket, get there early, because the line for seats begins forming about 20 minutes in advance.

Tips **Facets' Film Festival**

Facets Multi-Media, 1517 W. Fullerton Ave. ((C) **773/281-4114;** www.facets. org; Subway/El: Red or Brown Line to Fullerton), a nonprofit group that screens independent film and video from around the world, is for the die-hard cinematic thrill-seeker. The group also hosts the **Chicago International Children's Film Festival** (Oct), the largest in the U.S. In 2004 the festival screened more than 200 children's films from 40 countries—many of which you'll never see in mainstream theaters. Some 23,000 kids, adults, educators, and celebrities attend and run filmmaking workshops for kids. For more information about the film festival or to check out Facets' kids' programs, including Young Chicago Critics and Take One! Workshops, log on to **www. cicff.org**.

Chicago as Backdrop

Get your teen warmed up for your trip to Chicago by renting one of these Chicago-based flicks (all of which are rated PG or PG-13):

- *Girls Just Want to Have Fun* (1985)
- *Ferris Bueller's Day Off* (1986)
- *Adventures in Babysitting* (1987)
- *Prelude to a Kiss* (1992)
- *The Fugitive* (1993)
- *While You Were Sleeping* (1995)
- *My Best Friend's Wedding* (1997)
- *Blues Brothers 2000* (1998; note the original *Blues Brothers* movie is rated R)
- Save the Last Dance (2001)

6 Dance

Ballet Chicago **Ages 10 & up.** Under artistic director Daniel Duell, a former New York City Ballet dancer, the group is notable for its specialty: the ballets of Balanchine. The ballet performs one full-length story ballet a year, usually in April or May. © 312/251-8838. www.balletchicago.org. Tickets $12–$25.

The Dance Center—Columbia College Chicago **Ages 10 & up.** Columbia College, a liberal-arts institution specializing in the arts and media, has been growing by leaps and bounds in recent years. Its Dance Center—the hub of Chicago's modern dance milieu—features an intimate "black box" 275-seat performance space with stadium seating and marvelous sightlines. The Dance Center hosts at least a dozen performances a year by both international and national touring groups and homegrown choreographers. 1306 S. Michigan Ave. © 312/344-8300. www.dancecenter.org. Tickets $10–$25. Subway/El: Red Line to Roosevelt. Bus: 151.

Hubbard Street Dance Chicago **Ages 12 & up.** Dance lovers recommend that if you're going to see just one dance performance while you're in town, make it Hubbard Street, Chicago's best-known dance troupe whose mix of jazz, modern, ballet, and theater dance has won many devoted local fans. Sometimes whimsical, sometimes romantic, the crowd-pleasing 22-member ensemble incorporates a range of dance traditions, from Kevin O'Day to Twyla Tharp, who has choreographed pieces exclusively for Hubbard Street. Although the troupe spends most of the year touring, it has regular 2- to 3-week Chicago engagements in the fall and spring. In the summer the dancers often perform at Ravinia Festival (p. 251). Office: 1147 W. Jackson Blvd. © 312/850-9744. www.hubbardstreetdance.com. Tickets $20–$50.

Joffrey Ballet of Chicago **Ages 10 & up.** Although this major classical company concentrates on touring, the Joffrey schedules about 6 weeks of performances a year in its hometown. Led by cofounder and artistic director Gerald Arpino, the company is committed to the classic works of the 20th century. Its repertoire extends from the ballets of Arpino, Robert Joffrey, Balanchine, and Jerome Robbins to the cutting-edge works of Alonzo King and Chicago choreographer Randy Duncan. The Joffrey continues to draw crowds to its popular rock ballet, *Billboards,* which is set to the music of Prince, and tours internationally. The company is usually in town in the spring (Mar or Apr), fall (Sept or Oct), and December, when it stages its rendition of the holiday favorite *The Nutcracker.* Office: 70 E. Lake St. © 312/739-0120. www.joffrey.com. Tickets $15–$80.

Muntu Dance Theatre of Chicago **Ages 8 & up.** The tribal costumes, drumming, and energetic moves of this widely touring group, which focuses on both traditional and contemporary African and African-American dance, are always a hit with audiences. The company performs in town several times a year, at the Harris Theater for Music and Dance in December and in spring (Apr or May). Office: 6800 S. Wentworth Ave. ℂ 773/602-1135. www.muntu.com. Tickets $20–$30.

River North Dance Company **Ages 10 & up.** Chicago can be a brutal testing ground for start-up dance companies, who have to struggle to find performance space and grab publicity. But the odds didn't buckle the well-oiled knees of the River North Dance Company. This terrifically talented jazz dance ensemble performs programs of short, Broadway-style numbers by established and emerging choreographers. You never know where they'll pop up next, so call for information on upcoming shows. Office: 1016 N. Dearborn St. ℂ 312/944-2888. www.rivernorthchicago.com. Tickets $25–$45.

7 Puppet Shows

Puppet Parlor Theatre **Ages 4 & up.** Don't be fooled by the converted grocery store venue: Puppet Parlor's repertoire includes 50 different productions, including classics such as *Wizard of Oz, Hansel and Gretel,* and *Pinocchio* in an intimate theater that holds about 60 people. The well-staged, European-style marionette shows take place every Saturday and Sunday at 2pm. Call ahead for reservations. 1922 W. Montrose. ℂ 773/989-0308. Tickets $10. Subway/El: Brown Line to Montrose.

Redmoon Theater *Finds* **Ages 10 & up.** Redmoon Theater might well be the most intriguing and visionary theater company in Chicago. Founded in 1990, the company produces "spectacle theater" comprising masks, objects, and an international range of puppetry styles in indoor and outdoor venues around town—including, at least once a year lately, in Steppenwolf Theatre's studio space. Utterly hypnotic, highly acrobatic and visceral, and using minimal narration, their adaptations of Melville's *Moby Dick,* Mary Shelley's *Frankenstein,* Victor Hugo's *The Hunchback of Notre Dame,* and *Rachel's Love,* an original work based on Jewish folktales, were revelations that have earned the company an ardent and burgeoning following. Every September, Redmoon presents a "spectacle," transforming a public park into a site for performance art, larger-than-life puppet shows, and dramatic visual effects. Office at 1438 W. Kinzie St. ℂ 312/850-8440. www.redmoon.org. Tickets $18–$22.

8 Spectator Sports

Alas, Chicago's professional sports glory has faded since the days when Michael Jordan was the most recognized athlete in the world. Now most of our teams rarely rise above mediocre, despite a few high points, such as Sammy Sosa making home-run history for the Cubs. But Chicago fans are nothing if not loyal, and for that reason, attending a home game in any sport is an uplifting experience. And to look on the bright side: When our teams aren't doing so well, it's a lot easier to get tickets to the games (unless you're talking about the perennially sold-out Cubs).

Chicago Bears **Ages 8 & up.** The Bears play at the newly renovated Soldier Field, although the project was controversial and continues to be booed by architecture fans. But the original stadium, built to commemorate the soldiers of World War I, was undeniably shabby and low on amenities. The stadium's most distinctive feature, its classically inspired colonnade, was retained, but a giant addition that resembles a spaceship was crammed awkwardly on top. (Thus, the complaints that the place is an architectural disaster). But from a comfort perspective, the place is much improved. Regale your kids with stories of the notorious "Monsters of the Midway" who battered opponents into submission under the aegis of NFL founding father and legendary coach George "Papa Bear" Halas. There is still something quintessentially Chicago about bravely freezing your derriere off at Soldier Field, or, for that matter, grilling up ribs and brats in the parking lot before the Bears go to battle against our arch enemy, the Green Bay Packers. True story: I once sat through a Bears-Packers game late in the season in which it rained, then sleeted, then snowed (and still, it seemed that not one spectator left!). Just make sure you bring a thermos of hot chocolate for the kids and a flask of something warming for the adults before you experience "Bear Weather" for the first time. At Soldier Field, Lake Shore Dr. and 16th St. ℭ **847/295-6600.** www.chicagobears.com. Tickets $40–$300. Bus: 12, 127, 130, or 146.

Chicago Blackhawks **Ages 8 & up.** The 'Hawks have a devoted, impassioned following of fans who work themselves into a frenzy with the first note of the "Star Spangled Banner." But don't expect any heroics on ice along the lines of past 'Hawks legends such as Bobby Hull and Tony Esposito. Any player that turns into a star and, hence, earns the right to restructure his contract for a higher salary is immediately traded by penny-pinching owner Bill Wirtz— derided by fans and local sportswriters as "Dollar Bill." Blackhawks's practices at "The Edge," the ice facility in west suburban Bensonville (near O'Hare Airport), are open to the public; for information, call ℭ **312/455-7000.** (Practices at the United Center are not open to the public.) For a more family-friendly and affordable hockey experience, catch the semipro **Chicago Wolves** at the Allstate Arena (ℭ **847/724-GOAL;** www.chicagowolves.com). The team has been consistently excellent over the past few years and the games are geared toward all ages, with fireworks before the game and plenty of on- and off-ice entertainment (tickets $13–$30). Blackhawks at the United Center, 1901 W. Madison St. ℭ **312/455-4500.** www.chicagoblackhawks.com. Tickets $15–$100. Bus: 9 or 20.

Chicago Bulls **Ages 8 & up.** Woe is us. After dismantling the world-famous six-time NBA championship Chicago Bulls following the 1998 season, the Bulls losing 5, 10, or 15 games in a row year after year is so dismal, I almost can't write about it. Still, maybe basketball in Chicago will become fun again—who knows? But until then, do not mention the name Jerry Reinsdorf or Jerry Krause to a Chicago sports fan unless you want to be pummeled like a speed bag—the owner and general manager, respectively, have been castigated by the public and local press ever since that infamous 1998 dismantlement. Back in the glory days, the planet's most celebrated athlete, Michael Jordan, pulled off the impossible: replacing the world's perception of Chicago as gangster Al Capone's playground with an image of his royal Airness executing a signature tomahawk dunk. We started to take for granted the frenzied celebrations in the street that inevitably occurred each June in the wake of the latest championship crown. It was a wonderful boost for a perennially pessimistic sports-loving metropolis, and a rare, indelible moment when the city's white and black populations seemed to embrace in simple camaraderie and festivity. United Center, where the Bulls play, feels like an airplane hangar–size funeral parlor these days, and for the time being, tickets are worth about as much as the paper they're printed on. So grab yourself a courtside seat—there are plenty to go around. At the United Center, 1901

W. Madison St. ✆ **312/455-4000.** www.nba.com/bulls. Tickets $10–$85; purchase through Ticketmaster at ✆ **312/559-1212.** Bus: 9 or 20.

Chicago Cubs   **Ages 4 & up.** The Cubbies haven't made a World Series appearance since 1945 and haven't been World Champs since 1908, but don't let the team's less-than-stellar track record stop you. You must, absolutely must, take your kids to a game at Wrigley Field. Attend a day game. Buy a hot dog and box of Crackerjacks, and join in the chorus of "Take Me Out to the Ballgame" during the seventh-inning stretch. (Since the death of longtime announcer Harry Caray, the crowd is led by a guest singer, often a visiting celebrity.) Because Wrigley Field is small, just about every seat is decent. Families might want to avoid the bleacher seats, because fans there can get a little overzealous in their routing for the home team (and drinking). The ivy-covered outfield walls, hand-operated scoreboard, view of the shimmering lake from the upper deck, and "W" or "L" flag announcing the outcome of the game to the unfortunates who couldn't attend make Wrigley a pure slice of Americana. About a dozen tours of the ballpark are led each season on various Saturdays in the summer. Stops include the visitors' and home-team locker rooms, press box, security headquarters, and—thrill of thrills—a walk around the field itself. Tickets are $15 and are sold through the Wrigley Field ticket office (✆ **800/THE-CUBS**), or stop by the box office at 1060 W. Addison St. The entire area around the stadium, known as Wrigleyville, is surrounded by souvenir shops, sports bars, and restaurants. One sandwich shop, the **Friendly Confines,** is actually located within the stadium itself, just off the sidewalk. **Sluggers,** a sports bar with real batting cages, is right around the corner from Wrigley at 3540 N. Clark St. (✆ **773/248-0055**). At Wrigley Field, 1060 W. Addison St. ✆ **773/404-CUBS.** www.cubs. mlb.com. Tickets $14–$50; games do sell out (especially against longtime rivals such as the Mets), and most weekend and night games are sold out by Memorial Day, so it pays to call ahead. To order tickets in person, stop by the ticket windows at Wrigley Field Mon–Fri 9am–6pm, Sat 9am–4pm, and on game days. You can also order tickets online or call tickets.com at ✆ **866/ 652-2827.** Subway/El: Red Line to Addison. Bus: 22.

Chicago Fire   **Ages 4 & up.** The city's Major League Soccer team launched in 1998 and quickly became a hit with families. The team usually plays at Soldier Field from late May through October. Bringing your kids to a game is highly recommended—tickets are cheaper than for other professional sporting events, you can walk right up to the box office before a game and buy them, and kids understand soccer because many of them play it. During the summer, games usually take place in late afternoon or early evening. Regular fans of the Fire make the games fun, with organized stadium cheers and a band. The team reaches out to kids 12 and under with Sparky's Kids Club (Sparky the Dalmatian is the team's mascot), and to moms with the occasional Soccer Mom Saturday, with half-time games and prizes for moms. The occasional Kids' Fest features music, games, and clowns, so check the website for upcoming events. ✆ **312/705-7200.** www.chicago-fire.com. Tickets $15–$40; to order, call ✆ **888/MLS-FIRE.**

Chicago White Sox   **Ages 4 & up.** Located in the South Side neighborhood of Bridgeport, the former Comiskey Park (now known as **U.S. Cellular Field**) has made a real effort to be family-friendly, although the sterile stadium and the blighted neighborhood that surrounds it remain deterrents. When the owners replaced the admittedly dilapidated former stadium with a concrete behemoth that lacks the yesteryear charm of its predecessor, they did improve sightlines (if your kids are afraid of heights, I'd recommend avoiding the vertigo-inducing upper-deck seats) and added every conceivable amenity—from above-average ballpark food concessions to shops to plentiful restrooms. The endearing quality about the White Sox is their blue-collar, working-class aura with which so many Cubs-loathing South Siders identify. Games are rarely sold out, but that makes this a bargain for bona fide baseball fans. U.S. Cellular Field has the added bonus of pregame batting practice for kids (see "Sports & Games," in chapter 8) At U.S. Cellular Field, 333 W. 35th St. in the South Side neighborhood of Bridgeport. ✆ **312/674-1000.** www.whitesox.mlb.com. Tickets $12–$45, half-price on Mon (kids get in for $1 for certain Sun games). To get Sox tickets, call Ticketmaster at ✆ **866/SOX-GAME** or visit the ticket office, open Mon–Fri 10am–6pm, Sat–Sun 10am–4pm, with extended hours on game days. Subway/El: Red Line to Sox/35th St.

DePaul Blue Demons **Ages 8 & up.** The local college basketball team, the Blue Demons, were an NCAA tournament selection last season. The team has a loyal following and is a good bet for an entertaining game at a reasonable price. The season begins at the end of November. At the Allstate Arena, 6920 N. Mannheim Rd., Rosemont. Tickets $9–$40; call ✆ **773/325-7526.** (Some of their games are at the United Center.)

Northwestern Wildcats **Ages 8 & up.** The smallest of the Big Ten colleges plays football here. Although the team has occasionally surprised everyone by winning that coveted spot in the Rose Bowl, more often, Northwestern crowds like to remind themselves why they attend Northwestern and not Michigan or Wisconsin or Ohio, with cheers of "Someday, we'll be your boss" to opposing teams. At Ryan Field, 1501 Central St., in north suburban Evanston. ✆ **847/491-CATS.** www. nusports.com. Tickets $25. Subway/El: Purple Line to Central St., Evanston.

Thoroughbred Racing **Ages 6 & up.** Arlington International Racecourse, with its gleaming-white, palatial, six-story grandstand and lush gardens, is one of the most beautiful showcases for thoroughbred horse racing in the world. Arlington likes to say that it caters to families, and it must be said that the ambience here is more Disney than den-of-iniquity. It has a storied history stretching back to 1927, and its track has been graced by such equine stars as Citation, Secretariat, and Cigar. The track's annual Arlington Million (the sport's first million-dollar race) has attracted the top jockeys, trainers, and horses in past years and recently became part of the new World Series Racing Championship, which includes the Breeders Cup races. Arlington's race days are thrilling to behold, with all of racing's time-honored pageantry on display—from the bugler in traditional dress to the parade of jockeys. Sunday is Family Day, with special activities for kids 12 and under. In the past, kids have been able to see a blacksmith shoe a horse, learn about horse care from a groomer and the track veterinarian, and get goggles signed by jockeys. Chicago parents should ask about the Junior Jockey Club, which keeps kids informed of these activities. You can sign up through the website. At Arlington International Racecourse, 2200 W. Euclid Ave., Arlington Heights. ✆ **847/255-4300.** www.arlington park.com. Seating $3–$6. Gates open Wed–Sun at 11am; post times are 1:05 and 3:05pm. Season runs June 13–Oct 28. Take the Kennedy (I-94W) expwy. to the I-90 tollway and exit north on Rte. 53. Follow 53 north until you reach the Euclid exit. Or take the Metra train line to its Arlington Heights stop, which is within walking distance of the racecourse. General parking $4, valet parking $8.

9 Story Hours

Feel like you've read *The Cat in the Hat* about 10,000 times? Take your kids to one of these story hours and they can get their story fix while you get a rest— and you'll be inspiring a love of reading in your children.

Borders Books & Music **All ages.** Kids can hear stories, with special visits from costumed characters, at this story hour, held at 11am on Tuesday. 830 N. Michigan Ave. ✆ 312/573-0564. Free admission. Subway/El: Red Line to Chicago/State.

Children in Paradise *(Finds* **Ages 2 to 8.** Storytelling and monthly events makes this a hot spot for storytelling. Preschoolers are welcome at the story hour, 10:30am on Tuesday and Wednesday. 909 N. Rush. ✆ 312/951-5437. www.chicagochildrensbooks. com. Free admission. Subway/El: Red Line to Chicago/State.

The Field Museum of Natural History **Ages 2 to 4.** Designed for preschoolers, "Story Time: Fact, Fables, and Fiction" is a daily event in July and August, and a weekend afternoon event during the remainder of the year. Held in the Living Together exhibit area, stories and projects tie in with current exhibits. Roosevelt Rd. at Lake Shore Dr. ✆ 312/665-7400. Free with museum admission of $17 for adults, $11 for children. Bus: 146.

Thomas Hughes Children's Library at Harold Washington Library Center **Ages 2 and up.** Twice a month puppets act out stories, and Saturdays are packed with programs, including puppet shows, videos, crafts, author readings, and book signings. Toddler story times are offered for kids 2 years and up and include storytelling, puppetry, music, movement, and a craft, and you must sign up in advance, or if there's an opening, walk-ins are allowed. One-hour story times for ages 3 and up are available on a walk-in basis year-round. Most Saturday programs start at 2pm, but morning story hours vary, so call or log on for updates. 400 S. State St. ✆ 312/747-4200. www.chicagopubliclibrary.org. Subway/El: Red Line to Jackson/State, Brown Line to Van Buren/Library.

Women and Children First **Ages 2 to 5.** Books and poems are featured at this story hour for preschoolers, held Wednesday mornings from 10:30 to 11am. 5233 N. Clark St. ✆ 773/769-9299. Free admission. Subway/El: Red Line to Bryn Mawr, then walk several blocks west to Clark. Bus: 22.

10 Arcades

ESPN Zone **Ages 7 & up.** This 35,000-square-foot sports shrine provides arcade fans with sports-inspired video games plus the Sports Arena, where everyone can try out their skills. Future quarterbacks can try to throw the ball through moving cutouts. A simulated rock-climbing wall moves up and down like a vertical treadmill so you can never reach the top. You and your kids can dribble and shoot baskets on a half court, scoring points based on the difficulty of the shots you make. The basket can even be lowered so younger kids get a fair shot. And, you can check your scores against those of the NBA players who showed off their stuff here. If hockey's your sport, you and your kids can pretend to be NHL players, with one of you taking shots on simulated ice while the other plays goalie. The Screening Room is a fan's nirvana, with a 16-foot screen surrounded by skybox viewing suites, along with another 37 monitors to cover everything from the Super Bowl to the Madagascar Knee Volleyball Championships. 43 E. Ohio St. ✆ 312/644-ESPN. www.espnzone.com. Free admission; cost is $6 for 15-point card, $11 for a 40-point card, and on up to $101 for a 700-point card. Games "cost" 4–16 points each. Sun–Thurs 11:30am–midnight; Fri 11:30am–1am; Sat 11am–1am. Subway/El: Red Line to State/Grand.

Side Trips from Chicago

Even with all that the city proper has to offer, if you're in town for more than a few days (or if you're staying with friends or relatives in the suburbs), you might want to venture beyond the city limits and check out some of the sights in the surrounding areas.

1 Indiana Dunes State Park

53 miles SE of Chicago (in Indiana)

This all-ages destination is my favorite for escaping to the great outdoors. The scenery, with dunes and grasses fronting the lake, is reminiscent of Cape Cod. Sending your kids running up, down, and around the dunes is a great way to burn off some energy, and tiring your kids out usually makes for a nice, quiet car ride back to the city!

ESSENTIALS

To get to the dunes, you'll need to drive. Take I-94 East to Ind. 49 North (east of Porter). Follow Ind. 49 north to Route 12. Travel east on Route 12 for 3 miles to the Dorothy Buell Memorial Visitor Center, which offers restrooms and a gift shop with postcards, posters, and slides.

SEEING THE DUNES

You probably don't associate the words "sand dunes" with the Midwest, but a trip to Indiana Dunes State Park might change that. At the base of Lake Michigan, near Chesterton, Indiana, you'll find 15 miles of dunes so big you can't see over them; 3 miles of the dunes line sandy beaches. You can visit maple and oak forests, miles of sand piles covered with vegetation, marshes, and bogs, all in one state park. Plenty of well-marked trails help you explore.

Stop at the visitor center for a free map and a 10-minute slide show that will orient you. You might check out Cowles Bog, filled with ponds, wetlands, and marshes, plus delicate vegetation such as orchids, and not-so-delicate vegetation such as Venus' flytraps. West Beach offers a 3-mile trail that passes through a prairie zone, a conifer zone, and an oak forest-deciduous zone, and ends at a beach. If it's beachgoing that you're focused on, check out Kemil Beach, a long stretch of beautiful white sand. Finally, Mount Baldy is the largest "living" sand dune in the park, so named for the mounds of sand that are active in the wind.

1600 N. 25E, Chesterton, Indiana. ✆ 219/926-1952. Free admission. Nature center summer daily 10am–4pm; beaches summer daily 11am–6pm. To park, you'll find some free lots, but some summer lots require payment.

WHERE TO EAT

There are no restaurants here, so bring a picnic. You'll find plenty of picnic areas in the park, some with barbecue pits. If you're staying in downtown Chicago, good places to pick up sandwiches and drinks are Corner Bakery (p. 122) or Potbelly Sandwich Works (p. 113).

2 Kohl Children's Museum

17 miles N of Chicago

Children as young as 1 year old can enjoy this top-notch museum. (There's even an infants area, but I'd advise waiting until your child is a year old to really appreciate the museum.) In fact, many Chicago parents prefer Kohl to the Chicago Children's Museum on Navy Pier for its ease of access—you'll find much less of a crowd here than at Navy Pier. In September 2005 the museum will move to a new location in Glenview, so call for information if you're visiting after that time.

ESSENTIALS

Wilmette is located on the North Shore, a swath of suburbia between Chicago and the state border of Wisconsin that is one of the nation's most affluent residential areas.

BY CAR Go north on Lake Shore Drive, which feeds into **Sheridan Road.** Follow Sheridan it as it winds through the campus of Northwestern University in Evanston and into Wilmette. To reach the museum, turn left (west) onto Central Street (at Evanston Hospital) and follow it to Green Bay Road. Turn right on Green Bay Road and drive ¼-mile to the museum, which is on your left.

BY TRAIN Catch the **Metra** train (© **312/322-6777;** www.metrarail.com) from the Ogilvie Transportation Center at Madison and Canal streets in Chicago to Wilmette. As you exit the train, the museum will be an easy walk of a couple of blocks to the west.

SEEING THE MUSEUM

The Kohl Children's Museum packs a lot into its small square footage: The 200,000 visitors it hosts annually make it the most heavily visited museum per square foot in metropolitan Chicago. Opened in 1985, this museum is a hands-on, dress-up-and-pretend, blow-bubbles sort of place where your kids will amuse themselves for hours. They can shop at a simulated supermarket, take a voyage on a Phoenician sailing ship, and join in puppet shows and singalongs.

Permanent exhibits include **The Great Kohl Sailing Ship,** which provides a stage for imaginary play as kids journey to new worlds. The vessel is part sailing ship, part fishing vessel, and part cargo ship. Kids wear real life vests while raising and lowering the sail, using nets or rod and reel to catch schools of colorful fish, steering the ship in the wheel house, ringing the ship's bell, peeking through the portholes or loading cargo into the hold, and talking through the speaking tubes to the ship's captain.

Dominick's, a recently renovated grocery-store exhibit, gives children a chance to run the shop. Kids can role-play by pretending to be shoppers or the cashier. They're responsible for the workings of the store, from shopping to restocking to checking out. Other permanent exhibits include the **StarMax Technology Center,** a computer center that features creative learning software; **Construction Zone,** where you can be a home builder; **H20,** where kids can explore the wonders of water play; **People,** a multicultural exhibit aimed at prejudice prevention and the celebration of Chicago's diversity; and **Things That Go!,** a CTA train that entertains riders on a trip through Chicago.

165 Green Bay Rd., Wilmette. © **847/251-7781.** www.kohlchildrensmuseum.org. Admission $5 per person, $4 for seniors, free for children under age 1. Mon–Sat 9am–5pm; Sun noon–5pm.

> **Moments   A Suburban Respite**
>
> If you've made it up to the Baha'i Temple, take a stroll across Sheridan Road to **Gilson Park** for a taste of northern suburban life. Check out the sailors prepping their boats for a lake tour, families picnicking and playing Frisbee, and kids frolicking on the sandy beach. Access to the beach is restricted in the summer (the locals like to keep the Chicago riff-raff out), but in the fall and spring, you're welcome to wander (just don't expect to take a dip in the frigid water).

AN ADDITIONAL ATTRACTION

Baha'i House of Worship   While you're in the neighborhood, continue your drive up Sheridan Road in Wilmette to the most visited of all the sights in the northern suburbs, the Baha'i House of Worship, an ethereal edifice that seems not of this earth. The gleaming white stone temple, designed by the French Canadian Louis Bourgeois and completed in 1953, is essentially a soaring nine-sided 135-foot dome, draped in a delicate lacelike facade, that strongly reveals the Eastern influence of the Baha'i faith's native Iran. Surrounded by formal gardens, it is one of seven Baha'i temples in the world, and the only one in the Western Hemisphere. The dome's latticework is even more beautiful as you gaze upward from the floor of the sanctuary, which, during the day, is flooded with light. Temple members offer informal tours of the building to anyone who inquires; older children and adults with an interest in architecture will get the most out of a tour of the interior. Not only is the temple itself really a sight, but the drive on Sheridan Road is also one of the most beautiful in the Chicago area.

A word of caution if you're driving: The temple seems to appear out of nowhere as you round a particularly tight curve on Sheridan Road, and it can distract even the most focused of drivers. Take it slow and wait until you're safely parked before gazing skyward.

100 Linden Ave. (at Sheridan Rd.), Wilmette. (*C*) 847/853-2300. www.us.bahai.org/how. Free admission. Visitor center daily May–Sept 10am–8pm; Oct–Apr 10am–5pm. Temple daily from 7am. Devotional services are held Mon–Sat at 12:15pm and Sun at 1:15pm (with choral accompaniment). To get there from Chicago, take the Red Line of the El north to Howard St. Change trains for the Evanston train and go to the end of the line, Linden Ave. (Or take the Purple/Evanston Express and stay on the same train all the way.) Turn right on Linden and walk 2 blocks east. If you're driving, take the Outer Dr. (Lake Shore Dr.) north, which feeds into Sheridan Rd.

WHERE TO EAT

From the lines outside the restaurant, it appears that anyone who visits the museum is also required to stop at **Walker Bros. Original Pancake House,** located next door at 153 Green Bay Rd. ((*C*) **847/251-6000**). The place is decorated with colorful Tiffany-style lamps, warm woodwork, deep booths, and extraordinary stained-glass art windows. Expect a wait on weekends. Top choices are apple pancakes, which arrive bubbling hot and glazed with cinnamon, and German pancakes, fluffy pancakes dusted with powdered sugar and served with fruit. Kids often go for the silver-dollar pancakes in chocolate chip, blueberry, or plain varieties. Oven-baked omelets are another favorite. The restaurant also serves lunch and dinner, and offers chicken teriyaki, roast beef, chicken Dijon, Reuben sandwiches, and salads. All menu items are served throughout the day; it's open daily from 6:30am to 10pm.

3 Chicago Botanic Garden

About 25 miles N of Chicago

The Botanic Garden is a favorite of Chicago families because it's only a short drive from the city but it offers a welcome change of scenery. Even young children will enjoy the room to run (or ride in a stroller) along scenic trails, interspersed with waterfalls and fountains. Older kids can explore the fruit-and-vegetable garden (so this is where bananas come from!) and gardens of animal-shaped topiaries.

ESSENTIALS

BY CAR   Take I-90 (Kennedy Expressway) to the Edens Expressway (I-94). Go north 20 miles and continue north on Route 41 and exit on Lake Cook Road. Turn right and go ½-mile to the garden.

BY TRAIN   You can take the **Metra** North Line (© **312/322-6777;** www. metrarail.com) from Ogilvie Transportation Center at Madison and Canal streets in Chicago to Glencoe. Connect to the 213 Pace Bus to reach the Botanic Garden.

TOURING THE GARDEN

Owned by the Forest Preserve District of Cook County and managed by the 110-year-old Chicago Horticultural Society, this living preserve includes eight large lagoons and a variety of distinct botanical environments—from the Illinois prairie to an English walled garden to a three-island Japanese garden. To keep the visit manageable for kids, call ahead to find out what's blooming and grab a map from the information desk when you arrive to pick the gardens your family most wants to see. A tram tour lets kids cover more ground without getting tired, which is a real possibility in this 385-acre garden.

Also on the grounds are a large fruit-and-vegetable garden, an Enabling Garden (which shows how gardening can be adapted for people with disabilities), and a 100-acre old-growth oak woodland. The living collections are composed of more than 1.2 million plants, representing 7,000 plant types. If you're here in the summer, don't miss the extensive rose gardens (just follow the bridal parties who flock here to get their pictures taken). The Botanic Garden also is home to an exhibit hall, an auditorium, a museum, a library, education greenhouses, an outdoor pavilion, a carillon, a cafe, a designated bike path, and a garden shop. Carillon concerts are given on Monday evenings at 7pm from June 21 through August 23, with a preliminary hour-long tour.

Every summer the Botanic Garden stages a special outdoor exhibition. One year, giant animal-shaped topiaries were placed in unexpected locations throughout the grounds; the next, model railroads wound through miniature versions of American national parks. In winter the greenhouses are nice and warm, and your kids can look for a Venus' flytrap, animal-shaped topiaries, and food trees such as banana and coffee plants. Check the website or call to learn about upcoming events.

1000 Lake-Cook Rd. (just east of Edens Expwy./I-94), Glencoe. © **847/835-5440.** www.chicago-botanic.org. Free admission. Apr–Oct tram tours $5 adults, $4 seniors, $3 children 3–15. Daily 8am–sunset. Closed Dec 25. Parking $10.

WHERE TO EAT

The **Garden Café,** located within the Chicago Botanic Garden, serves soup, sandwiches, and salads as well as kids' favorites, in a cafeteria-style setting. In the summer you can sit on a patio overlooking water, and more outdoor tables sit adjacent to the Rose Garden. It's open daily from 8am to 5pm.

4 DuPage Children's Museum

About 30 miles W of Chicago

Chicago's western suburbs are rapidly expanding. Naperville, a farming area not so long ago, is now one of Illinois's largest cities. Home to the DuPage Children's Museum, Naperville also has a historic downtown. The two make for a perfect day's outing. The museum is geared to all ages, but toddlers and up will enjoy it most.

ESSENTIALS

BY CAR Take the Eisenhower Expressway West (I-290) from Chicago. Take the I-294/I-88 West exit toward Indiana/Aurora. Merge onto I-88W, the East-West Tollway. Take the Naperville Road exit and turn right on Naperville Road. Turn right on East Ogden Avenue/U.S. 34. Turn left onto North Washington Street.

BY TRAIN Catch the **Metra** Burlington Northern Santa Fe Line (© **312/322-6777**; www.metrarail.com) from Union Station on Canal Street (between Adams and Jackson Blvd.) in Chicago to Naperville.

EXPLORING THE MUSEUM

DuPage Children's Museum is located in Naperville, a historic, formerly rural community with a Main Street U.S.A. downtown district worthy of Norman Rockwell. (Naperville maintains a collection of 19th-century buildings in an outdoor museum setting known as Naper Settlement, with a lovely river walk.) At the museum, visit six "neighborhoods," where kids can learn about everything from construction to art. It's a great layout that eliminates walls, so you can keep an eye on your kids even if they are in different exhibits. **Creativity Connections** brings art, math, and science together; wee ones can enjoy black, white, and red patterns to stimulate their brains, look at themselves in mirrors, and change the color of a light's filter to see themselves in a new perspective, while older kids can play with shadows and light. **Build It** puts kid-size saws, hammers, and other real tools in kids' hands and lets them build a chair for a Beanie Baby, or saw wood. (Never fear, staff members are on hand to make sure everyone stays safe.) The littlest ones get to participate by hammering golf tees into Styrofoam and building with soft blocks. **Make It Move** turns kids into scientists experimenting with gravity. **Air-Works** lets kids walk through a wind tunnel, and with the wave of a special wand, fill up an air sock. **WaterWays** shows kids how the power of water can be harnessed, and how to use sandbags to stop the rush of a waterfall. (Waterproof aprons are on hand to keep clothes dry.) Families with very young children should plan to spend about an hour here (or longer, if attention spans allow). Older children will be happy here for 2 to 3 hours.

301 N. Washington, Naperville. © **630/637-8000**. www.dupagechildrensmuseum.org. Admission $7 adults and children over age 1, $6 seniors. Tues, Wed, Fri, and Sat 9am–5pm; Thurs 9am–8pm; Sun noon–5pm.

WHERE TO EAT

The museum has a dining area with vending machines and a microwave, and nearby you'll find plenty of fast-food restaurants. For a change of pace, try pizza at **Lou Malnati's,** 131 W. Jefferson St. (© **630/717-0700**).

5 Wonder Works

10 miles W of downtown Chicago.

Wonder Works is the Chicago area's newest children's museum, located in Oak Park, a historic and scenic suburb, with a wonderful downtown full of shops and restaurants. If your kids are over age 8, I'd recommend spending a day in Oak Park, visiting the museum, and taking a tour of the Frank Lloyd Wright Home & Studio. With younger children, I'd limit the visit to just the museum.

ESSENTIALS

BY CAR   Oak Park is about 30 minutes due west of downtown Chicago. Take North Avenue west. You will travel about 9 miles straight on North Avenue to the museum, which is located at Elmwood and North avenues, just west of Ridgeland.

BY BUS   Take the no. 72 (North Ave.) bus from the corner of Clark Street and North Avenue. It's about a 45-minute bus ride straight to the museum.

EXPLORING THE MUSEUM

Originally founded in 1991, Wonder Works lost its lease in 1995 and searched for a new home, where it reopened in 2003. The 6,500-square-foot museum is designed for kids up to age 10. The museum is funded by contributions from the likes of the Oprah Winfrey Foundation, McDonald's, and the village of Oak Park.

One permanent exhibit is **Lights, Camera, Action!,** a performance area that allows kids to be stars with a low-rise stage, costumes, and backdrops. Kids can sing a song, entertain the audience, and record it all on videotape. Professional puppeteers and storytellers use the stage too during special events throughout the year.

The **Great Outdoors** exhibit lets kids experience the wonders of the natural nighttime world. Sounds and lighting set the mood and a canopy creates a beautiful night sky; tents are set up near a glowing "campfire." Kids can also climb a ladder into a treehouse. A nature trail lets kids wander through the "outdoors," with surprises around every corner.

The **Build It!** exhibit allows children to become construction workers, architects, and engineers. Filled with a variety of small- and large-scale construction materials, this exhibit lets children plan, design, and create anything they desire, while developing their fine and gross motor skills.

6445 W. North Ave., Oak Park. © 708/383-4815. www.wonder-works.org. Admission $5 ages 1 and up. Wed–Sat 10am–5pm; Sun noon–5pm. Closed holidays.

WHERE TO EAT

An Oak Park tradition, **Peterson's,** located at 1100 W. Chicago Ave. (© **708/386-6131**), is an ice cream shop that's been serving up good ol' American favorites since 1919. In addition to wonderfully rich ice cream (try the seasonal specials that include peach in summertime and eggnog in winter), Peterson's also offers soup and sandwiches for adults, and kiddie treats such as dinosaur-shaped chicken nuggets. But the focus here is on dessert, so have your kids save plenty of room: The specialty is the Merry-Go-Round, a chocolate sundae topped with animal cookies and a parasol.

6 Cuneo Museum & Gardens

About 30 miles from downtown Chicago

Best for kids over 8, this historic mansion and grounds provide a glimpse into how people lived 100 years ago. I wouldn't recommend this museum for very young children.

ESSENTIALS

The museum is not easily accessible by public transportation. To reach the museum **by car,** take the Kennedy (I-94W) expressway north to Route 60. Go west on Route 60 and then, at the Hawthorn Mall, turn north on Milwaukee Avenue (Rte. 21).

VISITING THE MUSEUM

This is a wonderful place for older kids to see how people lived in the early 20th century. The Cuneo Museum & Gardens was designed in 1914 by architect Benjamin Marshall for Samuel Insull, founder of the powerful Commonwealth Edison electric company and a partner of Thomas Edison. Its present-day name, however, comes from John F. Cuneo, a Chicago printing magnate, philanthropist, and gentleman farmer whose family lived at this vast, luxuriant estate from 1937 to 1990.

If you want to see how the other half lives, here's your chance. The palatial mansion is designed in an opulent Italianate style, with accents such as bold ironwork decor that are reminiscent of a Venetian palazzo. Eighteen of its 32 rooms are on exhibit to the public. The centerpiece is the **Great Hall,** featuring a 30-foot ceiling with skylights over a central courtyard surrounded by marble columns and arcaded balconies. You'll also "ooh" and "ahh" over the fanciful ceiling frescoes in the unusual double dining rooms and exquisite private chapel.

Cuneo was a connoisseur of art treasures, and the core of his collection is on display here, from old-master paintings and 17th-century tapestries to a custom-made gilt-wood piano and fine Capo di Monte porcelain. The estate's grounds, which at one time spanned 3,000 acres, are now a relatively modest 75 acres. They're quite lovely, with lakes, fountains, formal gardens, antique classical statuary, and even a few peacocks and swans. There's also a conservatory housing exotic plants, and Deer Park, a wooded enclosure that's about the only vestigial reminder of Hawthorn-Mellody Farms, a former farm and dairy operation that for years attracted families with its "Wild West Town," country store, and petting zoo.

1350 N. Milwaukee Ave., Vernon Hills. (℗ 847/362-3042. www.lake-online.com/cuneo. Admission $10 adults, $9 seniors, $5 children. Tues–Sun 10am–5pm. Guided tours presented Tues–Sat at 11am, 1pm, and 3pm. Grounds fee is $5 (no fee for parking). Tour prices $10 adults, $9 seniors, $5 students and children 12 and under.

WHERE TO EAT

Hawthorne Center Mall is adjacent to the museum and features the usual array of fast-food and chain restaurants. For a more true-to-Chicago experience, head into Vernon Hills to the **Pizzeria Uno** at 545 Lakeview Pkwy. (℗ 847/918-8667).

Appendix A:
For International Visitors

Whether it's your first visit or your 10th, a trip to the United States may require an additional degree of planning. This chapter will provide you with essential information, helpful tips, and advice for the more common problems that some visitors encounter.

1 Preparing for Your Trip

ENTRY REQUIREMENTS

Check at any U.S. embassy or consulate for current information and requirements. You can also obtain a visa application and other information online at the **U.S. State Department**'s website, at **www.travel.state.gov**.

VISAS   The U.S. State Department has a **Visa Waiver Program** allowing citizens of certain countries to enter the United States without a visa for stays of up to 90 days. At press time these included Andorra, Australia, Austria, Belgium, Brunei, Denmark, Finland, France, Germany, Iceland, Ireland, Italy, Japan, Liechtenstein, Luxembourg, Monaco, the Netherlands, New Zealand, Norway, Portugal, San Marino, Singapore, Slovenia, Spain, Sweden, Switzerland, and the United Kingdom. Citizens of these countries need only a valid passport and a round-trip air or cruise ticket in their possession upon arrival. If they first enter the United States, they may also visit Mexico, Canada, Bermuda, and/or the Caribbean islands and return to the United States without a visa. Further information is available from any U.S. embassy or consulate. Canadian citizens may enter the United States without visas; they need only proof of residence.

Citizens of all other countries must have (1) a valid passport that expires at least 6 months later than the scheduled end of their visit to the United States, and (2) a tourist visa, which may be obtained without charge from any U.S. consulate.

To obtain a visa, the traveler must submit a completed application form (either in person or by mail) with a 1½-inch-square photo, and must demonstrate binding ties to a residence abroad. Usually you can obtain a visa at once or within 24 hours, but it may take longer during the summer rush from June through August. If you cannot go in person, contact the nearest U.S. embassy or consulate for directions on applying by mail. Your travel agent or airline office may also be able to provide you with visa applications and instructions. The U.S. consulate or embassy that issues your visa will determine whether you will be issued a multiple- or single-entry visa and any restrictions regarding the length of your stay.

British subjects can obtain up-to-date visa information by calling the **U.S. Embassy Visa Information Line** (© **0891/200-290**) or by visiting the Consular Section of the American Embassy London's website at www.usembassy.org.uk.

Irish citizens can obtain up-to-date visa information through the **Embassy of the USA Dublin,** 42 Elgin Rd., Dublin 4, Ireland (© **353/1-668-8777;** or by checking the Consular Section of the website at http://dublin.usembassy.gov.

Australian citizens can obtain up-to-date visa information by contacting the **U.S. Embassy Canberra,** Moonah Place, Yarralumla, ACT 2600 (© **02/6214-5600**), or by checking the U.S. Diplomatic Mission's website at http://us embassy-australia.state.gov/consular.

Citizens of **New Zealand** can obtain up-to-date visa information by contacting the **U.S. Embassy New Zealand,** 29 Fitzherbert Terr., Thorndon, Wellington (© **644/472-2068**), or get the information directly from the "For New Zealanders" section of the website at http://usembassy.org.nz.

MEDICAL REQUIREMENTS   Unless you're arriving from an area known to be suffering from an epidemic (particularly cholera or yellow fever), inoculations or vaccinations are not required for entry into the United States. If you have a medical condition that requires **syringe-administered medications,** carry a valid signed prescription from your physician—the Federal Aviation Administration (FAA) no longer allows airline passengers to pack syringes in their carry-on baggage without documented proof of medical need. If you have a disease that requires treatment with **narcotics,** you should also carry documented proof with you—smuggling narcotics aboard a plane is a serious offense that carries severe penalties in the U.S.

For **HIV-positive visitors,** requirements for entering the United States are somewhat vague and change frequently. According to the latest publication of *HIV and Immigrants: A Manual for AIDS Service Providers,* the Immigration and Naturalization Service (INS) doesn't require a medical exam for entry into the United States, but INS officials may stop individuals because they look sick or because they are carrying AIDS/HIV medicine.

If an HIV-positive noncitizen applies for a nonimmigrant visa, the question on the application regarding communicable diseases is tricky no matter which way it's answered. If the applicant checks "no," INS may deny the visa on the grounds that the applicant committed fraud. If the applicant checks "yes" or if INS suspects the person is HIV-positive, it will deny the visa unless the applicant asks for a special waiver for visitors. This waiver is for people visiting the United States for a short time, to attend a conference, for instance, to visit close relatives, or to receive medical treatment. It can be a confusing situation. For up-to-the-minute information, contact **AIDSinfo** (© **800/448-0440** or 301/519-6616 outside the U.S.; www.aidsinfo.nih.gov) or the **Gay Men's Health Crisis** (© **212/367-1000;** www.gmhc.org).

DRIVER'S LICENSES   Foreign driver's licenses are generally recognized in the U.S., but you may want to get an international driver's license if your home license is not written in English.

PASSPORT INFORMATION

Safeguard your passport in an inconspicuous, inaccessible place like a money belt. Make a copy of the critical pages, including the passport number, and store it in a safe place, separate from the passport itself. If you lose your passport, visit the nearest consulate of your native country as soon as possible for a replacement. Passport applications are downloadable from the websites listed below.

Note: The International Civil Aviation Organization has recommended a policy requiring that *every* individual who travels by air have a passport. In response, many countries are now requiring that children must be issued their own passports to travel internationally, where before those under 16 or so may have been allowed to travel on a parent or guardian's passport.

FOR RESIDENTS OF CANADA

You can pick up a passport application at any of 28 regional passport offices or most travel agencies. Canadian children who travel must have their own passports. However, if you hold a valid Canadian passport issued before December 11, 2001, that bears the name of your child, the passport remains valid for you and your child until it expires. Passports cost C$85 for those 16 years and older (valid 5 years), C$35 for children 3 to 15 (valid 5 years), and C$20 for children under 3 (valid 3 years). Applications, which must be accompanied by two identical passport-size photographs and proof of Canadian citizenship, are available at travel agencies throughout Canada or from the central **Passport Office,** Department of Foreign Affairs and International Trade, Ottawa, ON K1A 0G3 (✆ **800/567-6868;** www.dfait-maeci.gc.ca/passport). Processing takes 5 to 10 days if you apply in person, or about 3 weeks by mail.

FOR RESIDENTS OF THE UNITED KINGDOM

As a member of the European Union, you need only an identity card, not a passport, to travel to other E.U. countries. However, if you already possess a passport, it's always useful to carry it. To pick up an application for a standard 10-year passport (5-year passport for children under 16), visit the nearest Passport Office, major post office, or travel agency. You can also contact the **United Kingdom Passport Service** at ✆ **0870/571-0410** or visit its website at www. passport.gov.uk. Passports are £33 for adults and £19 for children under 16, with another £30 fee if you apply in person at a Passport Office. Processing takes about 2 weeks (1 week if you apply at the Passport Office).

FOR RESIDENTS OF IRELAND

You can apply for a 10-year passport, costing €57, at the **Passport Office,** Setanta Centre, Molesworth Street, Dublin 2 (✆ **01/671-1633;** www.irlgov.ie/iveagh). Those under age 18 and over 65 must apply for a €12 3-year passport. You can also apply at 1A South Mall, Cork (✆ **021/272-525**) or over the counter at most main post offices.

FOR RESIDENTS OF AUSTRALIA

You can get an application from your local post office or any branch of Passports Australia, but you must schedule an interview at the passport office to present your application materials. Call the **Australian Passport Information Service** at ✆ **131-232,** or visit the government website at www.passports.gov.au. Passports for adults are A$144 and for those under 18 are A$72.

FOR RESIDENTS OF NEW ZEALAND

You can pick up a passport application at any New Zealand Passports Office or download it from their website. Contact the **Passports Office** at ✆ **0800/225-050** in New Zealand or 04/474-8100, or log on to www.passports.govt.nz. Passports for adults are NZ$80 and for children under 16 are NZ$40.

CUSTOMS
WHAT YOU CAN BRING IN

Every visitor more than 21 years of age may bring in, free of duty, the following: (1) 1 liter of wine or hard liquor; (2) 200 cigarettes, 100 cigars (but not from Cuba), or 3 pounds of smoking tobacco; and (3) $100 worth of gifts. These exemptions are offered to travelers who spend at least 72 hours in the United States and who have not claimed them within the preceding 6 months. It is altogether forbidden to bring into the country foodstuffs (particularly fruit, cooked meats, and canned goods) and plants (vegetables, seeds, tropical plants, and the like). Foreign tourists may bring in or take out up to $10,000 in U.S. or foreign currency with no formalities; larger sums must be declared to U.S. Customs on entering or leaving, which includes filing form CM 4790. For more specific information regarding U.S. Customs and Border Protection, contact your nearest U.S. embassy or consulate, or the **U.S. Customs** office (℃ **202/927-1770** or www.customs.ustreas.gov).

WHAT YOU CAN TAKE HOME

U.K. citizens returning from a non-E.U. country have a Customs allowance of: 200 cigarettes; 50 cigars; 250 grams of smoking tobacco; 2 liters of still table wine; 1 liter of spirits or strong liqueurs (over 22% volume); 2 liters of fortified wine, sparkling wine or other liqueurs; 60 cubic centimeters (ml) perfume; 250 cubic centimeters (ml) of toilet water; and £145 worth of all other goods, including gifts and souvenirs. People under 17 cannot have the tobacco or alcohol allowance. For more information, contact **HM Customs & Excise** at ℃ **0845/ 010-9000** (from outside the U.K. ℃ 020/8929-0152), or consult their website at www.hmce.gov.uk.

For a clear summary of **Canadian** rules, request the booklet *I Declare,* issued by the **Canada Customs and Revenue Agency** (℃ **800/461-9999** in Canada, or 204/983-3500; www.ccra-adrc.gc.ca). Canada allows its citizens a C$750 exemption, and you're allowed to bring back duty-free one carton of cigarettes, one can of tobacco, 40 imperial ounces of liquor, and 50 cigars. In addition, you're allowed to mail gifts to Canada valued at less than C$60 a day, provided they're unsolicited and don't contain alcohol or tobacco (write on the package "Unsolicited gift, under $60 value"). All valuables should be declared on the Y-38 form before departure from Canada, including serial numbers of valuables you already own, such as expensive foreign cameras. *Note:* The C$750 exemption can only be used once a year and only after an absence of 7 days.

The duty-free allowance in **Australia** is A$400 or, for those under 18, A$200. Citizens age 18 and over can bring in 250 cigarettes or 250 grams of loose tobacco, and 1,125 milliliters of alcohol. If you're returning with valuables you already own, such as foreign-made cameras, you should file form B263. A helpful brochure available from Australian consulates or Customs offices is *Know Before You Go.* For more information, call the **Australian Customs Service** at ℃ **1300/363-263,** or log on to www.customs.gov.au.

The duty-free allowance for **New Zealand** is NZ$700. Citizens over 17 can bring in 200 cigarettes, 50 cigars, or 250 grams of tobacco (or a mixture of all three if their combined weight doesn't exceed 250g); plus 4.5 liters of wine and beer, or 1.125 liters of liquor. New Zealand currency does not carry import or export restrictions. Fill out a certificate of export, listing the valuables you are taking out of the country; that way, you can bring them back without paying duty. Most questions are answered in a free pamphlet available at New Zealand consulates and Customs offices: *New Zealand Customs Guide for Travellers, Notice no. 4.* For more information, contact **New Zealand Customs,** The Customhouse, 17–21 Whitmore St., Box 2218, Wellington (℃ **0800/428-786** or 04/473-6099; www.customs.govt.nz).

HEALTH INSURANCE

Although it's not required of travelers, health insurance is highly recommended. Unlike many European countries, the United States does not usually offer free or low-cost medical care to its citizens or visitors. Doctors and hospitals are expensive, and in most cases will require advance payment or proof of coverage before they render their services. Policies can cover everything from the loss or theft of your baggage and trip cancellation to the guarantee of bail in case you're arrested. Good policies will also cover the costs of an accident, repatriation, or death. See "Insurance & Health" in chapter 2 for more information. Packages such as **Europ Assistance's "Worldwide Healthcare Plan"** are sold by European automobile clubs and travel agencies at attractive rates. **Worldwide Assistance Services, Inc.** (*C* 800/821-2828; www.worldwideassistance.com), is the agent for Europ Assistance in the United States.

Though lack of health insurance may prevent you from being admitted to a hospital in nonemergencies, don't worry about being left on a street corner to die: The American way is to fix you now and bill the living daylights out of you later.

INSURANCE FOR BRITISH TRAVELERS   Most big travel agents offer their own insurance and will probably try to sell you their package when you book a holiday. Think before you sign. **Britain's Consumers' Association** recommends that you insist on seeing the policy and reading the fine print before buying travel insurance. **The Association of British Insurers** (*C* 020/7600-3333; www.abi. org.uk) gives advice by phone and publishes *Holiday Insurance,* a free guide to policy provisions and prices. You might also shop around for better deals: Try **Columbus Direct** (*C* 020/7375-0011; www.columbusdirect.net).

INSURANCE FOR CANADIAN TRAVELERS   Canadians should check with their provincial health plan offices or call **Health Canada** (*C* 613/957-2991; www.hc-sc.gc.ca) to find out the extent of their coverage and what documentation and receipts they must take home in case they are treated in the United States.

MONEY
CURRENCY   The U.S. monetary system is very simple: The most common **bills** are the $1 (colloquially, a "buck"), $5, $10, and $20 denominations. There are also $2 bills (seldom encountered), $50 bills, and $100 bills (the last two are usually not welcome as payment for small purchases). All the paper money was recently redesigned, making the famous faces adorning them disproportionately large. The old-style bills are still legal tender.

There are seven denominations of coins: 1¢ (1 cent, or a penny); 5¢ (5 cents, or a nickel); 10¢ (10 cents, or a dime); 25¢ (25 cents, or a quarter); 50¢ (50 cents, or a half dollar); the new gold-colored "Sacagawea" coin worth $1; and, prized by collectors, the rare, older silver dollar.

Note: The "foreign-exchange bureaus" so common in Europe are rare even at airports in the United States, and nonexistent outside major cities. It's best not to change foreign money (or traveler's checks denominated in a currency other than U.S. dollars) at a small-town bank, or even a branch in a big city; in fact, leave any currency other than U.S. dollars at home—it may prove a greater nuisance to you than it's worth.

In Chicago, if you find yourself in need of a foreign-exchange service, the Chicago consumer Yellow Pages lists names and numbers of foreign-exchange services under the heading "Foreign Exchange Brokers." In the Loop, try **World's Money Exchange, Inc.,** 203 N. LaSalle St., located on the mezzanine (*C* 312/641-2151).

TRAVELER'S CHECKS   Though traveler's checks are widely accepted, make sure that they're denominated in U.S. dollars, as foreign-currency checks are often difficult to exchange. The three traveler's checks that are most widely recognized—and least likely to be denied—are **Visa, American Express,** and

Thomas Cook. Be sure to record the numbers of the checks, and keep that information in a separate place in case they get lost or stolen. Most businesses are pretty good about taking traveler's checks, but you're better off cashing them in at a bank (in small amounts, of course) and paying in cash. *Remember:* You'll need identification, such as a driver's license or passport, to change a traveler's check.

CREDIT CARDS & ATMs   Credit cards are the most widely used form of payment in the United States: **Visa** (Barclaycard in Britain), **MasterCard** (Euro-Card in Europe, Access in Britain, Chargex in Canada), **American Express, Diners Club, Discover,** and **Carte Blanche.** There are, however, a handful of stores and restaurants that do not take credit cards, so be sure to ask in advance. Most businesses display a sticker near their entrance to let you know which cards they accept. (*Note:* Some businesses may require a minimum purchase, usually around $10, to use a credit card.) In Chicago all major credit cards are commonly accepted, and if you are a Discover cardholder, you might find it more extensively accepted than in other cities. That's because it's owned by Sears, which is based in suburban Chicago.

It is strongly recommended that you bring at least one major credit card. You must have a credit or charge card to rent a car. Hotels and airlines usually require a credit card imprint as a deposit against expenses, and in an emergency a credit card can be priceless.

You'll find **automated teller machines (ATMs)** on just about every block—at least in almost every town—across the country. Some ATMs will allow you to draw U.S. currency against your bank and credit cards. Check with your bank before leaving home, and remember that you will need your personal identification number (PIN) to do so. Most accept Visa, MasterCard, and American Express, as well as ATM cards from other U.S. banks. Expect to be charged up to $3 per transaction, however, if you're not using your own bank's ATM.

One way around these fees is to ask for cash back at grocery stores that accept ATM cards and don't charge usage fees. Of course, you'll have to purchase something first.

ATM cards with major credit card backing, known as "debit cards," are now a commonly acceptable form of payment in most stores and restaurants. Debit cards draw money directly from your checking account. Some stores enable you to receive "cash back" on your debit card purchases as well.

SAFETY
GENERAL SUGGESTIONS   Although tourist areas are generally safe, U.S. urban areas tend to be less safe than those in Europe or Japan. You should always stay alert. This is particularly true of large American cities. If you're in doubt about which neighborhoods are safe, don't hesitate to make inquiries with the hotel front-desk staff or the local tourist office.

Avoid deserted areas, especially at night, and don't go into public parks after dark unless there's a concert or similar occasion that will attract a crowd.

Travel Tip
Be sure to keep a copy of all your travel papers separate from your wallet or purse, and leave a copy with someone at home should you need it faxed in an emergency.

Avoid carrying valuables with you on the street, and keep expensive cameras or electronic equipment bagged up or covered when not in use. If you're using a map, try to consult it inconspicuously—or better yet, study it before you leave your room. Hold onto your pocketbook, and place your billfold in an inside pocket. In theaters, restaurants, and other public places, keep your possessions in sight.

Always lock your room door—don't assume that once you're inside the hotel you are automatically safe and no longer need to be aware of your surroundings. Hotels are open to the public, and in a large hotel, security may not be able to screen everyone who enters.

For more about personal safety in Chicago, see "Safety" under "Fast Facts: Chicago," in chapter 3.

DRIVING SAFETY   Driving safety is important too, and carjacking is not unprecedented. Question your rental agency about personal safety and ask for a traveler-safety brochure when you pick up your car. Obtain written directions—or a map with the route clearly marked—from the agency showing how to get to your destination. (Many agencies now offer the option of renting a cellphone for the duration of your car rental; check with the rental agent when you pick up the car. Otherwise, contact **InTouch USA** at © **800/872-7626** or www.intouchusa.com for short-term cellphone rental.) And, if possible, arrive and depart during daylight hours.

If you drive off a highway and end up in a dodgy-looking neighborhood, leave the area as quickly as possible. If you have an accident, even on the highway, stay in your car with the doors locked until you assess the situation or until the police arrive. If you're bumped from behind on the street or are involved in a minor accident with no injuries, and the situation appears to be suspicious, motion to the other driver to follow you. Never get out of your car in such situations. Go directly to the nearest police precinct, well-lit service station, or 24-hour store.

Park in well-lit and well-traveled areas whenever possible. Always keep your car doors locked, whether the vehicle is attended or unattended. Never leave any packages or valuables in sight. If someone attempts to rob you or steal your car, don't try to resist the thief/carjacker. Report the incident to the police department immediately by calling © **911.**

Size Conversion Chart

Women's Clothing

American	4	6	8	10	12	14	16
French	34	36	38	40	42	44	46
British	6	8	10	12	14	16	18

Women's Shoes

American	5	6	7	8	9	10
French	36	37	38	39	40	41
British	4	5	6	7	8	9

Men's Suits

American	34	36	38	40	42	44	46	48
French	44	46	48	50	52	54	56	58
British	34	36	38	40	42	44	46	48

(continued)

Size Conversion Chart (continued)

Men's Shirts

American	14½	15	15½	16	16½	17	17½
French	37	38	39	41	42	43	44
British	14½	15	15½	16	16½	17	17½

Men's Shoes

American	7	8	9	10	11	12	13
French	39½	41	42	43	44½	46	47
British	6	7	8	9	10	11	12

2 Getting to the U.S.

British Airways (© **0845/773-3377** in the U.K., or **800/247-9297** in the U.S.) offers direct flights from London's Heathrow Airport to Chicago. Some of the other major international carriers that service Chicago are **Aer Lingus** (© **0818/365-000** in Ireland, **0845/084-4444** in the U.K., or **800/525-7424** in the U.S.), **Air Canada** (© **888/247-2262** in Canada and the U.S.), **Qantas** (© **13-13-13** in Australia, or **800/227-4500** in the U.S.), and **Air New Zealand** (© **0800/737-767** in New Zealand, or **800/262-1234** in the U.S.). For further information about traveling to and arriving in Chicago, see the "Getting There" section in chapter 2.

AIRLINE DISCOUNTS   The smart traveler can find numerous ways to reduce the price of a plane ticket simply by taking time to shop around. For example, overseas visitors can take advantage of the APEX (Advance Purchase Excursion) reductions offered by all major U.S. and European carriers. For more money-saving airline advice, see "Getting There," in chapter 2. For the best rates, compare fares and be flexible with the dates and times of travel.

IMMIGRATION & CUSTOMS CLEARANCE   Visitors arriving by air, no matter what the port of entry, should cultivate patience and resignation before setting foot on U.S. soil. Getting through immigration control can take as long as 2 hours on some days, especially on summer weekends, so be sure to carry this guidebook or something else to read. This is especially true in the aftermath of the September 11, 2001, terrorist attacks, because security clearances have been considerably beefed up at U.S. airports.

⎛Tips   Prepare to Be Fingerprinted

Many international visitors traveling on visas to the United States are photographed and fingerprinted at Customs in a new program called **US-VISIT** created by the Department of Homeland Security in 2004. Non–U.S. citizens arriving at airports and on cruise ships must undergo an instant background check as part of the government's ongoing efforts to deter terrorism by verifying the identity of incoming and outgoing visitors. Exempt from the extra scrutiny are visitors entering by land or those from 28 countries (mostly in Europe) that don't require a visa for short-term visits. For more information, go to the Homeland Security website at **www. dhs.gov/dhspublic**.

People traveling by air from Canada, Bermuda, and certain countries in the Caribbean can sometimes clear Customs and Immigration at the point of departure, which is much quicker.

3 Getting Around the U.S.

BY PLANE   Some large airlines (for example, Northwest and Delta) offer travelers on their transatlantic or transpacific flights special discount tickets under the name **Visit USA,** allowing mostly one-way travel from one U.S. destination to another at very low prices. These discount tickets are not on sale in the United States and must be purchased abroad in conjunction with your international ticket. This system is the best, easiest, and fastest way to see the United States at low cost. You should obtain information well in advance from your travel agent or the office of the airline concerned, since the conditions attached to these discount tickets can be changed without advance notice.

BY TRAIN   International visitors (excluding Canada) can also buy a **USA Rail Pass,** good for 15 or 30 days of unlimited travel on Amtrak (© **800/USA-RAIL;** www.amtrak.com). The pass is available through many overseas travel agents. Prices in 2004 for a 15-day pass were $295 off-peak, $440 peak; a 30-day pass costs $385 off-peak, $550 peak. With a foreign passport, you can also buy passes at some Amtrak offices in the United States, including locations in San Francisco, Los Angeles, Chicago, New York, Miami, Boston, and Washington, D.C. Reservations are generally required and should be made for each part of your trip as early as possible. Regional rail passes are also available.

BY BUS   Although bus travel is often the most economical form of public transit for short hops between U.S. cities, it can also be slow and uncomfortable—certainly not an option for everyone (particularly when Amtrak, which is far more luxurious, offers similar rates). **Greyhound/Trailways** (© **800/231-2222;** www. greyhound.com), the sole nationwide bus line, offers an **International Ameripass** that must be purchased before coming to the United States, or by phone through the Greyhound International Office at the Port Authority Bus Terminal in New York City (© **212/971-0492**). The pass can be obtained from foreign travel agents or through Greyhound's website (order at least 21 days before your departure to the U.S.) and costs less than the domestic version. Passes available in 2004 were as follows: 4 days ($160), 7 days ($219), 10 days ($269), 15 days ($329), 21 days ($379), 30 days ($439), 45 days ($489), or 60 days ($599). You can get more info on the pass at the website or by calling © **402/330-8552.** In addition, special rates are available for seniors and students.

BY CAR   Unless you plan to spend the bulk of your vacation time in a city where walking is the best and easiest way to get around (like New York City or New Orleans), the most cost-effective, convenient, and comfortable way to travel around the United States is by car. The interstate highway system connects cities and towns all over the country; in addition to these high-speed, limited-access roadways, there's an extensive network of federal, state, and local highways and roads. Some of the national car-rental companies include **Alamo** (© 800/462-5266; www.alamo.com), **Avis** (© 800/230-4898; www.avis.com), **Budget** (© 800/527-0700; www.budget.com), **Dollar** (© 800/800-3665; www.dollar.com), **Hertz** (© 800/654-3131; www.hertz.com), **National** (© 800/227-7368; www.nationalcar.com), and **Thrifty** (© 800/847-4389; www.thrifty.com).

If you plan to rent a car in the United States, you probably won't need the services of an additional automobile organization. If you're planning to buy or borrow a car, automobile-association membership is recommended. **AAA,** the **American Automobile Association** (© 800/222-4357), is the country's largest auto club and supplies its members with maps, insurance, and, most important, emergency road service. The cost of joining runs from $63 for singles to $87 for two members, but if you're a member of a foreign auto club with reciprocal arrangements, you can enjoy free AAA service in America. See "Getting There" in chapter 2 for more information.

FAST FACTS: **For the International Traveler**

Automobile Organizations Auto clubs will supply maps, suggested routes, guidebooks, accident and bail-bond insurance, and emergency road service. The **American Automobile Association (AAA)** is the major auto club in the United States. If you belong to an auto club in your home country, inquire about AAA reciprocity before you leave. You may be able to join AAA even if you're not a member of a reciprocal club; to inquire, call AAA (© **800/222-4357**). AAA is actually an organization of regional auto clubs; so look under "AAA Automobile Club" in the White Pages of the telephone directory. AAA has a nationwide emergency road service telephone number (© 800/AAA-HELP).

Business Hours Offices are usually open weekdays from 9am to 5pm. Banks are open weekdays from 9am to 3pm or later and sometimes Saturday mornings. Stores typically open between 9 and 10am and close between 5 and 6pm from Monday through Saturday. Stores in shopping complexes or malls tend to stay open late—until about 9pm on weekdays and weekends, and many malls and larger department stores are open on Sunday.

Currency & Currency Exchange See "Entry Requirements" and "Money" under "Preparing for Your Trip," above.

Drinking Laws The legal age for purchase and consumption of alcoholic beverages is 21; proof of age is required and often requested at bars, nightclubs, and restaurants, so it's always a good idea to bring ID when you go out. Beer and wine often can be purchased in supermarkets, but liquor laws vary from state to state.

Do not carry open containers of alcohol in your car or any public area that isn't zoned for alcohol consumption. The police can fine you on the spot. And nothing will ruin your trip faster than getting a citation for DUI ("driving under the influence"), so don't even think about driving while intoxicated.

Electricity Like Canada, the United States uses 110–120 volts AC (60 cycles), compared to 220–240 volts AC (50 cycles) in most of Europe, Australia, and New Zealand. If your small appliances use 220–240 volts, you'll need a 110-volt transformer and a plug adapter with two flat parallel pins to operate them here. Downward converters that change 220–240 volts to 110–120 volts are difficult to find in the United States, so bring one with you.

Embassies & Consulates All embassies are located in the nation's capital, Washington, D.C. Some consulates are located in major U.S. cities, and most nations have a mission to the United Nations in New York City. If your country isn't listed below, call for directory information in Washington, D.C. (© **202/555-1212**) or log on to **www.embassy.org/embassies**.

The embassy of **Australia** is at 1601 Massachusetts Ave. NW, Washington, DC 20036 (© **202/797-3000**; www.austemb.org). There are consulates in New York, Honolulu, Houston, Los Angeles, and San Francisco.

The embassy of **Canada** is at 501 Pennsylvania Ave. NW, Washington, DC 20001 (© **202/682-1740**; www.canadianembassy.org). Other Canadian consulates are in Buffalo (N.Y.), Detroit, Los Angeles, New York, and Seattle.

The embassy of **Ireland** is at 2234 Massachusetts Ave. NW, Washington, DC 20008 (© **202/462-3939**; www.irelandemb.org). Irish consulates are in Boston, Chicago, New York, and San Francisco.

The embassy of **Japan** is at 2520 Massachusetts Ave. NW, Washington, DC 20008 (© **202/238-6700**; www.embjapan.org). Japanese consulates are located in many cities including Atlanta, Boston, Detroit, New York, San Francisco, and Seattle.

The embassy of **New Zealand** is at 37 Observatory Circle NW, Washington, DC 20008 (© **202/328-4800**; www.nzemb.org). New Zealand consulates are in Los Angeles, Salt Lake City, San Francisco, and Seattle.

The embassy of the **United Kingdom** is at 3100 Massachusetts Ave. NW, Washington, DC 20008 (© **202/462-1340**; www.britainusa.com). Other British consulates are in Atlanta, Boston, Chicago, Cleveland, Houston, Los Angeles, New York, San Francisco, and Seattle.

Emergencies Call © **911** to report a fire, call the police, or get an ambulance anywhere in the United States. This is a toll-free call (No coins are required at public telephones).

If you encounter serious problems, contact **Traveler's Aid International** (© **202/546-1127**; www.travelersaid.org) to help direct you to a local branch. This nationwide, nonprofit, social-service organization geared to helping travelers in difficult straits offers services that might include reuniting families separated while traveling, providing food and/or shelter to people stranded without cash, or even emotional counseling. If you're in trouble, seek them out.

Gasoline (Petrol) Petrol is known as gasoline (or simply "gas") in the United States, and petrol stations are known as both gas stations and service stations. Gasoline costs about half as much here as it does in Europe (about $2 per gallon at press time), and taxes are already included in the printed price. One U.S. gallon equals 3.8 liters or .85 imperial gallons.

Holidays Banks, government offices, post offices, and many stores, restaurants, and museums are closed on the following legal national holidays: January 1 (New Year's Day), the third Monday in January (Martin Luther King Day), the third Monday in February (Presidents' Day, Washington's Birthday), the last Monday in May (Memorial Day), July 4th (Independence Day), the first Monday in September (Labor Day), the second Monday in October (Columbus Day), November 11 (Veterans Day/Armistice Day), the fourth Thursday in November (Thanksgiving Day), and December 25

(Christmas). Also, the Tuesday following the first Monday in November is Election Day and is a federal government holiday in presidential-election years (held every 4 years, and next in 2008). In addition, many city offices are closed in Chicago for Casimir Pulaski Day, marking the birthday of a Polish-born Revolutionary War hero, which is observed on the first Monday in March.

Legal Aid If you are "pulled over" for a minor infraction (such as speeding), never attempt to pay the fine directly to a police officer; this could be construed as attempted bribery, a much more serious crime. Pay fines by mail, or directly into the hands of the clerk of the court. If accused of a more serious offense, say and do nothing before consulting a lawyer. Here the burden is on the state to prove a person's guilt beyond a reasonable doubt, and everyone has the right to remain silent, whether he or she is suspected of a crime or actually arrested. Once arrested, a person can make one telephone call to a party of his or her choice. Call your embassy or consulate.

Mail If you aren't sure what your address will be in the United States, mail can be sent to you, in your name, c/o General Delivery at the main post office of the city or region where you expect to be. (Call © **800/275-8777** for information on the nearest post office.) The addressee must pick up mail in person and must produce proof of identity (driver's license, passport). Most post offices will hold your mail for up to 1 month and are open Monday to Friday from 8am to 6pm, and Saturday from 9am to 3pm. Chicago's main post office is at 433 W. Van Buren St. (© **312/654-3895**).

Generally found at intersections, mailboxes are blue with a red-and-white stripe and carry the inscription U.S. MAIL. If your mail is addressed to a U.S. destination, don't forget to add the five-digit postal code (or zip code), after the two-letter abbreviation of the state to which the mail is addressed. This is essential to prompt delivery.

At press time, domestic postage rates were 23¢ for a postcard and 37¢ for a letter. For international mail, a first-class letter of up to one-half ounce costs 80¢ (60¢ to Canada and Mexico); a first-class postcard costs 70¢ (50¢ to Canada and Mexico); and a preprinted postal aerogramme costs 70¢.

Measurements See the chart on the inside front cover of this book for details on converting metric measurements to U.S. equivalents.

Taxes The United States has no value-added tax (VAT) or other indirect tax at the national level. Every state, county, and city has the right to levy its own local tax on all purchases, including hotel and restaurant checks, airline tickets, and so on.

Telephone, Telegraph, Telex & Fax The telephone system in the United States is run by private corporations, so rates, especially for long-distance service and operator-assisted calls, can vary widely. Generally, hotel surcharges on long-distance and local calls are astronomical, so you're usually better off using a **public pay telephone,** which you'll find clearly marked in most public buildings and private establishments as well as on the street. Convenience grocery stores and gas stations always have them. Many convenience groceries and packaging services sell **prepaid calling**

cards in denominations up to $50; these can be the least expensive way to call home. Many public phones at airports now accept American Express, MasterCard, and Visa credit cards. **Local calls** made from public pay phones in most locales cost either 25¢ or 35¢. Pay phones do not accept pennies, and few will take anything larger than a quarter.

You may want to look into leasing a cellphone for the duration of your trip.

Most long-distance and international calls can be dialed directly from any phone. **For calls within the United States and to Canada,** dial 1 followed by the area code and the seven-digit number. **For other international calls,** dial 011 followed by the country code, city code, and the telephone number of the person you are calling.

Calls to area codes **800, 888, 877,** and **866** are toll-free. However, calls to numbers in area codes **700** and **900** (chat lines, bulletin boards, "dating" services, and so on) can be very expensive—usually a charge of 95¢ to $3 or more per minute, and they sometimes have minimum charges that can run as high as $15 or more.

For **reversed-charge or collect calls,** and for person-to-person calls, dial 0 (zero, not the letter O) followed by the area code and number you want; an operator will then come on the line, and you should specify that you are calling collect, or person-to-person, or both. If your operator-assisted call is international, ask for the overseas operator.

For **local directory assistance** ("information"), dial ✆ 411; for long-distance information, dial 1, then the appropriate area code and 555-1212.

Telegraph and telex services are provided primarily by Western Union. You can bring your telegram into the nearest Western Union office (there are hundreds across the country) or dictate it over the phone (✆ **800/ 325-6000**). You can also telegraph money, or have it telegraphed to you, very quickly over the Western Union system, but this service can cost as much as 15% to 20% of the amount sent.

Most hotels have **fax machines** available for guest use (be sure to ask about the charge to use it). Many hotel rooms are even wired for guests' fax machines. A less expensive way to send and receive faxes may be at stores such as **The UPS Store** (formerly Mail Boxes Etc.), a national chain of retail packing service shops. (Look in the Yellow Pages directory under "Packing Services.")

There are two kinds of telephone directories in the United States. The so-called **White Pages** list private households and business subscribers in alphabetical order. The inside front cover lists emergency numbers for police, fire, ambulance, the Coast Guard, poison-control center, crime-victims hot line, and so on. The first few pages will tell you how to make long-distance and international calls, complete with country codes and area codes. Government numbers are usually printed on blue paper within the White Pages. Printed on yellow paper, the so-called **Yellow Pages** list all local services, businesses, industries, and houses of worship according to activity with an index at the front or back. (Drugstores/pharmacies and restaurants are also listed by geographic location.) The Yellow Pages also include city plans or detailed area maps, postal zip codes, and public transportation routes.

Time The continental United States is divided into **four time zones:** Eastern Standard Time (EST), Central Standard Time (CST), Mountain Standard Time (MST), and Pacific Standard Time (PST). Alaska and Hawaii have their own zones. For example, noon in New York City (EST) is 11am in Chicago (CST), 10am in Denver (MST), 9am in Los Angeles (PST), 8am in Anchorage (AST), and 7am in Honolulu (HST).

Daylight saving time is in effect from 2am on the first Sunday in April through 2am on the last Sunday in October, except in Arizona, Hawaii, most of Indiana, and Puerto Rico. Daylight saving time moves the clock 1 hour ahead of standard time.

Tipping Tips are a very important part of certain workers' income, and gratuities are the standard way of showing appreciation for services provided. (Tipping is certainly not compulsory if the service is poor!) In hotels, tip **bellhops** at least $1 per bag ($2–$3 if you have a lot of luggage) and tip the **chamber staff** $1 to $2 per day (more if you've left a disaster area for him or her to clean up). Tip the **doorman** or **concierge** only if he or she has provided you with some specific service (for example, calling a cab for you or obtaining difficult-to-get theater tickets). Tip the **valet-parking attendant** $1 every time you get your car.

In restaurants, bars, and nightclubs, tip **service staff** 15% to 20% of the check, tip **bartenders** 10% to 15%, tip **checkroom attendants** $1 per garment, and tip **valet-parking attendants** $1 per vehicle.

As for other service personnel, tip **cab drivers** 15% of the fare, tip **skycaps** at airports at least $1 per bag ($2–$3 if you have a lot of luggage), and tip **hairdressers** and **barbers** 15% to 20%.

Toilets You won't find public toilets or "restrooms" on the streets in most U.S. cities, but they can be found in hotel lobbies, bars, restaurants, museums, department stores, railway and bus stations, and service stations. Large hotels and fast-food restaurants are probably the best bet for good, clean facilities. If possible, avoid the toilets at parks and beaches, which tend to be dirty; some may be unsafe. Restaurants and bars in resorts or heavily visited areas may reserve their restrooms for patrons. Some establishments display a notice indicating this. You can ignore this sign or, better yet, avoid arguments by paying for a cup of coffee or a soft drink, which will qualify you as a patron.

Tour Guides There are two respected multilingual tour guide services in Chicago: **Chicago Tour Guides Institute** (✆ **773/276-6683;** fax 773/252-3729; www.chicagoguide.net) and **Inlingua International Tours** (✆ **312/641-0488;** fax 312/641-1724).

Appendix B:
Chicago in Depth

by Elizabeth Canning Blackwell

1 History 101

By virtue of its location, Chicago became the great engine of America's westward expansion. The particular patch of land where Chicago now stands straddles a key point along an inland water route linking Canada, via Lake Erie, to New Orleans and the Gulf of Mexico by way of the Mississippi River.

The French, busy expanding their own territory in North America throughout the 17th and 18th centuries, were the first Europeans to survey the topography of the future Chicago. The French policy in North America was simple—to gradually settle the Mississippi Valley and the Northwest Territory (modern Ohio, Indiana, Michigan, Illinois, Wisconsin, and Minnesota). The policy relied on an alliance between religion and commerce: The French sought a monopoly over the fur trade with the Native American tribes, whose pacification and loyalty they attempted to ensure by converting them to Catholicism.

The team of Jacques Marquette, a Jesuit missionary, and Louis Joliet, an explorer, personified this policy to perfection. In 1673 the pair found a very short portage between two critically placed rivers, the Illinois and the Des Plaines. One was connected to the Mississippi, and the other, via the Chicago River, was connected to Lake Michigan and then onward to Montreal and Quebec.

Chicago owes its existence to this strategic 1½-mile portage trail that the Native Americans had blazed in their

Dateline

- 1673 French explorers Marquette and Joliet discover portage at Chicago linking the Great Lakes region with the Mississippi River valley.
- 1779 Afro-French-Canadian trapper Jean Baptiste Point du Sable establishes a trading post on the north bank of the Chicago River. A settlement follows 2 years later.
- 1794 Gen. "Mad" Anthony Wayne defeats the British in the Battle of Fallen Timbers; disputed Illinois Territory is finally ceded to the young American Republic by treaty a year later.
- 1803 Garrison of Fort Dearborn is established in Chicago, commanded by the grandfather of artist James McNeill Whistler.
- 1812 Incited by the British in the War of 1812, Pottawatomie Indians destroy Fort Dearborn and slay its residents.
- 1816 Fort Dearborn is rebuilt.
- 1818 Illinois is admitted to the Union as the 21st state.
- 1833 Town of Chicago is officially incorporated, with little more than 300 residents.
- 1837 Chicago is incorporated as a city, with about 4,000 residents.
- 1847 *Chicago Tribune* begins publishing.
- 1848 The 96-mile Illinois and Michigan Canal is opened, linking the Great Lakes with the Mississippi River.
- 1850 Chicago's population is roughly 30,000.
- 1856 Chicago is chief railroad center in the United States.
- 1860 Republican National Convention in Chicago nominates Abraham Lincoln for the presidency.

continues

own water travels over centuries of moving throughout this territory. Marquette himself was on the most familiar terms with the Native Americans, who helped him make his way over the well-established paths of their ancestral lands. The Native Americans, of course, did not anticipate the European settlers' hunger for such prime real estate. Because the Chicago River provided a crucial link between the Great Lakes and the Mississippi River, the frontier city was destined to grow into the nation's great midcontinental hub of transportation and transshipment, facilitating travel and trade between the eastern settlements and the West.

FIRST SETTLEMENT

Over the next 100 years, the French used this waterway to spread their American empire from Canada to Mobile, Alabama. Yet the first recorded settlement in Chicago, a trading post built by a French Canadian of Haitian descent, Jean Baptiste Point du Sable, did not appear until 1781. By this time the British already had conquered the territory, part of the spoils of 70 years of intermittent warfare that cost the French most of their North American holdings. After the American War of Independence, the Illinois Territory was wrested from British/Native American control in a campaign led by the Revolutionary War hero Gen. "Mad" Anthony Wayne, which ended with a treaty in 1795 ceding the land around the mouth of the Chicago River to the United States.

Between du Sable's day and 1833, when Chicago was officially founded, the land by the mouth of the Chicago River served as a military outpost that guarded the strategic passage and provided security for a few trappers and a trading post. The military base, Fort Dearborn, which stood on the south side of what is now the Michigan

1865 After Lincoln's assassination, his body lies in state at the Chicago Courthouse before burial in Springfield. More than 125,000 mourners pay their respects.

1865 Chicago stockyards are founded.

1870 City's population numbers almost 300,000, making it perhaps the fastest-growing metropolis in history.

1871 Great Chicago Fire burns large sections of the city; rebuilding begins while the ashes are still warm.

1882 The 10-story Montauk Building, the world's first skyscraper, is erected.

1885 William Le Baron Jenney's nine-story Home Insurance Building, the world's first steel-frame skyscraper, is built.

1886 Dynamite bomb explodes during a political rally near Haymarket Square, causing a riot in which eight policemen and four civilians are killed, and almost 100 are wounded. Eight labor leaders and socialist-anarchists, demanding an 8-hour day, are later convicted in one of the country's most controversial trials. Four are eventually hanged.

1892 The city's first elevated train goes into operation.

1893 Completely recovered from the Great Fire, Chicago hosts its first World's Fair, the World's Columbian Exposition. The world's first Ferris wheel is a big draw.

1894 Led by Eugene V. Debs, members of the American Railway Union hold a massive strike against the Pullman Palace Car Company; President Grover Cleveland calls in federal troops after 2 months, ending the strike.

1900 The flow of the Chicago River is reversed to end the dumping of sewage into Lake Michigan.

1905 Wobblies, or Industrial Workers of the World (IWW), is founded in Chicago.

1905 Robert S. Abbott founds the *Chicago Defender,* which becomes the nation's premier African-American newspaper and later plays a major role in encouraging Southern blacks to move north during the "Great Migration" years.

Avenue Bridge, was first garrisoned in 1803 under the command of Captain John Whistler, grandfather of the famous painter.

At first the settlement grew slowly, impeded by continued Native American efforts to drive the new Americans from the Illinois Territory. During the War of 1812, inhabitants abandoned Fort Dearborn, and many were slain during the evacuation. But before long the trappers drifted back; by 1816 the military too had returned.

Conflict diminished after that, but even as a civil engineer plotted the building lots of the early town as late as 1830, periodic raids continued, ceasing only with the defeat of Chief Black Hawk in 1832. A year later the settlement of 300-plus inhabitants was officially incorporated under the name Chicago, said to derive from a Native American word referring to the powerful odors of the abundant wild vegetation (most likely onions) in the marshlands surrounding the riverbanks.

COMMERCE & INDUSTRY

Land speculation began immediately, as Chicago was carved piecemeal and sold off to finance the Illinois and Michigan Canal that would eliminate the narrow land portage and fulfill the long-standing vision of connecting the two great waterways. Thus the domesticated East would be linked to the pioneer West, with Chicago at midpoint, directing the flow of commerce in both directions. Commercial activity was quick to follow: Within 2 to 3 years, local farmers in the outlying areas were producing a surplus. Chicago grew in size and wealth, shipping grain and livestock to the eastern markets and lumber to the treeless prairies of the West. Ironically, by the time the Illinois and Michigan Canal was completed in 1848, the railroad had arrived, and the water route that gave Chicago its raison d'être was rapidly

- **1908** The Chicago Cubs win their second World Series. They haven't won one since!
- **1917** The Chicago White Sox win the World Series. They haven't won one since!
- **1919** "Black Sox" bribery scandal perpetrated by eight Chicago White Sox players stuns baseball.
- **1920–33** During Prohibition, Chicago becomes a "wide-open town"; rival mobs battle violently throughout the city for control of distribution and sale of illegal alcohol.
- **1924** University of Chicago students Nathan Leopold and Richard Loeb murder 14-year-old Bobby Franks. They are defended by famed attorney Clarence Darrow and are found guilty but spared the death penalty, in the "Trial of the Century."
- **1929** On St. Valentine's Day, Al Capone's gang murders seven members of rival George "Bugs" Moran's crew in a Clark Street garage.
- **1931** Al Capone finally goes to jail, not for bootlegging or murder but for tax evasion.
- **1932** Franklin Delano Roosevelt is nominated for the presidency by the Democratic National Convention, held at Chicago Stadium (since demolished).
- **1933** Chicago Mayor Anton Cermak, on a political trip to Miami, is shot and killed during an attempt on president-elect FDR's life.
- **1933–34** Chicago hosts its second World's Fair, "A Century of Progress." The biggest attraction is fan dancer Sally Rand, who wears only two large ostrich feathers.
- **1934** Bank robber and "Public Enemy Number One" John Dillinger is gunned down by police outside the Biograph Theater.
- **1942** Scientists, led by Enrico Fermi, create the world's first nuclear chain reaction under Stagg Field at the University of Chicago.
- **1945** The Chicago Cubs make their last appearance in the World Series—and lose to Detroit.

continues

becoming obsolete. Boxcars, not boats, grabbed the title of principal mode of transportation throughout the region. The combination of the railroad and the emergence of local manufacturing, and, later, the Civil War, caused Chicago to grow wildly.

The most revolutionary product of the era sprang from the mind of Chicago inventor Cyrus McCormick, whose reaper filled in for the farmhands who now labored on the nation's battlefields. Local merchants not only thrived on the contraband trade in cotton, but also secured lucrative contracts from the federal government to provide the army with tents, uniforms, saddles, harnesses, lumber, bread, and meat. By 1870, Chicago's population had grown to 300,000, a thousand times greater than its original population, in the brief interval of 37 years since the city's incorporation.

THE GREAT FIRE

A year later, the city lay in ashes. The Great Chicago Fire of 1871 began somewhere on the southwest side of the city on October 8. Legend places its exact origin in the O'Leary shed on DeKoven Street, although most historians have since exonerated the long-blamed bovine that locals speculate started the blaze by kicking over a lantern. The fire jumped the river and continued northward through the night and the following day, when it was checked by the use of gunpowder on the South Side and rainfall to the north and west, just before spreading to the prairie. In its wake the fire destroyed 18,000 buildings and left 90,000 homeless, taking a toll of 300 lives.

One thing that the fire could not destroy was Chicago's strategic location, and on that solid geographic footing, the city began to rebuild as soon as the rubble was cleared. By chance, Chicago's railroad infrastructure—factories, grain warehouses, and

1953 Chicago native Hugh Hefner starts publishing *Playboy* (the original Playboy Mansion was located in Chicago's Gold Coast neighborhood).

1955 Richard J. Daley begins term as mayor; he is widely regarded as the "last of the big-city bosses."

1959 Chicago White Sox make their last World Series appearance, losing to Los Angeles.

1960 John F. Kennedy and Richard Nixon hold the first televised presidential debate in WBBM-TV's studios.

1966 Civil rights leader Martin Luther King, Jr., moves to Chicago to lead a fair-housing campaign.

1968 After King's assassination, much of the West Side burns during heavy rioting. Anti–Vietnam War protests in conjunction with the Democratic National Convention end in police riot and a "shoot to kill" order by Mayor Richard J. Daley.

1969 Fred Hampton and Mark Clark are killed in a police raid on the West Side headquarters of the radical Black Panther party.

1974 The 1,454-foot Sears Tower is completed, becoming the tallest building in the world.

1976 Mayor Daley dies in office.

1979 Jane Byrne becomes the first woman elected mayor of Chicago.

1983 Harold Washington becomes the first African-American mayor of Chicago.

1986 The Chicago Bears win their only Super Bowl.

1987 Mayor Washington dies in office.

1989 Richard M. Daley, the son of the long-serving mayor, is elected mayor.

1992 A freight tunnel ruptures; the Loop is flooded underground by water from the Chicago River.

1994 Chicago hosts portions of soccer's World Cup, including the opening ceremonies.

1996 The city patches up its turbulent political history by hosting the Democratic National Convention, its first national political gathering in 3 decades. William Jefferson Clinton is nominated for a second term.

lumberyards—was also spared because it was located beyond the circle of fire on the southern periphery of the city. By 1873 the city's downtown business and financial district was up and running again, and 2 decades later Chicago had sufficiently recovered to host the 1893 World's Columbian Exposition commemorating the 400th anniversary of the discovery of America.

The Great Fire gave an unprecedented boost to the professional and artistic development of the nation's architects—drawn by the unlimited opportunities to build, they gravitated to the city in droves. And the city raised its own homegrown crop of architects. Chicago's deserved reputation as an American Athens, packed

- 1999 Michael Jordan, arguably the best basketball player ever, retires (for the second time) after leading the Chicago Bulls to six NBA Championships in the previous 8 years.

- 2000 The Goodman Theatre opens its new $46 million theater complex in the Loop, completing the revitalization of a downtown theater district.

- 2001 Chicago's second airport, Midway, opens a new $800 million terminal, attracting new airlines and giving travelers more options for Chicago flights.

- 2004 Millennium Park, Chicago's largest public works project in decades, opens at the north end of Grant Park. The centerpiece of the development is a modern, steel-sheathed band shell designed by famed architect Frank Gehry.

with monumental and decorative buildings, is a direct by-product of the disastrous fire that nearly brought the city to ruin.

In the meantime, Chicago's population continued to grow as many immigrants forsook the uncultivated farmland of the prairie to join the city's labor pool. Chicago still shipped meat and agricultural commodities around the nation and the world, but the city itself was rapidly becoming a mighty industrial center in its own right, creating finished goods, particularly for the markets of the ever-expanding western settlements.

THE CRADLE OF TRADE UNIONISM

Chicago never seemed to outgrow its frontier rawness. Greed, profiteering, exploitation, and corruption were as critical to its growth as hard work, ingenuity, and civic pride. The spirit of reform arose most powerfully from the ranks of the working classes, whose lives were plagued by poverty and disease, despite the city's prosperity. When the sleeping giant of labor finally awakened in Chicago, it did so with a militancy and commitment that were to inspire the union movement throughout the nation.

By the 1890s, many of Chicago's workers were already organized into the American Federation of Labor. The Pullman Strike of 1894 united black and white railway workers for the first time in a common struggle for higher wages and workplace rights. The Industrial Workers of the World, aka the Wobblies, which embraced for a time so many great voices of American labor—Eugene V. Debs, Big Bill Haywood, and Helen Gurley Flynn—was founded in Chicago in 1905.

AN AFRICAN-AMERICAN CAPITAL

The major change in Chicago in the 20th century, however, stemmed from the enormous growth of the city's African-American population. Coincident with the beginning of World War I, Chicago became the destination for thousands of blacks leaving Mississippi and other parts of the Deep South. Most settled on the South Side. With the exception of Hyde Park, which absorbed the black population into a successfully integrated, middle-class neighborhood, Chicago gained a reputation over the decades as the most segregated city in the United

States. Today, although increased black representation in local politics and other institutions has eased some racial tensions, the city remains far more geographically segregated than most of its urban peers.

THE CHICAGO MACHINE

While Chicago was becoming a center of industry, transportation, and finance, and a beacon of labor reform, it was also becoming a powerhouse in national politics—again by virtue of its location. Between 1860 and 1968, Chicago was the site of 14 Republican and 10 Democratic presidential nominating conventions. (Some even point to the conventions as the source of Chicago's "Windy City" nickname, laying the blame on a politician who was full of hot air.) The first of the conventions gave the country one of its most admired leaders, Abraham Lincoln, while the 1968 convention was witness to the so-called Days of Rage, a police riot against demonstrators who had camped out in Grant Park to protest the Vietnam War. As TV cameras rolled, the demonstrators chanted, "The whole world is watching."

And it was; many politicos blame Mayor Richard J. Daley for Hubert Humphrey's defeat in the general election. (Maybe it was a wash; some also say that Daley stole the 1960 election for Kennedy.)

A few words about (the original) Mayor Daley: He did not invent the political machine, but he certainly perfected it. As Theodore White writes in *America in Search of Itself,* "Daley ran the machine with a tribal justice akin to the forest Gauls." Daley understood that as long as the leaders of every ethnic and special-interest group had their share of the spoils—the African Americans controlled the South Side, for example, and the Polish Americans kept their neighborhoods segregated—he could retain ultimate power. His reach extended well beyond Chicago's borders; he controlled members of Congress in Washington, and every 4 years he delivered a solid Democratic vote in the November elections. Since his death in 1976, the machine has never been the same. One election produced the city's first female mayor, Jane Byrne; another resulted in the city's first African-American mayor, Harold Washington. Neither was a novice at politics, but neither could hold the delicate balance of (often conflicting) groups that kept Daley in power for 20 years.

Today, Daley's son, Richard M., may have inherited his father's former office, but the estate did not include the Cook County machine. Mayor Richard M. Daley has abandoned his late father's power base of solid white working-class Bridgeport for the newly developed (some would say yuppie) Central Station neighborhood just south of the Loop. The middle-aged baby boomer appears to be finding himself, but many in the city still enjoy calling him—with more than a hint of condescension—"Richie."

The city has ongoing problems. With roughly 2.8 million people total, Chicago's black and white populations are almost equal in size—a rarity among today's urban areas—but the city's residential districts continue to be some of the most segregated in the country. Families are also trying to cope with the school system, which has been undergoing a major restructuring but whose outlook is still dismal. In 1995 the federal government seized control of the city's public housing, pledging to replace the dangerous high-rises with smaller complexes in mixed-income neighborhoods. It is a long-term goal, but authorities have been gradually tearing down the notorious apartment buildings of Cabrini Green, where then-mayor Jane Byrne moved briefly to show her support for the crime-victimized residents.

2 The Politics of Clout

by Chris Serb

To understand Chicago, you must first take into account its two greatest passions: politics and sports. In this town the two are often indistinguishable from each other. Forget Tammany Hall. More than any other city, Chicago has earned a reputation for machinations and shady dealings among its politicians. It has always been a city where "clout" rules. A place where any $40,000-a-year alderman can amass a million-dollar fortune by making a few key zoning changes. A place where a sewer worker's job is safe only if he delivers 200 registered Democrats to the polls each election day. A place where cops can pocket a couple hundred dollars a week by giving gamblers and prostitutes special "protection." A place where dead people regularly turn out to vote by the thousands.

"Chicago ain't ready for reform," once declared Alderman Paddy Bauler, a jolly, beer-drinking character who ran his ward office out of the back of a saloon during one of the city's more colorful political eras.

Bauler was speaking of the 1950s and 1960s, when Mayor Richard J. Daley's "Machine" Democrats had a stranglehold on the cops, the courts, the bribes, and, most important, the jobs. He could just as easily have been talking about 1999, when City Treasurer Miriam Santos was convicted of twisting businessmen's arms for political "donations" from her City Hall office. (She was later retried on the same charges and exonerated, and she waltzed right back into her office, much to the chagrin of Mayor Richard M. Daley.)

Corruption was nothing new to the Windy City, even in Bauler's day. Turn-of-the-20th-century First Ward bosses Michael "Hinky Dink" Kenna and "Bathhouse" John Coughlin put the organization in "organized" crime by collecting fees from the gambling and prostitution houses. During Prohibition, Mayor William "Big Bill" Thompson and his Republican Machine made a fortune in bribes from Al Capone and his bootleggers—and, in the process, Big Bill disillusioned the voters so much that the GOP hasn't won the mayor's office in the 70 years since then.

Until the 1970s, however, being on the take not only was profitable business, but it also was safe: Cops and precinct workers and lesser public servants might have done a little time in jail, but the big fish were never caught. U.S. Attorney Jim Thompson changed all that, winning convictions against Gov. Otto Kerner, who took a racetrack bribe; Alderman Paul Wigoda, who took payoffs in return for zoning changes; and the elder Daley's top lieutenant, Alderman Tom Keane, who found out where the city wanted to build parks or schools or housing projects, bought the land, and then sold it back to the city at inflated prices. By trying—and winning—so many high-profile cases, the Republican Thompson swept right into the governor's mansion and left the squeaky-clean U.S. Attorney's office and the FBI trying to match his record. So far, they've done a good job, winning convictions against almost 50 aldermen and key city officials in the past 25 years.

Large-scale corruption investigations include "Operation Silver Shovel," which nabbed six aldermen (including the once-saintly Lawrence Bloom) for taking bribes connected to an illegal construction-debris dumping site; "Operation Haunted Hall," which trapped several city officials paying friends and relatives full salaries for jobs that didn't exist; "Operation Incubator," which convicted 15 aldermen, city officials, and businessmen in a city-hall bribery sting; and, the granddaddy of them all, "Operation Greylord," where after hearing reports that defendants in Cook County courts were bribing judges, the FBI and local police officials set up phony robberies and drunk-driving cases, then secretly taped judges and other courthouse staff accepting payments to make the charges disappear. In all, more than 50 lawyers and 15 judges were sent to jail—and there was nobody they could pay to make those charges go away.

Other scandals, wrapping up only one or two politicians at a time, might have been smaller in scope but have had just as high a profile. Chicago-based Congressmen Dan Rostenkowski and Mel Reynolds did hard time, respectively, for skimming Congressional office funds and for having sex with a 15-year-old campaign worker. Mayor Daley's top lieutenant, Alderman Pat Huels, used his city position to drum up business for his security firm and was later forced to resign. Even "reform mayor" Harold Washington, an alleged ghost payroller himself during his early days in politics, once went to jail for repeatedly failing to file his income taxes.

The voters forgave Harold for his ethical lapses, although they almost didn't forgive him for the ethnical "lapse" of being black. White voters and aldermen and city workers were afraid that Washington would seize the clout that had always belonged to them and take the jobs, city contracts, and key political appointments that went with the clout. And, of course, that's what Harold did.

Race shouldn't have played much of an issue, though. Washington was just following a time-honored Chicago tradition. He was doing for the black community what Kenna and Coughlin and the original Daley had done for the Irish, what Fred Roti and Anthony Laurino had done for the Italians, what Jacob Arvey had done for the Jews, what Rostenkowski and Roman Pucinski did for the Poles. Harold simply stuck his hand out and recited the city's unofficial motto, *"Ubi est mea?"*—"Where is mine?" Paddy Bauler would've been proud.

Appendix C: Useful Toll-Free Numbers & Websites

AIRLINES

Air Canada
☎ 888/247-2262
www.aircanada.ca

Air Jamaica
☎ 800/523-5585 in U.S.
☎ 888/359-2475 in Jamaica
www.airjamaica.com

Air New Zealand
☎ 800/262-1234 or 800/262-2468
  in the U.S.
☎ 800/663-5494 in Canada
☎ 0800/737-767 in New Zealand
www.airnewzealand.com

AirTran Airlines
☎ 800/247-8726
www.airtran.com

Alaska Airlines
☎ 800/252-7522
www.alaskaair.com

American Airlines
☎ 800/433-7300
www.aa.com

American Trans Air
☎ 800/225-2995
www.ata.com

America West Airlines
☎ 800/235-9292
www.americawest.com

British Airways
☎ 800/247-9297
☎ 0345/222-111 or 0845/77-333-77
  in Britain
www.british-airways.com

BWIA
☎ 800/538-2492
www.bwee.com

Continental Airlines
☎ 800/525-0280
www.continental.com

Delta Air Lines
☎ 800/221-1212
www.delta.com

Frontier Airlines
☎ 800/432-1359
www.frontierairlines.com

JetBlue Airlines
☎ 800/538-2583
www.jetblue.com

Mexicana
☎ 800/531-7921 in the U.S.
☎ 01800/502-2000 in Mexico
www.mexicana.com

Midwest Express
☎ 800/452-2022
www.midwestexpress.com

Northwest Airlines
☎ 800/225-2525
www.nwa.com

Olympic Airways
☎ 800/223-1226 in the U.S.
☎ 80/111-44444 in Greece
www.olympic-airways.gr

Southwest Airlines
☎ 800/435-9792
www.southwest.com

Spirit Airlines
☎ 800/772-7117
www.spiritair.com

TACA
☎ 800/535-8780 in U.S.
☎ 503/267-8222 in El Salvador
www.taca.com

United Airlines
☎ 800/241-6522
www.united.com

US Airways
☎ 800/428-4322
www.usairways.com

Virgin Atlantic Airways
☎ 800/862-8621 in continental U.S.
☎ 0293/747-747 in Britain
www.virgin-atlantic.com

CAR-RENTAL AGENCIES

Advantage
☎ 800/777-5500
www.advantagerentacar.com

Alamo
☎ 800/327-9633
www.alamo.com

Auto Europe
☎ 800/223-5555
www.autoeurope.com

Avis
☎ 800/331-1212 in continental U.S.
☎ 800/TRY-AVIS in Canada
www.avis.com

Budget
☎ 800/527-0700
www.budget.com

Dollar
☎ 800/800-4000
www.dollar.com

Enterprise
☎ 800/325-8007
www.enterprise.com

Hertz
☎ 800/654-3131
www.hertz.com

Kemwel Holiday Auto (KHA)
☎ 800/678-0678
www.kemwel.com

National
☎ 800/CAR-RENT
www.nationalcar.com

Payless
☎ 800/PAYLESS
www.paylesscarrental.com

Rent-A-Wreck
☎ 800/535-1391
www.rentawreck.com

Thrifty
☎ 800/367-2277
www.thrifty.com

MAJOR HOTEL & MOTEL CHAINS

Best Western International
☎ 800/528-1234
www.bestwestern.com

Clarion Hotels
☎ 800/CLARION
www.clarionhotel.com
www.hotelchoice.com

Comfort Inns
☎ 800/228-5150
www.hotelchoice.com

Courtyard by Marriott
☎ 800/321-2211
www.courtyard.com
www.marriott.com

Days Inn
☎ 800/325-2525
www.daysinn.com

Doubletree Hotels
☎ 800/222-TREE
www.doubletree.com

Econo Lodges
☎ 800/55-ECONO
www.hotelchoice.com

Fairfield Inn by Marriott
☎ 800/228-2800
www.marriott.com

Four Seasons
☎ 800/819-5053
www.fourseasons.com

Hampton Inn
☎ 800/HAMPTON
www.hampton-inn.com

Hilton Hotels
✆ 800/HILTONS
www.hilton.com

Holiday Inn
✆ 800/HOLIDAY
www.basshotels.com

Howard Johnson
✆ 800/654-2000
www.hojo.com

Hyatt Hotels & Resorts
✆ 800/228-9000
www.hyatt.com

InterContinental
Hotels & Resorts
✆ 888/567-8725
www.interconti.com

ITT Sheraton
✆ 800/325-3535
www.starwood.com

La Quinta Motor Inns
✆ 800/531-5900
www.laquinta.com

Marriott Hotels
✆ 800/228-9290
www.marriott.com

Motel 6
✆ 800/4-MOTEL6
(800/466-8356)
www.motel6.com

Omni
✆ 800/THEOMNI
www.omnihotels.com

Quality Inns
✆ 800/228-5151
www.hotelchoice.com

Radisson Hotels International
✆ 800/333-3333
www.radisson.com

Ramada Inns
✆ 800/2-RAMADA
www.ramada.com

Red Carpet Inns
✆ 800/251-1962
www.reservahost.com

Red Lion Hotels & Inns
✆ 800/RED-LION
www.redlion.com

Red Roof Inns
✆ 800/843-7663
www.redroof.com

Renaissance
✆ 800/228-9290
www.renaissancehotels.com

Residence Inn by Marriott
✆ 800/331-3131
www.marriott.com

Ritz-Carlton
✆ 800/241-3333
www.ritzcarlton.com

Rodeway Inns
✆ 800/228-2000
www.hotelchoice.com

Sheraton Hotels & Resorts
✆ 800/325-3535
www.sheraton.com

Super 8 Motels
✆ 800/800-8000
www.super8.com

Travelodge
✆ 800/255-3050
www.travelodge.com

Vagabond Inns
✆ 800/522-1555
www.vagabondinn.com

Westin Hotels & Resorts
✆ 800/937-8461
www.westin.com

Wyndham Hotels and Resorts
✆ 800/822-4200 in continental U.S.
and Canada
www.wyndham.com

Index

See also Accommodations and Restaurant indexes, below.

ACCOMMODATIONS

Restaurants

FROMMER'S® NATIONAL PARK GUIDES

Algonquin Provincial Park
Banff & Jasper
Family Vacations in the National
  Parks

Grand Canyon
National Parks of the American
  West
Rocky Mountain

Yellowstone & Grand Teton
Yosemite & Sequoia/Kings
  Canyon
Zion & Bryce Canyon

FROMMER'S® MEMORABLE WALKS

Chicago
London

New York
Paris

San Francisco

FROMMER'S® WITH KIDS GUIDES

Chicago
Las Vegas
New York City

Ottawa
San Francisco
Toronto

Vancouver
Walt Disney World® & Orlando
Washington, D.C.

SUZY GERSHMAN'S BORN TO SHOP GUIDES

Born to Shop: France
Born to Shop: Hong Kong,
  Shanghai & Beijing

Born to Shop: Italy
Born to Shop: London

Born to Shop: New York
Born to Shop: Paris

FROMMER'S® IRREVERENT GUIDES

Amsterdam
Boston
Chicago
Las Vegas
London

Los Angeles
Manhattan
New Orleans
Paris
Rome

San Francisco
Seattle & Portland
Vancouver
Walt Disney World®
Washington, D.C.

FROMMER'S® BEST-LOVED DRIVING TOURS

Austria
Britain
California
France

Germany
Ireland
Italy
New England

Northern Italy
Scotland
Spain
Tuscany & Umbria

THE UNOFFICIAL GUIDES®

Beyond Disney
California with Kids
Central Italy
Chicago
Cruises
Disneyland®
England
Florida
Florida with Kids
Inside Disney

Hawaii
Las Vegas
London
Maui
Mexico's Best Beach Resorts
Mini Las Vegas
Mini Mickey
New Orleans
New York City
Paris

San Francisco
Skiing & Snowboarding in the
  West
South Florida including Miami &
  the Keys
Walt Disney World®
Walt Disney World® for
  Grown-ups
Walt Disney World® with Kids
Washington, D.C.

SPECIAL-INTEREST TITLES

Athens Past & Present
Cities Ranked & Rated
Frommer's Best Day Trips from London
Frommer's Best RV & Tent Campgrounds
  in the U.S.A.
Frommer's Caribbean Hideaways
Frommer's China: The 50 Most Memorable Trips
Frommer's Exploring America by RV
Frommer's Gay & Lesbian Europe
Frommer's NYC Free & Dirt Cheap

Frommer's Road Atlas Europe
Frommer's Road Atlas France
Frommer's Road Atlas Ireland
Frommer's Wonderful Weekends from
  New York City
The New York Times' Guide to Unforgettable
  Weekends
Retirement Places Rated
Rome Past & Present